In memory of David Nicholls (3 June 1936 - 13 June 1996),
historian of Haiti, priest, theologian and political scientist,
who is the inspiration behind this book.

Charles Arthur is coordinator of the London-based Haiti Support Group and the author of *After the Dance, the Drum is Heavy* (1995).

Michael Dash is Professor of Francophone Literature in the Department of Modern Languages and Literature at the University of the West Indies, Jamaica, and the author of *Haiti and the United States: National Stereotypes and the Literary Imagination* (1988).

CONTENTS

INTRODUCTION

The struggle for *libète*, the Creolisation of the French, *liberté*, (freedom in English) is, in many respects, the story of Haiti. Under Spanish and then French colonial rule, the African slaves brought to Hispaniola to replace the exterminated Tainos, struggled to gain their freedom from enslavement on the plantations. The independent nation of Haiti was born of twelve years of revolutionary warfare waged in pursuit of freedom from slavery and from colonial subjugation. After independence, the liberated slaves' yearning to escape the constraints of labouring for others impelled them to take control of their own plots, so transforming the pattern of landholding in a way almost unique to the continent.

Despite these antecedents, in the near two centuries since independence Haiti's history has been shaped by a state structure based on the exploitation of the poor majority, and controlled by an elite and military strongmen with scant regard for the basic freedoms of their countrymen. When US Marines re-introduced forced labour during the occupation of 1915-34, Haitians once again took up arms to fight for *libète*. To escape the oppressive weight of dictatorship and economic stagnation, in the latter part of the twentieth century hundreds of thousands of Haitians left their homeland in search of a life of freedom abroad. Then when Haitians rose up against the 'Baby Doc' Duvalier regime in 1985-6, the hopes raised by *Haïti Libére* proved a false dawn. The burgeoning popular movement for fundamental change was brutally stopped in its tracks by the 1991 military coup, and even with the restoration of formal democracy in 1994, freedom from crushing poverty remains elusive.

Libète: A Haiti Anthology aims not just to introduce some of the best writing about this dramatic history. Drawing on a wide range of texts by academics, historians, and travel writers, and featuring numerous extracts from the writings of Haitian novelists, poets, political activists, and journalists, it intends to explore the context, the ideas, and the culture from which this history has emerged. While many contemporary political analyses are rapidly overtaken by events and soon go out of date, this collection explores long-standing themes and their interpretation in the hope of providing the keys to an understanding of present-day Haiti for some time to come.

Each of the ten chapters addresses a particular theme and is preceded by an essay contextualising the extracts that follow. The total

of more than 180 extracts have been selected not only from the growing body of work by non-Haitian, and wherever possible, Haitian
writers, but also from interviews, newsletters, press releases, and
journalistic articles, in an attempt to acknowledge the views and
perspectives of some of the majority of Haitians never taught to read
or write, and consequently never published.

Chapter One, *Colonialism and Revolution*, deals with the era when
the territory that would become known as Haiti played a pivotal
role in the history of the Western world. When Columbus established
the Europeans' first permanent settlement in the Americas on the
island they called Hispaniola, he paved the way for the colonisation
of the 'New World' and the empires on which so much of the wealth
and power of the European metropole was based. The Spanish venture was short-lived, but long enough for the indigenous population
to succumb to the world's first recorded genocide. Long enough too
to initiate the infamous triangular trade that, over the course of four
centuries and more, shaped the destinies of three continents.

Under French control, the western part of the island became the
most profitable colony in the world, and the unrelenting toil of the
slaves generated the capital for the rapid growth of French cities
such as Nantes, Bordeaux, and Marseilles. The other side of this story
was the barbarity of the plantation system, and the slaves' defiant
reaction to it. Resistance in the shape of the different forms of
marronage, and Makandal's failed plot to poison the slave-owners,
were precursors of the mass uprising of 1791. The subsequent years
of warfare and the victories over the armies of Spain, Britain, and
France were elements in what C.L.R. James described as 'one of the
great epics of revolutionary struggle and achievement'.

The repercussions of the revolution that led to the creation of the
world's first black republic were manifold. The defeat of the French
seriously weakened Napoleon's military capability in Europe and
ended his ambition to create a new American empire. Defeat at the
hands of Dessalines' troops influenced France's decision to sell Louisiana to the United States of America - a sale that made the latter a
continent-wide power. Britain's failure to add 'The Pearl of the Antilles' to its imperial crown contributed to its decision to abolish the
slave trade. Eventually the other colonial powers followed suit, perhaps fearing the example of the Haiti would be repeated elsewhere.

An enduring pride in the slaves' revolution remains a powerful
part of the Haitian national consciousness. In 1998, a student born
of Haitian parents but living in France, when asked by friends to
join in the celebrations marking the 150th anniversary of France's

abolition of slavery, declined, commenting 'We Haitians did not wait for the French to decide to abolish it. We did it ourselves.'

Chapter Two, *The Status Quo: Elites, Soldiers and Dictators*, sees the revolutionary dynamic of the former slaves compel the new leaders of independent Haiti to break up the plantation system, only for military officers and the urban-based mulatto elite to adopt new economic and political systems with which to increase their wealth and defend their control of power.

The latter part of the twentieth century was dominated by the dictatorships of Duvalier father and son, whose corrupt and repressive regimes, backed by their bully-boys, the Tontons Macoutes, made Haiti notorious across the globe. When Jean-Claude Duvalier's dictatorship collapsed, the military took over where he and his father had left off, using extreme violence to protect the status quo. The overthrow of President Aristide in 1991, and the three years of military rule that followed, reveals the extent to which the established power structure is prepared to go to block any significant change.

In Chapter Three, *Rural Haiti: Peasants, Land and the Environment*, the consequences of two centuries of misrule for the majority are examined. Since the early years of independence, and still to this day, most Haitians live off the land, working on small plots using rudimentary methods and tools. Outsiders in their own country in many senses, Haitian peasants are, however, linked to the urban economy and national political scene via the rural markets, the travelling saleswomen, the coffee speculators and the increasing scarcity of agricultural land. The years of exploitation and neglect by the ruling elite have made life in rural Haiti ever more precarious, a situation compounded by an environmental crisis of staggering proportions.

Chapter Four, *Poverty and Urban Life*, covers the consequences of the resultant exodus to the urban centres and in particular to the capital, Port-au-Prince. The explosion in the size of the urban population has spawned miserable slums, and shocking social deprivation. As more and more people are drawn to the cities in search of that rare thing, a paid job, the already skeletal state social services teeter near the point of total collapse.

The attempts, as yet unsuccessful, to overturn the status quo, and break the elite's stranglehold over political and economic power are the subject of Chapter Five, *Forces For Change*. The mass of the people have only rarely banded together to try and force political change, preferring instead to get along with their lives with as little as possible to do with the state and national politics. Despite the efforts of the Communist Party, and the populist leader Daniel Fignolé, it was not until the 1980s that the masses began to exert their latent power. Consciousness-raising by progressive Catholic activists, combined with worsening social and economic conditions, convinced Haitians to agitate for an end to the Duvalier dictatorship. The fall of Duvalier unleashed a torrent of energy and creativity as across the country grassroots organisations attempted to confront a host of political, social and economic challenges.

The figure of Jean-Bertrand Aristide stands at the centre of this turbulent period, adored by the masses and loathed by the elite. While Aristide articulated the desire for change, and his election as President showed the popular backing for a sweeping transformation of the political terrain, the Lavalas current failed to coalesce into an organised movement that could enact the overthrow of the old order. The vicious counter-attack mounted by the forces of reaction during 1991-94 set back the prospects for meaningful change, yet the grassroots organisations of peasants and slum dwellers continue to offer the only hope of involving the people themselves in the construction of a viable future.

Chapter Six, *Refugees and the Diaspora*, puts the 'Haitian problem' into a regional perspective by examining some of the experiences and repercussions of the massive migration from Haiti over recent years. The outward flow of people has, on the whole, been to Haiti's disadvantage and the host countries' gain. Many skilled and educated men and women departed during the Duvalier era never to return, and successive waves of migrants escaping from poverty and persecution relieved political pressure at home, and provided cheap labour abroad. Although the current trend is for host countries to repatriate now unwanted 'guests', the continuing economic decline and an increasing population in Haiti suggest that the refugee issue will return with a vengeance. Meanwhile, the presence of Haitian migrants and refugees across much of the Caribbean, and in particular in North American cities, means that Haiti is not as isolated or 'cut-off' from the rest of the world as would at first seem.

The misconception that, because Haiti won its independence so much earlier than its neighbours, it has only itself to blame for its current predicament is exposed in Chapter Seven, *Foreign Interventions*. Beginning with the massive indemnity imposed by France in the early nineteenth century, followed by the long US occupation early in the twentieth century, and with, more recently, the influx of Christian missionaries, and the economic restructuring demanded by the Bretton Woods institutions, the country has rarely been free of outside interference.

Chapter Eight, *Popular Religion and Culture*, explores the aspects of day-to-day Haitian life that set it apart from other Caribbean nations subject to the homogenising influences of US culture and values. Vodou, the religion of the majority, whether newly converted to Christianity or not, continues to fascinate outsiders. Although still the source of voyeuristic intrigue, increasingly Vodou is seen not just a matter of faith and worship, but is also recognised as a vehicle for cultural resistance and a catalyst for artistic creativity.

For the moment, Haitians' rich and vibrant culture, embracing Vodou ritual, dance and art, naïve painting, and roots music, constitute a sort of 'comparative advantage' in the global tourist market-place. Whether the government of the day can utilise this advantage to the benefit of ordinary Haitians, or will allow foreign and local investors to corral tourists in beach resort enclaves serviced by cheap bar staff and chambermaids as in the Dominican Republic, remains to be seen.

Chapter Nine, *Literature and Language*, by contrast explores the cultural contribution of some of the many Haitian poets and writers, whose work belies the image of a country populated by illiterate peasants and bloodthirsty dictators. Despite its poverty and social turmoil, Haiti has produced a series of internationally recognised writers, including René Depestre, Jacques Roumain and, more recently, Edwidge Danticat. At first modelled on French traditions, Haitian literature was influenced by the Latin American vogue for 'magical realism' and now reflects such contemporary issues as political absolutism and the nature of exile. Today's Haitian writers face another difficult choice: whether to write in French, the language of the old colonial power, or Creole

In Chapter Ten, *The View From Abroad*, the stereotypes and perceptions as seen by non-Haitian writers are explored. The country is a source of perennial fascination for foreign writers, but as this selection of extracts shows, voyeurism and sensationalism are thankfully giving way to more considered and sympathetic explorations. Starting with the polarised views of the 1791-1802 revolution, generations of 'outsiders' have been attracted and sometimes inspired by Haiti's unique culture and history, but misunderstanding and wilful misinterpretation have also been constant features of the country's 'bad press'.

In the course of researching and compiling this anthology I have enjoyed invaluable access to the British Library in London, and the David Nicholls Memorial Collection in Oxford. I have also benefited considerably from use of the collection of contemporary news articles and periodicals held by the Haiti Support Group. Of the many books consulted, one of the most useful has been the Haiti bibliography, compiled by Frances Chambers and published by Clio Press.

I am grateful to my friends and colleagues at the Haiti Support Group for sharing my concern to support Haitians' struggle for participatory democracy, to the Haitian Information Bureau for reporting the 'other' side of the story from Haiti over the last seven years, and to Laurie Richardson for helping me to meet so many activists and organisers from the popular sector in Haiti.

I should like to thank my editor, James Ferguson, for his encouragement, patience and constant cajoling. I am also grateful to my co-writer, Michael Dash, who despatched his two erudite chapters (Chapters Nine and Ten) from Jamaica while I was still struggling to finalise my selections. I am indebted too to Max Blanchet, Emily Dunbar, Anne McConnell, and Webber Emile for their translations.

Finally I should like to especially thank Leah Gordon, not only for sharing my passion for the country, and allowing me to borrow from her extensive private book collection, but also for her essential photographs of Haitians, and for providing me with invaluable advice and support during the production of this book.

Charles Arthur
February 1999

CHAPTER ONE
COLONIALISM AND REVOLUTION

The original inhabitants of the land Christopher Columbus sighted on 6 December 1492 were the Tainos, a branch of the Amerindian people called Arawaks who had emigrated some 2,000 years earlier from the mainland of South America. Estimates of the Taino population at this time range from 300,000 to one million. They lived by fishing, and growing maize, yam and sweet potato on land that was owned and worked communally. Columbus described them as 'loveable, tractable, peaceable, gentle', (1) characteristics that the Spanish exploited as they consolidated the first permanent European settlement in the Americas. The Tainos were put to work as slaves, cultivating crops, but more especially, prospecting and extracting gold from rivers, streams and mines. If the search for precious metals was the economic rationale for the Spanish presence, the ideological justification was the imperative to convert the natives to the Christian faith. (2)

In response to the life of forced labour imposed by the colonists, thousands of Tainos committed suicide. Others rebelled or escaped to the mountains, yet within a stunningly short period of time the vast majority of Tainos on Hispaniola had perished – victims of overwork, brutal treatment, and the diseases the Spanish brought with them from Europe. The indigenous people had no natural immunity to smallpox, tuberculosis, typhus or influenza, and contemporary accounts estimate that by the middle of the sixteenth century only a few hundred indigenous people remained on the entire island. (3)

As the local population rapidly diminished, the Spanish brought in slaves from Africa to replenish the labour supply. The first arrived in 1501 and soon black slaves were used throughout the colony. The initial gold finds had quickly been exhausted, and the slaves were used on plantations growing sugar-cane, a profitable crop introduced to the region by the colonists. However, the Spanish were increasingly shifting their attention to the gold and silver-rich colonies of Mexico and Peru, so much so that by the end of the sixteenth century large tracts of land in the western part of the island had been abandoned. Over time marauding bands of European adventurers, many of French origin, began to settle and cultivate these vacant lands. (4) In 1697 Spain ceded the western third of the island to France, known thereafter as Saint-Domingue.

Under French rule, Saint-Domingue became an immensely prosperous colony producing vast quantities of sugar, coffee, cotton and indigo. A small group of plantation owners and merchants, the *grands blancs*, amassed huge fortunes. 'As rich as a Creole', was a commonly used expression in France. This growth was based on slave labour, and there was a massive increase in the numbers of slaves brought from Africa. (5) According to one estimate, in 1681 there were only 2,000 slaves in what was to become Saint-Domingue; by 1730 there were 117,000, and, fifty years later, over a quarter of a million. (6) Yet even these figures fail to reflect the enormous volume of the colony's slave trade. As many as one in nine of the new slaves died within their first year, and only the very fittest could survive the punishing plantation life for long. Rather than looking after their 'property', most planters preferred to work the slaves to death and replace them with new purchases. Gratuitous cruelty and torture were commonplace. (7)

The slaves responded to the inhuman and brutal character of their exploitation in a variety of ways. Like their predecessors, the Tainos, some slaves fled from the plantations to hide out in the mountains where they often banded together to form rebel communities. Others would quit the plantation for just a few days at a time, or would eke out a fragile existence doing odd-jobs on the outskirts of towns. (8) Efforts to damage the slave master financially included theft of and damage to plantation property, and malingering on the job. These various forms of *marronage*, involving protest through the active or passive withdrawal of labour, co-operation or participation, are phenomena that survived the ending of slavery and continue in Haiti to this day.

An altogether more desperate expression of resistance was suicide. There were also reckoned to have been thousands of cases of abortion and infanticide as mothers chose save their offspring from a life of cruelty and deprive their masters of new slaves. Numerous episodes of organised slave revolts involving the massacre of plantation owners and their families were recorded, but these were localised, isolated and quickly suppressed. The most widespread act of rebellion, and the most feared by the white colonists, was the use of poison against livestock, other slaves and the slave masters themselves. It seems this practice was made possible by a knowledge of the toxic properties of certain tropical plants, and by the common use of arsenic in the colonists' households. (9)

On the plantations the slaves' lives were short and arduous, but even with the small plots of land given to them to grow food by their masters, they began to sow the seeds of a future, free peasantry.

(10) As well as grand blancs and black slaves, the population of Saint-Domingue contained two other important classes. The *petits blancs*, or poor whites, were the plantation managers and overseers, and the artisans, shopkeepers, lawyers and clerks from the towns. Since voting was based on the amount of property owned, the petits blancs were excluded from any role in the political or administrative life of the colony. The *gens de couleur*, or mulattoes, were the offspring of white men and black slave women. Many of them were granted their freedom by their fathers, and became property and slave owners, yet they still suffered intense racial discrimination, and had no political rights. In the colony's main town, Cap-Français, the white minority led a life of ostentatious consumption and petty jealousies. (11) Rigidly hierarchical and claustrophobic, colonial society was obsessed with race, sexual liaisons and the most subtle gradations of colour which emerged from them. (12)

By 1789, when revolution began in France, elements within all four groups saw a chance to further their own ends. There were grands blancs who hoped to wrest political autonomy and economic control from France; most petits blancs wanted equal rights with the grands blancs; mulattoes proclaimed their equality with all the whites; and black slaves, of course, yearned for liberty.

The first attempt at rebellion, by the free mulattoes led by Vincent Ogé and Jean-Baptiste Chavannes, was crushed. Then, in August 1791, the volcano on which colonial Saint-Domingue was built erupted. (13) Slaves on the northern plain launched their revolt, and it quickly spread across the country. In return for the misery and agony they had suffered, the slaves wreaked a bloody revenge on their owners. Whites and free mulattoes were profoundly shocked by the rapidity and violence of the revolt. (14) The strong impression it made on the psyche of those who lived through it and emerged post-independence as a mulatto elite is still evident over 200 years later. Many rich Haitians still live in mortal fear that the poor black majority will re-enact the uprising of 1791.

There were numerous reasons why this revolution succeeded. The French Revolution weakened and divided the French in France and in Saint-Domingue; the conflicts between free mulattoes and the whites had grown ever more intense; and the other colonial powers of the time, Britain and Spain, intervened to further their own interests. But above all else it was the role played by the blacks that made it the first and only successful slave revolution in history. Over the course of an epic 12 year struggle the slaves defeated the local whites, the forces of the French Crown, a Spanish and a British invasion (15), and the massive expeditionary force sent by Napoleon Bonaparte. Immense credit for these victories is due to the man who quickly emerged as the leader of the black armies, Toussaint Louverture. (16) He not only welded the mass of rebellious slaves into a efficient fighting force, and in the process invented guerrilla warfare, but also skilfully exploited the rivalries between all the other main players in the conflict. (17)

Toussaint was taken prisoner in 1802 by the French forces dispatched by Napoleon Bonaparte to restore French rule and reimpose slavery. As he was put aboard a frigate that would take him to a dungeon and his death in France, Toussaint uttered these prophetic words, 'In overthrowing me, you have cut down only the tree of liberty in Saint Domingue. It will spring up again from the roots for they are numerous and deep.'

Less than a year later, his general, Jean-Jacques Dessalines, had united the previously warring black and mulatto forces, and initiated what was to become a triumphant campaign against the French. (18) At the town of Arcahaie, Dessalines took the French tricolor and tore off the white band, that to him represented the white colonist, and made a new flag by putting the blue and the red, representing the blacks and mulattoes, together. After Dessalines finally defeated the French at the Battle of Vertières, the last French regiments withdrew and on 1 January 1804 the independent republic of Haiti was declared. (19)

(1) THE TAINOS

John Cummins, *The Voyage of Christopher Columbus,* 1992

Columbus' journal testifies to the kindness and hospitality of the indigenous Tainos, qualities that were to contribute to their rapid extermination.

Friday, 21 December 1492

Some of the land we have seen is well cultivated, though in deed all of the land is well worked. I sent two men from the boats to climb a hill to see if there was a village. None was visible from the sea, but at ten o'clock last night some Indians came out to the ship in a canoe to marvel at us. I gave them some barter goods, with which they were well pleased.

The two men came back and told me that they had seen a large village some way inland. I ordered the men to row towards it, and when we had nearly reached land I saw some Indians coming down to the shore, looking frightened. I ordered the boats to stop, and told the Indians in the boat with us to tell them that I would not harm them. They came closer to the water, and we went closer to the shore, and when they had completely overcome their fear so many of them came down to the beach that they covered it, offering thanks for our arrival. Men, women and children came running from all directions to bring us bread made from yams, which they call *ajes*; it is good, very white. They also gave us water in gourds and clay pitchers like those in Castille, and brought us everything they had and thought we wanted, all with wonderful openness and gladness of heart. Let no one say that they gave freely because it was of little value, for those who gave us pieces of gold gave as gladly and willingly as those who gave us gourds of water, and it is easy to see when something is being given with true generosity.

These people have no staffs or assegais or any other weapons, nor do any of the others on this island, which I think is very large. They are as naked as the day they were born, men and women alike. Elsewhere, on Juana and some of the other islands, the women wear a little cotton thing in front to cover up their private part, the size of a flap on a man's breeches, especially when they are over twelve years old, but here neither the girls nor women wear anything. Also, in the other places the men hide their women from us out of jealously, but not here, and some of the women are very fine-bodied, and they were the first to come and give thanks to Heaven for our arrival and to bring us whatever they had, especially foodstuffs, *aje* bread, and peanuts, and five or six kinds of fruit, which I have ordered to be preserved to bring before your Majesties ...

I cannot believe that any man has ever met a people so good-hearted and generous, so gentle that they did their utmost to give us everything they had, and ran to bring it to us as soon as we arrived. Later I sent six men to explore the village. The Indians received them with all the ceremony they could and gave them whatever they had.

(2) FORCED CONVERSION

King Ferdinand of Castille (Spain), *Letter to the Tainos*, 1971

This letter was sent by the Spanish King Ferdinand with Columbus on his second voyage to Hispaniola, and was to be read to the Taino inhabitants of the island. Claiming the land in the name of the Roman Catholic Church, the letter goes on to issue the direst threats if the inhabitants fail to convert to the Catholic faith.

In the name of King Ferdinand and Juana, his daughter, Queen of Castile and Leon...conquerors of barbarian nations, we notify you as best we can that our Lord God Eternal created Heaven and earth and a man and woman from whom we all descend for all times and all over the world. In the 5,000 years since creation the multitude of these generations caused men to divide and establish kingdoms in various parts of the world, among whom God chose St. Peter as leader of mankind, regardless of their law, sect or belief. He seated St. Peter in Rome as the best place from which to rule the world but he allowed him to establish his seat in all parts of the world and rule all people, whether Christians, Moors, Jews, Gentiles or any other sect. He was named Pope, which means admirable and greatest father, governor of all men. Those who lived at that time obeyed St. Peter as Lord and superior King of the universe, and so did their descendants obey his successors and so on to the end of time.

The late Pope gave these islands and mainland of the ocean and the contents hereof to the above-mentioned King and Queen, as is certified in writing and you may see the documents if you should so desire. Therefore, Their Highnesses are lords and masters of this land; they were acknowledged as such when this notice was posted, and were and are being served willingly and without resistance; then, their religious envoys were acknowledged and obeyed without delay, and all subjects unconditionally and of their own free will became Christians and thus they remain. Their Highnesses received their allegiance with joy and benignity and decreed that they be treated in this spirit like good and loyal vassals and you are under the obligation to do the same.

Therefore, we request that you understand this text, deliberate on its contents within a reasonable time, and recognize the Church and its highest priest, the Pope, as rulers of the universe, and in their name the King and Queen of Spain as rulers of this land, allowing the religious fathers to preach our holy Faith to you. You own compliance as a duty to the King and we in his name will receive you with love and charity, respecting your freedom and that of your wives and sons and your rights of possession and we shall not compel you to baptism unless you, informed of the Truth, wish to convert to our holy Catholic Faith as almost all your neighbors have done in other islands, in exchange for which Their Highnesses bestow many privileges and exemptions upon you. Should you fail to comply, or delay maliciously in so doing, we assure you that with the help of God we shall use force against you, declaring war upon you from all sides and with all possible means, and we shall bind you to the yoke of the Church and of Their Highnesses; we shall enslave your persons, wives and sons, sell you or dispose of you as the King sees fit; we shall seize your possessions and harm you as much as we can as disobedient and resisting vassals. And we declare you guilty of resulting deaths and injuries, exempting Their Highnesses of such guilt as well as ourselves and the gentlemen who accompany us. We hereby request that legal signatures be affixed to this text and pray those present to bear witness for us...

(3) COLONISATION

Benoît Joachim, *Les Racines du sous-développement en Haïti,* 1979

Haitian political scientist, Benoît Joachim, outlines the early history of European colonisation of what was to become Haiti.

When the western Europeans arrived in what they termed the New World, tropical America was known primarily as Haiti, or Ayti-Quisequeya-Boyo in the native language. For their own purposes, they renamed it Isla Espanola, which was corrupted to Hispaniola.

The Tainos, Ciboneys and other Arawaks who lived a primitive life on Haiti did not survive for much more than twenty years after the invasion of the country in 1492-1493 by the bearers of the Christian cross and the Spanish flag, led by the Genoese, Christopher Columbus. Despite fierce, but fragmented, resistance, the one million inhabitants of the five Caciques, or primitive kingdoms, which shared the 77,000 square kilometres of the island, were overwhelmed by the firearms, swords, trained mastiffs, horses' hooves, disease, and other novelties of a similar nature, introduced into the West Indies by the subjects of the Catholic Kings. It was only due to a small, indomitable group of survivors – like the one led by the Cacique rebel, Henri – sheltering in near impenetrable mountains and quickly joined by the first imported black slaves, that elements of Amerindian culture was able to pass into current Haitian civilisation.

The Conquistadors had not crossed the ocean in order to put down roots in the Indies in general, and Haiti in particular. They set out to scout (or "discover"), to help themselves to new riches – principally gold – and take them to Europe, even if it meant converting these pagans, who stood between them and the coveted riches, to their religion, and paving their way to heaven. What is more, having quickly exhausted the gold mines of Hispaniola, the first 'Europeanised' territory in the Western Hemisphere to have been pillaged, the Conquistadors abandoned it almost completely. From this time onwards, the role of the young colonial town of Santo Domingo, initially the official residence of both the Viceroy of the Indies and the Admiral of the Ocean, was simply that of a beachhead in the fight to win Cuba, and later, the "terra firma" [1] where the existence of other forms of precious metal had been detected.

This was not quite the death of Ayti/Hispaniola. But it would be more than a hundred years before it awoke from a long period of lethargy. From the second third of the 17th century, and certainly during the 18th century, the face of Haiti was completely changed by the transplantation of new peoples. France was to establish there a typical mercantile, capitalist colony.

[1] The mainland of Central and South America

Translated from French by Emily Dunbar

(4) THE BUCCANEERS

Dantès Bellegarde, *La Nation haïtienne*, 1938

Less than thirty years after the Spanish arrived in Saint Domingue, French and English pirates began to set up a temporary bases along the coast of the largely deserted western part of the island, from where they launched attacks on passing ships. During the seventeenth century these men became the new colonisers of the western part of the island.

The adventurers ended up choosing as their permanent headquarters the island of Tortue, which became the lair of these fearsome sea plunderers, known as *flibustiers*. It wasn't long before the French got rid of their English companions. Then, having crossed the short Tortue channel, they settled in Port-Margot on the northern coast of the main island, and from there spread down towards the west and the south.

Aboard flimsy boats (fly boats, from which they get their name of *flibustiers* or filibusters) these daring men braved the high seas and audaciously attacked the most powerful ships. They lived day and night in their little sail boats, ready to attack at a moment's notice. They formed a loose association that recognised no authority other than the elected captain, and even then he was only obeyed during combat. The distribution of the booty would often turn into a bloody fight between the victors. After looting some galleon or caravel, they would go to sell the cargo in the nearest port, and this would be the occasion for unrestrained revelry.

Soon though, tiredness and age rendered some of these adventurers incapable of running the risks of the chase. Even amongst the younger ones, the taste for adventure began to diminish. A class of settlers began to develop, living from hunting the wild cattle and pigs that had multiplied on the island. To conserve the meat of slaughtered animals, it was suspended above large, low fires, endlessly replenished with green wood, which gave off a thick smoke. These hunters called the place where they set up these fires, *boucan*, from where they get their name, *boucaniers* (buccaneers). They usually chose to set up their *boucan* at a place near the sea, so they could sell animal hides to the Dutch sea captains who frequented these waters, and who provided, in return, guns, powder, and sometimes provisions of victuals and clothing.

The life of a buccaneer was very tough. He wore shirts and shorts that were usually stained with blood. He protected his feet with crude leather slippers, or a type of raw skin, ankle shoe. His house was a four-walled structure, an *ajoupa*, around which he grew some vegetables. His greatest ambition was to possess a long-range rifle and a pack of twenty to thirty dogs. There were no women among the buccaneers, who teamed up in pairs, and shared everything they possessed. On the death of one or other of the two associates, his assets passed to the survivor.

Although the buccaneers had meeting places, they were basically nomads since they had to move around in the course of the hunt, and to cross immense distances to reach the coastal places where they could trade hides. Little by little, they put down roots, conquering the forest, clearing the land, and devoting themselves to a permanent form of agriculture. They called themselves *habitants* to distinguish themselves from those who continued to lead the life of travelling buccaneers...

Translated from French by Charles Arthur

(5) OUT OF AFRICA

Harold Courlander, *The Drum and the Hoe*, 1960

The Africans brought to Haiti as slaves came from many different parts of the continent, and were from different tribes and classes. In the plantation fields and slave compounds a new entity, the Haitian, was formed.

Whereas the Indians of Haiti were not resilient, the Africans were. More and more slaves were poured into Hispaniola. By the eighteenth century the slave population represented countless tribes and kingdoms of West Africa. There were Senegalese, Foulas,

Poulards, Sosos, Bambarras, Kiambaras, Mandingos, and Yolofs from
north-west Africa. There were Aradas, Mahis, Haoussas, Ibos, Anagos
or Yorubas, Bini, Takwas, Fidas, Amines, Fantis, Agouas, Sobos,
Limbas, and Adjas from the coast and interior of the great bulge of
Africa. From Angola and the Congo basin came the Solongos, the
Mayombes, the Moundongues, the Bumbas, the Kangas, and others. Although there is no official record, Haitians themselves say that
there were also those tall people known as the Jangheys, or Dinkas,
from the region of the Upper Nile, and Bagandas from Uganda. A
few proper names that have survived, such as Ras Mede, suggest
that there may have been men from Ethiopia among them. Old slavers' records show that numerous shipments were made from
Madagascar and Mozambique on the East African coast.

   These transplanted people came from all classes and stations of
life. Some were criminals condemned and sold by their own tribes-
men; others were prisoners captured in intertribal raids or by Arab
slave hunts. There were men of royal blood among them, as well as
artisans and tribal scholars. The slave cargoes included leaf doctors,
bards, musicians, wood carvers, metalworkers, drum makers, boat-
builders, hunters, and farmers.

   In Haiti they were thrown together into a common mould. Shoulder to shoulder in the plantation fields were Bambarras, Anagos,
Takwas, and Bumbas – peoples with different backgrounds, different languages, different legends, and different traditions. There were
Moslems and so-called pagans, herdsmen and river-boatmen. Each
of them brought something of his past and unwittingly poured it
into the new amalgam that was to be the Haitian.

   And into this amalgam flowed some of the literature, the traditions, the religious thoughts, and the superstitions of Europe. Under
Spanish, French and English rulers the slaves were constantly subjected to ways and ideas that were new to them. They absorbed and
digested, and out of the diverse and even contradictory elements
they worked out new patterns of life and thinking. This was the
strength and resiliency of the West African in the New World.

(6) SLAVERY AND PROFITABILITY

C.L.R. James, *The Black Jacobins*, 1938

Trinidadian historian C.L.R. James sees the need to import more and
more slaves in order to guarantee continuing increases in production
as a major factor contributing to the outbreak of revolution in 1791.

Prosperity is not a moral question and the justification of San Domingo was its prosperity. Never for centuries had the western world known such economic progress. By 1754, two years before the beginning of the Seven Years' War, there were 599 plantations of sugar and 3,379 of indigo. During the Seven Years' War (1756-63) the French marine, swept off the sea by the British Navy, could not bring the supplies on which the colony depended, the extensive smuggling trade could not supply the deficiency, thousands of slaves died from starvation and the upward rise of production, though not halted, was diminished. But after the Treaty of Paris in 1763 the colony made a great stride forward. In 1767 it exported 72 million pounds' weight of raw sugar and 51 millions pounds of white, a million pounds of indigo and two million pounds of cotton, and quantities of hides, molasses, cocoa and rum. Smuggling, which was winked at by the authorities, raised the official figures by at least 25 per cent. Nor was it only in quantity that San Domingo excelled but in quality. Each coffee tree produced on an average a pound weight, equal sometimes to that of Mocha. Cotton grew naturally, even without much care, in stony ground and in the crevices of the rocks. Indigo also grew spontaneously. Tobacco had a larger leaf there than in any other part of the Americas and sometimes equalled in quality the produce of Havana... If on no earthly spot was so much misery concentrated as on a slave-ship, then on no portion of the globe did its surface in proportion to its dimensions yield so much wealth as the colony of San Domingo [...]

Between 1783 and 1789 production nearly doubled. Between 1764 and 1771 the average importation of slaves varied between ten and fifteen thousand. In 1786 it was 27,000, and from 1787 onwards the colony was taking more than 40,000 slaves a year. But economic prosperity is no guarantee of social stability. That rests on the constantly shifting equilibrium between the classes...With every stride in production the colony was marching to its doom.

The enormous increase of slaves was filling the colony with native Africans, more resentful, more intractable, more ready for rebellion than the creole Negro. Of the half-a-million slaves in the colony in 1789, more than two-thirds had been born in Africa.

(7) TORTURE

Baron de Vastey, *Notes à M. le Baron V. P. Malouet,* 1814

Pompée Valentin Vastey was a mulatto slave who joined Toussaint Louverture's army in 1796 at the age of fifteen. He survived the revolutionary wars to become one of the principal advisers to King Henri Christophe, an early leader of independent Haiti. Writing in 1814, in reply to an apologist for the French colonists, he describes some of the tortures that the owners routinely inflicted on their slaves.

Haven't they committed unheard-of cruelties, crimes until then unknown to humankind? Haven't they burnt, roasted, grilled and impaled alive the unfortunate slaves? Haven't they sawn off the limbs, torn out the tongues and teeth, torn off the ears, and cut off the lips of their blacks? Haven't they hung men upside down, drowned them in sacks, crucified them on planks, buried them alive, crushed them in mortars? Haven't they forced them to eat human shit? And, after having flayed them with the whip, haven't they thrown them to the ground to be devoured by worms, or onto anthills, or lashed them to stakes in the swamp to be eaten alive by mosquitoes? Haven't they thrown them into boiling cauldrons of cane syrup? Haven't they put men and women into barrels spiked with nails, closed at both ends, and rolled them from the tops of mountains, hurling the unfortunate victims inside into the abyss below? Haven't they had these miserable blacks savaged by trained dogs, until these mastiffs, full of human flesh, refuse any longer to act as instruments of the torturers who then finish off the half-eaten victims with the thrust of a knife or a bayonet?

Translated from French by Charles Arthur

(8) THE MAROONS

Gabriel Debien, *Marronage in the French Caribbean,* 1973

The historian, Gabriel Debien, describes the phenomenon of 'marronage', a term deriving from the Spanish word *cimarron'*, applied to wild cattle.

Planters distinguished two types of marronage: *grand marronage* and *petit marronage. Grand marronage* was, in the true sense, flight from the plantation with no intention of ever returning. Usually, such fugitives fled alone, sometimes in twos or threes. Some lived for long periods in isolation, but others more or less quickly formed bands under the direction of a chief, or joined a band that was already established. These bands lived in the hills, in the most remote, least-travelled districts. There was a scattering of women among them. These fugitives had settled into a way of life that was almost "collective".

Pillaging was far from being their main activity; but they nonetheless terrorised certain areas, or at least created an atmosphere of anxiety, for whoever said "band", presupposed an armed band and hostile intentions. As a result, the mounted police were sent out against them, and sometimes the militia, or even professional troops if the situation called for it. Whenever the maroons had raided the supplies of a plantation, or stolen horses or cattle, such an expedition was organised, though never too hastily... since they could never really hope to destroy all the maroons, but only capture a few and punish them [...]

The term marronage was also used, "but improperly," in speaking of absences of two or three days, or even of a week, which slaves made "out of laziness and libertinage rather than with the aim of desertion". We will call this *petit marronage* or *marronage léger*, which was an act of individuals or at most of very small groups.

These maroons did not go very far from the plantation from which they fled, but remained on its edges, or hid in the house of a relative or a friend from the neighbouring plantation. They subsisted not by systematically pillaging crops, but by stealing small amounts of food and committing minor thefts, in a kind of symbiosis with the plantation. These maroons exchanged fish, game, and stolen objects with the slaves for manioc, peas, and vegetables. This form of escape might be termed absenteeism, which could have been the result of the temperament of the slave, the nature of the work assigned, or the conditions of that work. In the case of those who lacked a particular skill, it was also due to the instability of their own condition. With the exception of the maroons who had been town slaves, whether serving as a free artisan or as a domestic, hardly any skilled slaves became maroons. The field slaves were the ones who most often took flight.

(9) POISON

Alejo Carpentier, *The Kingdom of This World*, 1957

In one of the first 'magical realist' novels, the Cuban writer, Alejo Carpentier, reconstructs the story of François Mackandal (or Macandal). An African slave who escaped and became a Maroon chief, Mackandal spent six years organising a united slave uprising to be launched with the mass poisoning of the whites. His rebellion was stopped soon after it began when he was betrayed, captured, and burnt alive in 1758.

One vine produced a rash, another made the head of anyone resting in its shade swell up. But what interested Macandal most was the fungi. There were those which smelled of wood rot, of medicine bottles, of cellars, of sickness, pushing through the ground in the shape of ears, ox-tongues, wrinkled excrescences, covered with exudations, opening their striped parasols in damp recesses, the homes of toads that slept or watched with open eyelids. The Mandingue crumbled the flesh of a fungus between his fingers, and his nose caught the whiff of poison. He held out his hand to a cow; she sniffed and drew back her head with frightened eyes, snorting. Macandal picked more fungi of the same species, putting them in an untanned leather pouch hanging from his neck[...]

What amazed Ti Noel was the revelation of the long, patient labour the Mandingue had carried out since the night of his escape. It seemed he had visited the plantations of the Plaine one by one, establishing direct contact with all who worked on them. He knew, for example, that in the indigo works of Dondon he could count on Olain, the gardener, Romaine, the cook of the slave-quarters, and one-eyed Jean-Pierrot; as for the Lenormand de Mezy plantation, he had sent messages to the three Pongue brothers, the bow-legged Fulah, the new Congolese, and to Marinette, the mulatto who had slept in the master's bed... He had also got in touch with two Angolese from beyond Le Bonnet de l'Evêque, whose buttocks were zebra-striped with scars from the red-hot irons applied as punishment for stealing brandy[...]

The poison crawled across the Plaine du Nord, invading pastures and stables. Nobody knew how it found its way into the grass and alfalfa, got mixed in with the bales of hay, climbed into the mangers. The fact was that cows, oxen, steers, horses, and sheep were dying by the hundreds, filling the whole countryside with an ever-present stench of carrion. Great fires were kindled at nightfall, giving off a heavy, oily smoke before dying out among heaps of blackened skulls, charred ribs, hooves reddened by the flames. The most experienced herbalists of the Cap sought in vain for the leaf, the gum, the sap that might be carrying the plague. The beasts went on falling, their bellies distended, encircled by swarms of buzzing bottleflies. The rooftrees were alive with great black bald birds awaiting the moment to drop and rip the hides, tense to the bursting, with their beaks, releasing new putrefaction.

Soon, to the general horror, it became known that the poison had got into the houses. One evening, after his afternoon repast, the master of Coq-Chanté plantation had suddenly dropped dead without any previous complaint, dragging down in his fall the clock he was winding. Before the news could reach the neighbouring plantations, other owners had been struck down by the poison which lurked, as though waiting to spring, in glasses on night tables, soup tureens, medicine bottles, in bread, wine, fruit and salt. The sinister hammering of coffins could be heard at all hours. At every turn in the road a funeral procession was encountered.

(10) THE FIELD SLAVES

Carolyn Fick, *The Making of Haiti: The Saint Domingue Revolution from Below,* 1990

Fick describes the life of the field slaves, by far the largest component of the black slave population. These people were, more often that not, born in Africa, and so were known as *bossales* as distinct from *creoles*, that is, blacks born in the Caribbean.

The lot of the average field slave was, on the whole, one of misery and despair. From the age of fourteen, youths were enrolled in the regular work force of the large plantations, where they continued to labour until the age of sixty. Rare, indeed, was the slave who survived to reach that age. Women in the fields were treated no differently from the men, except for a brief reprieve when pregnant or while nursing a new born. Herded together in what were known as the *case à nègres*, or slave quarters, families lived in straw-covered barracks, one next to the other, row upon row, at some distance from the master's house, or *grande case*. On the average, they were no more than twenty-five feet long, twelve feet wide, and fifteen feet high, with only one or two partitions in the interior. There were no windows and, with the exception of a single door, no ventilation. Narrow cots of a rudimentary sort, only slightly elevated above the bare earth floors, served as beds. Crowded together in these confines, father, mother, and children all slept indiscriminately.

Slaves were awakened at five in the morning by the sound of the *commandeur's* whistle or by the crack of his whip or, on large plantations of over a hundred slaves, by a huge bell. After the recital of perfunctory prayers by a steward, slave began work in the fields at eight, were allowed to stop for a meagre breakfast, and then returned until noon. The midday break lasted until two, when they returned at the crack of the whip to labour in the field until sundown. On many plantations slaves were often forced at the end of the day to gather feed for the draft animals, often having to travel considerable distances from the plantation. Finally, firewood had to be gathered, and dinner, consisting of beans and manioc, or a few potatoes, but rarely, if ever, any meat or fish, had to be prepared. During the grinding season on the sugar plantations, slaves then faced what must have seemed like interminable hours of night work at the mills, or of husking and sorting on the coffee plantations.

What little time the slave had for rest was consumed by other types of work. The two hours per day of rest at noon, as well as Sundays and holidays, were granted the slaves by law. And on most plantations, slave families were allotted a small piece of land on which to grow their food. Cultivation of their garden, upon which they were more often than not totally dependent for their subsistence, could only be undertaken on Sundays and holidays, or in the meagre time remaining after the preparation of the midday meal...By allotting small plots to the slaves for their own subsistence, the owner freed himself from the cost and responsibility of feeding them; yet these "kitchen gardens," meagre as they were and with as little time as the slaves had to plant and tend to their crops, came to be seen by the slaves as their own and thus eventually contributed to the development of a sense, if not of "proprietorship," at least of the firm notion that the land belonged to those who cultivated it.

(11) WHITE SOCIETY

Moreau de Saint-Méry, *A Civilization That Perished: The Last Years of White Colonial Rule* , 1985

Moreau de Saint-Méry, a French colonist, wrote his extensive and critical survey of Saint-Domingue in the period just before the 1789 French Revolution. In this extract from a recent translation he is struck by the decadence and social snobbery of Saint-Domingue's rich white community.

In Saint-Domingue everything takes on a character of opulence such as to astonish Europeans. That crowd of slaves who await the orders and even the signals of one man, confers an air of grandeur upon whomever gives the orders. It is in keeping with the dignity of a rich man to have four times as many domestics as he needs. The women, especially, have the talent of surrounding themselves with a useless lot of their own sex. And what is difficult to reconcile with the jealousy caused to them sometimes by these dark-skinned servants is the care given to choose pretty ones and to make their costumes elegant. How true it is that vanity can take charge of everything! Since the highest good for a European man is supposedly to have servants, he rents them until he can buy them [...]

The life style of people at the Cape is not one to lead to health. All the emotions are in play and are continually excited. One does not know there the sweet qualities of Society, of that meeting of persons who suit each other, and who pool their desire to please each other and make their leisure hours delightful... If one plays, it is for gain. If one talks, it is of business. If one goes to the theatre, it is to vie with the others in show; to the ball, it is to wear oneself out. If one entertains at dinner, it is to have a mob which drives away true happiness.

And what shall I say? It is to the character of most of the women that is due the loss of one of the most delicious pleasures in life. With little kindness and politeness, they have a thousand boasts and are all too free, among themselves, in showing their lack of education. They argue among themselves over their seats at the plays. They tot up their visits and their invitations. If there are several parties for the same day, for example, there are some who must have the hairdresser sleep at their house so that they will be the first ones ready; and they go ahead of time to take possession of the best seats. In a word, one could never imagine (conduct) more childish and more suited to preventing all friendship...

(12) THE 'PIGMENTOCRACY': RACIAL CATEGORIES

Moreau de Saint-Méry, *Description de la partie française de l'Isle de Saint-Domingue,* 1797

Saint-Méry includes 32 pages describing the recognised colour combinations of non-whites – a macabre illustration of the white planters' racist obsession with making clear their difference from the offspring of their liaisons with black slaves. In the section entitled, 'The Results of Interbreeding', he categorises non-whites into ten classes according to their genetic composition going back seven generations.

I must say here, that in the evaluation of the white and black parts of the many mixes, I have already noted:

the black	0-7 parts white, 128-121 parts black
the sacatra	8-16 parts white, 120-112 parts black
the griffon	24-32 parts white, 104-96 parts black
the marabou	40-48 parts white, 88-80 parts black
the mulatto	56-70 parts white, 58-72 parts black
the quadroon	71-96 parts white, 57-32 parts black
the métif	104-112 parts white, 24-16 parts black
the mamelouc	116-120 parts white, 12-8 parts black
the quarteronne	122-124 parts white, 6-4 parts black
the sang-mêlé	125-127 parts white, 3-1 parts black

Translated from French and adapted by Charles Arthur

(13) BOUKMAN'S CEREMONY

H. Pauléus Sannon, *Histoire de Toussaint L'Ouverture,* 1920

Mixing fact and legend, Haitian historian Pauléus Sannon wrote the following account of the Bois Caiman ceremony where Boukman Dutty, a Vodou priest, made the sacred pact of the general slave revolt. The ceremony remains a seminal event in the minds of many Haitians. This version is the one taught to most Haitian schoolchildren.

He exercised over all the slaves who came near him an inexplicable influence. In order to wash away all hesitation and to secure absolute devotion he brought together on the night of 14 August

1791 a great number of slaves in a glade in Bois Caiman near Morne-Rouge. They were all assembled when a storm broke. Jagged lightning in blinding flashes illuminated a sky of low and sombre clouds. In seconds a torrential rain floods the soil while under repeated assaults by a furious wind the forest trees twist and weep and their largest branches, violently ripped off, fall noisily away. In the centre of this impressive setting those present, transfixed, gripped by an inspired dread see an old dark woman arise. Her body quivers in lengthy spasms; she sings, pirouettes and brandishes a large cutlass overhead. An even greater immobility, the shallow scarcely audible breathing, the burning eyes fixed on the black woman soon indicate that the spectators are spellbound. Then a black pig is brought forward, its squeals lost in the raging of the storm. With a swift stroke, the inspired priestess plunges her cutlass into the animal's throat...The hot, spurting blood is caught and passed among the slaves; they all sip of it, all swearing to carry out Boukman's orders. The old woman of the strange eyes and shaggy hair invokes the gods of the ancestors while chanting mysterious words in African dialect. Suddenly Boukman stands up and in an inspired voice cries out, "God who made the sun that shines on us from above, who makes the sea to rage and the thunder roll, this same great God from his hiding place on a cloud, hear me, all of you, is looking down upon us. He sees what the whites are doing. The God of the whites asks for crime; ours desires only blessings. But this God who is good directs you to vengeance! He will direct our arms, he will help us. Cast aside the image of the God of the whites who thirsts for our tears and pay heed to the voice of liberty speaking in our hearts..."

(14) THE UPRISING

Stéphen Alexis, *Black Liberator*, 1949

Eight days after the Bois Caiman ceremony, the insurrection began, taking the whites completely by surprise. Within a week the northern plain was under the control of thousands of former slaves and the main city, Cap-Français, was surrounded.

On the night of August 22 a furious horde of Negroes, under the leadership of Boukmann, swept across the plantations, bound for Cap-Français. The first fire of the revolt had been the burning of the Chabaud plantation. Thousands of savage Negroes, armed with stakes, spears, iron bars, axes, knives, and spades, poured in a maddened torrent across the countryside. Not a single white was spared, regardless of age or sex. The whole plain was in flames. The horde advanced steadily to the rhythm of wild songs that were carried into Cap Français to the ears of the terrified landowners. Nearly all the wealthy mansions of Haut du Cap were on fire. Estates which had borne illustrious names – Fronsac, Vaudreuill, D'Argenson, Grammont, Charmettes, Noailles – became so many heaps of ashes. The atmosphere was sickly with the smell of burning sugar and burning flesh. Wisps of burning cotton floated through the crimson sky like tongues of fire. It was a truly apocalyptic night: all the fields of sugar-cane were aflame as far as the eye could see, all the immensity of the Negroes' suffering had blazed up in an instant.

The revolt had taken the authorities of Cap Français unawares, and they had few troops available. Messengers were hastily sent to Santo Domingo, Jamaica, and Curaçao to implore assistance, but without success. All the white men capable of bearing arms were mobilised into resistance corps. M. de Grandmaison, a rich land-owner, sent the following letter, dated September 9, 1791, to a friend in Paris: "Despite the help of the mulatto freed men, who have generously offered their assistance, we are not strong enough to attack and destroy these savage beasts. When they are asked why they have revolted they claim the Rights of Man, or freedom, or three days' holiday a week with pay – or else they say they will do without masters, since the whites have decided to do without kings." [...]

In the distance the rebellion roared and rumbled like a tempestuous sea. Failure met all the attempts to repel the insurgents, who now encircled Cap Français. The Negroes, although badly led and poorly armed, were upheld by a spirit which made them formidable enemies. Some, armed only with knives, hurled themselves at loaded guns, and were blown to bits when the gunners fired; but what did it matter? Others would take their place and do as they had done. singing as they did so: 'Gunpowder is but water! Ping! Pindang! Cannon is but bamboo! Ping! Pindang!' Irresolutely the battle waged to and fro, so that now the other side had the advantage; but there was no quarter either given or taken.

(15) BRITISH GRAVEYARD

David Geggus, *The British Army and the Slave Revolt*, 1982

When war broke out in Europe in February 1793, the British government saw an opportunity to seize the 'pearl of the Antilles' from the
French. Between 1793 and 1798 over 20,000 British soldiers were sent
to Saint Domingue to capture the island for the British empire. David
Geggus tells the story of one of the forgotten catastrophes of Britain's imperial history.

The influx of unacclimatised troops into the Caribbean fuelled a
massive 'pandemic' of yellow fever. Most of the British soldiers sent to Saint Domingue – at least three in every five – died
there...Death from disease, without doubt, was the central experience of the soldier's life in Saint Domingue. It created an atmosphere
of fear and despair, and even before leaving Europe a contemporary
wrote, 'the officer and soldier bound for this service look upon themselves as doomed to certain destruction'[...]

During the first half of the occupation, up to 1796, most of the
British troops were confined to the coastal towns. They found them
places under siege, cut off from the surrounding countryside and
ringed with fortifications. Hemmed in by mountains, crowded, claustrophobic and tense, they awoke with the morning gun and fell silent
at curfew. Surrounded by an exotic enemy, hydra-like and elusive,
numbering tens of thousands, the troops were unable to set foot beyond their picket lines without being attacked. Patrols were
ambushed; sentries and forage parties were sniped at. As their numbers dwindled, military duties fell more heavily on the survivors.
Consequently, men went for months without taking off their clothes
for a full night's sleep [...]

As only four of the thirty or so regiments sent to Saint Domingue
managed to arrive in the dry, healthy months from December to
March, it was never very long before new arrivals were struck down
with yellow fever or malaria. The effect could be shattering. Men fit
in the morning were sometimes dead by nightfall. Two weeks after
reaching Saint Marc, a bewildered officer was writing, 'hundreds
almost were absolutely drowned in their own blood bursting from
them at every pore; some died raving mad, others forming plans of
attacking, other desponding'. Thirty black slaves, he said, spent all
the daylight hours digging graves and could scarcely keep pace with
the dying, though up to five bodies were placed in each grave. At

Saint Marc the sick were crowded into barns and stables. At Port-au-Prince the great wards of the General Hospital were packed with the victims of yellow fever, whose groans and stench in the summer heat made the building a nightmare to experience [...]

For the British troops, this was a mainly a war of posts and ambushes. Colonial troops sometimes conducted raids but the Europeans usually fought on the defensive behind fortifications. Battle casualties were remarkably few, although among the ex-slaves losses were enormous. When attacking, the black slaves displayed a bravery that was only too often suicidal. Whether 'as naked as earthworms', as the black leader Toussaint Louverture described his men in 1795, or fully equipped and regimented, as in 1798, they were cut down by the hundred year after year. Yet their numbers continued to grow, and as was frequently noted, so did their skills in the art of war. They tended to emerge suddenly from the woods at dawn and attack *en masse*, scattering if resisted to snipe from behind bushes and rocks. They not only appeared in great numbers but further unnerved their opponents by beating drums, howling and whistling, and trumpeting eerily on large conch shells. If attacked, they invariably withdrew and, unless caught by cavalry, melted away into the forest, to the intense frustration of their pursuers. They evidently lacked the training that enabled European troops to stand still and be killed.

(16) SLAVE TURNED GENERAL

René Depestre, *Toussaint Louverture: Haiti's Tragic Hero,* 1981

Haitian poet, René Depestre, pays tribute to hero of the Haitian Revolution, Toussaint Louverture.

⁄⁄   Brothers and friends, I am Toussaint Louverture; my name is perhaps already known to you. I am intent on vengeance. I want liberty and equality to be respected in Santo Domingo, and I shall work until this goal is achieved. Join us, brothers, and fight alongside us for the same cause."

The man who, in 1793, at the age of fifty, was addressing himself in these terms to his unfortunate companions, had reached a point in his life when he felt ready to give himself completely to a task which transcended that of his own destiny.

Toussaint Bréda was born on 20 May 1742 on the residence of the same name, at the place called Haut-du-Cap. He was a descendent of Gaou-Guinou, an African prince of the Aradas group. His godfather Pierre Baptiste taught him how to read and write. The French he learned opened the way to such works as the *Commentaries* of Julius Caesar, the *Reveries* of Marshal Saxe, the *History of Wars* by Herodotus and, above all, the famous *Histoire philosophique des deux Indes* by the Abbé Raynal. The latter work represented an exceptional "opening" (*ouverture*) for his imaginative genius and for the name under which the slave of Bréda was to distinguish himself.

In addition, his familiarity with his country's medicinal plants, and the rudiments of veterinary science, which he had acquired while working in the stables of his master, Bayon Libertat, enabled him to exercise unquestionable influence over the Maroon negroes of the mountains once he joined them. His small stature, taciturn and fragile air, and ugly features cloaked a great strength of character, combined with outstanding powers of physical and mental endurance which brought him phenomenal success when directing operations which took place in Santo Domingo (Haiti) from 1791 to 1803.

The principal historical claim to fame of Toussaint Louverture is that he transformed groups of Maroon negroes into a seasoned and disciplined army of liberation. His consummate skill in guerrilla tactics, plus a shrewd appreciation of when to compromise, enabled him to exploit to the maximum the colonial rivalries between the different empires represented on the political and military stage of the Caribbean.

The closing years of the 18th century brought eventful times to the colony of Santo Domingo where Toussaint Louverture had set in motion the irreversible process of emancipation. Toussaint was aware that the new power directing France since the *coup d'état* of the 18th Brumaire would put in question the fragile conquests of the Haitian Revolution. His fears were justified, for Bonaparte lost no time in introducing a decree which made it obligatory to place on all the flags of Santo Domingo the following inscription: "Gallant black people, remember that the French people and only the French people recognise your liberty and the equality of your rights". Toussaint Louverture reacted sharply to this measure: "It is not", he said, "a circumstantial liberty conceded to us alone that we wish, but the unequivocal adoption of the principle that no man, whether he be born red, black or white, can become the property of his fellow-men."

(17) MILITARY STRATEGY

Toussaint Louverture, *Letter to Laveaux,* 1795

In June 1795, Toussaint Louverture led his troops into battle against the pro-French royalist forces under Dessources. The outcome was a famous victory over the planters that lifted the prestige of the blacks as a military force and furthered the reputation of Toussaint. In a letter that illustrates both his writing skills and his military acumen, Toussaint describes the battle to his then ally, the French republican general, Laveaux.

The enemy had not taken the precaution to establish on the St Marc road reserve camps to protect his retreat. I used a trick to encourage him to pass by the highway; this is how. From the town of Verettes he could see all my movements, so I made my army defile on the side of Mirebalais, where he could see it, so as to give the idea that I was sending large reinforcements there; while a moment after I made it re-enter the town of Petite-Rivière behind a hill without his perceiving it. He fell right into the snare, seeming even to hasten his retreat. I then made a large body of cavalry cross the river, putting myself at the head of it in order to reach the enemy quickly, and keep him busy, and in order to give time to my infantry, which was coming up behind with a piece of cannon, to join me. This manoeuvre succeeded marvellously. I had taken the precaution to send a four-inch piece of cannon from Petite-Rivière to the Moreau plantation at Détroit in order to batter the enemy on his right flank during his passage. While I harassed him with my cavalry, my infantry advanced at great speed with a piece of cannon. As soon as it reached me I made two columns pass to right and to left to take the enemy in flank. As soon as these two columns arrived within pistol shot, I served the enemy in true republican fashion.

He continued his way, showing all the time a brave front. But the first cannon shot that I caused to be fired among his men – and which did a great deal of damage – made him abandon first a wagon and then a piece of cannon. I redoubled the charge and afterwards I captured the other three pieces of cannon, two wagons full of ammunition and seven others full of wounded, who were promptly sent to the rear. Then it was that the enemy began to fly in the greatest disorder, only for those at the head of the retreat to find themselves right in the mouth of the piece of cannon that I had posted at Détroit on the Moreau plantation. And when the enemy saw himself taken in front, behind and on all sides, that fine fellow, the impertinent

Dessources, jumped off his horse and threw himself into the brush-wood with the debris of his army, calling out, "Every man for himself." Rain and darkness caused me to discontinue the pursuit. This battle lasted from eleven in the morning to six in the evening and cost me only six dead and as many wounded. I have strewn the road with corpses for the distance of more than a league. My victory has been most complete and if the celebrated Dessources is lucky enough to re-enter St Marc it will be without cannon, without baggage, in short what is called with neither drum nor trumpet. He has lost everything, even honour, if vile royalists are capable of having any. He will remember the republican lesson which I have taught him.

(18) DESSALINES

Félix Morisseau-Leroy, *Thank You Dessalines*, 1953

The Haitian poet, Félix Morisseau-Leroy, wrote this eulogy to Jean-Jacques Dessalines, hero of the Haitian war of independence. This illiterate former slave, whose back bore the scars of lashings administered by his owners, became the founder of the independent black republic of Haiti. He is remembered each year with a national holiday on 17 October, the date in 1806 of his death by assassination.

> Thank you, Dessalines
> Papa Dessalines, thank you
> Every time I think of who I am
> I say thank you Dessalines
> Every time I hear a black man
> Who is still under the white man's rule
> A black man who is not free to talk
> I say: Dessalines, thank you
> I alone know what you mean to me
> Thank you, Papa Dessalines
> If I am a man
> I must say: Thank you, Dessalines
> If I open my eyes to look
> It is thanks to you, Dessalines
> If I raise my head to walk
> It is thanks to you, Dessalines

Every time I look at other negroes
I say: Thank you, Dessalines
When I see what's happening in other lands
I say: thank you, Dessalines
When I hear white people talk
I say: Papa Dessalines, thank you
When I hear some negroes like me talk
I say: Thank you, Papa Dessalines
Only I know what you are for me
Dessalines, my bull
Dessalines, my blood
Dessalines, my two eyes
Dessalines, my guts
Only I know
All negroes must say
Thank you, Dessalines
You are the one who showed us the way
Thank you Dessalines
You are our guiding light
Dessalines
You gave us the land on which we walk
The sky above our heads
The trees, the rivers
The sea, the lake, it is you
Dessalines, you gave us the sun
You gave us the moon
You gave us our sisters, our brothers
Our mothers, our fathers, our children
You made us who we are
You made us kind of different
From the other negroes

(19) BIRTH OF HAITI

Boisrond Tonnerre, *Declaration of Independence*, 1804

Extracts from the Proclamation of Independence written and read on behalf of Jean-Jacques Dessalines by his secretary, Boisrond Tonnerre, in Gonaïves on 1 January 1804.

Citizens,

It is not enough to have thrown out of your country those barbarians who have soaked it in blood for two centuries; it is not sufficient to have curbed the factions that still play tricks on the spectre of liberty that France has revealed to you all: to guarantee the triumph of freedom in the country that you have seen born, you must make one last act of national authority. If the inhuman government that has held our spirits in the most humiliating torpor for so long is to give up all hope of subjugating us again, we must live free or we must die.

Independence or death...these are the sacred words that unite us [...]

Citizens, men, women, children, look around this island, look for your wives, your husbands, your brothers, your sisters, your children, your nursing babies. Where have they gone?...I shudder to say it...They have fallen prey to these vultures [...]

When they come near our shores, the French must tremble, if not from guilt for the atrocities they have committed, then from our resolution to put to death any French-born whose footprint desecrates our land of liberty [...]

Peace to our neighbours, but damn the French. Eternal hatred of France shall be our cry [...]

Generals and leaders, gathered here next to me to the delight of our country, the day has come, this day that must linger on in our glory, our independence.

If there exists among us any faint-hearts, shrink from and shiver at the taking of the oath that must unite us. Swear to whole world, to posterity, to ourselves, to renounce France forever and to die rather than live under domination. Swear to fight until the last breath for the independence of our country.

And you, the people, unfortunate for all too long, and now witness to the vows we are making, remember that I counted on your determination and courage when I started out on this career of combat against despotism and tyranny, against those whom you fought for 14 years. Recall everything that I have sacrificed to fly to your defence: relatives, children, wealth, so that now, the only riches I have are your freedom. Recall that my name horrifies all those who are slavers, and that tyrants and despots can only bring themselves to utter it when they curse the day I was born...With clasped hands, make the vow to live free and independent, and to accept death rather than live under the yoke. Swear to hunt down the traitors and enemies of your independence [...]

Translated from French by Charles Arthur

CHAPTER TWO
THE STATUS QUO:
ELITES, SOLDIERS AND DICTATORS

The new independent state of Haiti was born in far from propitious circumstances. The colonial powers, whose empires continued to depend on slavery, were openly hostile to the world's first black republic, and for several decades there was a constant threat of invasion. Internally, the country had been left devastated by thirteen years of near continuous warfare and destruction. The plantations, on which the economic prosperity of the French colony had been based, were in ruins, and many towns had been razed to the ground. Prospects for economic reconstruction were hampered by shortages of capital and labour. Many of the white planters had fled the country, while those who remained were massacred by Dessalines' troops in the aftermath of independence. War and disease over the course of the conflict meant that the size of the population had fallen by as much as a third.

Among those Haitians who had survived the revolution there soon emerged two distinct and very different conceptions of the form the new society should take. A small but powerful minority, mainly mulattoes, who had been free men and property owners before the revolution began, hoped to inherit the power and wealth formerly enjoyed by the defeated French colonists. On the other hand, the majority of the population, the black ex-slaves, bore a deep-seated antipathy towards work in the plantation system, and hoped instead for the opportunity to farm their own land. During the early decades of independence, the interplay between these racially and ideologically divided groups determined the economic, social, and political foundations of modern-day Haiti.

Under Dessalines a large percentage of cultivated land was brought under state control, and he planned to continue with Toussaint's attempts to revive large-scale agriculture. Less than three years into his leadership, Dessalines fell victim to a power-struggle which, significantly, was linked to the two recurring themes in Haitian history: the issue of ownership of agricultural land, and the continuing tensions between blacks and mulattoes. (1)

His successor, the most senior army officer, Henri Christophe, assumed power, but the mulatto minority that dominated in the south seceded, and the country split into two separate entities. In the north, Christophe had himself crowned king and created a black nobility. He used military force in an attempt to re-invigorate the plantation system and redevelop an export economy based on coffee and sugar. A type of feudalism was imposed, with large plantations run by military and state officers, and worked by strictly supervised labourers. This version of militarised agriculture generated large surpluses, and the revenue was used to strengthen the army and build extensive fortifications in preparation for an expected French invasion. The most spectacular of these was the formidable Citadelle of La Ferrière, built at enormous human cost. (2) Christophe's forced labour policy was deeply unpopular with those who worked the land, and in 1820 he committed suicide in the midst of an uprising.

In the south, the mulattoes established a republic under the leadership of Alexandre Pétion. Mindful of the potential for a black backlash against their rule if he attempted to force workers back to the plantations, Pétion instead distributed state-owned land in an effort to buy political acceptance. During his presidency over 150,000 hectares were distributed or sold to more than 10,000 individuals. Although the best lands were granted to members of the mostly mulatto elite, each member of the mainly black army was also allocated a six-hectare plot.

Following the death of Christophe, Pétion's successor, Jean-Pierre Boyer, reunited the country. He attempted to remove the continuing threat of invasion by annexing the eastern part of the island in 1822, an occupation that lasted until 1844 when an independent Dominican Republic was established. Boyer also bought French recognition of Haiti's independence with the payment of a massive indemnity to compensate French planters for property lost in the revolution. On the domestic front, the prosperity of the landowning clique who surrounded Boyer was undermined by a shortage of agricultural labour arising from the growing number of smallholdings. More and more peasant farmers were working their own land on plots granted by Pétion, on squatted plantation land that had been left idle or abandoned, and on new plots carved out of marginal land on hills and mountainsides. Early on in his long rule, Boyer made a failed attempted to tie rural workers to the service of a few large landowners, and thereafter the distribution of state land was resumed.

By the time Boyer's government, weakened by the manoeuvres of rival sections of the political clique, collapsed in 1843, the majority of the population was made up of small peasant farmers. The era of the plantation system had passed, and the minority elite, or more properly elites, had turned to new ways of perpetuating their wealth.

The black elite, heirs of the revolutionary army officers and Christophe's nobility, was largely located in the northern city of Cap-Haïtien (formerly Cap-Français), and in rural areas where it retained land that was rented out rather than farmed directly. The mulatto elite was mostly based in the capital, Port-au-Prince, and the southern towns of Jérémie, Jacmel and Les Cayes. Although members of both the black and mulatto oligarchies retained some land, the elite as a whole increasingly turned its attention and investments away from agricultural production, and focused instead on the economy of distribution and exchange. Shopkeepers, merchants, and moneylenders grew rich, but it was through the control of state tax and customs apparatus that Haiti's elite perfected a system of accumulation that has lasted into the contemporary period. (3)

From the mid-nineteenth century onwards, Haitian politics has been dominated by the struggle between groups within the small elite for control of the state apparatus through control of the presidency. The fight for office to a very great extent became a fight for the spoils that came with it. Once in control, the incumbent and the clique around him, anticipating that it would only be a matter of time before rival groups would conspire to unseat them, moved quickly to plunder the state coffers, and fleece the treasury. A period of great instability ensued, illustrated by the fact that of the 21 administrations between 1843 and 1915 only two managed to complete its term of office. (4)

Coups d'état and political uprisings became the most common means of both installing and removing governments. The country was still heavily militarised, and the contending elite groups depended on the intervention of military leaders and the factions of the army they controlled to win power. In return for their support, military officers were rewarded with grants of state land and political office.

The minority mulatto elite continued to exercise power while paying lip service to the political aspirations of the small number of black elite families and high-ranking black army officers. The formula of 'government of the understudy', or *politique de doublure*, saw black presidents in power but controlled and manipulated by the mulatto politicians. This system barely masked a continuing and deep-seated social antipathy between mulatto and black elites. (5)

The US occupation of Haiti from 1915 to 1934 (see Chapter 7) temporarily united both sides of the divided elite in a nationalist movement, but old antagonisms soon reappeared once the Marines departed. Those who favoured the mulatto hegemony, were opposed by those who championed a redistribution of economic and political power. This latter tendency was bolstered by an emerging black middle class of schoolteachers, clerks, civil servants and small businessmen.

One highly significant legacy of the occupation was the centralisation of administrative, economic, and political power in the capital, and, as a consequence, the diminished influence of elite groups based in coastal towns. As part of this process the Haitian military was reorganised, and became increasingly linked and involved with political affairs in Port-au-Prince. (6) The military exercised its new role as arbiter of political control of the centralised state by intervening to depose presidents Lescot in 1946, and Estimé in 1950. (7) Yet the presidency of the black military officer, Paul Magloire (1950-56), represented a return to the politique de doublure, where the mulatto elite was the power behind the throne.

In 1957 a general election was won by François Duvalier, a country doctor who since the 1930s had been a leading light in a group of black middle-class intellectuals known as *noiristes*. The noiristes stressed the cultural importance of Haiti's African past, and proposed an alliance between the black middle class and the masses to overturn mulatto dominance. Initially perceived as little more than a tool of the military, 'Papa Doc', as he became known, soon proved he was his own man.

First, his political opponents and their supporters were arrested or driven into exile. Then, to guard against the threat of a military coup, Duvalier transferred or replaced senior officers, and placed elite units under his direct command. The army leadership, and Papa Doc's own cabinet and inner circle were regularly purged. As a counterweight to the military, an irregular force was recruited and transformed into a private presidential militia, known as the Tontons Macoutes.

Duvalier used the Macoutes as spies, neighbourhood bullies, and shock-troops to suppress all real and potential sources of opposition. Trade unions were dismantled, progressive Catholic priests were expelled, newspapers were closed down, and even the Boy Scouts were disbanded. Terror and repression were the watchwords as Duvalier and his henchmen employed ever more blatant forms of extortion and corruption to enrich themselves. (8)

Papa Doc's fourteen-year long dictatorship relied on extreme violence that claimed the lives of tens of thousands of Haitians. Yet, significantly, the regime also had its supporters. Membership of the Tontons Macoutes, a force that grew in size to outnumber the military; employment as a section chief or deputy in the 515 rural section; rapid promotion through the military ranks: all these represented new avenues of social and economic advancement for the black lower middle class. In a more general sense, Duvalier's anti-mulatto rhetoric appealed to sections of the urban black middle class, and their rural counterparts. The agreement Duvalier reached with the Vatican in 1966 to nominate his own bishops not only brought the Catholic Church – the last remaining national institution of any influence – to heel, but was presented by Duvalier as an example of his black nationalist credentials. (9)

When Papa Doc died in 1971, the disabling of all serious opposition, and the tacit endorsement of important power-brokers such as the United States, the military high command and much of the business community, ensured that power was transferred smoothly to his 19-year-old son, Jean-Claude. Under the new leader, dubbed 'Baby Doc' by the foreign media, the ruthless repression of internal dissent, both real and imagined continued. (10)

During Jean-Claude's regime the process of siphoning off state revenues by those in power reached new extremes. Hundreds of millions of dollars were stolen by Jean-Claude and a small circle of associates. Such was the scope of the corruption, extortion, fraud and patronage in the service of personal enrichment, that the Haitian state came to be described as a 'kleptocracy'. (11) While Jean-Claude and his cronies grew fabulously rich, the majority of Haitians slipped deeper into poverty. The percentage of the population living in extreme poverty rose from 48 per cent in 1976 to 81 per cent in 1985. Under the Duvaliers, Haiti became one of the poorest, and most economically polarised, countries in the world.

Eventually Jean-Claude alienated important supporters among the old-guard noiristes and the black middle class by shifting his power base towards younger mulatto 'technocrats' and businessmen. As the regime faltered and an opposition movement grew, the US and the Haitian military withdrew their support, and in February 1986 Jean-Claude left the country for a life in exile.

During a four-year period known as 'Duvalierism without Duvalier', a series of military juntas headed by senior officers attempted to secure the old order in the face of challenges from both the poor majority and a section of the elite. Since the 1970s the latter had diversified its business interests from traditional import-export operations to low-wage assembly industries for the US market, and with the fall of Jean-Claude was pushing for reforms to modernise the state. These reforms, backed by the US and the international finance institutions, included a proposed transition to electoral democracy. The Duvalierists violently resisted changes to the political system, notably in the case of the aborted 1987 election. (12)

With the Macoute network disbanded, officially if not in practice, and the adoption of a progressive new constitution which
included a provision banning leading Duvalierists from political office for a ten-year period, the military reasserted itself as a dominant
force in Haitian politics. Soldiers, police and section chiefs enjoyed
the fruits of political power through the tried and tested mechanisms
of embezzlement and the woefully corrupt judicial system. (13) High-
ranking officers set up new money-making schemes such as
drug-trafficking, principally the transshipment of Colombian cocaine
and the control of the contraband trade. (14)

Over the years a small number of elite families had grown fan-
tastically wealthy through the exploitation of the country's peasant
producers. In their luxury villas in the suburbs of Pétionville, La
Boule and Kenscoff in the hills above Port-au-Prince, these rich
mulatto families viewed the newly mobilised and organised peasantry and urban slum dwellers with apprehension. (15) The military
was regarded as a necessary insurance against an uprising, à la 1791,
of the poor masses.

Yet a significant faction of the traditional elite, and the newer
group of technocrats and industrialists, perceived the old system
that the military propped up as an impediment to economic progress.
Merchants were denied opportunities to compete by the existence
of tightly controlled monopolies. Instead of the chance to exploit an
internal market of consumers, they saw only the increasing impoverishment of the population. Industrialists wanted a state that would
implement policies to facilitate the accumulation of capital and open
Haiti to foreign trade and investment. (16)

These pressures, combined with the political consideration of the
need to head off the threat posed by an increasingly radicalised popular movement, lead to the holding of internationally-monitored
elections in 1990. The late entry into the contest of the radical liberation theology priest, Jean-Bertrand Aristide, and the subsequent
registration to vote of tens of thousands of previously apathetic peasants and urban poor confounded the plans of the technocrats and
industrialists. The Lavalas candidate won an overwhelming majority, trouncing their man, a former World Bank official who enjoyed
the support of the US.

Aristide's victory represented the first serious challenge to the
status quo in Haiti's history. Although essentially social-democratic
in its programme, the reforms proposed by the Aristide government
were enough to upset most sections of the elite: large landowners
by talk of agrarian reform; industrialists by a proposed increase in
the minimum wage; the military by proposals to separate the police

from the army and to root out drug-traffickers; and Duvalierists by the disbanding of the section chief system and reform of corrupt state institutions. (17) The triumph of the Lavalas movement also threatened to eclipse the traditional politicians, and the conservative hierarchy of the Catholic Church. The elite as a whole was shocked by the sudden appearance on the political stage of representatives of the formerly marginalised poor majority.

Less than eight months after taking office, Aristide was overthrown by a military coup d'état, rumoured to have been financed by leading elite families. (18) For three years, the military and a resurgent Macoute sector carried out an intense and violent campaign of repression against the popular organisations which had mushroomed since the fall of Duvalier and formed the backbone of the Lavalas movement. (19) A half-hearted economic embargo applied by the international community failed to dislodge the military regime, which together with the leading families of the elite found new ways to make profits from a thriving contraband trade.

Nearly two centuries since independence, Haiti remains a starkly polarised society. At the top of the pyramid a group of millionaire families sit astride the economy. (20) The unseating of the military regime by a United Nations intervention force in 1994, the abolition of the military and the creation of a new police force in 1995 have failed to result in any significant change to the country's status quo.

(1) LAND AND COLOUR

David Nicholls, *From Dessalines to Duvalier*, 1979

Jean-Jacques Dessalines, the first leader of independent Haiti, was an early victim of the long-running power-struggle between mulattoes and blacks.

Independence had been won as the result of the tenuous alliance between the *anciens libres* and the *nouveaux libres*.[1] Most of the leading *anciens libres* were mulattoes and the vast majority of the former slaves were black. The *anciens libres* were property owners, and had retained their property through the revolutionary period. What is more, some of them had received property from their white fathers who had fled the country and others had illegally seized vacant properties, particularly in the South. With the abolition of slavery in 1793 the legal distinction between these two groups had been done away with, but as the country moved towards independence these two economic classes, which were largely identifiable by colour differences, faced one another... These economic and colour distinctions were reinforced by regional factors, so that the mulattoes were strongest in the South and the West, while the blacks dominated the political and military forces in the Artibonite and the North. It was Dessalines' ambition to eliminate colour prejudice from the life of the country, and this was reflected in the constitutional article... which referred to all Haitians as black; he offered the hand of his daughter to Pétion as a token of his determination to break down colour lines. Yet the economic disparity between the two groups had to be faced. In a well-known statement Dessalines referred to the unjust situation whereby *anciens libres* retained all the private property of the country, while the former slaves remained without land. Why should the sons of the white colonists have property and those whose fathers are in Africa have none? 'The sons of the colonists', he declared, 'Have taken advantage of my poor blacks. Be on your guard, negroes and mulattoes, we have all fought against the whites; the properties which we have conquered by the spilling of our blood belong to us all; I intend that they be divided with equity.' Whether Dessalines intended to divide the land into small properties and distribute them to the people, or whether he meant to extend state ownership with blacks enjoying equality with mulattoes, is not entirely clear. What was clear to his hearers was the emperor's intention of confiscating some of the recently acquired land from the *ancien libres,* and this is certainly one of the reasons for his assassination in October 1806.

[1] *Anciens libres* were those who were free before the beginning of the revolution. *Nouveaux libres* those who had gained their freedom during the war.

(2) CHRISTOPHE'S KINGDOM

John Candler, *Brief Notices of Hayti,* 1842

A British visitor, writing in 1842, describes the economic success and harsh rule brought to northern Haiti by King Henri Christophe (1806-20).

Although he began his career with an evident desire to improve the condition of the people, and give them a standing among civilised nations, the maxims of his government were unfortunately tyrannical. Wanting a revenue, and not knowing how otherwise to obtain it, and believing also that the people had become too much dissipated by war to labour willingly for wages, he compelled field labour at the point of the bayonet. By this means, he secured large crops of sugar and rum; and making himself, like Mohammed Ali of Egypt, the principal merchant in his own dominions, he became rich, kept a court, and maintained a standing army. He took possession of the best plantations in his own right, and gave others to some of his military comrades, and a few civilians who pleased him, on whom he bestowed the titles of Barons, Counts, and Dukes... Many of the estates of his great men were cultivated like his own, by coerced labour. Liberty did not at once obtain dominion in Hayti. The black army had triumphed; but the black generals forgetting the pit of slavery from whence they had emerged, exercised little regard to their companions in arms who had fought under them in the ranks [...]

Buoyant at first with success, Christophe became soured in after life through repeated disappointments. Possessing great powers of mind, he resolved on great enterprises, and having once undertaken a project would suffer no controllable difficulty to interrupt its progress. The citadel of La Ferrière had been begun by the French: he determined to carry out the design, and make it one of the strongest fortresses of the world. I asked Captain Agendeau of Cape

Haytien who worked two years and a half as a prisoner within the walls, how many persons had lost their lives by hard labour during its erection? "As many persons," he replied, "as there are stones in the building: every stone cost the life of a human being." This famous citadel was reared by bands of men and women, who were compelled to labour on very insufficient rations of food: vast numbers died in consequence of exhaustion, and many more of wounds and bruises received in the cruel work of forcing stones and other heavy materials up the steep sides of the mountain.

(3) TAXING THE PEASANTRY

Michel-Rolph Trouillot, *Haiti's Nightmare and the Lessons of History*, 1994

Unable to restore the plantation system in the period immediately after independence, urban elites instead established an alternative way to amass fortunes during the presidencies of Pétion (1807-18) and Boyer (1818- 43).

The elites turned the fiscal and marketing systems of the country into mechanisms that would allow them to siphon the wealth produced by the peasants. As traders, politicians and state employees, they lived off the peasants' labour. An import-export bourgeoisie, dominated by foreign nationals and unconcerned by local production, garnered profits from the labour of the peasantry. Taxes collected in the urban markets and at the custom-houses – and ultimately paid by the peasants – provided the bulk of government revenues. In 1842, more than 90% of government revenues were collected at the custom-houses. In 1891, import and export duties accounted for 98.2% of state income.

Coffee, Haiti's main agricultural export, was the favourite target of these elites and the centrepiece of Haiti's fiscal policy. The direct and hidden taxes imposed on that peasant crop accounted for from 60 to 90% of government revenues from the late 1800s to the first half of this century. Up until recently, the various charges on coffee amounted to a 40% tax on peasant income in a country where, after almost 200 years of independence, the government has yet to collect income tax from most merchants, civil servants, or middle-class employees.

Successive Haitian governments also heavily taxed food and other necessities such as flour, oil, candles, kerosene and matches. Meanwhile, luxuries consumed by the elites entered the country free of charge. At the turn of the century, for example, import duties on a pair of opera glasses were equal to those on five gallons of kerosene. Eighty years later, as coffee exports fell during Jean-Claude Duvalier's regime, taxes on flour, sugar, petroleum, tobacco and matches provided as much as 25% of government revenues. Meanwhile, the number of luxury cars in the streets of Port-au-Prince reached an all-time high.

The economic response of the Haitian elites to the emergence of an independent peasantry refusing to labour on the plantations guaranteed that they would get their surplus willy nilly, even if it meant squeezing the nation to death. The state reproduced itself by sucking up the peasantry; the urban classes reproduced themselves by sucking up the state *and* the peasantry. For a century and a half, successive governments have prolonged the agony.

(4) EPHEMERAL PRESIDENCIES

Various Sources, Haitian Heads of State and Regime Changes,1843-1915

The coup d'état has been the established method of changing governments throughout much of Haitian history.

Head of State	Political Fate
R. Hérard (1843-1844)	Overthrown
P. Guerrier ((1844-1845)	Died in office
L. Pierrot (1845-1846)	Overthrown
J.-B. Riché (1846-1847)	Died in office
F. Soulouque (1847-1859)	Overthrown
F-N. Geffrard (1859-1867)	Overthrown
S. Salnave (1867-1869)	Overthrown
N. Saget (1870-1874)	Retired after full term
M. Domingue (1874-1876)	Overthrown
B. Canal (1876-1879)	Overthrown
L.F. Salomon (1879-1888)	Overthrown
F. Légitime (1888-1889)	Overthrown
F. Hippolyte (1889-1896)	Died in office
T.A.S. Sam (1896-1902)	Completed term

N. Alexis (1902-1908)	Overthrown
A. Simon (1908-1911)	Overthrown
C. Leconte (1911-1912)	Died in office (killed by bomb explosion in the national palace)
T. Auguste (1912-1913)	Died in office (poisoned)
M. Oreste (1913-1914)	Overthrown
O. Zamor (1914)	Overthrown
D. Théodore (1914-15)	Overthrown
V.G. Sam (1915)	Overthrown and assassinated

(5) DIVIDED ELITE

Spencer St John, *Hayti or the Black Republic*, 1884

The British ambassador to Haiti from 1863 to 1884 laments the bitter racial antagonism between mulatto and black members of the elite.

Everyone who mixes in Haytian society is struck by the paucity of black gentlemen to be met with at balls, concerts, or the theatre, and the almost total absence of black ladies. At some of the largest given by the late President Geffrard, I have counted but three black ladies to perhaps a hundred coloured; and although the gentlemen were more numerous, it was evident that their presence arose from their official positions, and not from a desire to mix with the society.

There is a marked line drawn between the black and the mulatto, which is probably the most disastrous circumstance for the future prosperity of the country. A faithful historian, after carefully studying past events, can come to no other conclusion that the low state of civilisation which still obtains in the island arises principally from this unmeaning quarrel. The black hates the mulatto, the mulatto despises the black; proscriptions, judicial murders, massacres have arisen, and will continue to arise as long as this deplorable feeling prevails. There is no sign of its abatement; on the contrary, never was it so marked as at the present day. A black Minister once said to me, "We blacks and whites like and respect each other, because we are of pure race, but as for those mulattoes..."

I remember, on my arrival in Port-au-Prince in 1863, having a conversation with a young mulatto lady, no longer in the freshness of youth, on the subject of intermarriage; and having faintly indicated that I thought she had been unwise in refusing the hand of one of the best-mannered, best-educated, and richest blacks in the country, I received a reply which completely surprised me, "Sir, you insult me to imagine I would marry a black. No, I will never marry anyone but a white." [...]

This contempt of the black is felt by nearly every coloured girl, and is bitterly resented. I have seen young mulatto women refusing to dance with blacks at a ball, and the latter, in fury, threatening to call out the father or brother of the offending beauty. Yet what can be more absurd than such a pretension or prejudice, when, but two generations removed, their mothers were African slaves!

(6) RISE OF THE MILITARY

Michel-Rolph Trouillot, *Haiti: State Against Nation*, 1990

The reform of the Haitian military, carried out during the US occupation (1915-34), established a significant new political force.

The renewed militarisation that the Marines imposed on the state apparatus included the formation of a Haitian gendarmerie (later called Garde), the predecessor of the current army. After an uncertain start, the ranks swelled rapidly. By 1937, the new military apparatus, controlled from Port-au-Prince and filling the functions of both army and police, had 4,653 members. The complete disarming of the peasantry by the Garde, the strengthening of the power of the *police rurale*, and the centralisation of the new military force all contributed to the concentration of political power in Port-au-Prince. The effects were all the more strongly felt because the Marines prevented the development of regional solidarities within the new force. Hereafter, as Hans Schmidt rightly notes, "Political strongmen in Port-au-Prince were able to control the entire country more effectively than ever before."

This concentration of power was particularly dangerous because it was wielded by men who shared an extremely narrow sense of Haiti as a nation. We cannot overemphasize this fundamental political difference between the Garde and the army that was dismantled by the Marines. For all its flaws – and despite the fact that it had killed as many Haitians during the second half of its 122-year-long history as it had Frenchmen during the wars for independence – Haiti's first army saw itself as the offspring of the struggle against

slavery and colonialism...Its most important post-independence campaigns were the four – however unfortunate – against the Dominican
Republic. In short, it was primarily an army that claimed to fight
foreigners and to defend the national community. Because of its
stated role, because of its origins, and because of Haiti's position in
the world, the nineteenth century Haitian army believed it had been
assigned a national mission, even though history may have proved
it wrong.

   In sharp contrast, the Haitian Garde was specifically created to
fight against other Haitians. It received its baptism of fire in combat
against its countrymen. And the Garde, like the army it was to sire,
has indeed never fought anyone but Haitians. Its most important
campaign was its participation alongside the Marines in the war
against the peasant nationalists led by Charlemagne Péralte and
Benoit Batraville when Marines and Garde together killed at least
6,000 peasants...But the Garde did not turn its arms against peasants alone. From the earliest days of the occupation, the new form of
state violence it represented was also applied against urbanites, and
this repressive role intensified as time went on...

(7) COUP-MONGERS

Jean Métellus, *The Vortex Family,* 1995

In this extract, Haitian novelist Jean Métellus captures the mood of
political intrigue as military officers meet with their co-conspira-
tors, Georges Férère, officer in charge at the Department of the
Interior and National Defence, and Bishop Le Croutonec, to plot the
downfall of President Estimé (1946-50).

Colonel Pierre Pirval, chief of staff, Colonel Paquito Félix, chief
of police, Lieutenant-Colonel Ralph Oswald, commander of the
troops at the Dessalines Barracks, Major Quentin Samuel, Adjutant-
General, and assistant general chief of staff Major Thierry Steven,
head of the secret service and commander of the military college,
met together in Pétionville. At the swimming pool, Pierre Pirval and
Paquito Félix impatiently awaited Férère, who was late. When he
turned up with Monseigneur Le Croutonec, their faces brightened.
"Things have turned out better than we could have imagined," they
confided to one another.

"All the forces are on our side. We will need to think about the communiqué," said Paquito.

"Let's go and greet the man of God while affecting not to know anything. He'll tell us how bitter he feels after a couple of whiskies," said Pirval.

"He's probably already pretty smashed," Paquito added. "Férère should have given him a good brimful before coming."

"Oh, he doesn't need Férère for that. He's fed up at the cathedral," was Pirval's conclusion.[...]

The lawns in the garden and around the yard were meticulously maintained. Torch-thistle, verbena, diuretic plants, a few citronelles, cockscombs and cat's-foot grew all over the estate, and gave rise to Le Croutonec's wonder whenever he came to house: "Oh, happy people who live in communion with nature, far from the squalidness of the capital."

It was in this atmosphere that the staff officers, the friends of Jacky Maïxent, an import-export industrialist and money-lender, and Le Croutonec, had a frank exchange of views.

"Good day, Monseigneur," Colonels Pirval and Félix chorused.

"My name is Pierre," replied Le Croutonec, "isn't it?" He continued speaking to Férère. "Surely we should be on familiar terms, considering the hour and what is at stake."

"I very much think so," the latter replied.

"Then, my friends, let's get to know each other: the situation calls for it." ...

"We're not in the same situation as in 1946. We need to consider another method, another way of proceeding," said Paquito.

"It is necessary", asserted Le Croutonec, "to create a state of urgency and alarm."

"Two fires," Georges Férère declared, "will be lit this evening, one on ruelle Boyer, the other on rue de l'Enterrement. The fire officers have received orders not to intervene."

"And what is the Embassy's position?"[1]

"It will support us as long as there isn't too much bloodshed."

"How many officers can you count on?" the priest enquired.

"All the principal posts in the capital and provincial towns are held by men we can rely on."

[1] The United States Embassy

(8) BANKING ON TERROR

Graham Greene, *The Nightmare Republic,* 1963

In this extract from a news feature article, Greene, whose novel, *The Comedians*, made Duvalier and his Tontons Macoutes internationally infamous, describes the endemic corruption of the regime.

Surely never has terror had so bare and ignoble an object as here – the protection of a few tough men's pockets, the pockets of Gracia Joseph, Colonel Athi, Colonel Desiré, the leaders of the Ton Ton Macoute, of the police and of the Presidential guard – and in the centre of the ring, of course, in his black evening suit, his heavy glasses, his halting walk and halting speech, the cruel and absurd Doctor.

Everyone is some sort of prisoner in Port-au-Prince. The exit visa for a foreigner is twice the price of the entry. For a Haitian a passport costs $100 and the visa (controlled personally by the Doctor) another five. You pay your money, but it is dubious whether you will ever see your passport.

Travel on the island is almost at a standstill. The roads were always a deterrent, but now there are roadblocks round Port-au-Prince to the north and controls at every small town to the south. Within a circuit of a few kilometres from Port-au-Prince I was searched four times, and it took me two days at the police station, where the portrait of the Doctor is flanked by snapshots of the machine-gunned bodies of Barbot and his companions[1], to gain a two-day permit for the South. The North, because of the raids from the Dominican Republic, was forbidden altogether.

All trade which does not offer a rake-off is at a standstill. A whole nation can die of starvation so long as the Doctor's non-fiscal account is safe. The public revenue of Haiti in a reasonable year should be around $28 million, but the non-fiscal account which is paid directly into the President's pocket amounts to between $8 million and $12 million. On all the main commodities, sugar, flour, oil, tires, cement, a special tax is levied which never goes into the general account. The export of cement is forbidden because the world price would not admit this extra tax. The export would aid Haiti, but not the ring.

The President has, of course, other less traditional sources of revenue. The British Ambassador was expelled because he protested at the levies which the Ton Ton Macoute were exacting illegally from all businessmen. An arbitrary figure was named and if the sum was not forthcoming the man would be beaten up in his home by the Ton Ton Macoute during the hours of darkness.

Tolls are enforced on all cars between the rich suburb of Pétionville and Port-au-Prince. These particular sums go to the only project in Haiti visible to the naked eye. This project is the new town of Duvalierville, 40 miles out of Port-au-Prince. The Doctor has obviously read accounts of Brasilia and in the absurd little tourist houses with roofs like wind-wrecked butterflies one can detect Brasilia's influence. There is no beach, and the town, if it is ever finished, is supposed to house 2,000 peasants in little one-roomed houses, so that it is difficult to see why any tourist would stay there. The only building finished in Duvalierville is the cock-fight stadium. In the meanwhile the peasants' homes have been destroyed and they have been driven from the area to live with relatives.

[1] Clement Barbot helped Duvalier come to power and was chief of the Tontons Macoutes. He had run the country while François Duvalier recovered from a near-fatal heart attack in 1959, but his very success spelt his downfall. He was deposed, and sent into exile. He returned to conspire against his former ally, and even tried to kidnap Duvalier's children. In 1963 his attempt to overthrow Duvalier ended in failure when he and his men were discovered and shot dead by Duvalier loyalists.

(9) TAMING THE VATICAN

The Jean-Claudiste National Action Committee, *Il était une fois... François Duvalier,* 1980

When Papa Doc Duvalier persuaded the Vatican to allow him to nominate Haiti's bishops, he not only secured the allegiance of the Catholic church hierarchy but convinced many that there was more to his espousal of black nationalism than just rhetoric. This extract from a cartoon book published by Duvalierists perpetuates the legend.

I am keen that I myself appoint the new archbishop of Port-au-Prince and the Bishop of Les Cayes... will you agree to that?

Excellency, I'll have to ask you to wait for the response.

Pope Paul VI agrees that the Archbishop and three Bishops be nominated by the head of State in August 1966. A protocol lays down the modalities of this historic accord.

At last, authentic sons of the nation are going to accede to episcopal dignity.

Later, Monsignor François Wolff Ligondé took the civil oath.

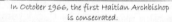

In October 1966, the first Haitian Archbishop is consecrated.

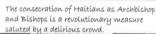

The consecration of Haitians as Archbishop and Bishops is a revolutionary measure saluted by a delirious crowd.

Bravo!

Long live our Bishops!

In 1966 Papa Doc repeated 1804!

(10) BABY DOC AND REPRESSION

Marc Romulus, *Les Cachots des Duvalier*, 1991

The author was imprisoned in the notorious Fort Dimanche prison in Port-au-Prince from 1974 until, following international appeals on behalf of 'political' prisoners of the Duvalier regimes, he and 104 others were released in 1977. He describes some aspects of the repression carried out by the security forces.

Among those defined as political prisoners, Duvalier's jails contain not only people who have opposed the government, but equally the unemployed who may have complained about their poverty or just made a remark considered to be subversive by one of Duvalier's agents. Sylvestre Jilmiste, 24, an unemployed apprentice shoemaker, racked by hunger, curses the Duvalier family. Denounced by Macoutes, he is tortured at the National Palace and then transferred to Fort Dimanche, where he dies in October 1976 in cell no.1. Ambroise Desravines, 62, a barber from Cap-Haïtien, is arrested because he said, in the presence of a Protestant pastor and Duvalier spy, that Henri Siclait, the former head of the state tobacco company, was a candidate for the presidency. Having been tortured by Colonel Albert Pierre, Desravines dies in Fort Dimanche eight months later, in September 1976.

Peasants expropriated by the Tontons Macoutes or Duvalier's soldiers flee from starvation in the countryside, taking to the sea on leaking boats. Some are killed on the spot, others are arrested either by government agents or by foreign security forces who send them back to Haiti where they go straight to prison. Serge Donatien, a young peasant from the Gonaïves area trying to escape from poverty and repression, is arrested as he tries to get onto a boat. Held at Fort Dimanche, he dies in March 1977.

You can also be arrested because of some argument with a friend of a member of the government or even a friend of a friend, because all those who are connected, whether closely or not, with Duvalier's government, can exercise their own justice by sending their enemies to Fort Dimanche as political prisoners. One citizen died there because he had killed a dog belonging to his neighbour, the brother of a Macoute. The father or husband of an attractive daughter or pretty wife who refuses to play the game can become a political prisoner. Haitians returning from abroad are arrested at Port-au-Prince airport, in front of their horrified relatives and friends, on the basis of nothing more than some suspicion. Passers-by look away so as not to meet the same fate. For each accused person the government agents can round up dozens of victims, as in a well-known Haitian phrase "comme terminel". This expression, borrowed from games of chance, is applied to people who are arrested because a relative, friend or mere acquaintance is involved in political intrigue. Lafortune Cicéron, his brother Louis Cicéron and their cousin are held for nine years in the National Penitentiary. The reason for their arrest: the brother of Lafortune's mistress had escaped from Fort Dimanche in May 1968. Sémonvil Osias, a lawyer from Cap-Haïtien, was arrested because he was a friend of Max Dominique, Duvalier's son in law who fell into disgrace. Sémonvil Osias died in Fort Dimanche in June 1975, while Max Dominique was relaxing in his luxurious villa in the United States.[...]

Citizens are arrested at home, in church, in the street, at school, while taking exams, anywhere. Only one thing is consistent: the arbitrary. The chiefs of repression and their lieutenants have unlimited powers; as one of the heads of the Detective Service at the Dessalines barracks put it so well: "Here, we're the prosecutors, judges, chamber of commerce and registry office." [...]

Duvalier's agents can go ahead with the arrest of any citizen without having to explain the reasons for the arrest, without the slightest formality. They don't even think it necessary to show their victim any identification. At machine-gun point, the citizen is tied up and thrown into a car that always disappears as onlookers cower in front of the well-armed agents. Such was the case with Riché Andrisse (one of the prisoners released on 21 September 1977), who was arrested at Port-au-Prince airport as he was leaving to go abroad in 1975. [...]

In Haiti each arrest amounts to a disappearance. The efforts made by relatives and friends to obtain information on the reasons for the arrest and the prisoner's whereabouts are always in vain.

In April 1974 Oveny Paul was arrested on the Delmas road in Port-au-Prince. The police response to his parents' enquiries: "person unknown". His parents have heard nothing of him to the present day. I met him in Fort Dimanche, where he was executed on 7 August 1974. René Franex, arrested near Oveny Paul's house, at Cité St-Martin in Port-au-Prince: no word of him. I saw him in Fort Dimanche, where he was executed on 7 August 1974. Marie-Thérese Féval didn't come home one evening in November 1975; she was executed in Fort Dimanche in March 1976. Clarel Tervil, Reynold Timoléon, Ronald Duchemin... many more, all met the same fate.

Translated from French by James Ferguson

(11) BLOOD MONEY

Elizabeth Abbott, *Haiti: the Duvaliers and Their Legacy,* 1988

Luckner Cambronne was a leading Duvalierist who served as a loyal servant to the regimes of both Papa Doc and Jean-Claude Duvalier. He was also reputed to be the lover of Simone Duvalier, the dictators' wife and mother.

Most callous was Cambronne's blood-plasma business, which earned him the nickname, "Vampire of the Caribbean." Through his company, Hemocaribian, he shipped five tons of plasma a month to American laboratories directed by Armour Pharmaceutical, Cutter Laboratories, Dow Chemical, and others. Haitian blood is extremely rich in antibodies, for survivors of the country's high disease and infant mortality rate develop much richer supplies of antibodies than necessary in less unhealthy societies. Haitian blood was therefore in great demand, and Cambronne did all he could to satisfy it. He organised clinics that paid donors, indiscriminately chosen, $5 a pint for their blood, then resold it at $35 a pint to the United States.

Cambronne also dealt in cadavers, in almost as much demand. To save the living, medical students must dissect the dead, and obtaining corpses in sufficient quantity is the perennial problem of medical schools. Haitian cadavers, readily available once Cambronne entered the business, had the distinct advantage of being thin, so the student had not layers of fat to slice through before reaching the object of the lesson. Cambronne, using the refrigerated container service recently introduced to Haiti, supplied these corpses on demand. When the General Hospital failed to provide him with enough despite the $3 he paid for each body, he simply stole them from various funeral parlours. More than one mourning family opened a coffin for a final viewing to discover it was empty.

Rumours even circulated that Cambronne resorted to killing the urban homeless when he was having trouble filling his quota, and an apocryphal tale about the cadaver trade is still widely repeated. Cambronne, the story goes, was criticised for the mouldy condition in which his corpses often arrived in the States. Determined not to lose the business, he instructed his secretary, "All right, then. Phone and say I'll start shipping the bodies up alive. Then when they need them, they can just kill them."

Blood and bodies were macabre businesses, but for pure cynicism even they could not rival the railway scheme he carried out years earlier under Papa Doc. In the pathetically underdeveloped nation struggling to combat every developmental problem known to man, Luckner Cambronne sold approximately 150 kilometres of railroad to his African cousins and pocketed the money for himself, for his insatiable gambling and for the mulatto mistresses he kept behind Simone's back. For days Haitians watched in wonder as workmen pulled up and carefully stored the entire rail system linking Verettes via St. Marc, originally installed to transport passengers and freight. Down to the harbour it went, and on to Africa. Cambronne was much richer, and Haiti poorer.

(12) ELECTION DAY MASSACRE

James Ferguson, *Papa Doc, Baby Doc,* 1988

In November 1987, an attempt to hold a presidential election was sabotaged by Tontons Macoutes and hardline Duvalierist army officers.

The night of 28 November was the worst yet. Accustomed by now to the sound of gunfire, the inhabitants of Port-au-Prince were woken by the louder explosions of grenades and mortars. By daybreak on Sunday the three most important independent radio stations were off the air, their transmitters blown up during darkness. Petrol stations, churches and polling stations were other targets; many of the capital's hundreds of rudimentary stations were burned down, as was the trade union office which contained ballot papers for over sixty local stations.

Many polling stations were never to open. During the previous two days, roadblocks and armed gangs and prevented the transportation of ballot papers and boxes to an estimated one-fifth of the country. On the road north to Gonaïves a lorry had been attacked and the driver killed. Now, on the morning that voting was due to take place, a significant number of stations in the capital were destroyed or their staff too frightened to open them. Nevertheless, tens of thousands of voters were determined to exercise their constitutional rights. At early morning church services throughout the country they had been urged once again to support the democratic process and to hasten the departure of the junta by peaceful means. In some areas there was an expectant and almost euphoric atmosphere; to celebrate the historic occasion, men were wearing their best clothes and women white dresses usually reserved for weddings and christenings.

As the surviving polling stations opened at 6 a.m., lines of voters were already in place. The gunfire and occasional explosions had deterred some, but many more were not to be intimidated. The vigilante groups stood guard in certain districts, ready to warn of attacks. These began within an hour, when cars full of armed men started to tour the streets, firing at random at anybody in sight. At 7.30 a.m. a queue of 100 people had formed outside the polling station in the Ecole Nationale Argentine Bellegarde in the centre of town. Suddenly a group of fifty men, armed with machine-guns and machetes stormed the school buildings. The voters attempted to barricade the gates, defending themselves only with stones. Within minutes sixteen lay dead in a classroom, shot or hacked with machetes [...]

At another school, meanwhile, six more voters were shot down and many more wounded. With their dark glasses and Uzi sub-machine-guns, the Tontons Macoutes were now taking control of the streets.

The full irony of Régala's[1] pledge to 'guarantee order and security' was by now apparent. Evident too, was the fact that the thin dividing line between the army and the Tontons Macoutes had finally vanished. Army vehicles were to be seen, but they were merely following the cars of the death-squads, lending open support to the Duvalierist gangs.

[1] Williams Régala was a member of the military junta and Minister of the Interior in 1987.

(13) UNNATURAL JUSTICE

National Coalition for Haitian Refugees, *No Greater Priority: Judicial Reform in Haiti,* 1995

The corrupt and incompetent judicial system has allowed the elite and military to exploit and repress the majority of the population at will.

The armed forces, including the army, the police, rural section chiefs, attachés and members of the armed paramilitary group, *Front pour l'avancement et le progrès haïtien* (FRAPH), threatened, beat and sometimes killed judges, prosecutors and lawyers...Wealthy, absentee landowners hire soldiers or local enforcers to intimidate judges and lawyers representing peasants involved in land disputes. Judges and prosecutors admit they are too afraid to issue an arrest warrant or investigate cases involving the military, para-military or certain civilian supporters of the military.

Corruption and extortion thrive at every level of the justice system. Salaries are low and venality is high. People pay the police to arrest a rival; prosecutors and judges demand payment before opening an investigation or issuing an order. Section chiefs arbitrarily impose taxes that are not found in law and then threaten those who refuse to pay with prison or a beating. Jailers demand payment before a family is allowed to bring food to a detainee and also to extort money from desperate prisoners to avoid beatings or even worse treatment. Sometimes families are able to buy a relative's release from a prison.

Most judges and prosecutors are poorly trained and lack motivation. Many judges, especially the lowest-level *juges de paix*, have never been to law school, have received no specialised training to be judges and show little interest in receiving such training...

Courts lack even rudimentary materials necessary to function. Most have no electricity or phones. Copy machines, let alone computers or faxes are unheard of. Most judges and prosecutors do not even own the texts essential to their work: the Civil Code, the Code of Criminal Procedure and the Penal Code. Record-keeping is in complete disarray with barely legible orders and decisions, some dating more than 10 years ago, tacked to walls and doors.

Most Haitians view lawyers, judges – virtually anyone connected with the justice system – with well-deserved scorn and contempt. People will avoid contact with the system unless it is the last resort. It is expensive, corrupt and largely mysterious since all the laws and most of the proceedings are conducted in French, a language most Haitians can barely understand and only a wealthy elite can speak or read...

The most powerful sectors of Haitian society – the wealthiest families, government officials, and most of all the entire military apparatus – have enjoyed virtual impunity. Soldiers have never been prosecuted in civilian courts for abuses committed against civilians despite constitutional requirements for these cases to be heard in civil courts. This impunity fuels the cycle of violence and the population's cynicism about 'justice' in Haiti.

(14) THE SMUGGLING INDUSTRY

Michel Laguerre, *The Military and Society in Haiti,* 1993

In addition to extortion and theft, the Haitian military made money from control of the contraband trade that flourished when the regional ports, closed by the Duvaliers, re-opened in 1986.

The case is about an officer who was in charge of a military district in North-West Haiti. That district headquarters is located in a coastal city where contraband goods are often unloaded. This form of illegal economic activity became a source of profit for the officer in many different ways.

The officer was able to acquire a certain percentage of profits from any deals made by the contrabandists. In return, he protected them and let them operate without interfering in their illegal business activities. From the contrabandists, the officer received either outright cash or merchandise that he managed to sell to others.

Through that scheme, the officer developed a commerce within the barracks that lasted six months. He sold American-acquired merchandise to the soldiers, mostly clothes and foodstuffs, and pocketed the money. The barracks then served as a storage place and a market-place where he could sell them even in broad daylight. When the local civilian population started talking about it in a negative manner, he stopped using the barracks to carry out his business.

His next scheme involved the sale of chicken legs. These were American products acquired through a contact who controlled a contraband racket in the city. The contact served as an associate, and they shared between themselves the profits made from selling wholesale to merchants and retail to their trusted clients. The officer was able to maintain that business for a long time, until he was transferred to another city.

During this time, as the officer in charge of the military district, he was able to acquire three luxury automobiles from a contact in Miami, Florida. Through that same contact, who was also bringing contraband automobiles to Haiti, he helped a physician friend acquire a new car, valued in excess of $10,000 for the ridiculous price of $4,000.

This is a case of an officer who engaged in illegal activities, who sold contraband goods, who protected contrabandists and extorted funds from them, and who used the military barracks and his position for personal gain, to enrich himself.

(15) THE VIEW FROM ABOVE

Amy Wilentz, *The Rainy Season,* 1989

Up in the suburbs above Port-au-Prince, the elite lives a life of ostentatious luxury, and looks down with a mixture of disdain and fear on the masses crowded into the seaside slums.

We drove down the residential streets of Pétionville. Even in the daylight, when it's not raining, you can see only the less expensive houses, because the rest of them sit behind high cement security walls. We honked out in front of Jeanne's gate (*la barrière,* Haitians call them, appropriately), and finally Joseph the gardien came and opened up, and we drove down the circular driveway to Jeanne and Sylvain's house. We parked under the dark, dripping bougainvillaea. The spotlights were on above the terrace, and I could see Jeanne's three Dobermans pacing the top of the security wall.

"Pierrot, encore du champagne pour ce côté de la table, non?" says Jeanne. More champagne for this side of the table, and I look down at my lobster, its meat artistically removed from the shell, some delicate green beans arranged at its side, some delicately boiled potatoes nestled next to the beans, gold silverware. Pierrot is not in uniform – Haitian servants don't usually wear uniforms...

The champagne that Pierrot pours is good, and it makes Jeanne more voluble than usual.

"But I don't understand," she says. "If the point of having elections is to elect someone who will continue the work of the junta, why have elections?" She points Pierrot to Charles' glass. "Why not just keep the junta? Besides," she says, laughing, "Sylvain knows Namphy."[1] Her husband smiles.

"That wouldn't be democracy, my dear," Sylvain says. "Anyway it is not what the Americans want. Besides, people need to think that they have elected their President. It will help the national spirit." He raises his eyebrows. Sylvain is always ironic. He learned it in France. He also drinks too much; he learned that in France, too.

"The Haitian people aren't that stupid, as you all know." This is Charles. Of course my date says the wrong thing. Everyone looks at everyone else except for Charles, and I look at my lobster.

"If they're not so stupid, why are they living the way they do?" This from a former government minister. His wife picks silently at her food. The former minister is having an affair with Jeanne, that's what Charles told me.

"Well, they seem to have figured *something* out," says Charles. "Look at the demonstrations. Look at Father Aristide." ...

"What do you mean, look at Aristide?" asks Sylvain. "There's not much to look at, really, is there?" He gazes around the table for approval, and gets some murmurs, but the guests seem to find the lobster more engrossing than the talk. [...]

"Aristide is a little dictator, in true Haitian style," says Sylvain. "A fascist in the making. Couldn't be plainer. And the only thing 'the people' know, the only 'idea' they have," he says, skewering a piece of lobster on the end of his gold fork and holding it in the air, "is that they'd like to be eating this." He waves the piece of meat around, pops it into his mouth, picks up his champagne, and takes a sip. "And with our bloody corpses at their feet, I might add." [...]

"These rabble-rousers like Fignolé [2] and this new one, they always appeal to people's worst instincts," Sylvain went on. "Aristide, he appeals to their racism. You don't see any light faces in his congregation, have you noticed? He says 'the elite', and they know that what he means is 'the mulattos.' Every day he's getting worse and worse. He'll have to shut up soon. He'll have to. Or be shut up. Pierrot, where is the champagne?" Sylvain looks round the table. "I mean, it can't go on like this, can it?"

[1] General Henri Namphy, leader of the military junta.
[2] Daniel Fignolé, leader of the first political party to represent the poor of Port-au-Prince in the period 1946-57.

(16) TRADITIONAL OLIGARCHY AND NEW ENTREPRENEURS

Catherine Orenstein, *An Interview with Ben Dupuy, Aristide's Ambassador-at-Large,* 1993

The director of the weekly newspaper, *Haiti Progrès*, and ambassador-at-large for the Aristide government from 1991-3 analyses the class forces at the root of the transition from dictatorship to democracy.

What is the background to the current situation in Haiti?

... Historically, the elite was composed of two sectors. On the one hand there were the landowners, who in Haiti are called *gwandon*. At the same time we had a bourgeois sector. It was not a capitalist sector per se; it was more merchant-capitalism. This sector would export agricultural products and import manufactured goods. Historically these two sectors of the elite have been fighting for political control. The very tumultuous history of the country is a result of that struggle – *within* the elite.

But things have changed in recent years.

The focus is no longer on the simple securing of raw materials. Capital's need to compete in the world market, and the fact that the cost of labour in developed countries had increased in spite of high technology, led to the creation of a new form of industry – assembly industry – in which foreign capital could be imported into countries like Haiti at much less risk. Before when there was a capitalist venture, the possibility of it being nationalised existed, such as the sugar industry in Cuba. But the new assembly industry receives its material from the outside, and the market is also outside. So what is isolated is the domestic labour force. This type of industry is *outside* the economic structure of the country.

The one handicap was the need for infrastructure. These countries lacked sufficient electricity, ports, roads, etc. And that is where the international institutions and the private banks took a role in lending to those governments. This was the beginning of our debt crisis.

Did this affect the power base of the merchant class in Haiti?

Yes. This created a division within the merchant class. Certain merchants became involved in the assembly industry. Another part remained in traditional commerce. Because of this development, some in the elite felt the need for a new political structure. Power had always been monopolised by the oligarchy who were very backward. They didn't even conceive of modern management, and were more concerned about living a sumptuous life, and using political power to exploit and enrich themselves. This was not compatible with the developing assembly industry.

The international investors and the assembly entrepreneurs began to realise that Haiti needed elections, democracy. So it was necessary to remove political power from the traditional oligarchy. There were two objectives: on the one hand, to diffuse the possibility of a mass movement that could wind up in a radical revolution, and on the other, to create a political structure more in tune with these new types of investment and development.

How was this agenda pursued and to what effect?

The struggle to destroy the oligarchy was not only a political power struggle to modernise the state, but also a struggle to destroy the oligarchy's economic base. It coincided with the food-aid programme which created a situation in which the country became more and more dependent on the outside world. Dumping surplus food on the Haitian market was a sure way to destroy the economic base of both the agricultural oligarchy and the traditional merchant class, those who had not invested in the new assembly industries.

What were the political alliances behind the election (of Aristide in 1990)?

Well, in the arena you had the United States, trying to change the political structure and fighting the oligarchy, but at the same time allying with the oligarchy in order to oppose the masses, the people. It was a tricky situation, where on the one hand the United States and the international institutions wanted to change and mobilise the society, and on the other, there was the risk that the people might have their own agenda at odds with US policy. [...]

The Lavalas movement that brought Aristide to the presidency is an alliance of the masses – the peasantry – and the traditional merchant bourgeoisie, which was on the verge of bankruptcy. This alliance defeated the oligarchy, the assembly entrepreneurs, and the US agenda.

(17) ENEMIES OF REFORM

Alex Dupuy, *Haiti in the New World Order*, 1997

The proposed 'Lavalas Project' for social-democratic reforms and more equitable development was far from revolutionary, yet neither the entrenched elite nor the 'modernisers' could accept the advent of a reforming government with popular backing.

Though (the Lavalas government of 1991) achieved mixed results with its attempted reforms in the military, public administration, magistracy, and public enterprises, there is no question that the measures it took struck at the heart of the old regime's power base and intensified the antagonism between the pro-Macoute camp and the Aristide government. The Macoute camp and the prebendary military and public sector officialdom would be the biggest losers with the advent of democracy and a government bent on implementing sweeping reforms in these institutions. They therefore had an interest in subverting the democratisation process, and this could only be done by reverting to dictatorship. [...]

Despite the government's moderate economic policies, members of the Haitian bourgeoisie, especially the few powerful families that dominated the private sector, withheld their support from the government. If the Lavalas Project had been implemented, the bourgeoisie would have benefited, and its influence as a class would have been strengthened. However, this would have been a long-term consequence, and the Haitian bourgeoisie usually pursued its interests in the short term. For most of its history, the Haitian bourgeoisie has been a vision-less, retrograde social class concerned primarily with safeguarding its immediate wealth and privileges. The monopolist faction of the bourgeoisie had collaborated closely with the Duvalier dictatorships and their successors. It has been said that "if the Duvaliers did not exist, (the wealthy elite) would have invented them". [...]

As expected, the business elite opposed the social democratic and redistributive thrust of the Aristide government, particularly the reforms that targeted the loopholes and prerogatives the elite enjoyed under the old regimes. The business elite considered the law that raised the minimum daily wage by a mere US$1.80 to be "anti-economic and anti-national." In a meeting with Aristide, representatives of this group argued that implementation of the law would negatively impact Haiti's competetiveness vis-à-vis its Caribbean neighbours, increase unemployment, and compel investors to relocate in countries where labour was cheaper. [...]

Above all, members of the bourgeoisie felt threatened by the fortification of civil society and especially by what they saw as Aristide's encouragement of the increasing militancy of the grassroots organisations, student organisations, TKL community-based organisations, trade unions, peasant organisations and vigilante groups. The bourgeoisie, in other words feared the empowerment of the social classes whose abject exploitation and suppression the dictatorships had guaranteed.

(18) ARISTIDE'S OVERTHROW

Jean-Bertrand Aristide, *Aristide: an Autobiography,* 1992

President Aristide recalls the first days of the military coup against him and his Lavalas movement in 1991.

On the evening of Sunday, September 29, shots were heard at the Frères camp, a few kilometres from Port-au-Prince. This time the rumour of mutiny was transformed into the noise of automatic weapons. The director of the national radio, Michel Favard, a brave man, also announced that a coup d'état was imminent. He would be kidnapped immediately afterward by a military commando troop. Before they were cut off, the radio stations had called for vigilance against the suspicious movements of part of the army.

On the previous evening, I had called General Cédras to ask his feeling about the rumours, to which I still gave little credence. He supported me in my scepticism, and we laughed about it together. How can I help feeling some remorse now, when I think of the thousands of dead and remember the tranquil calm I then felt...

On Sunday I received the same reassuring response from Cédras, but by evening there could be no more doubt about the rebellion: my house was surrounded and bullets were spattering against its walls again. Friends and militants who were already there or who came in great numbers were massacred. Before the demonstrators could assemble or barricades be erected, the military emptied their magazines at everything that moved. They had learned the lesson of Lafontant's coup d'état [1]: at all costs, they had to prevent the people from gathering, barricades from being erected, and a popular insurrection from being unleashed. Assisted by Macoute bands apparently coming from the Dominican Republic, they sowed death everywhere. The corpses were counted in the tens and hundreds. The terror was carried out in the most brutal form in order to discourage any popular reaction. Lafanmi Selavi [2] was a target once again, along with populous neighbourhoods (Cité Soleil, Carrefour), where the people attempted with the most pitiful means to provide some opposition to the soldiery. The young partisans of Lavalas paid a heavy price...

Never since the time of François Duvalier had such a slaughter been seen: hundreds of victims during the night hours of September 29-30, daily machine-gunning of the slums during the curfew, forcing inhabitants to an urban exodus, forcing manu militari to dig in the cemeteries to bury their own dead, whole truckloads of corpses, the sadism of the new chief of police, Michel François.

[1] The Duvalierist, Roger Lafontant, had attempted a coup d'état in January 1991, but had been thwarted by huge crowds who took to the streets to defend Aristide.
[2] Lafanmi Selavi is the home for street children in Port-au-Prince set up by Aristide before he was elected president.

(19) HUMAN RIGHTS UNDER FIRE

The Platform of Haitian Human Rights Organisations, *Resistance and Democracy*, 1994

Extracts from a partial list of human rights violations in March and early April 1994, collated and published by the Platform of Haitian Human Rights Organisations.

Since the beginning of March 1994, the residents of Cité Soleil have been the target of many assassinations. Most of the time, corpses lay in the streets for many days and sometimes were eaten by pigs. Many bodies have not been identified.

On the other hand, the former Macoute leader of this area, named Sedoine, who has established an office at Soleil 11, seems to have declared that corpses were too visible in the streets of Cité Soleil, so they had to find a way to hide them. Following this declaration, many disappearances have been reported in the area and the bodies have not been found...

March 26 – Anès Valcourt was kidnapped by armed civilians who had broken into his house in Drouillard, and accused him of being an Aristide supporter. His feet tied up, he was severely beaten up before he was taken by his abductors. Since then, we have no news of Anès.

April 6 – Ruddy Joseph (30 years old) was also kidnapped, by armed civilians who had broken into his house. His pregnant wife Denise Enes, was raped by three of the armed bandits. She was also beaten around the waist. Before leaving the place with Ruddy, they threatened his wife and stole objects from the house. Ruddy was taken away in a white pick-up to an unknown destination.

Elsewhere:

March 8 – Croix des Bouquets – Jean Yvon Pierre, a mechanic and an active member of a neighbourhood commmittee in Vareux, was arrested by Yves Moise accompanied by many armed civilians and FRAPH members.[1] He was accused of being in possession of a weapon and explosives. He was taken to the Croix des Bouquets prison where he was beaten with a stick and tortured. Brought in front of a judge, he was sent back to prison under the pretext that his case, badly prepared, contained an irregularity. On March 23, he was transferred to the National Penitentiary. Since then, his health has worsened.

March 14 – Port-au-Prince – St-Juste Sineus (30 years old) is from Limbé. Under Aristide's government, he worked for the Interior Ministry and the Defense Ministry. Since the coup, he has been living in hiding in Les Cayes and then in Gonaïves following persecution. On March 14th, he got in contact with the OAS/UN International Civilian Mission in Port-au-Prince to report his case. The Mission asked him to bring them a copy of his work ID. So his wife, Dyela Dorcin, went back to the abandoned house to recover the requested documents. As she was close to her residence, situated near the Jérémie wharf in La Saline, she was arrested by an attaché named Leonard and the documents were seized. Since then, Dyela Dorcin has been reported missing.

March 18 – Pean Street – Around 5 a.m., Gérard Louis and Levis St-Fleur, members of the "Association Groupement Agricole de Paysans de l'Artibonite" (AGAPA), were stopped by three soldiers out of uniform. The soldiers, armed with machetes, guns and daggers, ordered them to lie on the floor. Others passing by also had to obey. The soldiers then went fiercely and unrelentingly at their victims, hitting them with rifle butts. Levis St-Fleur, who had not obeyed the order, received a bullet in the foot. After that, the soldiers just left the site. Carried to the University State Hospital, he was refused medical assistance.

Night of March 22-23 – Corridor Lumière – During the night, an unidentified individual was kidnapped at Corridor Lumière. He was later killed but his body was not found; only his clothes and traces of blood were seen on the pavement.

March 25 – Port-au-Prince – Salomon Erase (43 years old), Arsene Coicou and two other persons went to Devez Laroche's house for the evening. The next morning, at 8am, the car in which the above mentioned people drove was found abandoned in front of the Pédodontique Center on Bicentenaire street. There was no sign of the passengers or of blood...

March 26 – Port-au-Prince – Mrs. Saintercie Kersie (56 years old), member of the "Groupements de Paysans Kombit Lave Je", was savagely beaten. Since then, she has been having eye problems. She had also been beaten up in June 1992.

March 28 – Bel Air – On January 27, 1993, Paul Prophète was arrested at l'Eglise du Perpetuel in Bel Air and was taken to the Anti-Gang [2] where he was severely beaten. He was accused of organising pro-Aristide demonstrations...

[1] FRAPH was the acronym of the Duvalierist Front for the Advancement and Progress of Haiti, a paramilitary anti-Aristide organisation, including many former Tontons Macoutes.
[2] The Anti-Gang Service was a counter-insurgency police unit.

(20) THE POWERFUL FEW

James Ridgeway, *Haiti's Family Affairs,* 1994

Although Haiti's elite is composed of thousands of wealthy families, a small number have become supremely rich through their domination of the country's economy.

There are several dozen major families, most of them mulatto. Two of them are powers to be reckoned with.

There are the Brandts, originally from Jamaica, where they still maintain businesses. In Haiti they have interests in edible oil, poultry, and banking. They have been key participants in a World Bank-financed tomato-paste project, and historically have had holdings in coffee, textiles, and autos. The Brandts have long been regarded as the richest family in Haiti, richer even than former president-for-life Jean-Claude (Baby Doc) Duvalier.

As one Haitian diplomat put it, speaking about the family scion O.J. Brandt, "he is the king maker." When François (Papa Doc) Duvalier wanted to build a paved road in downtown Port-au-Prince, O.J. Brandt put up the money to pay for it. If Duvalier needed money, he would stop Brandt at the border, on one occasion allowing him to re-enter only after he bought $2 million in government bonds. Today the Brandts are believed not only to have funded the coup but to be currently underwriting its activities by providing part-time jobs to its leading members...Unfazed by the embargo, the Brandts have close ties to FRAPH, the army's civilian front, and recently have discussed buying a bank in Paris.

Second only to the Brandts are their enemies the Mevs, dominant in sugar, in the manufacture of shoes, plastics, and detergents, and in assembly work, including the production of baseballs. Accused of supporting the coup, they angrily insist the family opposed military rule and embraced Aristide. In Haiti, according to a former minister who asked to be anonymous, the Mevs provided cover for members of the rightist governments so they could secretly run businesses that they were forbidden to engage in...

Beneath the Brandts and the Mevs are several lesser-known members of the Haitian oligarchy – the Accras, flush from textiles; the Bigios (one of the country's few Jewish families; Gilbert Bigio is Haiti's honorary Israeli consul), with a monopoly on iron and steel fabrication; the Behrmanns, with concessions to import automobiles and trucks; the Apaids, with electronics factories; and the Madsens, with coffee holdings and beer production...

These Haitian families run their businesses in an old-fashioned way. "They are traditional people who are used to running the country without doing any great amount of work," another Haitian diplomat explained. "They could invest more, but why? Then they'd have to work harder and ruin their lives." Even the younger family members, educated at Harvard and Yale, resist the lures of the free market on grounds that they then would have to compete with other newly educated Haitians and risk the loss of their way of life.

CHAPTER THREE
RURAL HAITI:
PEASANTS, LAND AND THE ENVIRONMENT

In the colonial era, society had been based on a plantation system with a population located on the coastal plains and the central Artibonite valley. The three-quarters of the country covered by vast mountain ranges had remained largely uninhabited, save for the scattered bands of Maroons. In the post-independence period, the desire of former slaves for land of their own brought about a profound transformation of the country's economy and demography. The Haitian elite was obliged to abandon the plantation system, and in contrast to the rest of the Latin American and Caribbean region where the *latifundio* system was maintained, in Haiti most of the large estates were divided up. Within a short time, a predominantly peasant society based on individual smallholdings developed. As the population increased, so too did the demand for land, and the area under cultivation was extended further into the hinterland of the country.

Over the last century and a half, the population has rapidly grown to number some seven million by 1994. Although hundreds of thousands have moved from the countryside to the towns, 70 per cent of Haitians continue to depend on agriculture for a living. With an average of 254 people per square kilometre, Haiti is second only to Barbados as the most densely populated country in the Americas.

In many respects the life of the Haitian peasant has changed little over the last two centuries: farming tools and techniques are still rudimentary; health care and education are practically non-existent; illiteracy is the norm, and families live in one- or two- roomed shacks without electricity or piped water. The way of life of a typical peasant family living on a remote mountainside is little easier than that described by an observer in the 1920s. (1) His hosts lived in the traditional way of the Haitian peasantry, the form of social organisation known as the *lakou*. This grouping together of five, six or a dozen houses, usually inhabited by members of a large extended family, suits a communal style of life. In the shared compound between the buildings, food can be stored and prepared, animals kept, and children can play. The lakou arrangement lends itself to the pooling of labour for work in the fields, involving both the extended family and the neighbouring lakou. The *coumbite*, or *konbit* in Creole, a traditional cooperative working arrangement, still survives in the Haitian countryside. (2)

The basic mode of agriculture practised by the peasant farmers on their individual plots is subsistence production. Crops grown to feed the family include maize, millet, bananas and plantains, various varieties of beans, yams, manioc and sweet potato. Rice is also grown in the Artibonite valley and the few other regions where rivers provide sufficient water for irrigation. A variety of micro-climates across the country mean that certain crops ripen at different times, but the exacting work involved in preparing the ground, planting and harvesting these different crops goes on all the year round. (3)

Although men take responsibility for the heavier work, such as breaking the ground in preparation for planting, and building and re-building houses, in general the task of cultivation is shared equally by both sexes. Women have additional duties including child- care and preparation of food. (4). They are also responsible for the sale of surplus crops at markets and in towns, and the purchase, with the proceeds, of items that peasants cannot produce, such as shoes, tools, soap, medicine, and kerosene for their lamps. Many commentators have described women as the central pillar, or *poteau mitan*, around which the whole of Haitian society is built.

A key feature of the country's economy is the existence of some 300 official rural markets. These not only function as the primary point of exchange of commodities between the town and the country, but also as a focal point of the peasants' social life. It is a place where business is done but also where news is exchanged, and friendships and relationships formed. (5) The rural market has also functioned as the main source of revenue for local authorities: each trader has to pay a charge to secure a space in the market, and there are levies for each beast of burden that enters the market, and on the slaughter of animals at marketplace abattoirs.

Peasant farmers often avoid the market taxes and the effort involved and time lost in travelling great distances to the local market by selling their surplus to women intermediaries, the re-sellers or *revendeuses*. These traders travel across the country, and from market to market, buying products that can be resold at a higher price in the towns or in the country's main market, Port-au-Prince. Nicknamed *Madan Sara* after a bird of the same name that feeds on food crops, they are an important part of the rural economy and a link between countryside and town. (6)

In addition to the sale of foodstuffs at the domestic market, the Haitian peasant also makes an income from the sale of crops for export. Sugar, sisal and cocoa have been important exports at one time or another, but, throughout Haitian history, coffee has been the favoured cash crop of the small peasant farmer, and in the early 1990s it was grown by an estimated 380,000 peasants. The coffee plant can be easily grown and, once picked, the beans are usually sold without any preparation to middlemen, known as *spéculateurs*, who are agents of the great coffee export houses in the towns.

Since the early nineteenth century, coffee has been the principal source of government revenues. Although the fees and duties on coffee for export are levied at the customhouses at the port of departure, it has been the Haitian peasant who has borne the brunt of this indirect form of taxation. Each time the government increased the taxes on coffee exports, the small group of merchant families, who have traditionally dominated the trade, passed the charges on to their suppliers, the spéculateurs, who in turn transferred the cost on to the peasant producer.

Individual peasants, faced with a coffee exporting oligarchy running a tightly controlled cartel, and with a limited number of spéculateurs who must purchase a licence to ply their trade, have no option but to accept whatever price is offered for their coffee. By means of this process, the state extracted revenue from the peasantry, and the coffee export houses made vast profits. Attempts by peasants to band together to change this system have been fiercely resisted by the elite and their agents. (7)

During the nineteenth century, the port towns from where coffee was shipped to the United States and Europe developed on the back of this trade. Although coffee exports declined in quantity in the twentieth century, the crop continued to play a central role in linking the urban and rural economies. (8)

One of the most divisive and complex issues in rural Haiti is the question of land ownership. In part this is due to the way that peasant farmers originally took possession of their individual plots. In the early decades of independence, while many soldiers were rewarded with land by the country's leaders, other farmers simply occupied abandoned or idle lands and became *de facto* owners. Over the years, one government replaced another in rapid succession, each one buying support or placating potential opponents with grants of land formally belonging to the state. Complicating matters still further is the fact that the transfer and sale of lands have never been adequately recorded. In the late 1930s, a researcher found that when land was divided up and passed on as an inheritance with each new generation, the legal status of many land holdings grew ever more obscure. (9)

An accurate assessment of the pattern of land tenure remains difficult to make, not least because an individual farmer may be cultivating small plots of land that he himself owns and other plots that are rented or leased, while at the same time he could be leasing his own land to other peasant farmers. Where a peasant farms land that he does not own, the most common arrangement is the share-cropping system, in which a landowner leases a plot of his land to another peasant in return for a share of each harvest.

One phenomenon not in dispute is that the absence of official land deeds and titles has left illiterate peasants vulnerable to expropriation. Large landowners, military officers and coffee speculators have taken advantage of the confusion, and of the existence of an easily corruptible judicial system, to enlarge their personal holdings at the expense of small farmers. This phenomenon was particularly pronounced under the Duvaliers when large amounts of peasant land were taken over by Tontons Macoutes, section chiefs, and other supporters of the dictatorships. In areas where land is particularly productive, as on the fertile plains and gentler mountain slopes, disputes over land ownership are frequent and sometimes violent. (10)

An important feature of the development of rural society over the course of the twentieth century has been the decreasing size of individual land holdings. By the early 1990s, it was estimated that the average size of Haiti's 620,000 farms was less than one hectare. The combination of population growth and a finite quantity of land suitable for arable farming is one explanation, but more significant has been the use of the Napoleonic legal inheritance system whereby land is passed on to not just the eldest son but to all the children. Land that is owned by a family has been divided between ever greater numbers of heirs, resulting in barely viable plots. Peasant farmers have been obliged to sell off parts of their holdings when a poor harvest or unexpected expenditure, such as medical treatment or a funeral, creates a debt that can only be repaid by selling land. However, the polarisation of the peasant class with, at one end of the scale, peasants accumulating more land, and, at the other, peasants without any, has not brought about a concentration of land holdings. Typically, a successful peasant owns a number of tiny and widely-dispersed plots most of which are farmed by landless peasants working, not as wage labourers, but as share-croppers. Changes in agricultural production have been brought about by the diminishing size of holdings. (11)

The growing pressure on arable land is one of the root causes of an extremely serious environmental crisis in which deforestation and soil erosion are but two of the most visible aspects. The exploitation of the country's forests was begun by foreign logging companies which felled and shipped tons of mahogany and logwood in the early nineteenth century. According to research conducted by Haitian non-governmental organisations, however, the most relevant factor has been the expansion of poor peasants into the forested interior in search of new farm land. (12) Cultivation of the mountainsides and the cutting down of trees for charcoal production led to the erosion which, by the 1980s, was each year estimated to be stripping the country of nearly 40 million tons of soil, representing over ten thousand hectares of arable land. The process continues to the present day. (13)

In many areas of the country, and in particular in the north-west, deforestation and soil erosion have created desert-like conditions which in turn have brought famine. Yet peasants continue to cut down trees even while aware of the consequences. The explanation for this seemingly irrational behaviour is related specifically to the above-mentioned issues of small land holdings and insecure land tenure. In the first case, peasants working tiny plots of land are reluctant to surrender valuable space for growing crops to trees, whose roots suck valuable moisture from the soil, while in the second, uncertainty about the future of their plots does little to generate an appreciation of the long-term environmental benefit of leaving trees standing. More generally, a large percentage of peasant farmers live on the edge of abject poverty, and when faced with the choice of starving children or the income from the sale of a bag of charcoal, the trees are cut down. (14)

The division of land holdings, and the degradation of the environment are two reasons why, since the late nineteenth century, agricultural production has failed to keep pace with population growth. But equally important factors contributing to the impoverishment of the rural sector are the existence of an economic and political system based on exploitation and extraction, the absence of any investment in the agricultural sector, and the lack of technological innovation.

In the early 1980s, this sector suffered a further set-back when, following an outbreak of African swine fever, the US Agency for International Development organised the slaughter of the entire Haitian pig population on the grounds that it might spread to threaten the pork industries of North America. The blow which the eradication programme dealt the already depressed peasant sector (15), was felt even harder when promised compensation often never materialised, and re-population was attempted with a US breed completely unsuited to Haitian conditions. The results were a further decapitalisation of the poorer peasantry, and an increased reliance on charcoal production as a 'cash crop'.

Since the 1940s, thousands of foreign development experts have attempted to address the problems of the rural sector in Haiti, and few of their projects have had any lasting positive effect. Some analysts have suggested that the very structure of peasant society, built around a concept of social self-sufficiency and the rejection of the state in all its forms, cannot accommodate outside intervention (16) A more obvious and, in some cases, more accurate explanation for the failure of many foreign development initiatives is that they are just inappropriate for the particular circumstances found in rural Haiti. The agricultural techniques suggested by the foreign 'experts' are often simply disregarded as irrelevant. (17)

The Haitian peasantry faces greater challenges than ever before. Land is scarce, production is decreasing, costs are increasing, erosion and desertification are spreading, drought and famine threaten. These mounting pressures point to the collapse of the entire agricultural sector. In 1997, a small peasant organisation in a hamlet in the south of Haiti was recorded singing a song while its members worked to build ditches to prevent the further erosion of soil from the steep slopes where they farm. (18) The song reveals a certain resignation with their lot, with the hardships they have suffered, but at the same time it also suggests a political sophistication in its understanding of the community's predicament. Significantly, the peasants in question organised themselves in a collective response to common problem. The Haitian peasant, while often self-centred and individualistic, is also capable of acting with others to resolve pressing concerns when left with no other option. (19)

(1) RURAL ISOLATION

William Seabrook, *The Magic Island*, 1929

Up in the mountains in the 1920s, Seabrook stays with an isolated community living in a typical peasant *lakou*, a communal living arrangement found in rural Haiti.

This habitation, lost in the high mountains, was primitive and patriarchal. There were half a dozen thatch-roofed buildings in the cleared compound; the little community was ruled by Mamam Celie and Papa Theodore, her venerable, less active husband; its members were their grown up sons and daughters, their grandchildren naked from babyhood to puberty, playing in the sunshine among the pigs and goats; the eldest son, Emanuel, was past forty; the youngest, unmarried daughter, Catherine, was sixteen. Maman Celie herself I guessed to be far past sixty. Her sweet black face, like that of an old prophetess, was deeply wrinkled, but her thinness and straightness, her vitality, made her seem sometimes curiously young.

Patches of corn, millet, and cotton clung farther downward, above the jungle line, on the mountainside; a full mile below in a green jungle valley were the plantains, banana trees, coconut palms, and the clear spring with its rivulet from which donkeys toiled upward, festooned with calabash bottles like ambulant bunches of gigantic yellow grapes, often with children in procession single file behind, each with water-filled calabash balanced on his head.

Many paths led from this spring, winding down over the mountains and far away, but the path to Maman Celie's led upward only to our habitation and ended there. The next nearest family community was on the other side of a deep, mile-wide gorge; we counted them friends and neighbours; we could hear their cocks crowing at dawn, their dogs barking in the evening, and when darkness fell we could see their cook-fires burning; on the drums we could say to them across the chasm, "Come on such and such day," or "Expect us on such another," exchanging simple messages; but to reach their habitation, scarcely a mile distant as the birds flew, we had to journey seven miles around, down past the spring where the bare gorge narrowed to become a fertile valley, and then up again on the other side, regaining lost altitude.

Thus we were isolated, not only from the organised world down yonder – the nearest gendarme post, chapel, rural clinic, market, were a long day's journey beyond another range – but even somewhat from our neighbours, of whom there were perhaps fifty little family communities scattered far and wide on our own mountain.

Almost every day, despite our isolation, some of these neighbours trailed up from the common spring, sometimes on donkey-back, more usually in procession afoot, family visiting family; but strangers never came.

(2) WORKING TOGETHER

Harold Courlander, *The Drum and the Hoe*, 1960

The *coumbite*, or *konbit* in Creole, a West African tradition that lives on in Haiti, enables the peasant farmer to carry out major agricultural tasks which cannot be accomplished individually.

A member of the group holds a coumbite by notifying his fellow members that on such-and-such a day his fields will require clearing or hoeing. There are several variants of the work gathering. One, called *carré* or *corvée*, meets at irregular intervals and only on special invitation. There are no regular reciprocal obligations in the *corvée*; the workers are compensated by a "feast" and party given at the end of the day by the host. More usual than the *corvée* is the regular sharing of work on one another's fields – the *ronde*, or "taking turns"[...]

Essential to all coumbites are musicians and singing leaders. The instruments used are various, according to local custom. In the south they are usually drums, *tymbales*, and bamboo trumpets. In some areas of the north, the *lambi*, or conch-shell trumpet, is favoured.

According to the custom in the south, on the day of the coumbite the drummers arise in the false dawn before sunrise and begin a roundabout march to the home of the host. They pass before the huts of all the neighbours who are going to join the work party, playing a *rappel* on the drums. By one's and two's the workers come down the trails to join the procession, bringing hoes, machetes, or sickles as required. As the marching group grows larger, there is talking, laughter, and perhaps singing. Most of the men who join the procession are from close by. Others who may have to travel from a distance, perhaps from the next valley, go directly to the house of the host. When the workers arrive there, the women of the house serve coffee. This is the usual breakfast of the Haitian peasant.

Then the drummers play another *rappel*, and the men go down to the field that is to be tilled. There may be ten, twenty, or fifty of them. Some coumbites are even larger... The singing leader, called a *samba* or *simidor*, begins a song, the drummers play, the hoes begin to rise and fall in unison, and the workers join in the singing...The men stand shoulder to shoulder, moving the hoes up and down together, syncopating their movements by pauses as they sing...Sometimes tafia or rum is portioned out. The squads move forward slowly, inching their way across the field. The sanba beats on his hoe blade with a stone to keep time for his song. His job is to "encourage" the men... At noon the drummers signal a halt, and the workers shoulder their hoes, wipe off their machetes, and adjourn to the house for food. If it is a grand coumbite, the men rest for several hours, talking, catching up on sleep, or playing cards... At about three o'clock they go back to the fields to work until evening. Then comes the feast, under the canopy adjoining the house. The host and his wife have killed and cooked one or more goats... The men are served meat, rice, beans, and whatever else had been prepared. Afterward, women join the party, and there is more tafia or rum. Some men drift homeward, but most stay for the dancing.

(3) THE PEASANT FARMER'S YEAR

Alfred Métraux, *Making a Living in the Marbial Valley*, 1951

A summary of the annual cycle of agricultural work in the central Marbial region, an area at the foot of the Morne La Selle mountain, outside the southern town of Jacmel.

Annual cycle

January	In the lower valley: tending of irrigated crops. In the middle region: harvesting of millet. On the uplands: preparation and sale of coffee. This month is set aside for building and is a busy period for small local industries.
February	Towards the end of the month: clearing of the land for spring sowing. Picking of irrigated beans sown in December.
March	The clearing and hoeing process continues. Sowing can begin at the end of the month if the weather is favourable, i.e. rainy.
April	The main period for sowing beans, maize, millet, Congo peas, ground-nuts, sweet potatoes, etc. This is also the period for planting all permanent crops

(bananas, coffee) which thus have two seasonal
rainfalls. The beans planted in March are weeded and
the ground-nuts sown at the same time have their
ridges built up. Certain types of clearing are
completed. Young beans are picked.

May Sowing is frequently continued and the April seedlings
weeded. The beans and green maize planted in March
are harvested.

June Harvest is in full swing. Banana trees are planted in the
irrigated areas. The dry maize planted in March is
harvested.

July The land is cleared for the second season. The
harvesting of dry maize is completed. Storage of
maize. Harvesting of late crops.

August Sowing of the second season's ground-nuts, beans and
maize. Planting of sweet potatoes. "Cleaning" of coffee
shrubs in the lowlands.

September Weeding of August seedlings. Harvesting of new
coffee. Drying, grinding and sale of coffee in the
lowlands.

October Harvesting of beans and maize planted in August.
Harvesting and preparation of coffee continues in the
lowlands. Harvesting of the first season's ground-nuts
and sesame.

November End of the coffee harvest in the lower valley. Beginning
of the coffee harvest on the uplands. Preparation of the
land for irrigation.

December Cultivation of irrigated land. Bulk sales of coffee,
poultry and pigs. Overhaul of farms and generally
payment of debts.

(4) WOMEN'S WORK

Madeleine Sylvain Bouchereau, *Haïti et ses femmes*, 1957

In the late 1950s, a United Nations research project in the southern
valley of Marbial attracted a host of anthropologists. Bouchereau, a
Haitian academic, interviewed women to ascertain their role in the
working life of the peasantry.

In common with peasants nearly everywhere in world, the Haitian peasant woman has little time for leisure activities, yet her life seems to be tougher and more laborious than in most other countries. Herskovits [1] has depicted it as the pounding of maize in the mortar, and working in the fields, with childcare duties in between. In our survey, we found that nearly all the women from the smaller villages and rural areas are wholly responsible for household work; they are however helped by their daughters who little by little take on more tasks.

The women do the cooking, the housework, the washing, they repair used clothes, they make some of the family's clothes apart from the men's clothes, only 13% of which are home-made, and they transport water and firewood, mostly on their heads. Their work is not limited to domestic work, they also participate in money-making activities. The majority of women interviewed, 183 out of 230, are engaged in agriculture and the rearing of domestic animals, as are girls of school age, 197 out of 367. This contradicts the findings of Herskovits who found that in the Mirebalais region women seldom worked in the fields. This is perhaps a local custom, because my personal observations confirm the results of the survey, and I found that women work in the fields in nearly all regions of the country. This was also the case in Marbial. In general, it is the men who prepare the ground and sometimes the planting, but the weeding and day-to-day maintenance of the fields is carried out by the women. The harvest is usually carried by the whole family, although where the field is extensive, the work is done by a 'coumbite' or by another type of collective as had been the case in Africa.

In certain regions, particularly in the south, the women take part in the 'coumbites' and work just like the men; in other places, they are solely responsible for the preparation of the food on these occasions.

The female peasant is normally responsible for the sale of produce at the market and in the village. In our survey of 597 women and girls, 439 were engaged in small scale retail business.

A considerable number of peasants of both genders are engaged in secondary occupations which allow them to increase their incomes. In the Marbial survey, out of 147 families, only 37 worked solely on the land without any other occupation. A small number of women also augment the family income by sewing. There were only 51 women out of the 230 in our survey who took in sewing for money. In the Marbial survey nearly half of the women in the region said they worked as dressmakers, so that they could earn some money during the harvest. Many of them were highly skilled and made clothes for men and women. They had learnt their trade from dress-makers in the region, in the town of Jacmel or in Port-au-Prince.

[1] Melville Herskovits, an anthropologist.

Translated from French by Charles Arthur

(5) THE RURAL MARKET

P. Baltenweck, *Bulletin météorologique du Collège Saint-Martial,* 1922

The market is the hub of the agricultural economy in Haiti. One of the main rural markets is in the south-east, not far from the border with the Dominican Republic.

The importance of Fonds-Verrettes is due to its excellent location where access routes in the south coast region converge, from Pédernales and Saltrou and on towards Port-au-Prince; to its proximity to several large Dominican villages that find it easier to do business there than around Barahona or Neyba; and finally to the mild and varied climate which makes it the centre of a region boasting all sorts of crops...

This market takes place from Tuesday morning to Wednesday morning, but in reality it starts on Monday afternoon. Traders hasten to arrive early so they can occupy the best pitches. These are above all the hawkers who bring into the town, fabrics, hardware, bread, biscuits, salted fish, etc., and who take away foodstuffs, vegetables and fruits of all kinds. On our journey we encountered a large number driving ahead of them their beasts of burden, heavily laden donkeys, mules and horses, and sometimes the way was blocked when a temperamental or weary mule refused to budge. So they wouldn't think us superior, we had to say hello and have a word with each of them. We thus had the good fortune to observe the picturesque spectacle of the market filling up little by little. It was not at all complicated: posts driven into the ground were linked by interlaced strips of pliable wood, and the whole thing was covered by palm leaves to form little huts that vaguely resembled hutches or baskets. These rudimentary shops are laid out in three lines along a 100-metre stretch, and everyone crammed themselves in. Those who couldn't find a place inside, set up outside in the open. At its peak two thousand people are gathered together and it's a real scrum. The evening comes and it's the same crowded situation

– there's no question of going to sleep. The market lasts all night by the light of little wax torches that are made on the spot. Of course, there is still more to sell but isn't it also because of the enjoyment of meeting each other and the whole fascinating attraction? There's hardly a young girl in the countryside, large or small, who doesn't long to go to the market. There they find the movement, the life, the gaiety, and this is a diversion from the life of solitude they live in the mountains.

Translated from French by Charles Arthur

(6) HAITI'S HIGGLERS

Sidney Mintz, *Markets in Haiti*, 1963

The travelling saleswomen, the *Madan Sara*, have long been a vital component in the exchange of commodities between the countryside and the towns.

...The *revendeuse* is as typically Haitian as *vodoun* (voodoo), the Citadelle of Henry Christophe, or the Creole language. Haiti without its thousands of higgling, chaffering, laughing "Mesdames Sarah" is unimaginable.

The tourist there will see *revendeuses* descending from the mile-high villages of Pétionville and Kenscoff to the sea level capital of Port-au-Prince. Some of these women come great distances, perhaps walking from the Jacmel region of the south, literally across mountains, to sell in the city market places. Others are the wives of the relatively prosperous and sophisticated Kenscoff and Pétionville peasants; and still others live in Port-au-Prince and climb to the highlands, once or twice a week, to purchase stock. The scale of the enterprise is often very small indeed, and marked by a staggering investment of labour; a substantial headload weighs 60 pounds, and the women who carry this stock on foot over the four miles down to the mountain from Pétionville to the capital do so to save ten American cents.

The minuscule scale of operations, the enormous labour input, characterise an activity in which the numbers of participants competing for economic rewards are very large indeed. One authority estimates somewhat more than 50,000 women primarily engaged in trade in Haiti, a land of less than four million inhabitants. In fact the figure is almost certainly much larger since many women move in and out of trade, depending upon their passing successes and failures, their health, the demands of their home life, and the state of the economy. Typically, since alternate economic opportunities are very scanty and the press of need severe, *revendeuses* are prepared to work for very small rewards. One careful observer reports on higglers who travelled nine miles to buy cornmeal stock for resale, paying one US cent for each can, when it could have been bought locally at two and a half cents for two cans. The substitution of plentiful resources (labour) for scarce ones (capital) in an economy which is capital-scarce and labour-plentiful is economical in every sense; but the rate of expenditure of human energies in the absence of more lucrative enterprise is harrowing.

The picturesqueness of the market women, then, helps to cloak certain grim economic facts about Haiti and other societies like it. What is apparent to anyone who visits the country and reflects upon its economy is that the market women and the filthy, bustling venues of trade they fill each market day are at the very core of Haitian commerce.

(7) COFFEE AND CONFLICT

Haiti Info, *Commune of Borgne*, 1993

Coffee is the source of vast profits for the export houses which control the trade, and for the intermediaries, the spéculateurs, who buy from the peasant farmers. These groups typically react with violence to attempts by the farmers to organise themselves and raise their prices. The events in Borgne in northern Haiti, reported in November 1993, are an example of such conflict.

In the middle of the mountains in the North department, Borgne (Oboy in Creole) has seven communal sections. Recent statistics show the region has 28,000 inhabitants. Many specialists familiar with the zone say the land is very fertile, with a great capacity for agricultural production.

The most common crop is coffee, creating great tension between growers and speculators. Growers, most of whom own small plots, say the speculators buy their crop at very low prices and then sell the coffee at much higher rates, turning big profits. One of the main speculators is Borgne-native Lionel Bennett. His brother, Ernest (Michèle Bennett-Duvalier's father[1], controlled the prices of many agricultural products, especially coffee, during Jean-Claude's regime. The speculators have always been opposed to all efforts for progressive change in the area. For a number of years, for example, they have opposed plans to improve the road between Borgne and Limbé because that would give peasants the opportunity to sell their coffee to the highest bidder.

Nevertheless, the peasants of the region are politically very sophisticated, thanks to the work of Marc Lamour, a popular educator who has worked in the area since 1983. Because of his good reputation for consciousness-raising, under the Jean-Bertrand Aristide government he was the official "delegate" to whom peasants could come with their problems or questions for the capital. Lamour has been targetted by local soldiers and has been arrested several times.

"For years, the big speculators and large landowners have financed the local military and section chiefs to break down the peasant movement which was demanding fairer coffee prices and making other demands which were part of the democratic movement," explained a local organiser who asked to remain anonymous.

Because of that constant conflict, Borgne has been the site of numerous massacres.

In 1987, the local military officer and a section chief helped murder several dozen peasants after they demonstrated to ask the current government to fix the price of coffee at 5 gourdes (US$1 at the time) per pound.

In 1988, soldiers and their assistants massacred peasants in Danti, a section separating Borgne and Gonaïves. Over 100 houses were burned, at least six people were killed, many gardens and animals destroyed. The most recent attack occurred in the Basen Kayman and Mola sections at the end of last month. At least 300 houses were burned and five people were killed.

Although the Borgne peasants have lived through a number of difficult and terrorising events, they continue to work to organise themselves so that they can better represent their demands.

[1] Michèle Bennett was Jean-Claude Duvalier's wife.

(8) A COFFEE PORT

Dany Laferièrre, *An Aroma of Coffee*, 1993

The protagonist in this novel by the Haitian writer Laferièrre is a small boy who lives with his grandmother, Da, in the small port town of Petit-Goâve in the 1960s.

THE STREET

Our street isn't straight. It twists like a cobra blinded by the sun. It begins at the barracks and stops suddenly at the foot of Croix de La Jubilée. A street of speculators who buy coffee and sisal from the peasants. Saturday is market day. A regular hive of activity. People come from the twelve neighbouring rural sections that form the district of Petit-Goâve. They walk barefoot, wide-brimmed straw hats on their heads. Their mules go before them, heavy with sacks of coffee. Long before sun-up, you can hear the racket from the street. The animals paw the ground. The men shout. The women cry. Da gets up early on Saturday to make them coffee. Strong black coffee [...]

THE COFFEE OF LES PALMES [1]

According to Da, the best coffee comes from Les Palmes. In any case, that's what she always drinks. Da can't buy large amounts of coffee, like before. We went bankrupt ten years ago, long before my grandfather died. But the peasants go on offering to sell Da coffee. When they see she doesn't have the money, they leave a half-bag of coffee beans on the gallery [...]

THE PARK

It's really an empty lot where the peasants tie up their horses when they come down for the market. Actually, they leave them with old Ogine, whose job is to find them a good spot in the park. He brings them plenty of hay and gives them water to drink when the sun is at its zenith. Most of the horses have sores all over their backs. Ogine rubs down their backs with a brush, then puts big leaves over their open sores. Without flinching, the animals let him tend to them [...]

SACKS OF COFFEE

My grandfather was a great speculator in commodities. He brought coffee from the peasants and sold it to the Maison Bombace. The Maison Bombace is by the harbour. That's where all the speculators go to sell their coffee. At the end of the month, a big boat comes to pick up all the coffee in Petit-Goâve and take it to Italy. The whole town pours down to the harbour to watch the loading of the coffee. I always went with my grandfather. The longshoremen were sweating. People were running every which way, like frightened ants. Men from the Maison Bombace would have the speculators sign all kinds of papers. My heart beat faster every time I saw our coffee sacks go by.

[1] Les Palmes is a village in the mountains south of Petit-Goâve.

(9) LAW OF THE LAND

George Eaton Simpson, *Haitian Peasant Economy*, 1940

A Byzantine system of inheritance laws, together with an expensive and corrupt judicial process, means that the legal status of land tenure grows ever more complicated with each new generation.

When the land is not divided, each branch of the family, by virtue of a tacit, but immutable law, occupies a particular plot, and these allotments are religiously respected by the co-heirs. The family increases, but not the land, and succeeding generations establish themselves elsewhere, except the oldest son, who takes the place of his father. Those members of the family who are cultivating the undivided land are not compelled to give portions of the crops each year to the other heirs. However, each heir conserves his rights, and if a circumstance arises which necessitates a division of the land it is customary for an heir to sell his part to a co-inheritor or to an outsider. Before a man can sell any part of his land to someone outside the family he must, according to law, offer it first to members of his family. If the co-inheritors refuse to buy, or if a neighbour can pay more for it, the share passes into the hands of another family. Should this happen the remaining heirs may wage war against and try to expel the outsider whose purchase breaks up the family's estate.

After two or three generations division of the land becomes almost impossible, and the confusion is aggravated with the passing of time. If someone in the family tries to end this chaotic state of affairs he may find himself confronted by an outsider who invokes the twenty-year law, for if one has occupied a piece of land for twenty years as owner he needs no legal title to that part of it where his house stands, nor for the field which he is cultivating. The arbitrator will also find it impossible to retrieve tracts of land for which the family has received false titles, or which have been lost in civil troubles, or whose titles are hidden away among the papers of unknown members of the family. He may also encounter outsiders who claim patches of the family's land by right of "possession." According to Haitian law if a person for a year has cultivated a piece of land as owner, publicly and in the sight of everyone, he may claim it. Such encroachments are made possible by ignorance of boundaries, and by a family's neglect of a part of its land. The first litigation, in which the encroacher tries to establish claim to the harvest on the land he has cultivated for a year, is before the Justice of the Peace. The loser may take the case to the Civil Tribunal, and finally, action may be

brought in the Tribunal de Cessation. Lawsuits over the claims outsiders make to a family's land, as well as those brought by individuals
who insist upon a division of the family estate, are disastrous to the
peasants.

(10) LAND AND POLITICS

Libète, *San kontinye ap koule nan Latibonit,* 1994

In this extract from an article in the Haitian weekly newspaper, *Libète,*
a member of the local council discusses a recent conflict over land in
the lower Artibonite region. The piece is subtitled, 'A lot of people
die in a fight over land, but, according to the peasants, at the root of
the conflict there's a political game being played.'

Libète: What's been happening in the last few days?

"On Wednesday, 21 December, from six o'clock in the evening to
around midnight, people from Briza and Baraj attacked the hamlet
of Blen. They looted Madame Solon's house, taking her neck chain,
her ring, her ear rings – everything in the house. On the Thursday,
the same group was shooting with a lot of pistols, and a young man,
Jansèn Inosan, died on Boulen bridge. On the Friday, people from
Boulen, Negriyèl, Remosen, Koutèt, and Akasya set up barricades
to keep out the Briza people. Then people from Briza and Baraj shot
someone from Blen. They cut off his head and took it away to Briza.
He was buried without his head... On Christmas Eve, the Briza men
returned, not with guns but with machetes, and there was panic in
the zone of Pitray. Now it's not a fight between Blain and Briza any
more. It involves Bwajoli, Akasya, and Pitray, from where everyone
is moving out taking their pigs and beds with them. There's no one
in Pitray any more, except perhaps some guys from Briza and Baraj..."

Libète: What's the explanation for the fighting?

"It all started with a lawsuit that Noveyis Ano, a man from Blen,
brought against Briza before I was born. Noveyis died in 1950. In
1991 I asked how many carreaux [1 carreau = 1.29 hectares] are dis-
puted and was told approximately 33 carreaux. Briza people showed
me a document that the section chief of the time, Jan Lafòs Edwa,
had witnessed for them. I said to them, "If you appear in court with

that, it will be meaningless because it's handwritten." We set up a meeting at the court between four people from Briza and four from Blen, so it could adjudicate on this matter, but at that moment the Préval government blocked the transfer of land, and then there were soldiers everywhere [after the 1991 coup d'état].

Five days after the president returned [October 1994], I met up with some guys in Briza, and I said to them "Let's hope that what happened in '91 won't happen again..." They suggested that four people from Briza and four from Blen go to sort out the problem at the court in St Marc, but I told them, "the law never gives anyone possession of rice lands that another person has transplanted." Three days later they started to go into the Blen peoples' lakou, and beat them and take their rice. This is how the crisis started."

Libète: Is there a political problem behind the struggle over land?

"That's certain. Edi Dipiton, from Bwajoli, was the government judicial authority in St Marc before he was a Senator (1). His cousin, Wolan Dipiton, was in the public prosecutor's office in St Marc. The Briza people met with him to make a series of false legal documents. They told me, "these lands are owned by a soldier called Jan Pyè who died a long time ago", but they couldn't produce a document to prove it. In reality, the people who are fighting there are not the Briza people but people who come from a small area of Lestè...Because they are supported by Dipiton, they feel strong. Edi gave Wolan the land. Wolan got his buddy, Ti Pòl Dolimon, to manage the land. They partitioned the land, they sold it, and kicked everyone off! When the Blen people filed a summons concerning the guys invading their land, Wolan arrested the people who were the victims instead of the Dolimon group."

[1] Edi Dipiton, elected to the Senate in 1990 representing the pro-Lavalas FNCD party, became a prominent supporter of the military regime in power between 1991 and 1994.

Translated from Creole by Charles Arthur

(11) SMALLER AND POORER

Georges Anglade, *Coup d'oeil sur le passé*, 1990

Haitian geographer Anglade summarises the changing agricultural practices of the peasant farmer as land holdings have been divided into smaller and smaller plots.

In 1880, a Haitian family with four children lives on 20 hectares of land. Sixteen of these 20 hectares are in "bois-debout" [tree crops] with coffee, etc. A small proportion, one or two hectares, is given over to staple crops and assure the family's subsistence. There are a lot of plantains and fruit, and the key animal in this type of agricultural set-up is the pig. Each farm possesses around 20 to 30 pigs. This is the grand era of "griots, banane pesée". "Griot, banane pesée" [fried pork, fried plantain] is the popular image of national cuisine in the 1880s.

From 1910 to 1920 there is another generation. The 20 hectares have been subdivided, with each child inheriting five hectares. Only some five hectares remain as "bois-debout" and the rest is used for growing food staples. The production of commodities for export, previously grown on the 16 hectares (cut wood and coffee grown in the trees' shade, with pigs living in the undergrowth of the coffee bushes) has decreased. The presence of the pig is no longer suitable on this five-hectare farm; goats are introduced in the 1920s; the pig needed a large area with ample fruit and didn't eat grass, unlike the goat. This is the age of the goat, of tasso [dried meat], a whole new feature of the peasant as well as the urban diet...The landowners are reduced to five hectares with lower production of coffee. Why? Because coffee is produced on no more than two hectares per unit, whereas previously it was produced on 16 hectares per unit.

We come now to the 1940s and 1950s. Already in the 1930s the peasant's daughters are increasingly moving away from the land. The size of the farm is now no more than one or two hectares. Now the goat has outlived its usefulness; it is the cow that starts to be best suited to the new conditions. The peasantry's capital accumulation which had taken the shape of the pig in the nineteenth century, the goat by the beginning of the present century, now falls to the level of the cow and the chicken... What's left for producing exports? Next to nothing. Subsistence replaces everything.

By the time we reach the 1980s, it's impossible to divide half a hectare into five. The cow's days are numbered, but so are the human being's; hence emigration, exile, boat-people, the enormous pressure which people feel. There are fifty eligible parties for each carreau of land. The population of Port-au-Prince reaches 1 million and 80% of peasants are on the move. The only animal that can survive on one-tenth of a carreau is a chicken or perhaps a rabbit in a cage. It's absurd...

Translated from French by James Ferguson

(12) A HISTORY OF DEGRADATION

COHPEDA, *Causes de la dégradation de l'environnement en Haïti,* 1993

The Haitian Collective for the Protection of the Environment and an Alternative Development (COHPEDA) outlines the factors leading to deforestation and soil erosion.

Colonial period (1493-1803)
During the Spanish and French colonisation, the use of new agricultural techniques, the practice of monoculture, and the destruction of virgin forests in the mountains were some of the factors that favoured the weakening of the soil and the degradation of the environment.

(1804-1915)
Environmental degradation during this period was accentuated by the anarchic intensification of precious wood extraction, and the excessive use of wood as the only source of energy. It is necessary, however, to emphasize that one of the principle causes of environmental degradation in this era was and today still remains the movement of the poor peasantry into the mountains. In effect, the dominant Haitian groups and the foreigners imposed on the peasants a servile regime (agrarian corporatism, the rural code, etc.) and monopolised the best land on the plains (all of them practising agriculture based on share-cropping or leaving it to lie fallow). Faced with this situation, the small peasants gradually cleared the mountain lands to carry out their agricultural activities based principally on the production of food staples (manioc, sweet potato, etc.) The practice of seasonal cultivation (necessitating a periodic and repeated use of the soil) most often on the fragile land (the thin layer of arable soil) and on very steep slopes, brought about the erosion that we know today.

(1934-today)
During the American occupation agricultural and rural policy was based on the establishment of big companies practising monoculture, extensive agriculture, and the reestablishment of the corvée. [1] All of this accelerated the process of movement of the poorest peasant sector towards the mountains and the anarchic clearing of the land. After the physical departure of the American troops, the process of degradation continued. Urbanisation and the partial expansion of industry brought about an increase in the use of wood as an energy source in urban households and in industries such as dry cleaning, vetiver factories, rum distilleries, etc. During the Duvaliers' dictatorship some hectares of forests were also razed for political reasons – destruction of forest cover in order to flush out the opponents of the regime who took refuge there. What is more, environmental degradation which is especially conspicuous in rural areas, also affects the towns as a result of the rural exodus, the pauperisation of the population, and irresponsibilty on the part of the authorities, e.g. the growth of slums, the build-up of domestic waste, and the dumping of toxic waste.

[1] The corvée was a system of forced labour, dating back to the early post-independence period but revived by the US occupying forces as a means of securing labour for road-building and other infrastructural projects.

Translated from French by Charles Arthur

(13) UNNATURAL DISASTER

Fédération des Amis de la Nature (FAN), *Quelques données sur la réalité dramatique de l'environnement en Haïti* , 1986

FAN, a green organisation based in Port-au-Prince, collated data from various sources in the 1980s to highlight the severity of the environmental crisis in Haiti.

Three-quarters of the country is mountainous. 63% of the land has inclines of more than 20%, while 29% has inclines of less than 10%.

33% of the country is either extremely eroded, or abandoned, or sterile, or lost forever.

Each year, erosion makes an additional 6,000 hectares of land impossible to farm.

Percentage of the surface area covered by forests:
    1492 100%
    1923 23%
    1974 7%
    1982 3.6%
    1986 1.5%

Haiti's energy sources:
    Wood and charcoal   72.0%
    Bagasse [sugar-cane] 7.5%
    Hydro-electricity   3.5%
    Petrol/oil   1.5%

The use of wood in Haitian industry:

Dry cleaning: 20,000 tons of wood annually – mango, campeche, acajou, chene and other trees. 71% of energy needs are met by wood, 26.9% by gas and oil.

Essential oils: The vetiver factories consume 84% of energy in this industry, lime juice factories 15%. 75% of energy needs are met by wood, 24.5% by heating-oil.

Bakeries in the Port-au-Prince area: Every year – 12,000 tons of wood. 66% of energy needs are met by wood, 33% by gas and oil.

Distilleries: Wood is used in the majority of cases.

Between 40 and 50 million trees are cut each year to serve our demand for energy. It would be necessary to plant as many every year to stabilise production. If you wanted to reforest Haiti, imagine how many trees would need to be planted to guarantee an increase.

Erosion is wearing away the surface, removing the irreplaceable, fertile top-soil. Once this layer is removed by the wind or the rain, the rocks appear. "In the mountains the harvest is rocks," says the peasant.

The pseudo-drought phenomenon:

Water can't filter down into the soil. In spite of the rain, the springs are not replenished because of the lack of forest cover. The forests act as a sort of sponge to retain water in the rainy season and return it to the springs during the dry periods. Without this sponge phenomenon, rain water doesn't have time to penetrate the soil. and quickly floods away into the sea.

Results of erosion:

a) Reduction of the natural fertility of the land.

b) Reduction of agricultural production, and famine.

c) Increase in salinity. Salt water tends to be drawn back up to the surface by osmosis, which leads to an increase in uncultivable land.

d) Decrease in the efficiency of infrastructure such as dams, hydro-electric plants, irrigation systems, and roads.

e) Increasing drought and pseudo-drought, and springs dying up.

f) Destruction of natural habitat and the disappearance of certain endemic animal species.

g) Reduced standard of living in rural communities.

h) Exodus towards the towns.

Translated from French by Charles Arthur

(14) CHARCOAL: THE LAST RESORT

Leah Gordon and Anne Parisio, Interview with a Charcoal Maker, 1996

Testimony of a charcoal-maker on the plateau between Jean Rabel and Môle St Nicolas in the North West department. Deforestation in Haiti continues because for many peasants the production of charcoal is their only source of income.

//You can see this earth doesn't want to give birth to anything. We keep going at it to try and get a little corn and beans, but if there's no rain, you can't plant and the earth won't give anything. The sun beats down, and the children get thinner. The only thing you can do is to go around and cut these little trees, which is the only way you can give your kids a little something to eat. All you get round here for all these people living together is one ration card (for food aid) to go to the feeding stations, and they give you 4lbs of food for a month. All you can do is turn to charcoal-making to feed your children.

When you have a goat with babies, the dogs won't leave it alone, and the next day you find all the babies have gone. We had chickens, but we lost them all to disease. If you are poor, chickens are something to fall back on, because at least you can go to market to sell something.

We have no jobs, no work...We are just down to our little trees, so we are trying to replant trees now...We've only got little trees left, so we can only make a little amount of charcoal from them. As soon as you have eaten up the money from the last sack, you are having to make another one. The same day you have cut the trees, you've already eaten the money...

My son here is 16, but a boy of 12 would be bigger than him. I know poverty really well. If you cut a tree – enough to make a sack – you know you can keep your kids alive. But sometimes it rains and you can't cook up the charcoal for a month, yet the children are still asking for food.

Sometimes we buy wood from other people and then we can make seven or eight sacks really quickly. Our uncle is really keeping us going. We borrow money from him to buy wood from other people."

(15) THE CREOLE PIG DISASTER

Bernard Diederich, *Swine Fever Ironies*, 1985

The peasant economy was seriously weakened when, in the early 1980s, the United States oversaw the eradication of the Haitian 'Creole' pig population.

There is much bitterness in Haiti over the 13-month-long, $23 million slaughter of its pig population, a disaster so devastating that it has ended a way of life for the Haitian peasant. "In monetary terms, it's a loss to the Haitian peasant of $600 million," says an American veterinarian involved in the pig re-population programme. "The real loss is incalculable," says a Haitian economist familiar with the peasant economy, which is, he says, "reeling from the impact of being without pigs. A whole way of life has been destroyed in this survival economy," he adds. "This is the worst calamity to ever befall the peasant." [...]

African swine fever first struck Hispaniola on the eastern side of the island in the Dominican Republic in 1978. In 1979 there was an outbreak of the disease in Haiti's Artibonite Valley, which is linked to the Dominican Republic by the Artibonite River. Usually when African swine fever strikes, 99% of the pigs that catch the virus die quickly, but in Haiti the virus was not so lethal. In fact, the country has been rife with rumours that the pigs were sacrificed for no good reason, and many Haitians have questioned whether the disease was even threatening their pigs. Among villagers discussing the pig eradication programme, some said it was unnecessary; that there had been no disease, that it was a plot. After all, their black pigs had lived for 500 years under extremely poor conditions and had become immune to most diseases. Furthermore, the disease had been at its peak in 1980; and by the time the eradication programme began in May 1982, no more pigs were dying. The average peasant believed the epidemic to be over and saw no reason for their pigs to be killed [...]

Over a period of 500 years the black pig had become a lean and degenerate scavenger. It was perfectly adapted to some of the most miserable raising conditions in the world, and could go two or three days without food. That hardy species is extinct; it will take generations of American pigs to become "Haitianised" to the point where they can survive and forage for food in the filth as the black pig did.

Pig care in the past required no special attention. The hog grew in city garbage dumps or in humid places in country backyards. The usual cost of a pig at birth averages $10, and the retail prices at maturity range from $150 to $250. The initial investment could be as low as $2 if the purchase was made "in the belly" during the sow's pregnancy. Says Jean-Jacques Honorat, a Haitian sociologist, "Beyond its nominal cash value, which is part of the peasant subsistence economy, the pig also has an enormous indirect economic value which has never as yet been estimated. It is indeed a master component of the Haitian peasant's production system."

Not only was the pig inexpensive to keep, it provided many services for the farmer. The pig was the farmer's garbage disposal system, consuming a large variety of human and domestic wastes as well as farm residues and by-products. The pig went after wild plants, roots and certain species of insects and worms. Its natural immunity against most of the endemic diseases kept it healthy. After a harvest, pigs would dig for tubers and roots left in the soil – almost like a mechanical digging device – thereby helping prepare it for the next planting. It fed on the may beetle larva, a worm that was particularly destructive to plants. In addition, its excrement, high in nitrogen, provided fertiliser for crops.

(16) RESISTING THE OUTSIDE WORLD

Mats Lundahl, *Underdevelopment in Haiti*, 1991

Lundahl suggests that, in the post-independence period, the peasantry developed 'autoregulation' mechanisms which preserve the equilibrium of peasant society and, at the same time, act as a form of passive resistance to interventions by the elite and by foreigners.

The peasant society that developed in Haiti did not provide ac tive resistance to the state. Rather it operated parallel and independently of it. It sought to ignore in so far as possible the formal power imposed by the *creole* administration and it rejected the principle of hierarchy. Instead, autonomous structures were developed that built on the individual and on reciprocity: structures that lead to autoregulation.

Through family education, the individuals learn the rules to be followed. Deviant behaviour is not accepted, especially when it would jeopardise the reproduction of the system. Sorcery is used as a defence against aggression. Collective and reciprocal work structures are employed since wage labour is not compatible with egalitarianism (wage labourers would belong to a 'lower' category in a hierarchy) and because the individual peasant units have to be autonomous, i.e. they must be able to survive without recourse to outside labour (reciprocity being a different matter). Religion provides another important mechanism for cohesion and survival since it contributes both to the collective identity (mainly Catholicism) and to individualism (voodoo with its innumerable *loas* (spirits).

The autoregulation mechanisms define a 'permanent' equilibrium in peasant society. To a very large extent this equilibrium rests on poverty (*précarité*) which is shared by all. There exists a uniform concept of 'needs' and the efforts made by outside society to create an increased rural demand for consumption are resisted. The peasants have many devices to prevent intrusion by the outside state. The complexity of land ownership is a good example, with the same peasant owning, leasing, and share-cropping land, while also letting it out to others on share-crop contacts. All this takes place against the background of a lack of clear titles.

Contact with the *creole* state (which is of course inevitable) always poses a danger for peasant society. To avoid being absorbed by the state, a number of behavioural traits have been devised by Haitian peasants. These tactics include 'getting liked' by outsiders, hiding facts (like the voodoo cult and the site of real power), as well as using multiple names for the same person. Moreover, structures that are built by intruders are eroded by peasant action... Development projects are left to decay as soon as the outside experts have left the project site. Dissuasion – persuading the outside aggressor that his intervention is in vain – and mockery complete the picture. Ultimately, resort is made to force. When all other mechanisms have been rendered ineffective, outbursts of violence are directed against the sources of disturbance of the peasant equilibrium.

(17) IGNORING THE EXPERTS

Ideas and Action   *The Low Voice of Saint-Jules Clocy, A Haitian Farmer,* 1987

Gérald Belkin, project officer of the Institute of Cultural Action for Development, asked a peasant farmer why the advice of agricultural development experts is often ignored.

Gérald Belkin: I hear the experts came here to teach you how to plant in straight lines. How do you feel about that?
Saint-Jules Clocy: Planting in straight lines? To tell you the truth, that started as long ago as 1971, but they never succeeded in getting it adopted. If a development agent comes this way to work with the people in one or two small gardens here and there, the people are quite capable of planting in straight lines, but once the agent has gone, that's an end of it. Take, for example, a small garden the size of this one. I do all the planting myself. With that system, if I plant in a straight line, with the area I've got, I should have to sow more densely, much more densely. Whereas, if I don't sow in straight lines, with a little bit of hoeing here and there, I can sow one pocket here and another one further on.

In the last analysis, planting in straight lines does you no good. There's no advantage in it, is there? Because even if your crop is that much bigger, the amount of time you've spent is worth twice as much as the extra yield. And then, here on the slope, there's a lot of wind. If the maize is planted too densely, the wind beats the leaves against each other. After a strong gale, all the leaves are crushed. Whereas if you plant wherever you want to, you always take care not to put maize plants too close to each other. When the wind comes, it finds a space; this way, the maize doesn't get exhausted. But in a straight line, each planted thirty by fifty, when the maize starts to come up, all the leaves touch each other and it becomes a wall. And in the end there are far more leaves than corn-cobs, because the leaves are battering each other in the wind continuously, and the cobs stay small.

G.B: And the peasants all know this?

S-J.C: Of course they know it, but when someone comes and tells them they can obtain higher yields by doing it like this, they're always ready to try it out.

G.B: Do you know that many people criticise this system of planting several plant species together?

S-J.C: I know. But they should see why the peasants plant all these species in the same plot. Me, for example: it is only in this corner of the lakou that I can grow yams, maize and sweet potatoes, and I need all three of them. Well, I need beans too. Beans take about two months before they are ready to be picked. Maize takes five months to ripen. The way I see it, beans can be a threat to maize. The maize has all the time it needs to develop, because as soon as the beans are pulled up the maize starts growing. At that point, rain is what we always need. In December, it hardly rains at all. When we get rain it will be February and time to plant. I should have to make a yam plot here, a maize plot there, a potato plot somewhere else. At that rate I would do better to plant all my crops together. Like that I can save time and go and do another job somewhere else.

G.B: OK, all right, but why don't the development experts know this?

S-J.C: I don't know, but it is a fact that they criticise us peasants because of our combined cropping! It should perhaps also be borne in mind that people who plant in straight lines probably have the means to do so. Perhaps they have enough money to pay for labourers, or they have a lot of land, or their land is flat. In those conditions it is right to plant in lines; perhaps they plan to use a plough or something! For example, the Ministry of Agriculture, if they have enough money, they have the right to plant in lines if they want to. But not me... I have no money. It's an uphill struggle for me to look after plots, and then I have to go to work to earn enough to feed myself until crops are ready.

If they are going to understand our reasons, these people will have to live where the peasants live. At least then they would see why we plant the way we do. If you ask me, there's no-one who doesn't look after his own interests in the place where he lives. If people found that planting in straight lines really worked, they wouldn't be so stupid as to reject the method.

(18) SINGING THE BLUES

Gwo Zago's gwoupman, *Peyizan yo*, 1997

Members of a small peasant organisation in Fond de Bouden, south-ern Haiti, sing of their life of hardship, and their sense that all politicians court their support at election time and afterwards al-ways neglect them.

Peyizan yo, se peyizan nou ye,
Peasants, we are peasants,

Fòk nou chita, pou n reflechi bagay sa yo,
We must sit down, and mull these things over,

Nèg la vil yo ap gayone sou do nou lontan,
The city people have been riding on our backs for a long time,

Tout pyebwa nou finn koupe,
All our trees have been cut down,

Yo te touye kochon nou,
They killed our pigs,

Yo mete nou anbago,
They put an embargo on us, [1]

Kounye a la, nou pral nan eleksyon,
And now we are supposed to vote,

Lè eleksyon yo fini, y ap rele nou nèg mòn, gwo zago.
So that when the elections are over with, they can call us hillbilly,
   and bigfoot. [2]

[1] Between 1992 and 1994, Haiti was subjected to an economic em-bargo, imposed by the Organisation of American States and the United Nations. The embargo failed to compel the military regime to restore democracy, and caused great suffering for the poorest sec-tions of the population.

[2] *Gwo zago*, or 'bigfoot', is an abusive term for poor peasants who can-not afford shoes. The leader of the peasant collective (gwoupman) in Fond de Bouden has subverted the insult by making it his nickname.

Translated from Creole by Laurie Richardson

(19) PASSIVE VICTIMS OR AGENTS OF CHANGE?

Amy Wilentz, *The Rainy Season*, 1989

Many commentators are struck by the Haitian peasant's apparently ambivalent attitude to political participation.

Most of the time, it is true, the peasants act for themselves only; it is not easy to keep a family alive out in the dry countryside, and the competition for what little there is is fierce. Often, peasants don't know who is President; the big news from Port-au-Prince is just a lot of meaningless names to the farmer. He is more concerned with the lack of rain, the indifference of the gods, the rising or the falling of the price of rice in the market. He wonders how much it will cost to send his four children to school next year, and how much it will cost to get the houngan to make a cure for his wife's head-aches. Port-au-Prince politics – to him it's just *bla-bla-bla*, as Haitians say. But if it comes down to his right to the land he farms, or how much higher a tax his wife will have to pay when she brings their produce to market, or whether or not he is going to get his free pig-let from the foreign development project, the Haitian farmer becomes as politically involved and motivated as any politician in the capital.

Everyone in the countryside makes his various contributions to Haitian politics – not just the farmer on his little plot of land, but the village houngan and the princely bishop and the progressive Catholic priest; the local sheriff and the gentleman farmer and the former Tonton macoute with his rifle tucked under his bed; the market woman with her over-packed burro and the coffee trader and his son; the sub-lieutenant and the foreign development workers in Gonaïves, Jean-Rabel, Verrettes. Not always, but often, their actions filter down to Port-au-Prince, and affect what happens there. If the provincial towns and the peasantry are not involved, nothing really changes in Haiti. Of course, a new general may become President in Port-au-Prince or a new political party may take to the streets, but real change comes only when the peasantry participates. Thus, the most important events in Haitian history have been preceded by organisation and unrest in the provinces and on the mountainsides; the Revolution of 1791-1804; the end of the US occupation in 1934; the fall of Jean-Claude Duvalier in 1986 and the subsequent popular movements.

CHAPTER FOUR
POVERTY AND URBAN LIFE

By the end of the twentieth century, Haiti's combination of an economic system based on the exploitation of peasant farmers and the enrichment of a privileged minority, and a predatory state making negligible investments in human resources and basic infrastructure, had created a socio-economic crisis of staggering proportions. With a national average income per head for the year 1995 of just US$240, Haiti ranks as the poorest country in the Americas and one of the twenty-five poorest in the world. Stunningly unequal distribution of what wealth there is means that some 70 per cent of a population, currently totalling an estimated 7.2 million people, live in abject poverty. (1) Nearly half the population do not have access to health services, less than a third have access to safe drinking water, more than quarter of children suffer from malnutrition, and one in ten people depend on daily food rations provided by international relief agencies. Haiti has the worst health indicators, the lowest school enrolment and the highest illiteracy rates in the continent.

At the macro-economic level, at the heart of the contemporary crisis is the accelerating decline in agricultural production over the last half of the twentieth century. As outlined in the previous chapter, the rural sector has for some time been beset by a range of problems, but in 1970 agricultural production still accounted for about half of Haiti's Gross Domestic Product. By the beginning of the 1990s it had dropped to less than a third. Over the course of thirty years Haiti has deteriorated from a state of near self-sufficiency in food to depending on imports for more than half of its consumption. The production of traditional agricultural exports such as coffee and cacao has plummeted too. A striking example is provided by the case of sugar. During the colonial era the country was the top sugar producer in the Americas. In 1951 Haiti still produced almost 90,000 metric tons, but when the last commercial sugar refinery was closed down in the late 1980s, Haiti began to import sugar. The decline of the agricultural sector, on which the economy as a whole is heavily reliant, poses serious problems, not least for the central government which has traditionally depended on customs revenues from exports for the bulk of its revenue.

The macro-economic crisis is compounded by the absence of significant development in any other economic sector. The small size of the domestic market has limited the development of manufacturing to foodstuffs, beverages and basic household goods. During the 1970s, the tourism sector thrived but then collapsed in the mid-1980s when negative international publicity about the incidence of Aids and political violence in Haiti deterred most visitors.

The human cost of the deteriorating state of an already underdeveloped economy has been the worsening standard of living of the two-thirds of the population who still live in the countryside. By the mid-1990s the average annual income per head for the rural population was less than US$100. Periodic droughts leading to famine and emergency relief operations underline the precariousness of rural life. (2) The plight of the rural population has been deepened by the almost complete absence of social services provided by the state. In the countryside, the public-sector health service is practically non-existent, and malaria, dengue fever, tuberculosis, measles, worms, and other diseases relating to chronic malnutrition remain largely unchecked. State schools are few and far between, and those that do exist are dilapidated and under-staffed.

In response to the lack of prospects and the deteriorating quality of life in the countryside, many poor rural families send one or more of their children to live with an urban family for whom they work as unpaid servants. As of January 1996 there were as many as 250,000 of these children, known as *restavèks*, in Haiti. (3) Huge numbers of individual adults and whole families have also abandoned the rural milieu in recent years and moved to a new life in the cities, particularly Port-au-Prince. The population of the capital, numbering some 500,000 in 1970, grew to an estimated 1.4 million in 1990, and at the end of the century may total some two million. This massive human influx has overwhelmed the limited services provided by the metropolitan authorities. (4)

The majority of the new arrivals take up residence in the mushrooming shanty towns on the outskirts of the city. In Port-au-Prince, sprawling slum areas have grown up in Carrefour to the south, and in Cité Liberté and La Saline near the sea-front. Here thousands of families live in rudimentary homes made of breeze block and corrugated iron, and constructed in zones that lack even basic amenities such as water, electricity and sewerage. The most notorious of all the slums is Cité Soleil to the north of the capital, an area of five-square kilometres where as many as 400,000 people live crammed together in squalid conditions. Cité Soleil began as a state-sponsored, low cost housing project on low-lying mud-flats in the late 1950s, but the project was soon abandoned and the area was taken over by squatters. The tightly-packed maze of tin and cardboard shacks offers the cheapest, and the worst, housing in all of Port-au-Prince. (5)

With the rural exodus showing no sign of slowing down, the urban sprawl continues to spread. (6)

The crush of people, the street markets, traffic jams, slums, and run-down infrastructure give the cities, especially Port-au-Prince, an anarchic feel, but underneath the veneer of urban chaos and insanity there is order and meaning of sorts. (7) Away from the main thoroughfares, the inhabitants of the teeming *quartiers populaires* of downtown Port-au-Prince have developed a strong sense of community as a necesssary antidote to the deprivations of slum life. (8)

Despite the difficult living conditions in the capital, the possibility of finding some form of work acts a powerful magnet for the rural unemployed. The state has for some time been one of the main sources of formal employment, but to get a job requires a level of education and, perhaps more importantly, the contacts, that few of those arriving from the provinces enjoy. The small manufacturing sector is also mostly concentrated in the capital, but employment opportunities are again limited. During the 1970s the assembly factories that set up operations in and around the capital's industrial parks did provide new jobs, and by the mid-1980s this sector employed around 60,000 workers. However, at this point, the political instability following the demise of the Duvalier regime prompted many of the foreign-owned companies to relocate to other countries. This trend continued during the trade embargoes imposed after President Aristide's overthrow in 1991, and by 1994 nearly all the factories had closed. The sector revived slightly after the international intervention to restore Aristide, but by the end of 1997 the total number of jobs was still only 21,500. The salaries are low, usually close to the legal minimum wage and sometimes less if workers fail to meet the required target for daily production. The mostly female labour force complain that the wage, even after it was raised to 36 gourdes (just over $2) a day in 1995, is woefully insufficient. (9)

Other than the assembly sector there are few other sources of unskilled work, and in 1997 the national rate of unemployment was estimated at a staggering 70 per cent, an increase of 20 per cent since 1991. In urban areas, as in the countryside, the vast majority of the labour force is underemployed, working for a few hours or days every now and again, for example, as labourers or cart pullers (10). There are also hundreds of road-side micro-enterprises providing services such as the manufacture of concrete blocks and furniture, and the repair of cars, bicycles, shoes and clothes. A huge number of people, most of them women, try to earn a few gourdes each day by selling minute quantities of items such as used clothing and shoes, fruits and vegetables, cooked meals, toothpaste, soap, chewing gum, and cigarettes. One of the major problems faced by those in this informal sector is the lack of access to credit and loans with which to build up their business. (11)

As in other poor countries, the precarious existence of the urban poor is reflected by the phenomenon of street children. In Haiti some of these are restavèks who are abused by members of the family they live with, and run away to join the growing number of children, orphaned or abandoned by mothers unable to support them, who live in the street. In 1993 a UNICEF report estimated that there were as many as 2,000 street children, mostly in the capital, who survive by washing cars and begging, or by petty theft and prostitution. (12)

Although the paucity of social services in the countryside is a another important motivating factor for the rural exodus, the situation in the urban areas is in fact little better. State health provision is rudimentary at best. The public hospitals lack equipment, beds, and basic sanitation, and the staff are badly paid, with salaries often months in arrears. (13) There are private hospitals and clinics, but the charges put their services out of reach of the vast majority who must rely on the shadow service provided by clinics operated by non-governmental organisations. The treatment provided by these clinics range from the dubious practices of those who experiment on their patients with techniques, dosages, and medicines that are prohibited in other countries, to the preventative healthcare and advice offered by clinics run by community-based and women's organisations. (14) In the early 1980s, Haiti became internationally associated with HIV/Aids when certain US authorities connected the virus with the four 'H's – haemophiliacs, heroin addicts, homosexuals, and Haitians. (15) Recent statistics suggest that, despite high-profile campaigns to promote the use of condoms, the incidence of the HIV/Aids virus among the population is in the region of 5-6 per cent. This rate is a serious source of concern, with the World Bank claiming that Aids is becoming the primary cause of hospitalisation.

Education too is in a parlous state. Most schools are in urban centres, but the service is woefully inadequate. Classes are overcrowded, books and materials must be paid for, and the language of instruction is French, making tuition practically meaningless for the Creole-speaking majority. The 90 per cent of schools administered by the private sector are generally as bad if not worse than the State schools. (16) It is then perhaps not surprising that only 138 out of 1,000 children who enter the first year of primary school finish the secondary level, and that, as of 1995, the estimated adult illiteracy rate stood at around 55 per cent.

The poor services offered by the state social sector are mirrored by the performance of other national institutions. Government ministries are inadequately staffed, badly equipped, and poorly organised. State-owned utilities such as the telephone and electricity companies provide a pitifully inadequate service to a fraction of the population. Throughout the Duvalier era the public sector served as little more than a source of private income for the dictators and their clique.

Haiti's capital and other cities are thus centres of widespread and spectacular deprivation. Yet the conspicuous absence of the state has forced local communities, often the poorest, to take action on their own behalf. In the aftermath of Baby Doc Duvalier's flight in 1986, local committees proliferated, attempting to solve immediate issues such as water and electricity provision. These organisations contain enormous political potential, especially among people suspicious of traditional politicians and more inclined to support local leaders. (17)

(1) UNDER THE TABLE

Jean-Bertrand Aristide, *In the Parish of the Poor*, 1990

In an open letter to the progressive Catholic clergy of Latin America,
the Haitian priest Jean-Bertrand Aristide, who was later elected president, despairs at Haiti's poverty and inequalities.

Let me guide you through those dark corners and byways of Haiti
so that together we can get to a place where there is light...I speak
to you of dark corners and byways, and you think perhaps I am
speaking in metaphor. Or perhaps you reflect on the dark byways of
your own countries, and then you know that what I am talking about
is real.

The dark places I know best are my country's slums. The church
where I used to preach sat on the edges of one of these, La Saline,
and in the old days, before it became impossible, I used to walk
through La Saline and the other slums like it that are spreading like
confetti in a city that for years has been clogged with the detritus of
the deadly contagion called capitalism. In La Saline, there are many
dark byways, paths that run between two rows of shanties made of
plywood and cardboard and old, disintegrating tin. One bright hot
day I walked down one of these corridors, a dark byway even in the
hot Haitian sun, and at the end I found a courtyard with three naked children, my country's new generation, bathing in a puddle of
garbage left from the rains the night before. On another day, I walked
down another corridor in the darkness of our bright sun, and at the
end I found a wider road, and three young boys in tattered shorts,
playing marbles in the dirt. The new generation. On another day, I
walked down another corridor and three young girls – wearing second-hand dresses thrown away by nice middle-class girls in a
northern country and brought here by profiteering middlemen –
these young girls were selling themselves for quarters and dimes
and less to any man, and that was the new generation of my beloved country [...]

Today the country is not peaceful. In some places, the people
hardly manage to eat one hot meal a week. In other dark places
throughout the country, men and women work all day in their dry
fields and have only a few plantains for dinner. They crouch and eat
with their fingers, because they can't afford a fork. In dark places in
the provincial towns, they travel all morning to market and then sit
there all day selling their wares and earning only a few pennies, and

then they have only a few plantains to eat for dinner, or a bit of cassava, or rice without beans, or a little cornmeal.

Yet while the peasant eats his cornmeal mash with his fingers, men and women up on a hill above my dying Port-au-Prince are sitting at tables and eating steaks and paté and veal flown in from across the water. The rich of my country, a tiny percentage of our population, sit at a vast table covered in white damask and over-flowing with good food, while the rest of my countrymen and countrywomen are crowded under that table, hunched in the dirt and starving.

(2) THE RURAL CRISIS

Haiti Briefing, *Famine and Food Aid,* 1997

Periodic droughts, attributed to the unrelenting process of defor-estation, are catastrophic for peasant farmers, particularly those living in areas such as the Northwest that lack irrigation systems. When crops fail they must depend on the food hand-outs provided by relief agencies.

With no significant rainfall this year, many parts of Haiti are experiencing a severe drought. Famine has already claimed scores of lives, and in the worst-hit region, the Northwest, over 350,000 people face starvation. In order to survive, Haitians in the famine-affected areas are reported to be eating cattle that have died in the fields, as well as weeds and roots. Some have even taken to frying and eating government-provided seeds rather than planting them in the parched earth where they will shrivel and die.

The famine is also threatening lives in the Artibonite and Central Plateau departments, on the island of Gonâve, and in the Grand Anse in the south west. In April, residents of a village in the Artibonite announced they had violated a cultural taboo and eaten dog meat to survive. Elsewhere in the region several people died after stuff-ing themselves with unripe mangoes. In the Central Plateau people are eating clay to deaden hunger pains.

Even if the rains come, it may be too late to avert a catastrophe. In Fond de Bouden, in the mountains south of Léogâne, a peasant farmer told *Haiti Briefing* that because it had only rained twice be-tween January and May, his maize, sweet potato and bean crops were dying, and as a result he would have no seeds to plant for the anticipated second harvest later this year.

The Préval government has belatedly woken up to the fact that there is a life-threatening famine in the Northwest and has asked foreign relief agencies to increase their work in the region. The US-supported aid agency, CARE, is providing drought victims with 250,000 meals a day, and the UN World Food Programme has started to deliver 600 tons of food to be distributed to those who take part in road-building and other construction projects.

However, to many Haitians, US food aid, although saving lives, does not look like a humanitarian donation. Criticism of food aid, or *manje sinistre* as it is known in Haiti, exploded in the aftermath of Duvalier's fall in 1986... Today, food aid for the Northwest is again under attack. A coordinator of the Tèt Kole peasant movement harshly denounced the government's emergency food-for-work pro-gramme administered by CARE. Hungry people must work for three weeks to receive a small quantity of US-government-supplied sur-plus cracked wheat. He told *Haiti Info* that Tèt Kole had met with the government in March and suggested that local food instead of food aid be used, and instead of road work, peasants should be paid to work on their fields to prepare them for the upcoming season.

"We are against working on roads. Why don't they work in fields instead. I think it is a plan of the US and the big countries to destroy the economy of the country..."

(3) CHILD SERVANTS

J.P. Slavin, *Restavèk: Four-Year-Old Child Servants,* 1996

The deterioration of the rural economy and the state's almost com-plete neglect of the countryside persuade many peasant families to send children to work as servants for better-off urban families.

When she was only ten years old, the harsh realities of rural Haitian life irrevocably changed Céline Bouchon's childhood. Her family was offered a bone-chilling deal from a local business-man: release Céline to his care and he would arrange for her to work as a live-in domestic servant in the far-off capital of Port-au-Prince. Céline would not be paid, he said, but she would go to school.

Céline's relatives agreed to the offer because of their dismal eco-nomic plight. Eighty percent of the country's rural population lives below the absolute poverty line, according to the United Nations Children's Fund. With Céline in Port-au-Prince, her family would have one less child to feed. Her relatives hoped that by letting her go, she might have a chance at a better life and an education, a highly prized but virtually unobtainable goal for many Haitian families. More than half of the primary school students in Haiti never reach fifth grade.

Céline moved from the lush mountainside farmlands of southwestern Haiti to the teeming middle class Port-au-Prince slum of Carrefour. For the past three years, she has worked as a *restavèk*, Creole for a child who works as an unpaid servant and lives apart from his or her family. [...]

Restavèk recruiters usually promise families that the child they want to take away from then will go to school but, in nearly every instance, the pledge is never honored...To come to aid of restaveks, the Reverend Miguel Jean-Baptiste founded Foyer Maurice Sixto in 1990. Father Jean-Baptiste also serves as a parish priest in Rivière Froide, and he used his influence in this heavily Roman Catholic country to convince families who employ *restavèks* to send the child servants to his school. The family Céline works for did not enrol her in a school until Father Jean-Baptiste persuaded them to send her to Foyer Maurice Sixto [...]

What particularly disturbed me at Foyer Maurice Sixto was that there were children as young as four. Because these children are separated from their families and work eight to ten hours a day, they do not receive the love, affection, and attention that all children deserve. Consequently, they frequently appear emotionally and physically younger than they really are. Several of the four-year-old *restavèks* I saw at Foyer Maurice Sixto looked like younger children. Among some employers, the motivation for hiring very young *restavèks* is equally disturbing: They want the very young children to be as young as possible so that they can be easily intimidated and trained to be particularly docile

...Father Jean-Baptiste told me, "The *restavèk* is a result of the economy, the misery and the poverty of Haiti. Usually the children come from outside Port-au-Prince. There are intermediaries who set the child up with the family who employs them. There's a myth in the countryside that the streets of Port-au-Prince are paved with gold. The families in rural areas feel they can improve themselves if a child goes to the capital."

"The reality is the children are mistreated, undernourished, poorly housed and overworked. They are separated from their families and cut-off from communication with them. They're never paid. They usually work until they're 18 or 19 when they leave the family and become street people, and many of the females extend their misery by becoming pregnant. Or they get passed from family to family and live an uncertain life."

(4) URBAN CHAOS

P.J. O'Rourke, *All the Trouble in the World,* 1994

As thousands relocate from the countryside to the capital each year, the basic infrastructure of Port-au-Prince is falling apart.

Making figurines of one's enemies and torturing these playthings has nothing to do with Haiti or voodoo. It is a piece of European superstition brought to the New World by those mysterious savages, the French. Haiti has no need for such elaborate fancy goods of evil. Sturdy, utilitarian forms of wrong are readily available – the city water system, for instance.

For most Haitians the only source of water is a public well or tap. Downtown Port-au-Prince is served by one slimy concrete outdoor sink, a sort of horse trough with faucets. Here water is available only between eight P.M. and five in the morning. The women and girls carry it home in five-gallon plastic buckets. That's forty-some pounds of water balanced on the heads of people who don't weigh much more themselves. And they're carrying it through unlit streets.

These streets are heaped with trash as high as the women's bucket tops. A long mound of putrefying dreck will stretch for a block to an intersection, then turn the corner and continue for half a block more – a giant disposable traffic island. Not that it gets disposed of. According to the Pan American Health Organization, as of June 1993, Port-au-Prince had twelve garbage trucks in running condition. This to collect an estimated sixteen thousand tons of solid waste produced daily in the capital. Every now and then the locals try to burn the refuse, but the result is a parody of the North American landfill debate – biodegradability versus incineration. In Haiti's climate everything is biodegradable. And the ooze of tropical rot defeats the fires. The trash piles stay just as large, with guttering flames adding a new stench to the miasma. [...]

My driver and translator, Dumarsais, asked, "Who do you want to talk to?"

"Let's just drive around," I said.

The mystery of Port-au-Prince's trash heaps is that there are so many really immense holes in Port-au-Prince's streets. Putting one into another would create a certain levelling, at least, if not sanitation.

The streets and roads of Haiti are so bad that they almost seem to have been made so on purpose. The mere dragging and scraping of axles and undercarriages should lower some of the great humps, and chunks of disintegrating vehicles should fill a few of the ruts. "Haitian roads are a free massage," said Dumarsais.

(5) LIFE IN CITÉ SOLEIL

Catherine Maternowska, *Coup d'Etat and Contraceptives: A Political Economy of Family Planning in Haiti*, 1996

Living conditions in the capital's worst slums are as bad as any-where in the world.

Housing in Cité Soleil is the most highly visible dimension of poverty in this community. Anyone entering one of the cramped homes can feel what residents call *lamizè* (misery). The homes are hot, so hot that guests are often provided a towel or rag to wipe the sweat from the brow as it accumulates within minutes of entering. All of Cité Soleil's houses have roofs made of tin which serves to trap the heat from the relentless rays of the sun inside making the interior of homes feel like ovens.

All of the residences are one story high and typically have one or two rooms, the most spacious in this study measuring 40 square meters. Among respondents in this sample, 51 per cent lived in two rooms and 43 percent lived in a single room (on average measuring four square meters). Inside these cramped and stifling quarters an average of eight people eat and sleep daily. Some homes double as businesses; for example, one home served as a kitchen (called a "popular restaurant") during the day and a brothel at night.

Homes usually have one double bed, raised on at least four cinder blocks to keep it dry from rains. A bed typically sleeps a minimum of four people and sometimes up to six children and two adults. Sleeping is rarely a rejuvenating event since living quarters are so confined. Residents of Cité Soleil opt for one of several possibilities: *dòmi kanpe* ("sleeping standing" whereby people lean on walls or each other), sleeping shifts (whereby people take four hour sleeping shifts and walk around the community when awake) or eking out any available space on tables, inside oil barrels outside the home, or on straw or cardboard mats placed on any dry surface. Rat bites are common in these conditions.

Homes in Cité Soleil are made of rudimentary materials and recyclables...(they) are generally dark and dank inside, for lack of electricity though crude windows with shutters are usually sealed to keep roving spirits away. One of the community's poorest sites is Cité Carton ("Cardboard City"), a neighbourhood whose residents are obliged to search for new and dry corrugated cardboard walls following each rainfall. Residents of these homes search for days for dry cartons and when located they fasten the flattened boxes to long wooden poles that serve as the house structure.

The tiny shacks of Cité Soleil proliferate on almost every discernible space. If there is any distance between homes it is on average not more than 50 centimeters. Space is particularly coveted in the drier areas, just inches above sea level. During the rainy season though, no homes are protected from the rains. When dark clouds hover, valuables are lifted from the floor. Water replete with faeces and garbage, during an afternoon or evening rainstorm, can rush up to three feet high inside the homes. One informant, who sold her bed to meet her rent payments, described sleeping standing, holding a child in each arm while filthy water rose thigh-high for hours during the late evening hours.

(6) BEYOND THE SLUMS, MORE SLUMS

Mike Kamber, *Haiti: the Taiwan of the Caribbean Breaks Away,* 1991

Families that leave the countryside and move to the city in search of a better life invariably find themselves setting up home in the abysmal slum areas on the city outskirts.

Olmane is one of the women who sells the dresses that come in from "kenedi".[1] Today she's sold no dresses and walks slowly through the massive slum known as Cité Soleil. People spill out everywhere from houses, shacks really, with overflowing open sewers running by their front doors.

We walk out past the centre of the slum, over a footbridge spanning another sewer and across worn paths past where the city stops and the open fields begin. As her kids come running up to meet her, she points to her home, a small zinc and cardboard shack. Rocks have been carefully arranged in front of it to make a yard, and saplings form a rickety fence.

"It's not really done yet," she explains apologetically as she shows me outside. On one end there's just cardboard where they ran out of zinc. "We're saving up to buy more zinc: maybe you could take the pictures so the cardboard doesn't show?" she asks.

As curious children start to gather, she opens the door and invites me inside. When my eyes adjust to the darkness, I'm puzzled – the shack is completely empty. The floor is just the earth that they've built on top of; in the corners are small rocks they've swept to the side. I'd expected her to ask me to sit down, but there are no chairs, and then I realise, no beds either, just some scraps of cardboard on the ground.

I feel uncomfortable, and I don't know if it's shame at how she lives or shame at how I live. Her children are standing there watching us, and trying to relieve the tension, I say, "Well don't let me hold you up from making your dinner." She smiles awkwardly, doesn't say anything, and leads me outside.

Her husband arrives, a small man, thin like Olmane, and I ask them the question, "Why Aristide?"

"This man, he's always been with us. We've listened to him on the radio for years. He's always fought for us. He is one of us."

What do they expect from Aristide? "...I'm 35 years old" he says, "I've never had a job!" Olmane speaks up. "We don't want to sleep in fear every night ...we want our kids to go to school." She shows me her son's swollen infected foot: "We want to be able to go to the doctor, and we'd like to be able to get some more zinc to finish our house." It doesn't seem like a lot to ask for.

It's getting late now and the kids are still there waiting. I ask again, "Aren't you going to give them dinner?" Again there is a long silence and then finally she confesses, "No, I didn't sell anything today. They ate yesterday. When I sell something tomorrow, they'll eat again."

[1] Kenedi is the Creole word for secondhand clothes that were first sent to Haiti from the United States as a form of charitable aid during the administration of President Kennedy. Since that time the import of secondhand clothes has developed as a business, and traders sell small quantities of clothes at markets and on the side of the roads.

(7) EVERYDAY MYSTERIES

Amy Wilentz, *A Place Called Haiti,* 1992

Behind the apparent anarchy and unpredictability of Haitian urban life, there are rational motives and explanations – even if many visitors fail to understand them.

Haiti can be, and has been, a difficult place for foreigners to visit. Inexplicable things happen there, or you think that they are inexplicable. In the evenings when it is almost cool, up in Cap-Haïtien, men in light jerseys run backwards up hills. Boys play soccer in the street during general strikes. An American journalist steals an unused ballot box as a souvenir, and his guide has to leave town for a month. A girl you've never seen before kisses you as you walk through the slums, and a child you've known for years refuses to speak to you after you give him money. Near the market at night, women, and sometimes men, will talk to no one, loudly and in a high-pitched voice. Men wear coloured clothespins in their beards and little umbrellas on their heads. In church on a Sunday morning, the congregation stomps to death a large black moth. A one-way street will go in the opposite direction for an afternoon. Drivers stick their hands out of the window, and it means they're stopping, they're turning left, or please pass. You can't tell which.

You can't tell which, that is, until you've been there a while, and learned something of the grammar of Haiti's reality. You have to want to figure the place out on its own terms and in its own language...

Men run uphill backwards in Cap-Haïtien because they are training for the city's famous soccer team. Boys play ball on the streets during the strikes, because they don't have playing fields, and during strikes, there is no traffic in the capital's broad boulevards. The American's guide had to leave town for a month because he was afraid government informers would punish him after the American stole the ballot box. The girl kisses you in the slums because she thinks you are beautiful (you are white). The little boy won't speak to you because he is insulted that although you gave him money today, you didn't give him anything last week – he knows you could give him money every day, and the proof of your treachery is: you gave him money today. During a voodoo ceremony, a man or a woman may talk in a high-pitched voice if the flirtatious goddess of love, Erzulie, has come down to possess him or her. Men wear coloured clothespins in their beards to keep score in dominoes and umbrellas on their heads against the sun. The congregation killed the moth in the church balcony because the moth represented the spirit of the dictatorship. The street goes the wrong way because the US Embassy has blocked all the roads around it, for security, and a new traffic pattern has been invented overnight. A driver's palm facing downward means: I'm stopping. His palm facing upward means: I'm turning left. A waving hand means: Please pass.

These are explanations, some of them partial.

(8) STREET LIFE

Michel Laguerre, *Urban Life in the Caribbean,* 1984

In the crowded and run-down urban slums, the inhabitants are sustained by a street culture and a strong community spirit.

A fter a morning of ceaseless activity, the inhabitants of Port-au-Prince's crowded slum areas retreat into their house to escape the heavy heat of the sun. The community in the slum area of Belair in downtown Port-au-Prince returns to life about 3 o'clock in the afternoon.

Men emerge from their houses bringing tables and chairs onto their balconies for dominoes and *besique* (a game played with cards). While girls play *marelle* (hopscotch) and jump ropes, naked boys play with *billes* (marbles) or organise soccer games. Many more men and women merely sit on their balconies or under their *peristyle* and cool off through the afternoon.

During the daytime much social interaction occurs in the corridor. Shoe-shiners pass by, ringing their bells, announcing to the neighbours that they are on the road. When someone stops them for a shoeshine, they sit down on their small chairs and adjust their box on the ground so that the client may put his foot on it while standing up. Much conversation goes on between the shoeshine man and his client while he is doing his five cents a shine job.

It is expected that when a neighbour passes by, he will greet the balcony people. The passers-by most often stop to greet the residents if they know them and have a short conversation about recent community news...

During the rainy season, children take their afternoon bath in the corridors and have a great deal of fun. The rain water is also captured for cooking purposes. Others store the water in a circular steel container which they hang up and use for their shower. Rain is not welcome in Upper Belair because it forces people to bring everything they have inside their houses and they have to remain inside too.

In the American ghettos, the barber shop, the laundromat, and the corner bar are places for gossip and exchanges of news in the community. In Upper Belair this role is played partially by the *fritay* place, where women sell fried food. The fritay women starts frying her bananas, plantains, potatoes, pork and fish about 5.00 pm Since very few households cook supper, the families who can afford it go instead to buy fritay. Young women come to socialise with young men. In this way they get free fritay from time to time when a sweet-heart offers to buy some for them. Young men also banter with women vendors so that they may buy on credit or get free fritay from time to time. These young people stand close to the pot, talk, attract other buyers by their presence, eat, and pass on news and jokes. Their presence gives the place a lively atmosphere.

When the sun goes down and the darkness of the evening shrouds the active households and still busy streets of the neighbourhood, young men and women dominate the scene. Some young men will stand in groups on a corner of the corridors and will yell at passing young women. On the balconies, men and women tell stories...

The fritay places are not the only ones where young men and women assemble at night. Some go to the Pentecostal Church to see believers who get happy and start trembling. Some assemble at the Voodoo temple to sing and dance with the devotees.

(9) MICKEY MOUSE IN PORT-AU-PRINCE

Charles Kernaghan, *Living on the Edge of Misery,* 1996

The sub-contracting assembly plants in the capital's free-enterprise zones produce garments for multinational companies such as Walt Disney and Warner Brothers. These are some of the few jobs available in the capital, but for the mostly female workforce the drawback is low wages and poor conditions.

On a recent trip to Haiti in late April, I had the opportunity to visit the home of a Disney worker who lived in the Delmas neighbourhood of Port-au-Prince. She worked at NS Mart in the Sonapi Industrial Park where she sewed Pocahontas and Mickey Mouse shirts.

She was a single mother with four young children. They lived in a one-room windowless shack, 8 by 11 feet wide, lit by one bare light bulb and with a tin roof that leaked...The mother had years of experience as a sewer. The production quota set by NS Mart is excessively high. On her assembly line, working furiously under constant pressure, she handled 375 Pocahontas shirts an hour – shirts that sell at Wal-Mart for $10.97 each. Yet her average weekly wage was only $10.77! She earned the minimum wage of 28 cents an hour.

No one can survive on 28 cent-an-hour wages – even in Haiti, which is not a cheap place to live. Seventy percent of what Haiti consumes is imported, including basic staples like rice, beans and corn meal. Food can actually be as expensive in Haiti as in the US. Workers producing Disney garments in Haiti are thin and tired looking. They and their families are always on the edge of hunger, sinking ever deeper into debt and misery...

The following day, we met with a large group of NS Mart workers, all of whom sewed Disney garments. They told us that the majority of workers at NS Mart – almost everyone – earn just 28 cents an hour, which is $2.22 for a full eight-hour day. And, they reported, at times they are short-changed on their hours and pay.

The workers also told us the plant is hot, dusty and poorly lit. Some complained about having trouble with their eyesight and respiratory problems.

According to the workers, the production quotas and piece rates the company sets are impossible to reach. Supervisors put enormous constant pressure on the workers to go faster.

Supervisors yell, scream, threaten and curse workers...If you are young and pretty and a supervisor wants you as his mistress, you either give in to him or you are fired. Sexual harassment is common.

The toilets are filthy. Rats are everywhere. The holding tank for drinking water is covered only with a light piece of metal which the rats have no trouble getting under...If you dared to speak up, to complain to NS Mart management about these conditions or about the pay scale, you would be fired, period. Every worker we spoke with told us that if the company even suspected that they were interested in organizing to claim their rights, they would be thrown out of the factory immediately.

(10) BEASTS OF BURDEN

Haiti Info, *The Bouretyes' Burden,* 1994

Based on an article in the Creole monthly, *Aksyon,* this extract explores the life of the *bouretyes,* or cart-pullers, the men who bring merchandise from the suburbs to the city, from the bus station to the market place, from one construction site to another, or help people move house.

*❝*When you see how Haitians are slaving away in the streets, it reminds you of an epoch a long time ago when our ancestors were slaves," writes journalist Mirlene Joanis. "In those days, it was only human force that made the country rich. Time passed, machines replaced people who lifted heavy loads, pulled heavy loads, pushed heavy loads. But in Haiti, we are stuck with the same practices from long ago. We see, we live and practically every day we meet living and breathing people who are doing the work of oxen from the big cane plantations."

"The *bouretye* ensures a great deal of transportation. They take people to work and back, they take people across rivers...There is such a lack of state services, sometimes they become ambulances, carrying women who are about to give birth or people who have been in accidents."

Many of the *bouretyes* do not own their carts, which cost at least US$50. Instead, they rent them for between 20 cents and one dollar a day. The *bouretye* is then responsible for the cart and any problems, like a flat tire which can cost a day's earnings.

"Because of the theft of tires *bouretyes* have to take the tires off every night when they sleep, whenever they are not working, and then put them back on, or even sleep in them!"

Many *bouretyes* sleep in the streets, because their salaries, about 60 cents to one dollar a day, if they are lucky, are too low to cover housing. When several work together, the man in charge gets 30 cents extra.

"The little money they get goes for a plate of food, a little *grog,*[1] some medicine if they are sick, but renting a house is not possible. Those who want a place to sleep have to join with three or four others to pay the rent."

Joanis deplores the terrible conditions *bouretyes* are forced to endure.

"In countries where the state is organized, where it undertakes its responsibilities, the *bouretyes* would not exist. If the state did not concentrate all activities in the capital, the people who leave the provinces, who leave their drought-stricken land, or who lose their land when the big landowners seize it, they would not have to come to Port-au-Prince to 'look for life'."

"Unfortunately, this social group is important, and it won't disappear overnight. If they have to slave away, they will slave away. If they have to go through hard times, they will. But no matter how hard they try, they can't really change the conditions of their lives."

[1] Grog – in Creole the generic term for an alcoholic drink, usually home-made rum.

(11) SURVIVING IN THE INFORMAL SECTOR

Simon Fass, *Political Economy in Haiti: The Drama of Survival,* 1990

The precarious economic balancing act of the hundreds of thousands who work in what is known as the informal sector is illustrated by this story of a soup-maker in Port-au-Prince.

Her market was downtown, which was also where she purchased her ingredients. For a while she tried to produce the soup in the central market, but found the costs too high. She needed to hire someone to help her carry charcoal, a heater, a large pot, a wooden bowl, and a large pestle between home and market twice a day. This was expensive because she lived four kilometers from downtown. She had to hire someone else to watch over her equipment while she looked for ingredients, and the price of water was very high in the market. She then tried to make the soup at home, but the time required to get ingredients, return home, and then go back to the market used up too many of the best hours for selling food. She eventually convinced her husband that the only way to earn more from this activity was to move closer to the market. The higher rent that such a move might entail would be offset by lower production costs and a superior time frame for selling. They moved to St. Martin in 1973...

The soupmaker's day began at 4.00 am when she left home to purchase roots, crab, pork, goat, beef, and vegetables. She returned home at 6.00 am to crush the roots for an hour, and then to add them to the other ingredients already simmering in water. Cooking was done by 10.00 am and she hired a porter to carry the product to the market, arriving there no later than 10.30 am. At 3.00 pm she was usually sold out. In peak periods following harvests the flow of money in the market was high and she could always earn a net of US$2.00 per day. She earned less when the flow of money ebbed, but she still obtained at least US$1.00 per day.

Her present problem was finding a way to increase her earnings. Costs were as low as she could make them without compromising her recipe, and raising her price would only push customers to other food suppliers. She had the US$15.00 required for another pot and charcoal heater, but since she could not sell out until 3.00 pm, and since there were hardly any sales after that time, she doubted that she could sell a second pot at the same location. She had once reduced her price to see what would happen, but the rate of selling did not increase very much. What she needed was a trustworthy person (who would not skim off money or steal her recipe) to manage sales of a second pot at another place in the market. Her husband, a shoemaker who did not earn very much, was out of the question because even if he were willing to sell food, no one bought this kind of meal from a man. Her daughter was too young. She hoped that one day soon her sister in Cap-Haïtien would accept her invitation to come and work with her. In the meantime she would wait.

(12) MEAN STREETS

Haiti Info, *Street Children,* 1997

A reporter from a Port-au-Prince newsletter spoke to about a dozen young people, most of them boys, who live on the streets of the capital.

Over half said they come from the countryside. All of them have living relatives who could not or did not want to care for them. Many said they wanted to go to school and live in a home or "centre." They all said the police abused them, and wrongfully accused them of crimes. All the boys denied being involved in prostitution. Almost all of them said they "get high" whenever they can.

"I sleep on Champ de Mars. Not at anyone's house. In the streets," explained one boy from L'Estère. "I need to go to school, but I can't. When you are in the street, things are not good."

The boy, now 17, sometimes makes 50 gourdes a day washing cars, if he is lucky. He does not go back home because he has no money. The only clothes and shoes he owns are those he wears.

Another boy is from the capital. He used to live with his uncle, who paid for his school, but when the uncle left the country, "the other people who took over the house did not have the possibility to take care of me." The youth said everyone has his "base." He said he knows youth engaged in prostitution, but he claimed he makes money by washing cars. "I don't see any future for us," he said. "The state is not there for us...those people live in their big houses...All this insecurity, police being killed, they even blame that on us. Everything falls on our backs."

A 15-year old girl said she "used to" earn money through prostitution but that she has a boyfriend now who takes care of her, but who also beats her if she does something wrong. She is not afraid of AIDS because "if I were going to get it, I would have it already. I don't do it anymore because the police beat me," she said, and added bluntly, " I got pregnant from one guy. I threw it out."

Another girl who looked about 12 said she earns 5 gourdes (about US$0.30) for having sex with someone. It takes five minutes. She is from the Artibonite Valley. She also got pregnant once: "I threw it out." About her life, she said: "I have resigned myself."

A 17-year old from Gonaïves said he came to the capital a couple of years ago. "I have grown up in the streets," he said. He sleeps near the cemetery. He said he buys drugs for 30 gourdes (about US$2.00), every three days.

Asked if he thought there were more children in the streets than before, he said: "There are more...There was a project to take everyone off the streets, so that they could get jobs, go to school, but the state does not do anything for us. The only thing the state does is shoot us, hit us with clubs, beat us, put us in prison. We could die; they don't care...Things have got worse. Today it is the same way it was during the embargo. Those guys are eating off of us, a bunch of *gran manjè* (big eaters – corrupt politicians), while we are dying in the streets."

(13) SICK HOSPITALS

Ives-Marie Chanel, *General Hospital: Ante-Chamber of Death,* 1995

A journalist visiting the public hospital in Haiti's second city, Cap-Haïtien, found staff and patients experiencing appalling conditions.

For almost a month now the lamps no longer light up the vast courtyard around the dozen buildings of the Justinien Hospital. Kerosene, used in place of electricity, is often in short supply at this the only state hospital in northern Haiti.

"Patients are obliged to supply their own light by buying their own kerosene when they have to have an operation. No one looks after us here any more, and the Ministry of Health is no longer functioning," laments one gynaecologist.

In the courtyard the hustle and bustle of the hospital staff has given way to an empty silence as the dead make their presence felt among the living. The smell of rotting corpses overwhelms everything. The morgue's refrigerator has not worked in three years. Bodies left here beyond 48 hours are unceremoniously dumped in common graves located some 10 kilometres east of Cap-Haïtien, Haiti's second largest city.

The staff complains incessantly; there are not enough equipment to perform autopsies, not enough medical equipment to do anything; insufficient alcohol, cotton, bandages, medicine, not even an ambulance to fetch the sick.

The 260-bed hospital is infested with rats and mosquitoes plague patients. Many beds are without mattresses, taken, says one man who lives on the compound, by hospital personnel who have not been paid in 15 months.

"We get paid every three months," admits one nurse who has worked there for 21 years and who earns the equivalent of 60 US dollars monthly. Doctors say their monthly salary, worth some 175 dollars, is enough only to pay their aides and buy gasoline for their car.

In front of the service entrance to the Orthopaedic Ward a 55-year-old man called Elinor is standing on crutches. He has lived at the hospital for the past five months and has not received medical care for a long time. With no orthopaedist available, Elinor's broken leg and fractured pelvis are healing without medical help. Elinor says he expects to live the rest of his life disabled. His story is not unusual in Haiti. [...]

It is Elinor's misfortune that he has ended up at the Justinien. Many patients are forsaking the hospital, scared away by the wretchedness of the conditions there. "Here in this hospital we only have visiting doctors, who only pass by irregularly, then leave. No patients come to the hospital any more, there is no reception centre, there are no resources, consequently, people no longer have any confidence in the hospital," said one doctor.

For months patients have been going to three other less important hospitals in the region run by non-governmental organisations and foreign church missions. Many medical practitioners are also referring the sick to their own private clinics to be hospitalised. Some doctors and nurses without hesitation advise patients, not to come to the Justinien when sick. Others cynically say if you do not have the means go to a private clinic, then avoid becoming ill altogether.

(14) THE HEALTH CRISIS

Haiti Support Group, Interview with Rose-Anne Auguste, 1996

The co-ordinator of the Women's Health Centre in Carrefour Feuille, a poor area of the capital, compares the clinic's work to putting a small bandage on a gaping wound.

❙❙This clinic opened in 1992 and was formed in the context of the coup, to serve people who suffered torture or were in hiding. But since then it is clear that the state has abandoned health care. The clinic sees 30 pregnant women in the morning and 70 children; others wait all day to be seen in the afternoon. Because there are so many health-care problems in the area, we have had to expand to seeing 180 people per day. When Aristide returned we tried to get the Ministry of Health to take up its responsibilities, since we were doing the job of the state, but all it has provided is half a salary for two doctors, two nurses and two lab technicians. We are part of a network of clinics in twelve zones of Carrefour Feuille, with 50,000 patients – that is the total population of the area, but many people come down from the surrounding hills for medical treatment.

Infant mortality in Haiti is 93 per 1,000 births up to 1 year old, but 133 per 1,000 up to 5 years. Maternal mortality is 4.6 per 1,000 live births. (So) the clinic's main programme is for maternal and infant health, but it is also involved in health education and family planning. Family planning is difficult for Haitian women because they must get the collaboration of their male partners, but are faced with sexism. The clinic would prefer to encourage more "natural" methods of family planning, i.e. longer-spaced pregnancies, but many women turn to the pill and to three-month injections because this does not involve any negotiation with partners.

Grassroots work against sexism includes women trainers who work with men to sensitize them and get their participation in supporting women's health. We encourage men to use condoms, though many see it mainly as a protection against disease, not as a family planning method – many Haitian men like to have a woman carrying a baby for them. We also educate women that it is better if they wait two or three years before getting pregnant again, not because there is an overpopulation problem, but because of the poverty and hard life of the poor. The real problem is distribution of wealth. Poor women have no access to education and other resources, so they lose control over their own fertility. The doctor can consult with them and help them plan what method of family planning is best for their health.

The greatest frustration of this work is that it is like just putting a small bandage on a very deep wound. The underlying problems are unemployment, poor conditions in the slum areas, inadequate housing, lack of clean water, etc. The health clinic cannot change these conditions – that is the responsibility of the state. Yet the state is dealing neither with the underlying causes of these terrible conditions, nor with the resulting poor health of the people. Thus, the clinic is only the minimum intervention – ideally the state must take up the real problems. We are not like some NGOs who replace the state by providing private services. We are engaged in a struggle to have people's rights to life and health recognized."

(15) AIDS AND MISINFORMATION

George Leonard, *AIDS in Haiti,* 1991

This article claims that, while there is a high incidence of the HIV/ Aids virus in Haiti, the link between the country and the disease was blown out all proportion to the reality in the early 1980s.

Just how common is AIDS in Haiti? There is no mystery here: the incidence has been carefully monitored by various research teams. The incidence of a positive HIV (Human Immunodeficiency Virus, or AIDS virus) antibody blood test is approximately 4% in otherwise healthy blood donors in Port-au-Prince, 3% in rural communities outside the capital, 1% in the remote mountainous regions of the country, less than 1% in the upper socio-economic classes, 9.5% in certain high risk populations, and as high as 50% in male and female prostitutes. Overall, the incidence in the country as a whole is considered 5%. By comparison, in New York City and San Francisco, the overall incidence of a positive HIV blood test is 1.5%. In some urban centres in the US, the incidence of a positive blood test is as high as 60% in female prostitutes, and 10-20% in other high risk groups. In the US as well as Haiti, I.V. drug users, male homosexuals and frequent recipients of blood transfusions are in the high risk group. (In Haiti, however, there are not many I.V. drug users.)[...]

Though it is quite true that the per capita incidence of AIDS is higher in Haiti (and in many Caribbean island countries) than it is in the United States, the difference is a matter of percentage points only, and not the sort of "night and day' difference that is commonly portrayed. Have you ever heard of an official Travel Advisory, or a travel agency recommendation, advising that one should not travel to New York City, San Francisco, Houston, or Miami because of the high prevalence of AIDS and the abundant violence in those cities? Of course not; yet such advice is regularly given to US citizens considering a visit to Haiti. Why?

As bad as this travel "advice" has been, the bad press on Haiti has been much worse. In the early 1980s individuals representing such prestigious US institutions as the National Cancer Institute of Technology, the Centre for Disease Control (CDC), and others were regularly suggesting that AIDS found its way to the US by way of Haiti, and may even have originated in Haiti – perhaps in one of the mysterious Voodoo practices. This was simply preposterous, and unsupported by scientific evidence. The renowned anthropologist/physician Dr. Paul Farmer provides compelling evidence in a 1990 article showing that AIDS was in fact introduced into Haiti by homosexual tourists from New York and San Francisco, for whom Haiti was a delightful vacation spot in the late 70s and 80s.

Lasting harm has been done to the Haitian image, and is, to a great extent, irreparable, at least until a worldwide cure for AIDS is found. The number of tourists fell from 75,000 visitors in the winter of 1981-82 to less than 10,000 the following year.

(16) THE COST OF PRIVATE EDUCATION

Jamil Salmi, *Equity and Quality in Private Education: The Haitian Paradox*, 1998

Although the first constitution, promulgated in 1805, noted explicitly that "...education shall be free. Primary education shall be compulsory. State education shall be free at every level", these principles were never put into practice.

Only a small number of primary and high schools were built by the Government to serve the children of the political elite, predominantly in urban areas. These schools were patterned after French and British models. At the end of the 19th century, there were only 350 public schools. The number had risen to 730 by 1917 but the proportion of children attending these schools represented only 11 percent of the reference age group. During the 1940s, the Government started to define educational policies better adapted to the Haitian context and efforts were made to expand public education coverage. However, the policy of relative neglect continued during the Duvalier era and there was even a deterioration of conditions in public schools as many qualified teachers left the country to escape political repression.

To compensate for the slow growth of the public school network, many religious communities established their own educational institutions. In more recent years, a number of non-denominational, for-profit schools were also started in the cities. While private education represented only 20 percent in 1959-60, in 1979-80, private schools accounted for 57 percent of enrolment in primary education, and 80 percent in secondary education. Between 1960 and 1971, enrolment stagnated in the public sector, as only 158 new schools were built during the entire period, mostly with external financing...Today, private education represents about 75 percent of primary school enrolment and 82 percent at the secondary level...For all practical purposes, private education is the norm in Haiti while public schools, which cater for less than 10 percent of the school age population, are the minority. [...]

The Haitian private education sector is quite diverse. Two-thirds of the private schools are religious schools. The Catholic schools have a long-standing reputation, with some of the best schools established in Port-au-Prince and in the main provincial towns. The mission schools (Baptist, Protestant, Adventist and Pentecostal) represent a second group of institutions which have traditionally received significant foreign support. A third group, the Presbyterian schools, are generally poorer and vary a lot in quality. In the category of non-denominational schools there are two main groups: community schools and commercial schools. The community schools (are) established and supported by NGOs and local associations...The commercial schools, which in practice escape any form of government control..., called "écoles borlettes" are named after the local lottery, because it is assumed that children attending these schools have the same probability of graduating as winning the lottery. [...]

The quality of instruction is deficient in most private and public schools because of unqualified and unmotivated teachers, lack of textbooks, uncoordinated development of curriculum and instructional materials, and poor facilities... In many countries where public and private schools coexist, it is often argued that the quality of education is better in the private sector. In Haiti, however, the opposite seems to be true. A three-tier hierarchy has evolved over the years, with a small group of elite private schools establishing itself at the top, then the public schools occupying the middle range, and finally the vast majority of private schools being at the bottom of the scale. According to the results of a 1994 survey, 85 percent of the latter operate in inappropriate facilities. Two-thirds of these schools do not have the basic pedagogical materials to teach the curriculum.

(17) PROMISE FOR THE FUTURE

Zacharie Louis and Fred Montas, *Comités de quartiers,* 1986

The emergence of local urban organisations is here analysed in terms of short-term neighbourhood renewal and longer-term political influence.

Ever since the flight of Duvalier, and thanks to the climate of freedom created by the masses, the most promising initiative here, in an era of real democracy, remains the creation and proliferation of the so-called Comités de Quartier (Neighbourhood Committees) throughout Port-au-Prince and certain provincial towns.

These basic units, unconnected to the oligarchic structures of domination, have been reclaimed by the Catholic Church in an effort to ensure its patronage of them. In the context of long-term liberalisation, they could provide the essential element in the process of popular democratisation, if they can link up with the struggles of the workers and peasants.

Until now, the activities of these committees have been limited to organising teams of street cleaners and house cleaners, and improvement and decorating work in general. However, the extent to which they become involved in more far-reaching activities will be determined by the awareness and initiative of both leaders and members.

Already, there is talk of certain groups initiating literacy programmes at a local level. Others, hoping for influential speakers and an early electoral campaign, are taking purely political decisions concerning, for example, the admission and reception into their midst of 'leaders' from outside the neighbourhood.

The various stances adopted reflect a level of maturity and independence which would suggest future progressive initiatives. Another encouraging development came when about fifty committees linked up with unions and professional groups during a recent march organised by the KID.[1]

Of course, there is a danger that destabilising entities with plenty of money will attempt to manipulate them or take them over. But so far patriotism has prevailed.

It is even more encouraging to see the development of the following programmes:-

- Community education: the teaching of arts and crafts (painting, cabinet-making, sculpture, etc...), public libraries.
- Political education: courses in history and geography with an emphasis on the Third-World, imperialism, etc.
- The organisation of leisure activities: games, sports, trips, walks, etc.
- Care of the elderly who have no family / friends to support them.
- The rehabilitation of both juvenile and adult offenders, and the homeless, and their reintegration into active life within the community.

Of course, to be really useful, these centres of local power, true units of the Haitian community, must be able to work not only amongst themselves but also with workers' associations, peasants and professionals, for the mutual benefit of all concerned. They must be able to sustain the strength of a popular power base and to be the eyes, ears and mouth of this power in the various diverse communities, rather than dependent and obedient entities. Ultimately they must judge the extent to which they are truly representative.

They will be, as it were, the *chouqueurs* and *dechouqueurs* [2] of a liberated Haiti, the driving force behind the construction, restoration, destruction and reconstruction of the social group, a role which rightly belongs to every viable human organism, and whose spiralling effect places it on an ever higher level, well beyond the limitations of underdevelopment, and in opposition to the oligarchic forces of domination who have done their best to hang on to their control of all national wealth, to the exclusion of the poor who exist on the fringes of society.

So let's hear it for the Neighbourhood Committees, for an increase in their numbers and support, and for their involvement in the fight to ensure the success of the rightful demands of the people!

[1] Democratic Unity Confederation, a grouping of progressive grass-roots organisations.
[2] Planters and uprooters – from the Creole word *dechoukaj* (to uproot) that was used to describe the political process of removing the roots of Duvalierism from Haitian society.

Translated from French by Emily Dunbar

CHAPTER FIVE
FORCES FOR CHANGE

The revolutionary upheaval of 1791-1804 overthrew slavery, ousted the colonial power, and forced the abandonment of the plantation system. Yet, while these victories changed and improved the lives of the majority beyond all recognition, within a short period of time a new economic and political system evolved, again based on the exploitation of the mass of the people in the interests of a small elite. A new status quo developed and endured, but what of the attempts to change it?

The existence of work *coumbites*, and of the societies attached to *Vodou* temples shows that the peasantry has had a widespread and well-developed tradition of organising labour and social structures at the grass roots, or very local level. However, during the nineteenth century, and for much of the twentieth, the majority of the population has remained outside of the formal political arena. In part, this is a consequence of the tendency, apparent since the early years of independence, for the peasantry to associate the national political authorities with unpopular restrictions and regulations that curtailed the freedoms won during the revolution. In the experience of the masses, the state and its agents were entities that merely taxed, exploited, or imprisoned, and they learnt to expect nothing good to come of interaction with them. On the other hand, the ability of the peasantry to intervene in national political life was severely limited by a whole host of exclusionary measures ranging from a very limited suffrage based on property ownership to the basic obstacle posed by the lack of education and high levels of illiteracy.

On numerous occasions during the nineteenth century, irregular peasant-based militia, known in the south as *piquets*, and the north as *cacos*, did mobilise to challenge the authority of the central government. In nearly every case, though, these actions were instigated by aspiring political leaders from the elite, and served their own narrow interests in winning political office or advancement. Rival elite factions would use the militia to bring down governments, but the changes would rarely result in any significant benefits for the peasants.

An exception was the Piquet rebellion in the 1840s, when landowners and peasants in the south-west of the country united to challenge the mulatto elite's economic and political dominance. The peasants revolted in support of a radical programme in favour of land reform and social change. However, once the rebellion had succeeded in ending the mulatto monopoly over the presidency, the black land-owning elite faction swiftly turned against their erstwhile allies and suppressed the threat posed by the peasants' radical agenda. (1)

Sporadic military activity on the part of caco bands representing the more successful sector of the peasantry in the early years of the twentieth century, took on a more popular character during the US occupation. The US Marines reintroduced the *corvée*, the forcible re-cruitment of labour for work gangs, and this generated great resentment among the poor peasantry. Thousands joined a caco re-sistance movement that, from 1918 until its defeat in 1920, waged a guerrilla campaign against the Marines in the east and north-east of the country. (See Chapter 7)

By the end of the 1920s, widespread dissatisfaction with the in-troduction of new taxes, a rising cost of living, and the expropriation of peasant lands, united students, workers and peasants in a nation-alist, anti-occupation movement. But with the withdrawal of the Marines in 1934, the *raison d'être* of the movement disappeared, and the elite's monopoly of the political scene quickly resumed. The po-litical intellectuals who had been united by their opposition to the occupation split into black nationalist and socialist wings. New po-litical parties were formed, and a profusion of newspapers and journals appeared promoting a variety of doctrines and ideologies, yet politics remained the preserve of the well-to-do, and barely touched the lives of vast majority. For example, the Communist Party, founded by Jacques Roumain in 1934, while popular with the radi-cal sons of elite families, failed to achieve any great following among the urban or rural workers, or the peasantry.

However, the development of a middle class, the growth of the urban population, particularly in Port-au-Prince, and expansion of light industry, also mainly based in the capital, did contribute to appearance of new forces with the potential to challenge the en-trenched, elite-dominated system. During the presidency of Dumarsais Estimé (1946-50), a small trade union movement flour-ished, and staged a number of strikes in favour of improved pay and better working conditions. At the same time, the social-demo-cratic *Mouvement Ouvriers-Paysans* (MOP) (Workers and Peasants Movement) emerged as the first political party to achieve any genu-ine popularity among ordinary Haitians. Although it enjoyed the support of some unionised workers, the MOP did not, however, live up to its name. Its following was largely restricted to the unemployed and informal-sector workers in the capital, attracted by the charisma and oratory of its leader, Daniel Fignolé. In 1957 the MOP was erased from the political scene during the machinations that ended with the election victory of François Duvalier. Fignolé had been named as provisional president but had lasted just 19 days before the Army kidnapped him, sent him into exile, and then massacred hundreds of his supporters in the capital's slums. (2)

Under the Duvaliers, all institutions and organisations perceived to represent any form of threat were suppressed. The authoritarian system was sustained by a variety of means ranging from intimidation and threats, to torture and assassination. Attempts to overthrow the regime by force were made by exile groups representing both the dissident elite, and organised left wing parties, but all ended in failure. (3) For nearly three decades, the iron grip exercised by the dictatorship left scant opportunity for organised resistance. Protest actions by workers and peasants did take place, but were few and far between. (4)

The only institution that retained any independence from the Duvalierist system was the Catholic Church. Although nearly all the bishops had been appointed by François Duvalier, and the hierarchy had a distinctly conservative outlook, among many priests and lay people the influence of Latin American liberation theology grew in the 1970s. Apart from the Vodou temple, the church was practically the only place where people could gather and share experiences, and progressive Catholics began to use this space to put their ideas into practice. Working in the poorest urban and rural communities, they organised groups for prayer, discussion and self-help. This grassroots work, and the church's sponsoring of rural training centres, built on and extended traditional alternative forms of organisation. (5) Previously marginalised and neglected sections of society were introduced to the possibilities of collective organisation and action.

During the early 1980s, the *ti legliz*, or little church, as the progressive current within the Catholic church became known, became increasingly influential and popular as it questioned the basis of social inequalities and encouraged discussion of social reforms. The impetus towards social reform and political protest both within the Catholic Church, and in the country as a whole, received an important boost in 1983 when, during his visit to Haiti, Pope Jean Paul II remarked that 'things must change'.

The influence of the progressive ti legliz community movement on the Church hierarchy was reflected by the Bishops' Conference radio station, Radio Soleil. Building on the innovations in radio broadcasting initiated by Radio Haiti Inter before it was closed down by Duvalierist forces in 1980, Radio Soleil broadcast almost exclusively in Creole, and daringly covered news of anti-regime protests and relayed the opinions of ordinary Haitians. (6) In a further concession to progressive elements within the Church, in 1985 the Bishops' Conference adopted the ambitious proposals made by priests and nuns for a nation-wide literacy campaign, *Misyon Alfa*.

The Catholic Church lent moral authority to those agitating for change, but, by the mid-1980s, other factors too were contributing to a shift in attitude among significant parts of the population. Jean-Claude Duvalier had alienated many of those in the black middle class and more prosperous peasantry who had supported his father by favouring an ostentatiously corrupt, new mulatto business grouping – a change in power base that was symbolised by his wedding to Michèle Bennett. Meanwhile, for the poor and destitute rural masses, hardship was heaped upon hardship, as droughts, and the impact of the Creole pig eradication programme, drove their standard of living downwards. With a new, more restrictive US refugee policy making the option of emigration all the more difficult and so cutting off an important escape valve, passivity in the face of deprivation turned to desperation and resentment.

In 1985, and the beginning of 1986, street demonstrations led by Catholic activists and school students erupted in the provincial cities of Cap-Haïtien, Jérémie, Les Cayes and, in particular, Gonaïves. (7). In February 1986, with protests finally taking place in the capital, Port-au-Prince, and the security forces unable to contain the situation, the United States acted to forestall the mounting radicalism of the anti-Duvalier movement by organising the departure of the dictator and his family to France.

With the removal of the straight-jacket of 29 years of dictatorship, the seeds sown by the ti legliz, literacy workers, and peasant organisers quickly germinated and flowered as hundreds of peoples', or popular, organisations formed. In the urban slums there was a proliferation of civic organisations, youth and women's groups, and neighbourhood committees. In work places, schools, and at the state university, labour and student unions began to organise and recruit members. In the countryside too, peasant organisations established co-operatives, pooled resources to build silos to stockpile grains, and refused to pay taxes. As well as addressing the issue of poverty at a local level, these popular organisations took part in demonstrations, strikes and land take-overs to advance universal demands for justice, human and labour rights, and land reform. (8). The explosion of grassroots organising, collective action and mass mobilisation brought the poor majority onto the national political stage for the first time in Haiti's history.

In the months following Duvalier's departure, this embryonic popular movement focused on the attempt to eradicate the most visible manifestations of the Duvalier regime – a process known as *dechoukaj*, or uprooting. Corrupt civil servants, Tontons Macoutes, and section chiefs were forced out of their jobs and their homes by sometimes violent street demonstrations and protests. However, while the popular organisations were united by their opposition to the old order, agreement on a common strategy on how to replace it proved more difficult.

Among the political groups that formed to try and harness the newly mobilised peasants and urban poor, opinions differed over the possibilities presented by the political conjuncture. One current believed that change would have to be gradual, and so concentrated its energies on encouraging participation in a referendum on a new constitution, and preparing for proposed elections to vote in a new government. Another, more radical, current maintained that nothing would change while the power of the Duvalierists remained intact, and that elections would merely distract the people from the fundamental struggle against the elite. (9)

Divisions within the Catholic Church also re-emerged as the hierarchy took fright at the dechoukaj and the militancy of the popular organisations. It attempted to rein in the ti legliz movement by abandoning the Misyon Alfa literacy programme and transferring progressive priests from their parishes. One such priest was Father Jean-Bertrand Aristide, a young Salesian priest who issued fiery denunciations of the Church hierarchy, and the Army-controlled provisional government (the CNG) from his parish church in the Port-au-Prince slum area of La Saline. Efforts to silence Aristide were, however, unsuccessful. When he was ordered to move to another parish, a crowd of 10,000 people demonstrated their support and the order was rescinded. Aristide emerged as one of the main figures in the ti legliz and acted as an influential spokesperson for the popular movement. (10)

The political struggle grew increasingly violent as the Tonton Macoutes, who had been officially disbanded but never disarmed, began to re-emerge. One of the most notorious massacres took place in the north-western town of Jean-Rabel in July 1987 when Macoutes and peasants in the pay of large landowners killed over 100 members of a peasant organisation demanding land reform. The November election was sabotaged when voters were killed by Macoute and military forces, and after General Namphy declared martial law in June 1988, attacks on political leaders, church workers and peasant organisers increased.

The military regimes, headed by General Namphy and, after another coup in September 1988, by General Prosper Avril, reflected a constantly evolving set of alliances between the military, the Duvalierists, and other elements of the established order threatened by the popular and democratic movement. At the same time, the pro-change movement was itself composed of many strands which, while agreed on their opposition to the status quo, had quite different conceptions of the strategy needed to transform the situation, and of the form of society that would emerge in the future. (11)

While the reformist sectors counted on a combination of internal protest and international pressure to force the military to allow the staging of free elections, organisations of peasants and urban slum dwellers presented a vision of an alternative form of democracy based on participation at the grass roots. (12) The more radical of these popular organisations claimed that the only satisfactory solution to the country's crisis would be for the people to take power themselves. (13) During this period of political tumult, ideas, position statements and news were disseminated across the country by Creole-language publications and, more importantly for a largely illiterate population, by the broadcasts of the new independent radio stations that set up post-1986. This medium was also instrumental in the growth in popularity of a new musical genre, known as *rasin* or roots, which reflected a generalised expression of opposition and resistance through culture.

When outright and increasingly bold opposition to the military government prompted the US to withdraw all support for Avril in March 1990, a new provisional civilian government began preparations for presidential and legislative elections. The majority of the population, however, although politically active and engaged, showed little interest in the political parties or much belief in the validity of the electoral process. This situation was then transformed when the Macoute leader, Roger Lafontant announced his candidacy for the presidency, and, in response, Father Aristide declared he would contest the election under the banner of a left-of-centre coalition. Although the electoral council, citing the ten-year constitutional ban on Duvalierists holding public office, subsequently disqualified Lafontant, Aristide stayed in the contest. His candidacy had captured the imagination of the people, and tens of thousands of peasants and the urban poor registered to vote. (14)

In an election monitored by international observers and declared free and fair, Aristide won a massive 67 per cent of the vote. His victory represented an overwhelming desire for a break with the past system of exploitation, corruption and violence, and for a new democratic and inclusive society. The reaction of the 'old guard' Duvalierists was not long in coming. The Archbishop of Port-au-Prince gave an inflammatory sermon at a New Year's Day service warning that Aristide's would be a 'socialist-bolshevik regime' that would destroy the country. A week later, and a month before Aristide was due to assume the presidency, Lafontant launched a pre-emptive coup. His bid for power failed when thousands of Haitians took to the streets to defend the election result, and the army declined to back the coup d'état. (15)

Although the approach of the Aristide government was based on recognition of the need to attract foreign aid, and of the dangers of alienating the military and the economic elite, it did initiate a number of reforms in response to its mandate to govern on behalf of the poor majority. (16) This programme, although far from radical, threatened the vested interests of important elements of the established power structure, and Aristide was toppled by a military coup after just eight months.

For three years the military regime oversaw a fierce and concerted campaign of repression targeting the popular organisations, and the ti legliz. As many as 5,000 people were murdered and thousands more were beaten, tortured and raped by the military, paramilitary death squads, and the restored section chiefs. Many of the victims were organisers and activists from the popular organisations. With almost 2,000 grassroots leaders taking the opportunity to escape the same fate by accepting political asylum abroad, the popular movement was effectively decapitated. Although some organisations survived in hiding, most grassroots structures and networks collapsed as an estimated 300,000 people moved from one area of the country to another to escape the repression. The losses and disruption during the coup period seriously handicapped the capacity of the popular organisations to resume their activities once constitutional rule was restored.

Since 1994, faced with a completely new political conjuncture, the pro-change forces have undergone a still unfinished realignment. On the one hand, there was the apparent acceptance by Aristide, Lavalas political leaders, progressive priests, and some popular organisations that the presence of foreign troops, and the conditioning of essential foreign aid assistance on free market reforms made the radical agenda, articulated in the period 1986-90, quite unrealistic. This line of thinking would have it that a pragmatic approach was not without its rewards, and points to two major successes during 1995, Aristide's last year as President: the abolition of the Army, and the landslide victory of the Lavalas Platform in parliamentary and mayoral elections.

On the other hand, while some popular organisations took advantage of the improved security situation and the provision of financial support from foreign NGOs to re-launch grass roots development projects (17), others claimed that the Lavalas government, under the tutelage of the US and UN, was unable to address any of the fundamental demands emanating from the poor majority. In particular, they attributed the growing crime rate and continuing insecurity to the failure to disarm and prosecute those responsible for violent crimes during the coup. (see Chapter 7) As the living standards of the poor continued to decline, criticism focused on the structural adjustment reforms demanded by the international financial institutions. (18) Haitian grass roots and development organisations claimed the free market, neo-liberal, economic strategy was inappropriate in the Haitian context, and, rather than basing growth on the attraction of low wages, called instead for government efforts to support the peasantry and agricultural production. (19)

The new President, the former Lavalas Prime Minister, René Préval, and his government argued that foreign loans and grants would fund the infrastructure needed to attract foreign investment and so provide jobs, and proceeded with the structural adjustment reform programme. However opposition both within and outside Parliament slowed the pace of the reforms to such an extent that the multilateral donors suspended millions of dollars in promised credits. In 1997, with the economic situation worsening rather than improving, and Aristide now speaking out against the application of the neo-liberal reforms, discontent with the government provoked deep splits between different branches of the Lavalas movement, and protests on the streets of Port-au-Prince. (20)

(1) THE PIQUETS

David Nicholls, *Haiti in Caribbean Context,* 1985

In 1843-4 peasants in the south-west took up arms in revolt against the established political system and to press for racial equality, social justice, and a more equal distribution of land.

The southern revolt began under the leadership of the Salomons, who were rich black landowners in the region of Les Cayes. The rising started in August 1843 and government forces under General Lazare were sent to put it down. It was estimated that Salomon's men were armed with roughly 300 rifles and 500 wooden pikes, from which they derived the name of *piquets*. The revolt was temporarily suppressed and the Salomons were arrested. Leadership then passed into the hands of Louis Jean-Jacques Acaau. Born of a black small-holding family during the early years of the century in the commune of Torbeck, Acaau joined the army at an early age and soon became an officer. He was, in the words of the British consul, "a man of some instruction for a negro." Nevertheless, promotion was difficult for blacks in the Boyer era and consequent discontent among black officers was one of the causes of the rising. The principal complaints of the small farmers of the region were about the penalty of imprisonment for debt and the power of the bailiffs. According to Madiou though, the unacknowledged objects of the rising were to destroy mulatto dominance in general, to install a black president, and to confiscate land from rich of all colours, distributing it among the poor. It was Acaau who is said to have first enunciated the well-known Kreyol proverb *nèg rich se mulat, mulat pove se nèg.*[1] [...]

Dressed in straw hats, with ragged trousers and jackets, these piquet leaders carried large machetes and had pistols in their belts. Acaau's followers proclaimed him *chef des réclamations de ces citoyens.* 'The population of the countryside,' he declared, 'awakening from the slumber into which it has been plunged, is murmuring in its poverty and is determined to work for the securing of its rights.' Acaau undoubtedly enjoyed widespread popular support, particularly in La Grande Anse...

Despite being poorly armed, Acaau's men were able to occupy the cities of Jérémie and Les Cayes and to put considerable pressure on the government. The fall of Charles Hérard and the election of the black General Guerrier did something to pacify the piquets and Acaau submitted to the government, being later appointed commandant of L'Anse à Veau.

[1] A rich black is a mulatto, a poor mulatto is a black.

(2) THE STEAMROLLER

Lyonel Paquin, *The Haitians: Class and Colour Politics,* 1983

Daniel Fignolé led the first political party to challenge the political ascendancy of the elite, and his populist message made him immensely popular among the poor of Port-au-Prince. In 1957 he served as provisional president for just 19 days before the Army deposed him and sent him into exile.

His message to the proletariat, unite against the urban rich. It was not a question of Mulatto against Black, rather it was a confrontation between the haves and have nots. Some called him a communist, others called him a fascist and a rabble-rouser. Fignolé reiterated that he was a consistent democrat à la FDR. The crowd was mesmerised by his eloquence. In practice, he could be moody and was introverted.

For the first time in Haitian history the urban masses had found a leader. The firebrand orator might be lacking in ideas but he was certainly rich in slogans and charisma.

His clientele came from the live-in domestics with little monetary compensation, the common labourers, the sales people, the unemployed, the underemployed. The vast army of starving non-persons living on the fringe of the capital and civilisation were his followers. He disciplined his pariahs. From 1946 to 1957, many times Fignolé could have ordered his masses to the business sector or to the "beaux quartiers," and have them consumed. But he did not. Even when the tide turned against him he never instigated them to pillage and burn.

The charismatic leader of Port-au-Prince's urban masses was a born orator in the native creole language. He was in total control of his adoring audiences. His speeches were biting, witty and sardonic. He was an artist in the coinage of new words and expressions which are now part of the Haitian vernacular. His sword was his words and his words were pointed directly against Duvalier, his former associate in the labour movement and now his mortal enemy.

But alas, the Professor had no technical brain trust – no cadre of intellectual, professional personalities among his followers. He was literally a one man army in that sense. In hour of grave crisis, he could tilt the destiny of the nation whichever way he wanted. He could help shape events; he could destroy. He even became president after the bloody 25th of May...but he could not consolidate his power. The nucleus of the army was against him and the two traditional elites saw in him a spoiler of the old political game. However, his 19 days in the palace was an event not to be forgotten. The rural masses of Acaau were stopped at the gate of Port-au-Prince. Fignolé and his urban proletariat held on for 19 days.

When he took the reign of government, he then realised that a country could not be governed solely by slogans, radio speeches and the steam roller.[1] Once on the presidential throne, he became a sitting duck for his enemies. He was also at the mercy of the bureaucracy and the army. He was a helpless man facing the skilful political underworld of Port-au-Prince. Thus, he was completely vulnerable to their dark designs.

[1] The steamroller, or *rouleau compresseur*, was the nickname given to the Fignolé-led demonstrations that would move through the capital destroying everything in their path.

(3) THE COMMUNISTS

Bernard Diederich and Al Burt, *Papa Doc and the Tonton Macoutes,* 1969

In December 1968, Haiti's two small Communist parties merged into one, the PUCH, and declared they had chosen the armed struggle as the means to attain their goal of overthrowing Duvalier and taking power in the name of anti-feudal and anti-imperialist forces.

Members of the PUCH (*Parti Unifié des Communistes Haïtiens*) on 26 March 1969 led an uprising in the village of Casale, in the Chaîne des Matheux, some thirty miles north of Port-au-Prince. For six hours the Communists held the village after chasing both the Tonton Macoutes and the soldiers away. The Communists explained their cause and war to liberate Haiti at a mass rally, and signs of support were scrawled over the mud and wattle walls of the humble village dwellings. Led by an ex-army sergeant who was said to have served in the crack Palace Guard, the Communists slipped away with the army in pursuit.

In early April, Communist publications and press releases told the world of Casale. Duvalier had suppressed mention of his Communist enemy until then. The Communists stated that Casale 'is a classic action in the beginning of a revolutionary struggle. It is an obtrusive act which has historical significance. It was, in fact, the first time that true revolutionaries sought the support of peasants in the mountains, and, at the same time explained to them that the

PUCH struggled for all the people, and that the time had come for the people to join the action.' They went on to stress 'the time has come for all Haitians to rise, help the revolutionaries, and continue the operation that has begun in Casale, and which might very well make the starting point of a glorious struggle of National Liberation...'

But Casale proved a turning point in Duvalier's favour. His usual harsh message, liquidation of the inhabitants of Casale tainted by Communism, soon spread through the mountains, and the Communists did not receive the material or recruits they hoped for. Spotlighted by publicity throughout the world after the Casale uprising, the young men who had so cleverly infiltrated into Haiti from their studies in Europe, and kept their identities secret while carrying out acts of terrorism against the government, were on the run by April. They discovered too late that their Central Committee had been infiltrated since 1961 by a government agent whom they later identified as Frank Eysalene. Throughout that spring Papa Doc's troops rolled up to Communist hide-outs, usually early in the morning, with the precision of the returning swallows.

The final blow came on Monday, 2 June. When the army announced that twenty-two Communists had been engaged and killed in a house on Martin Luther King street in Port-au-Prince, it was no idle boast...Important members of the PUCH Central Committee had fought to the death in this early morning engagement against a superior force of well-armed soldiers. [...]

The Communists gave Haiti its first bank hold-up, made lightning attacks on isolated army posts, and liquidated a number of small Tonton Macoute chieftains. If they had continued their terrorist attacks, and not involved themselves in a village uprising, they might have lasted until Duvalier died of natural causes. Then they might have written a new page in Haitian history.

(4) A HISTORY OF RESISTANCE

Arnold Antonin, *The Long Unknown Struggle of the Haitian People*, 1978

A leading opponent of the Duvaliers counters the common assumption that there was no popular resistance to the dictatorship by listing the struggles of workers and peasants.

// Haitians have the kind of government that they, by their compliance and passivity, deserve."

This is an untrue statement which stems from a number of falsehoods which must be unmasked. For many years the picture of the Haitian presented has been that of a submissive black, capable of accepting everything without protest on account of his inability to fight and of his centuries-old ignorance. But all this portrays a false picture. The Haitian people have steadily fought and still fight to get rid of tyranny. The history is there:

Workers' struggles

1963: Workers strike in the 'Comme Il Faut' tobacco firm because 20 fellow workers had been fired. The strike also affected many other businesses and was finally supported by the Haitian Inter-Union Organisation comprised of 33 unions and 60,000 workers.

1964: Violent protest by workers at Weiner's in Port-au-Prince.

1965: Strike by workers at the Brandt factory to demand that US employers stop deducting an illegal 10% from their salaries.

1967: Workers from the cement factory go on strike in protest over the firing of a fellow worker and the abolition of the old-age pension plan.

1968: Strike at the Sedren factory in protest over a 50% cut in salaries.

1977: Strikes by workers at Habitation Leclerc against the US manager, by workers at the Rawling Company, by public transport drivers in Pétionville, by tourist guides and drivers, by HASCO workers who march to the Presidential Palace, and by workers at Raymond Concrete.

Farmers' struggles

From 1957 to the present day, the small farmers of Haiti have organised many public demonstrations and land occupations.

In 1965 agricultural labourers working in the sugar cane fields destroy the crop in protest against the authorities who refused to pay for the sugar cane or the workers' salaries.

In 1966 peasants rise up against the attempted expropriation of their land by the Tonton Macoute Ludger Frédéric.

In 1967 peasants set fire to sugar cane plantations belonging to the US-owned HASCO Company, and capture a Tonton Macoute who had tortured a peasant woman.

In 1973 peasants from Léogâne oppose the expropriation of their land, and kill a large landowner and two soldiers.

In 1975 200 peasants from Bocozelle defend their land with arms, and fire on the army.

From 1976 to 1978 peasants in the Artibonite and the north fight against the expropriation of land, forced labour, and unpopular laws.[...]

Few – or perhaps none – of these actions are divulged through the normal news channels. The massacres and genocide of the civilian population, the fight to liberate the political prisoners and against the fascist laws, the organisation of political movements and parties, and the long history of US military, political and economic aggression against Haiti, are all unknown to most.

(5) GRASSROOTS ORGANISING

Robert Maguire, *The Peasantry and Political Change in Haiti,* 1991

A section of the Catholic Church played a significant role in the development of grassroots organising and mobilisation both before and after the fall of Jean-Claude Duvalier.

The Haitian Church traditionally shared the wealth and status of the elite segment of the population. A new course was chosen by a significant number of indigenous and non-indigenous clergy and religious, and committed laymen and laywomen, in the late 1960s and 1970s. Encouraged by Vatican II and the 1968 Conference of Catholic bishops in Medellín, reorienting the church's social mission toward the preferential option for the poor, and inspired by the Freirian concept of conscientisation, these grassroots forces within or close to the church carried the institution along a path committed to evangelisation, social justice and defence of the poor. Their position within the church was given a strong boost in 1983, when Pope John Paul II visited Haiti and urged change.

The commitment has been carried directly to the peasantry via two routes. One is the *ti legliz* (little church) or the Haitian version of basic Christian communities...The other avenue is the church-sponsored training centres that have played a decisive role in the birth of Haiti's heralded grassroots mobilisation. Most centres were established during the early to mid-1970s. They were scattered geographically, with all of them outside Port-au-Prince. The clergy, religious, laymen and laywomen directing them began with a common premise: real change comes from the bottom up. Hence, the training centres began their work with individuals from peasant com-

munities who showed promise of having an ability to begin to cata-
lyse that change.

Prior to the coup ousting President Aristide, there were at least
seven church-linked centres with ongoing regional and national programmes of leadership training. Exceedingly instrumental to peasant
mobilisation in Haiti, most have evolved with the grassroots movement they are catalysing, from an initial focus on the training of
animatè (community-based development workers) to include such
programmes as continuing education, training leaders of regional
associations of peasant groups, civic education and literacy, and agricultural extension services.

Grassroots organising work prior to 1986 focused almost exclusively on the virtual clandestine formation of groups. The formation,
solidification and federation of groups has been a tedious process,
taking a decade in some cases as groups came together and broke
apart before reforming with greater cohesion. Following the flight
of Jean-Claude Duvalier, established grassroots groups quickly abandoned the strategy of evasion which they had been forced to adopt.
They surged forward, initiating programmes designed to confront –
and resolve – fundamental problems keeping members poor.

(6) RADIO SOLEIL

Unda News, Interview with Father Hugo Triest, 1993

Belgian priest, Father Hugo Triest, was director of the Catholic Bishops' Conference radio station, Radio Soleil, during the 1980s when
it was the country's main organ for uncensored news, and helped to
unify opposition to the Duvalier dictatorship.

In Haiti radio is the most common and important means of mass
communication. Poor people have radios or access to them, but
they don't always have the money to buy batteries. There are three
or four newspapers in the capital, but they are in French. The Bishops' Conference station, Radio Soleil, started in 1975. It was a new
voice because it broadcast in *Kreyòl*. It intended to be an educational
radio, but the educational programme was not a success because
communications in general were so difficult, i.e. you would ask people to listen to a broadcast with the lesson sheets but either they
were never sent out or they failed to arrive in time. And of course
there was a problem due to lack of money.

When I became director of Radio Soleil in 1985, the station was in a state of transition because the country was in transition. At that time, near the end of the Duvalier dynasty, people were organising themselves and Radio Soleil became the voice of the people. Radio Soleil was the property of the Bishops' Conference and, as most of the bishops had been appointed by Duvalier, we had a certain space in which to work. But we were not free from harassment. Employees of the station were beaten up, telephone lines cut, and at one point they jammed the signal from the studio to the antenna. We had to go to the antenna, six kilometres away, and broadcast from there. But they were unable to close us down.

In July 1985, I was arrested, then released, and two days later was issued with expulsion papers. Radio Soleil was shut down in December 1985 and then, after Duvalier left, I returned in March 1986. I had been back a week when the Papal Nuncio telephoned me to say that from then on the station had to be exclusively religious and should not deal with social or political issues. I stayed on, but I could not accept this new direction and finally I decided not to renew my contract in 1989. I offered them my services on the condition that the bishops would talk to the 40 people who worked on the station to ask them what kind of director they wanted. But the bishops chose three new directors, one a priest, none of whom had ever been inside a radio station in their lives, and who all had very strong Duvalierist/Macoute ties.

A short time later, one of the bishops went to the station with the new radio call sign – until then it had been 'Radio Soleil – Catholic radio station, the voice of Jesus Christ, the voice of the people of God". The new call sign was "Voice of the Bishops' Conference". The head of programming refused to continue and was sacked. Twenty-seven employees protested and were fired. The radio has now become an instrument of the de facto government.

(7) CRADLE OF REBELLION

Haiti Progrès, *Gonaïves: Symbole de la résistance,* 1986

Beginning with a riot prompted by police brutality in May 1984, the city of Gonaïves was a focal point of the protests and demonstrations that brought down the Duvalier dictatorship in February 1986.

Several key dates in the resistance of Gonaïves should be remembered:

May 1984: Serious protests erupt in the town after the brutal treatment of a sick woman by a member of the military. Several days later she dies in hospital (La Providence) as a result of her injuries. Following raids on food stores belonging to the CARE foundation, the widespread anger is passed off as "protests against food shortages", in the hope that gifts of food from "Jean-Claude the benefactor" will be enough to quell a revolt whose causes are much deeper-rooted.

An anonymous writer put it this way: "On closer examination, the Haitian 'spring' exposes more than the hunger which has been part of everyday life for so long; it reveals the causes. The revolt was born of contempt for the violence shown towards a woman recovering from an operation. It was an indication that things had gone too far, that the gulf between some 200 families and the rest of the country was intolerable and that two countries could not exist within one."

It was also around this time that the so-called 'Declaration of Gonaïves' appeared, a document signed by more than 2,000 "lucid, patriotic and committed Church laymen" who dared to denounce what they regarded as an intolerable situation: the persecution of priests engaged in social work, various forms of extortion and abuse suffered mainly by peasants, arrests, disappearances, etc.

27th November 1985: The students of Gonaïves take to the streets. Bearing the blue and red flag[1] they chant: *"Nous bezwen chanjman radikal nan peyi a."* (We need radical change in the country) It is a purely peaceful demonstration but this time the government goes too far, and this will be a contributory factor in its later permanent collapse. The military opens fire and Jean-Robert Cius, 20, a student of rhetoric, is shot dead. Daniel Israel, 19, and Mackenson Michel, 13, are also killed. This is too much, and a wave of discontent and defiance engulfs the whole country. These martyrs, symbols of a barbaric regime, will later symbolise the country's liberation.

"Calm" was never restored in Gonaïves after this. A succession of protests and demonstrations took place in the town, and particularly in the poverty-stricken area of Raboteau, a series of arrests doing nothing to quell the unrest. In January 1986, when the government, despite strong pressure, decided to defer the appearances before a court of those responsible for the assassinations of the young protesters, a crowd gathered, demanding justice and brandishing the blue and red Bicolore, a symbol of the freedom to fight for liberty. Meanwhile, teachers were also protesting against the repression suffered by certain members of their profession and, in particular, the case of Fritz Bernard, beaten to death at the Toussaint Louverture Barracks after his arrest. A letter signed by 102 teachers reads: "We, the undersigned protest against the murder in Gonaïves of the baker and three students, the arrest and murder of Fritz Bernard, and the persecution suffered by teachers from the Artibonite and the Grande Anse."

At the beginning of February 1986, several food stores were raided, a fire broke out on the commercial premises of a supporter of Duvalier, and the pursuit of the macoutes began. By this time it was obvious that regions such as Gonaïves were no longer under the control of the regime, and on the 7th February, came the final episode in 28 years of Duvalierism, the departure of the dictator. The town of Gonaïves celebrated the first step towards liberation. On Sunday 16th February, an enormous demonstration of solidarity took place. From early morning the town was swamped by huge crowds, flooding in from towns and villages. There was singing and dancing in the streets while the blue and red flag was everywhere to be seen.

[1] François Duvalier was one in a long line of Haitian leaders who had made alterations to the Haitian national flag. Under the Duvaliers, the existing flag of two vertical blocks of red and blue was replaced with one of red and black. Opponents of the regime used the former version as a symbol of resistance to the dictatorship.

Translated from French by Emily Dunbar

(8) THE FIGHT FOR LAND

Haiti Info, *The Milot Land Struggle,* 1993

The Peasant Movement of Milot (south of Cap-Haïtien) occupied and took back control of land that it claimed had been expropriated.

In 1986 the peasants saw the opportunity to break their chains. They took to the streets and had a slogan: "It's the people who work the land that should own the land."

"On March 9, 1986, Mouvman Peyizan Milot, MPM, (Peasant Movement of Milot) was created to address the land problem in Milot and also to fight injustice and division amongst people of the towns and from the mountains," explained co-ordinator Moise Jean-Charles. "During those seven years, a lot of these problems have started to be solved."

On March 12, 1987, there was a first attempt to recuperate their land that was taken away in the seventies, but it did not come through because the entire community did not understand. "That's why a lot of us ended up in jail," said Jean-Charles.

The peasants kept up the agitation, the work of explaining why it was necessary to join the action. They even called upon other towns. When they felt they had enough support, they spread the word to make believe they would invade the land on March 20.

"We only had spread the word without really having the intention to do it that day, but just to test the ground to see what would happen," Jean-Charles said.

As predicted, Yves Beauséjour[1] sent in dozens of thugs armed with machetes, sharp sticks of iron and clubs with clear orders to cut off people's heads, but found nobody. MPM decided to move on the thirtieth.

On March 29 at midnight, everyone gathered and before dawn everybody was burning sugar cane and planting on the plots. They seized over 100 hectares. "Many more than just ten thousand came that day," one member of MPM remembers. "The foreign white person could not do anything."

The landowners said they would get their land back using force, and on April 15 ten truckloads of soldiers arrived. The peasants had been called together with one blow of the conch. Seeing the thousands of people, the soldiers left, and the peasants started leaving, thinking the conflict was over. Later, soldiers came back and massacred peasants – wounding 500 and killing four.

"By taking over the land, we are not only looking at that little piece of land but we are sending a message to the big landowners, the thieves of state property, the church that we know does not have any wife or children, however has lots of land," Jean-Charles told a press conference in Port-au-Prince in April 1993.

"This gesture has had profound repercussions. In many other places they tried to emulate us. Even though they've not been able to keep theirs like us, they tried and should keep trying and keep struggling to gain freedom. They should reorganise, become stronger and launch other actions, because the land is theirs.

This is one of the main reasons of the (1991) coup d'etat. Right after the coup, Beauséjour tried to regain control by force but everyone stayed on their land and he had to give up his effort. Today 8,000 of us are working and living with our families on that land."

[1] The MPM alleges that Yves Beauséjour, a Canadian development worker, was in league with absentee landowners who had expropriated a large tract of state-owned land.

(9) REFORMISTS AND REVOLUTIONARIES

Greg Chamberlain, *Up By the Roots*, 1987

Attempts to build a democratic movement to carry forward the demands of the newly mobilised majority were hampered by disagreements between those who proposed a gradual reform of the political system through elections and those calling for more immediate and fundamental changes to the political system.

A group of centre-left intellectuals organised a five-day National Congress of Haitian Democratic Movements in the capital in January 1987 to try to coordinate the broad will for meaningful change and a clear break with the "old politics". The organisers of the meeting claimed to have rallied more than 300 organisations, mostly peasant-based, making it the largest gathering of its kind in Haitian history. The 1,000 participants spanned a wide political spectrum, which included Catholic progressives. Many of the meeting's demands found their way into the new Constitution. "We've done the work the political parties should have done," declared one prominent congress figure. Congress leaders also set up the Committee of 57, which directed the protests in the summer of 1987.

Dupuy and his supporters rejected the congress as "a club of opportunists and pseudo-democrats."[1] It was also boycotted by Yves Richard, head of the largest and most left-wing of the country's three main labour federations, the Independent Haitian Workers Organisation (CATH)...

But the congress, which set up a standing body, Konakom, to press for a "democratic, nationalist state," impressed most Haitians with its representativeness and its calls for purging the "Macoute remnants" of the Duvalier regime, decreasing dependence on foreign countries, declaring Creole an official language, and bolstering respect for Voodoo, the national religion. Among congress participants was a new organisation, Children of the Haitian Tradition (Zantray), which helped successfully petition the constituent assembly to abolish a 1935 anti-Voodoo law...

Schoolteacher Victor Benoît, the leading figure in Konakom, said the Left's participation in the 1987 elections would depend on whether the independent electoral council was allowed real control of the scheduled local, legislative and presidential polls. "Our first task is to expand democracy's territory here," he said. "People are mobilised. We also have a favourable international situation right now." He denied Richard's charge of intellectual vanguardism "Ben Dupuy and the maximalists want to immediately install a revolutionary people's democracy. That just isn't possible. We have neither a progressive military nor an armed people. We have to have a pluralist regime first. But I wouldn't favour a one-party state anyway."

Benoît denied charges that the January congress fudged criticism of the United States. "The state here is domesticated by the United States. But we have to take US power in the region into account. We cannot afford irresponsible sorties..."

[1] Ben Dupuy, director of the New York-based newspaper, Haiti Progrès, and other activists organised a more radical alternative to the Congress, the National Popular Assembly (APN).

(10) POLITICAL RESURRECTION

Father Jean-Bertrand Aristide, Press Conference, 1987

On 20 August 1987, the day after the Haitian Church authorities rescinded a decision to transfer him from his parish in the Port-au-Prince slum area of La Saline, Father Jean-Bertrand Aristide outlined his analysis of the political situation.

// In the Church, more so than in any other section of society, every person now has an immediate responsibility and a decision to make: whether to let the Macoutes' corruption go on and on, or to take part in the historic movement to eradicate it. In other words, what is happening now is the resurrection of a whole people.

Liberation theology is becoming a lever capable of raising up all the youth against a corrupt generation. It is the story of Jesus of Nazareth that we, the Christians in Haiti, are called on to relive today. In a word, we have become subjects of our own history, whereas we have always been only the objects.

Haiti's "historic handlebars" are in our hands, and it is we who are steering the bicycle. The corrupt want to force us to keep the handlebars titled to the extreme right – driving us straight towards the precipice. But we, the young people, say in the name of our faith: no to this interminable turn to the right. And we say yes to a leftwards turn. What does this mean concretely? That we are communists? No. But does it mean that because we are not communists, we agree with those who are killing communists? No.

Voluntarily, freely, we are rejecting the corrupt right and advancing towards a left where the strength and the depth of our faith makes it possible for us not to turn away from society, but to join in, without the danger of being sullied, and to fight for a socialist Haiti. This is the only way that offers a possibility for everyone to eat, and to believe in justice, liberty and respect.

Without a socialist system – while we remain Christians – we can only consider ourselves a people condemned to die like dogs under the blows of imperialism and their local lackeys.

To attain these objectives it is important to rise above barriers of class, colour and even political differences. Whatever political party people belong to, there must be a historic alliance that allows us to break out of the framework of the National Government Council and of the corrupt capitalist system that keeps it going.

Afterwards, we can see by what name to call the Haiti that today true patriots are calling by names that express their desires: a system that can guarantee honest work, justice, liberty and respect to everyone."

(11) UPROOTING THE OLD ORDER

Marx-Vilaire Aristide and Laurie Richardson, *Haiti's Popular Resistance*, 1994

During the period of 'Duvalierism without Duvalier' (1986-90) there was a marked lack of consensus over strategy within the broad pro-change movement.

The popular movement is ensnared in dialectical struggle with the reformist sector of Haiti's broader "democratic" movement. This reformist camp – consisting of certain politicians, intellectuals and members of the business elite – remains preoccupied with establishing formal democracy through elections and superficial reforms. The tension between these two currents remains the most formidable impediment to the success of the popular movement. Although the reformists oppose hard-line Duvalierism, they do not share the popular movement's more radical vision for a new Haiti. [...]
Explained "Fritz", a well-known militant who has spent over twenty years in the struggle, "We all witnessed Duvalier's departure. Theoretically, there was no more dictatorship and the era of

repression was over. Then, we began to realise that Duvalier was the tip of the iceberg and that we had to start mobilising on all fronts."

One of the strategies employed in this mobilisation was *dechoukaj*. Translated literally as "uprooting" and often equated singularly with "necklacing" – execution by means of a burning tyre – the concept of *dechoukaj* embraced much more than popular street justice. In fact, its most potent dimension was political. In the process of "uprooting" Duvalierism, peasants organised to eliminate the brutal section-chief structure, students fought to end state control of the university, and the masses were galvanised to dismantle not just the Tontons Macoutes themselves, but the political machine that created and sustained them for nearly thirty years.

Popular militants were convinced that *dechoukaj*, left to gain momentum, could successfully transfer real power from the Duvalierists and the elites to the poor majority. Indeed, it was this possibility that most unnerved the reformist camp, many of whose adherents benefited at least indirectly from the status quo, and would – if political *dechoukaj* were allowed to run its course – ultimately be held accountable to the more militant bases. Echoing the Duvalier-appointed Catholic Bishops, the reformists launched a propaganda offensive highlighting the street-justice aspect of *dechoukaj* and calling for national reconciliation. By virtue of greater resources and control of major media outlets, they were able to bring *dechoukaj* to a halt by mid-1986.

"Whenever the people were highly mobilised," lamented Fritz, "instead of having a clear and unified call to action, you would find these guys ready, behind closed doors, to talk to (hard-line junta General) Régala, to talk to Namphy. Instead of urging the population to keep pressing with their demands, they acted like fire-fighters, making conciliatory declarations. Sometimes we felt that they considered us more of an enemy than the Macoutes." [...]

The reformists "need the popular mobilisation when they are under fire," said Fritz, "but once they get the Macoutes off their backs, they make an alliance with the bourgeoisie to block any deeper change. They always say it's not to block you. They say you are unrealistic, you are extremist, you are a purist. They have all kinds of names for you. But when the Macoutes come back to haunt them, they are quick to cry for help."

(12) PEASANT DEMOCRACY

Haiti Support Group, Interview with a Leader of the Tèt Kole Ti Peyizan Ayisyen Peasant Movement, 1996

Heads Together Small Peasants of Haiti is one of a number of peasant movements organising self-help projects and developing the political consciousness of its members.

// The background of this organisation goes back to the loss of reli gious leadership. Before 1986 the church helped the poorest small peasants, but after 1986 it stopped leading them in organising themselves. But in the rural milieu, grassroots organisers continued their work. Groups realised that they could organise autonomously without being under church leadership. In 1986 the regional peasant organisations decided to get together and build a unified movement, so Tèt Kole was formed."

"Tèt Kole works with the smallest peasants, not even the medium-sized ones, because even within the peasant sector, (our) enemies use middle peasants to attack other peasants. We are organising for life, for survival, to move from absolute poverty to social change. Most of the peasants we work with are landless. They either sell their labour or work as share-croppers. They have no decent housing, no schools for their children, poor health conditions. Both their social and their economic situations are extremely fragile. So our work is in popular education and conscientisation so that these small peasants can see the real root of their problems, analyze the causes, and come to demand that the state resolve these problems. The state offers them no services – no potable water, very few schools or health clinics, inadequate roads, no technical support for agricultural production, no electricity in many areas, no means of communication. Tèt Kole was born in this context."

"Tèt Kole has grassroots base-level groups in eight of the nine departments, scattered throughout the rural sections. It holds assemblies at the level of each rural section to facilitate communication. Each assembly sends elected delegates to a communal assembly, and these elect delegates for a departmental assembly. Then each department sends representatives to the national confederation, which elects a three-member executive committee. These representatives are elected for a specific period of time, then they are expected to go back to the rural sector. Also, regional co-ordinators are expected to spend one week per month working on their farm. Thus service in the organisation is not a way of bettering your social position."

"We want a state that is not a puppet of the "blancs." By this we mean foreign powers, it is not meant in a racist sense; all people living in exploitation, whatever their colour or country, are in the same situation of struggle. So "blancs" means the US government, the World Bank, the IMF, all enforcing their own economic and political plans on the world. We want a state that really welcomes participation of the popular masses in real power. We want democratic participation in its real essence, not demagogy and intimidation."

"Many of the peasants who are landless now, actually had land 10 or 20 years ago. The economic situation has forced them to sell it off bit by bit...We believe from our experience that the land should be distributed to groups who can hold onto it and work it together. They should not have the right to sell the land, and the state should provide services and inputs: credit, tools, seed, insecticide, fertilisers, and technical support. These would be the necessary conditions to give peasants real land security."

(13) POPULAR POWER

Le Militant, Press Release, 1989

Splits within the military prompted a group of popular organisations to call on the population to reject a reformist solution in favour of popular power.

We, the undersigned, in the middle of this crisis that's been plaguing the country since 1st April[1] want to make our position clear. Scoundrels are playing a game that nobody can interpret clearly. We want to shed some light on the situation.

This crisis, which started as a confrontation between two tendencies in the Army, is an abscess on a boil: the boil is the general crisis in which the country has been in since the time of the (US) occupation...The tangled web of the American imperialists, the compliant bourgeoisie, and the feudal landowners, which has put the Macoutes on the people's back, is corrupt and can't continue. It's clear we can expect neither the imperialists, nor the bourgeoisie, neither the feudal landowners, nor the Macoutes and the generals, to resolve the country's crisis or satisfy the demands of the majority of the population.

1. We denounce the US government for continuing to stick its nose in our country's business when it openly declares that it supports the idiot Prosper Avril, whether or not the people say they want him, and sends arms and technicians, an act that will prevent the people finding a solution that really suits them..

2. We denounce the manoeuvres of the ruling class – the big bourgeoisie and the big Macoutes, who use the soldiers to make the people think things are being sorted out. We see an interest group which is preparing the road for the American Plan, and another group who are in cahoots with the old-guard Macoutes who want to officially return to power. Neither of these powerful forces are friends of the people. In between these two camps are some ordinary soldiers who are starting to see the game being played by the imperialists and ruling class, and who want to join the popular camp.[2]

We declare,

a) the ruling class will never be able to find a solution that is advantageous to the popular majority. The negotiations refereed by the American and French imperialist bosses cannot resolve the Haitian crisis...

b) until the people have their hands on the control of economic and political power, there will be no definitive solution to a worsening national crisis...

For this reason we warn all popular sectors, both in the town and in the country, "Don't fall for the beautiful trap set by the big shots." On the contrary, while the Army is tearing itself apart with US weapons, we should be strengthening our organisations, and setting up vigilance brigades, so that we can finish with the Macoutes for good, and, without hesitation, take the road to popular power.

Signed by representatives of the following organisations, Haitian Revolutionary Union of Neighbourhood Committees, Solidarity Between Youth (SAJ), Haitian Unemployed Workers' Revolutionary Committee, Konbit Veye Yo, Heads together Small Peasants (Tèt Kole Ti Peyizan), Solidarity among Haitian Women (SOFA), Mobilised Women (Fanm Leve Kanpe), Students' Association of the North, Haitian League of Former Political Prisoners, Federation of Neighbourhood Committees, Milot Peasant Movement, National Popular Assembly (APN), Collective for the Liberation of Haiti, Young Christian Students, Youth Committee of Martisan.

[1] In April 1989 two of army's three main units, the Leopard Corps and the Dessalines Battalion rose against Colonel Prosper Avril, the head of the military regime. Ostensibly a revolt about pay, it is be-

lieved to have been connected with US-inspired moves against drug-trafficking commanders and supporters of the exiled Duvalierist leader, Roger Lafontant. After a week of shooting, Avril came out on top.

[2] Refers to some rank and file soldiers and junior officers, who in late 1988 had overthrown General Henri Namphy and, although sidelined, were still identified as a sympathetic current.

Translated from Creole by Charles Arthur

(14) AVALANCHE

Leslie Griffiths, *The Aristide Factor*, 1997

Father Jean-Bertrand Aristide stood as the presidential candidate for the FNCD left-centre coalition in the 1990 election. His campaign and the political current he represented became known as Lavalas.

One theme was beginning to emerge as the campaign intensified, one metaphor began to dominate. This was the word *Lavalas*, avalanche. In Haiti it had little to do with snow, much more to do with the raging waters that flood down the bare mountain slopes and unprotected valleys after a tropical storm. These floods are unstoppable, they destroy everything that stands in their way. In Carl Brouard's poem *Vous*, Haiti's peasant population is pictured as having the potential to be just such an unstoppable force if only they had enough self-awareness. There's little doubt that Aristide's use of the Lavalas metaphor draws its inspiration from Brouard. The people could indeed be unstoppable as the mighty floodwaters and he saw it as his job to raise their consciousness and engage their energies for the great political tasks that belonged to them and them alone. In Aristide's mind, this was the moment when the Haitian peasants stepped out of the shadows, where they had been consigned to waste away, and onto the pages of history.

He'd already struck this note in a broadcast he'd made two years previously, a short while after the St John Bosco massacre.[1] Much of that speech related specifically to the grim September events that had occasioned it. But there's already a clear delineation of the theme that he was to develop as a candidate (and indeed as president). It opens with an exhortation to the Haitian people:

To my sisters, my brothers,
To all my brothers and sisters in the Good Lord
Who raise their voices together with us,
To the valiant youth of Haiti,
To the peasants – whether Catholic, Protestant or Vodouisant –
To the brave Haitians abroad,
To the courageous Haitians here in Haiti...
Congratulations on your courage.
Alone we are weak,
Together, we are strong.
All together, we are the flood lavalas.
Let the flood descend,
The flood of poor peasants and poor soldiers,
The flood of the poor jobless multitudes (and poor soldiers),
Of poor workers (and poor soldiers),
The flood of all our poor friends (and all the poor soldiers) and
The church of the poor, which we call the children of God!
Let that flood descend!
And then God will descend and put down the mighty and send
  them away,
And He will raise up the lowly and place them on high.

Like the whole image of Haitian society as a banqueting table around which the whole Haitian family must sit, so too this picture of the poor as an unstoppable avalanche is drawn directly from his preaching days. It is particularly interesting to note the appeal he makes to the poor soldiers. He was well aware of the ordinary soldier's plight, how mindlessly he was exploited by his superior officers who, themselves, were often making huge fortunes from drug-running and smuggling activities. By linking the lowly Haitian soldier with Haiti's poor, he wanted to appeal to elements within the armed forces who could make the difference between peace and chaos, democracy and dictatorship...

This speech provided the great rallying cry of the election campaign. Imagine a litany that runs like this. The diminutive priest, raised up on a distant platform, would intone one word into his microphone. *'Apart'* (On our own), he'd say, and the crowd, as one, would reply *'nou fèb'* (We're weak). *'Ansanm'* (together), he'd continue, to which *'nou fò'* (we're strong), they'd cry, much louder this time. *'Ansanm ansanm'* (and when we're all together), he'd insist, *'nou se lavalas'* (we're an avalanche), they'd hurl back with relish, their voices themselves a veritable avalanche of energised sound. I've heard that litany hundreds of times and every single time I've

been aware of the enormous power Aristide possessed in this capacity to unify and articulate the deep feelings of those thousands of
poor Haitian people who flocked to hear him and who'd never had
a champion before.

[1] In September 1988, 50 armed men in the pay of the Duvalierist
mayor of Port-au-Prince attacked Aristide's church, St John Bosco,
while he was celebrating mass. A dozen members of the congregation were murdered, and the church was burnt down.

(15) CONFRONTATION

Laënnec Hurbon, *L'insurrection du 7 janvier 1991*, 1993

A Haitian sociologist compares the uprising to defend the election
of Aristide from the coup attempt led by the Tonton Macoute leader,
Roger Lafontant, with the slave rebellion of 1791.

After the first few hours of terror in the wake of the return to
power of Macoutism, every quarter of Port-au-Prince resounded
with the same angry cry: 'Down with Lafontant!' The banging on
doors and railings of every house in certain areas, the ringing of
church bells, or the sounding of conch shells – traditionally used by
the slaves to give the signal to assemble or to revolt – woke the whole
populace. From two o'clock in the morning, barricades were set up
every 20 metres or so in the streets of Port-au-Prince and Pétionville
(and we later found out in all the towns in the country). The houses,
buildings, and businesses belonging to Macoutes and supporters of
Lafontant were surrounded by furious crowds. Volleys of stones,
pickaxes, iron bars, burning tires were some of the makeshift weapons used for a big operation called *dechoukaj* of the Macoutes. Some
were burnt alive, or stoned to death. In certain houses Macoutes
were caught unawares and, unable to escape, shot into the crowd
which would fall back, and then renew the attack. In the provinces,
Cap-Haïtien, Cayes, Jacmel, and Gonaïves, similar methods of resistance were put into action. A whole people stayed up the entire
night, ready to face death rather than bend down before this mon-
ster. One could only be astonished by this absolute determination –
more visible in the poor areas – to literally block out Macoutism.
The capital in particular gave the impression of a town disappearing under columns of smoke rising up from the barricades. It's
impossible to reduce this eruption of the crowd to the result of ma-

nipulation, to a blind and superficial mobilisation. There was rather the startled awakening of a society aiming to re-establish and reaffirm itself through the practical and radical rejection of Macoutism...

Without doubt, in order to understand the event, one is drawn to similar historical situations such as the night of 22 August 1791 when the mass of slaves rose up to put an end to slavery once and for all. Whether or not this is a legitimate comparison, the fact remains that the decision to blatantly confront the 34 years of Macoutism was given its full expression on the night of the 6th to 7th of January. The significance of the 16th of December vote revealed itself on the flaming barricades of the 7th of January.

Translated from French by Anne McConnell

(16) ARISTIDE IN POWER

EPICA / Voices for Haiti, *Beyond the Mountains, More Mountains,* 1994

The first government of President Aristide embarked on a wide range of reforms during the eight months before it was overthrown by a military coup.

The platform of the Lavalas government that Aristide attempted to carry out was based on three organising principles: justice, transparency, and participation. The new government proceeded to attack the host of problems confronting Haiti...During less than a year in office, the Aristide government made headway in several areas:

Education: The government created a major adult literacy programme, similar to the one begun by the Catholic church in the early 1980s. Some of the thousands of exiled Haitians who returned to their country came specifically to remake the public education system and the National University.

Public Health: Interventions included the restructuring of the country's major hospitals and the elevation of primary health care as the top priority of the new Ministry of Health.

Agrarian Reform: By early summer Aristide announced the distribution of fallow state lands to peasant farmers. He appointed ombudsmen to oversee land disputes and launched a programme to increase access to credit for small farmers and to halt soil erosion and desertification.

Workers' Rights: Aristide's government tried to increase the minimum wage from 15 to 25 gourdes per day (less than US$3 at the 1991 exchange rate), and attacked unemployment with a major public works programme.

Corruption: Aristide began trimming a bloated and corrupt public administration, eliminating over 2,000 federal jobs in his first few months in office. He disbanded the Bureau of Tourism and trimmed the Ministry of Information by half.

Crime: The government held to its promise to fight "insecurity" felt throughout Haitian society by arresting key figures in a number of crime rings.

Separation of Police and Army: Aristide, following the mandate of the Constitution, began this difficult task by abolishing the position of chef de section, a significant move since section chiefs have long been at the centre of human rights abuses.

(17) PEASANT ORGANISATION

The Peasant, *MPP Programmes Move Forward,* 1995

The Peasant Movement of Papaye (MPP) in the Central Plateau is one of the oldest and largest peasant organisations in Haiti. One year after the return of President Aristide, Francky Saint Nare, head of the MPP's transition committee, outlines some of the organisation's development programmes.

The programme of reforestation and soil conservation, the agro-silvicultural programme, has been relaunched, although not exactly as it used to be. We are concentrating more on the aspect of tree nurseries and in training peasants in reforestation techniques. We operate several large nurseries throughout the Central Plateau and there are 318 small nurseries run by peasant groups themselves. However, given that the peasants already had training in the aspect of soil conservation, in many areas they are carrying those out on their own, because the habits stuck with them. They have also developed the capacity to produce their own seedlings, so if the MPP is unable to continue this programme, they will be able to carry on the work.

One of the biggest problems facing the peasants today is that of high interest rates. In order to combat usury, we developed our own credit union, *"Sere Pou Chofe,"* where individual peasants can save the little money they have and take out small loans. People have started to use the programme again to save their money, but there isn't yet enough money to begin giving loans.

Our credit programme for women, however, is functioning and helping many women to carry out petty commerce. This has a two-fold benefit. If the woman gets a loan to buy and resell rice, she can use a little of the rice to feed her family. If it is to resell gas, she can use a bit to light her family's lamps, etc. This has been of vital importance for groups throughout the country. We are receiving many requests for participation but the demand is so great, we are unable to help everyone within the movement.

We opened a community store, and have so far sold one initial lot of merchandise. We ran into a few difficulties but we have re-stocked and I think we will begin to sell again this week. We don't sell at the inflated prices that you find in Hinche. The shopkeepers in Hinche sell for a profit, but we don't. On the contrary, this store is part of our struggle against the high cost of living.

We also have a poultry programme, where we buy day-old chicks in Port-au-Prince and we bring them to Papaye. We just raised one group of 2,000 chicks. We sell them more cheaply than the market price. ...

The apiary programme is also working very well. We have our own bee hives, and we train the peasants in collecting honey themselves. We buy the honey from them at a good price and send it to Germany to be sold. After it is sold, the peasant groups receive the profit that remains after we take out transportation costs, etc.

We have also begun to get our silos back in working order. For example, the silos in Los Palis and Colladere are up and running. Without them, the peasants are forced to sell their harvest "in bloom" (i.e. they must agree on a sub-market price before harvest), but with this programme, they can sell at better prices. When we sell for them, we return the profits for the peasants. This is a way for them to get out of the cycle of exploitation. We want peasants to have control over their production.

(18) ALTERNATIVE DEVELOPMENT

New Internationalist, *Interview with Camille Chalmers*, 1996

Camille Chalmers is economics lecturer at the State University, former director of President Aristide's staff in 1993-4, and executive director of the Platform to Advocate for an Alternative Development (PAPDA).

Chalmers brings his considerable analytic skills to bear through PAPDA – a coalition of union and peasant organisations. He hopes to help establish a new consensus of resistance to the economic restructuring programme the IMF and the World Bank are trying to impose on Haiti. He refers to this package of savage social cuts, economic deflation and privatisation initiatives as a "second coup d'état". "The purpose of this coup is to expel the majority of Haitian people from the political arena and uphold a system wherein 50 per cent of the national wealth is gobbled up by just one per cent of the population."

With the sweeping use of his hands to aid him Chalmers picks apart the World Bank formula for Haiti. He is particularly incensed by the Bank's characterisation of the only hope for the rural peasant majority as a rural exodus to "some non-existent industrial sector, or else as boat people." [...]

With a quick grin and slow patience, Chalmers unravels the fallacies on which he believes that the World Bank model is based – the idea that the Haitian state is overdeveloped, that the country suffers from over-indebtedness, and that the salvation lies in low-wage industrial production underwritten by foreign capital. It is a familiar analysis: this set of remedies has been applied throughout Latin America with mixed results. Chalmers feels it to be particularly inappropriate for Haiti, where the government has never played much of a role in fostering development or meeting popular needs. He shudders at the Bank's proposal to cut the Haitian civil service by some 50 per cent, which will mean the death knell for even the most basic health and education services. He is incredulous about the Bank's predictions that spectacular growth in the export sector is likely and will solve basic problems of poverty and unemployment.

For Chalmers an alternative to the Bank plans cannot be formulated by technocrats but must grow out of popular organisations. PAPDA is working with a range of such groups together with critical economists to build the resistance to structural adjustment and work out alternative development priorities. He is heartened by the hostile response that IMF boss Michel Camdessus got in a recent visit to Haiti when the Upper House of the Haitian Parliament refused to meet him and the Lower House was openly sceptical about his structural-adjustment sales pitch...For him democracy is not just about the niceties of parliamentary procedures but a living force in the sun-drenched streets of Port-au-Prince's sprawling slum community, Cité Soleil. He worries about the de-politicisation of the people that may accompany their growing sense of betrayal as the Aristide leadership is drawn deeper into the US web of influence.

He places his hope and PAPDA's energy in a "re-dynamisation" of Haiti's popular movement. "It is popular mobilisation that has been the source of all the gains in recent years in Haiti. Without this mobilisation there is no hope of carrying out the basic tasks of development and democratic institution-building that the Haitian people both need and deserve."

(19) A PROGRAMME FOR RECOVERY

Lisa McGowan, *Democracy Undermined, Economic Justice Denied: Structural Adjustment and the Aid Juggernaut in Haiti,* 1997

The key elements of an alternative development path in Haiti, devised and articulated by a broad cross-section of civil society between 1994-6.

• Only by fundamentally changing the current configuration of international development assistance to Haiti and addressing the chronic imbalance of power and wealth that haunts Haitian society, can the country's poverty be effectively addressed. This implies not only a redistribution of resources within Haiti, but also a shift in the country's relationship to the world economy. Rather than providing cheap labour for that economy, for example, Haiti must direct its work force and resources in the first instance toward the production of locally consumed food and other goods.

• As advocated by several women's groups in Haiti, economic rights must be the basis of development. Without these rights, women, as well as their male counterparts, will continue to subsidize industrial production through poverty wages and other forms of exploitation.

• Haitian workers feel that foreign investment could provide an important source of employment in Haiti, but not if it is done at the expense of workers' rights. International Financial Institutions

(IFIs) should actively support Haitian workers' demands that foreign companies operating directly in Haiti or through subcontractors respect Haitian laws regarding minimum wages, working conditions, benefits, the right of Haitian workers to organize, and the right to negotiate a collective contract. Workers are also calling for an increase in the minimum wage to 75 gourdes, or US$4.90 a day.

• Direct and significant material and financial support to peasants and peasant associations, along with a land-reform program that distributes state lands plus other attendant policy measures, is needed immediately to assist them in rebuilding their capital base and increase food and export-crop production. The main goal of this assistance would be to strengthen food self-sufficiency in Haiti by both increasing the availability of food locally and decreasing the cost of food. This strategy implies a thorough understanding of the gender dimensions of food security and the need to explicitly address these dimensions in programs. Export-crop production in this schema is an important supplement to food production, but would not take precedence over it.

• The professional agronomists association (ANDAH) is calling for 25-30 percent tariffs on grains imported by Haiti as a means of "levelling the playing field" on which poor Haitian farmers are being forced to compete with their heavily subsidized competitors. Donor-financed food-aid programs should purchase locally produced food as a means of strengthening local food production and agricultural markets and lessening Haiti's dependence on imported food.

• Industrial-sector planning should valorize and strengthen local production, such as handicrafts. A long-term policy for the development of the Haitian craft sector that establishes and strengthens linkages with government programs in agriculture, environment, natural-resource management, education, tourism and commerce is badly needed and should be integrated with a larger national development strategy.

• To increase the amount of domestically available credit to peasants and small and informal-sector entrepreneurs, limits should be placed on the government's ability to borrow money from domestic sources. This might entail taking the banking system out of the control of the state (also a goal of the IFIs), though private banks should be required to make flexible, affordable credit available to these small producers across the country, if necessary through special programs. Capital shortfalls should be funded by international assistance, not on the backs of the poor through the imposition of excessive austerity measures.

• Economic policies that help create political stability through equitable growth, streamline business regulations and secure positive rates of interest on savings are a preferable means of attracting foreign investment rather than a policy of exploitative wages, tax holidays, excessive subsidies and preferential access to resources by the export sector, as is the case today. Immediate and substantial increases should be effected in health and education spending – some of which might be in the form of subsidies to private providers – such that services are increased and the cost to families decreased.

• While popular groups and NGOs agree with the Emergency Economic Recovery Programme (EERP) on the need to increase government revenues, they argue for the more equitable method of imposing and collecting progressive income and property taxes and more heavily taxing luxury imports rather than taxing such critical consumer items as food and fuel.

• The Haitian people are also calling for debt cancellation. They argue that the poor of Haiti should not be made to pay for the excesses of the Duvalier regime nor those of subsequent, non-democratic governments.

• In addition, popular groups support the rebuilding of their country's infrastructure, the rationalization of its economic system, greater government efficiency and less public corruption – all elements of the EERP – but they want this accomplished within the context of a larger, more effective, service-delivering state that is accountable to and addresses the needs and priorities of the people of Haiti, not foreign donors or investors.

(20) ANGER IN THE STREETS

Haiti Progrès, *Resurrection of the Popular Movement,* 1997

A Haitian weekly newpaper reports on the growing discontent with the policies of the Lavalas government and protests against the Prime Minister, Rosny Smarth. Smarth subsequently resigned later that year.

Black smoke billowed from a tangle of burning tires and an automobile carcass behind the young man from Cité Soleil. "The government acts as if it doesn't hear us," he shouted. Local popular organizations had thrown up several barricades on Route 1, the main artery to the north which skirts the giant Port-au-Prince slum, thereby blocking all traffic on the morning of Monday, January 13. "They are a bunch of opportunist thieves [*'gran manjè,'* literally 'big eaters']," he said. "They are filling their pockets and only care about them-selves. They used us young men from Cité Soleil as a stepping stone to get to where they are. We have always been the victims of all the [repressive] governments, always fighting for the Lavalas, but now they are going to lie and call us Macoutes... We are through with them, and we demand that [President René] Préval change his prime minister now."

The young man was expressing the sentiments of a movement which is growing like fire on a thatched roof. Throughout Haiti, popular organizations are re-emerging as Haiti's principal motor of social change, just as they were in the four years between the down-fall of Jean-Claude Duvalier in February 1986 and the election of former President Jean-Bertrand Aristide in December 1990. In a matter of weeks, and after less than a year in power, the Préval gov-ernment is faced with a nation-wide mobilization demanding the resignation of Prime Minister Rosny Smarth and a new political di-rection. "We want a new prime minister who can offer something better to the youth of the country, so everybody can go to school, find jobs, and have a break from the climate of terror and violence," explained the young man on the Cité Soleil barricade. "We want a change in the country," [...]

The events of January 13 were spurred by a day of confrontations on January 9 when demonstrations and road-blocks occurred in Gonaïves, Pont Sondé, Villard, L'Estère, and Tabarre. In several cases, police clashed with demonstrators but nowhere more dramatically than in Port-au-Prince. About 100 were demonstrating peacefully in front of the National Palace when the US-trained Rapid Reaction Force of the Haitian National Police (PNH) arrived on the scene. Dressed in black riot gear, the cops fired tear-gas and concussion grenades into the crowd. One grenade blew off the hand and dam-aged the ear of Dieuseul Civil, 23, a member of the Collective,[1] who was taken to the General Hospital. Police claim that the grenade exploded when Civil attempted to hurl it back at the officers. But other witnesses and the Collective say that the grenade hit Civil's hand when fired by police. Four other people were also wounded.

[1] The Collective to Mobilise against the IMF led protests against the government's economic policy in 1996-7.

CHAPTER SIX
REFUGEES AND THE DIASPORA

Africans were brought to the French Caribbean colony of Saint-Domingue as slaves in the eighteenth century, their descendants occupied the empty lands of independent Haiti in the nineteenth century, and, in the twentieth century, Haitians have been on the move again. Although it is only since the 1970s, when the poor and the persecuted began to flee across the sea towards the United States, that Haitians have been disparagingly labelled 'boat people' by North Americans, migration has always been an essential part of the Haitian experience. (1)

Throughout the twentieth century, huge numbers of Haitians have left their country, either as political exiles, or in search of work and a better standard of living. At the end of the millennium, there are perhaps as many as two million Haitians and children of Haitian migrants living outside the country. This Haitian 'diaspora', spread not only throughout the Caribbean region but also across the continents of Africa, Europe, and the Americas, is a phenomenon that links Haiti to the rest of the world, and the rest of the world to Haiti.

The first phase of mass migration from Haiti began in the early years of the twentieth century when the combination of a growing population and the dwindling availability of cultivable land stimulated an exodus of unskilled labour to the burgeoning sugar-cane industries of Cuba and the neighbouring Dominican Republic. Between 1915 and 1929, over half a million Haitians, out of a total population of approximately two million, travelled to those countries to work as cane cutters

Haitian migration to Cuba was often officially sanctioned and organised, and the migrant workers suffered exploitation at the hands of corrupt officials in both countries. (2) With the world-wide depression in the 1930s reducing the demand for this cheap labour, tens of thousands of Haitian immigrants were repatriated from Cuba, and this chapter of Haitian emigration came to an end. However, thousands of Haitians stayed on in Cuba and established a significant presence there, particularly in the east of the country. As of 1997 there were an estimated 200,000 Cubans of Haitian descent.

As was the case in Cuba, the early period of Haitian migration to the Dominican Republic was intrinsically linked to the rapid expansion of the sugar industry. While the United States occupied both Haiti (1915-34) and the Dominican Republic (1916-25), American-owned sugar companies in the latter came to depend on Haitian labour. Although Haitian cane cutters were generally employed on a temporary basis for the duration of the harvest and then sent home, by the 1930s, growing numbers of Haitian immigrants had taken up permanent residence on the eastern side of the border. In 1937, the Dominican nationalist dictator, Rafael Trujillo, brutally reinforced Dominican sovereignty over the border regions by ordering a massacre that claimed the lives of between a quarter and a half of the approximately 50,000 Haitians living in the Dominican Republic. Many accounts of this bloody orgy of killing focus on the fate of those slaughtered at the Massacre River dividing the two countries in the north, but the pogrom claimed victims all along the Dominican side of the border. (3)

In response to international denunciations of the massacre, Trujillo launched a racist campaign against Haitians to justify his actions to the Dominican public. He and his supporters cited fears of a *de facto* Haitian invasion, and played on the legacy of Haiti's attempts to annex the eastern part of the island in the nineteenth century. Anti-Haitian propaganda, sustained by the Trujillo regime and that of his successor, Joaquín Balaguer, has continued to sour relations between the two peoples.

Despite the tensions, large numbers of Haitians have continued to migrate across the long porous border between the two countries to meet the demand for low paid and compliant labour in the Dominican Republic. While the 1937 massacre depleted the Haitian immigrant population, within a short time their numbers began to swell as poor Haitians from rural areas crossed the border in search of employment. Haitian migrants found work not only on the sugar plantations, but also in other sectors of agriculture, harvesting rice, coffee and tobacco, and as labourers in the construction industry. One authority estimated that the number of Haitians living in the Dominican Republic was approximately 20,000 in 1950, increasing to 30,000 by 1960, 100,000 by 1970, and 200,000 by 1980. By the early 1990s, there were as many as half a million. Such estimates are however speculative as most of this migration has been unregulated. There are even many Haitian families that have been living in the Dominican Republic for several generations but who are not officially registered or recognised as citizens.

As the vast majority of Haitians in the Dominican Republic do not have official papers legitimising their presence in the country, they are vulnerable to a whole range of abuses at the hands of their employers and the security forces. Unable to claim the rights accorded to Dominican citizens, and subject to the continual threat of deportation, Haitians generally experience extremely low pay and bad working conditions. At the workplace they are generally not unionised, and can be dismissed without pay, or forcibly transferred from one work place to another. On the street or in their homes, Haitians are vulnerable to 'arrest' by Dominican soldiers and police who frequently rob them of their belongings before deporting them or transporting them to a new workplace. (4)

On many occasions Haitian nationals living in the Dominican Republic have been subject to mass deportations, ordered by the Dominican authorities in the interests of domestic or international politics. For example, in 1991 President Balaguer ordered the forcible repatriation of 8,000 Haitian sugar-cane workers in response to criticisms of their poor treatment by Haitian President Aristide, and international human rights organisations.

The plight of the Haitian cane cutters first came to international attention in the early 1980s when a campaigning journalist wrote a graphic account of the abysmal conditions experienced by Haitians living on the plantation compounds – the *bateyes*. (5) The back-breaking and badly paid work harvesting sugar-cane has traditionally been carried out by a Haitian workforce, approximately half of it composed of Haitians living permanently in the Dominican Republic, with the rest being contracted from Haiti on a temporary basis for the duration of the harvest. Beginning in 1952, and continuing throughout the Duvalier era, a series of five-year bilateral agreements established that each year the Haitian government would provide between 15-19,000 temporary cane cutters. In return for what were described as the costs of assembling and then transporting the workers to the border, the Dominican government paid their Haitian counterpart annual sums of between one and three million US dollars. This trade in human labour bolstered the coffers of the Duvalier regimes, and underwrote the profitability of Dominican sugar. The arrangement was renegotiated in 1966 following the nationalisàtion of the Dominican sugar industry, and continued until the collapse of the Jean-Claude Duvalier regime in 1986.

International concerns about the existence of a modern form of slavery on the Dominican sugar plantations prompted the despatch of an International Labour Organisation delegation to the Dominican Republic in 1983. Their report confirmed the poor conditions, and detailed the extremely low wage levels paid by the State Sugar Council. (6) Despite some reforms implemented in the early 1990s, including a law allowing the unionisation of cane cutters, the situation for Haitians on the bateyes remains dire.

While migration across the border by foot to the Dominican Republic long ago became an established option for the poorest Haitians, after the Second World War a second phase of migration to other countries in the region began. Haitians, similarly frustrated by a lack of a livelihood, but able to raise the necessary money, paid for boat or plane trips to destinations throughout the Caribbean region. Large communities of Haitians have assembled in the Bahamas, and in the French departments of Guadeloupe, Martinique and Guyane. There are also smaller pockets of Haitians in Mexico, Colombia and Venezuela.

During the late 1950s and 1960s, the rapid development of the tourism industry in the Bahamas created employment opportunities for large numbers of Haitians who found work as construction labourers, or as cooks, gardeners and servants for upwardly mobile Bahamians. (7) The vast majority entered as illegal immigrants making it difficult to establish a clear picture of the extent of Haitian migration to the Bahamas, although in the 1980s it was estimated that out of a total population of 240,000, some 40,000 were Haitian. Following a downturn in the economy beginning in the 1970s, the welcome formerly accorded to the Haitian immigrants turned to resentment, and the Bahamian authorities have periodically carried out round-ups and deportations.

By contrast, during the 1970s when the French Caribbean departments were also experiencing economic difficulties and an unemployment rate of more than 25 per cent, thousands of Haitians were brought in to work, primarily in the sugar and banana industries. The French authorities granted three-month work permits, but most Haitians stayed on, so that by 1980 there were at least 30,000 Haitian immigrants. Some 10,000 of them were on the island of Guadeloupe, where their presence was used to undercut the wage demands of local unions. (8)

Large-scale migration to destinations further afield also began in the 1950s. At first those leaving in search of a better standard of living abroad were Haitians from the educated upper and middle classes. Skilled and professional men and women, such as doctors, lawyers, teachers, and engineers, took their expertise to the North American cities of Montreal, New York, Chicago and Boston, or found administrative jobs in emerging nations, particularly in Africa. With the advent of the Duvalier dictatorship in 1957, this 'brain-drain' grew in size as the traditional elite found itself frozen out of positions within the government, and members of all non-Duvalierist organisations faced repression and harassment. The extent of the professional exodus is illustrated by two facts: in one year in the mid-1960s over half of the graduates from the Port-au-Prince University teacher training college took jobs in the Congo; and, of the 264 medical graduates between 1957 and 1963, only three remained in Haiti. It is an oft-repeated statistic that there are more Haitian doctors in Montreal, Canada, than there are in Haiti. During the 1960s, semi-skilled Haitians from the middle and lower urban classes also left for North America in large numbers. Between 1956 and 1985 US governments issued over one million entry visas to Haitians, and an estimated 50 per cent of them overstayed their permitted time limit in the hope of establishing permanent residence.

When, in 1972, a number of boatloads of Haitians arrived in Florida, thus proving that the sea-borne route to the United States was a viable possibility, a new phase of migration began. Poorer Haitians who could not afford exit visas or air fares but could, by selling their possessions or land, raise the amount charged by boat captains for the 700-mile trip to Florida began leaving in large numbers – the 'boat people' phenomenon was born. Deepening poverty and political repression, which continued under the regime of Jean-Claude Duvalier, fed the exodus. (9) The boat people departed primarily from the north and north west of Haiti. They paid for a space on large cargo vessels whose owners established a lucrative trade, or, if they could not afford the fee, attempted the perilous voyage huddled together on small fishing boats. During the 1970s between 50,000 and 80,000 boat people arrived without authorisation in Florida. Many of them travelled first to the Bahamas, and then moved on to the US after the Bahamian authorities began a crackdown on illegal immigrants.

In 1981, with up to 1,000 Haitian boat people arriving in Florida each month, the US concluded an interdiction agreement with the Duvalier regime that permitted the US Coast Guard to intercept Haitian vessels and return 'irregular' migrants to Haiti. The interceptions and forcible repatriations by the US Coast Guard achieved the desired effect of reducing the numbers leaving Haiti by boat, but still thousands attempted to beat the blockade. Over a ten-year period some 23,000 Haitians were interdicted and sent back. Thousands more, told that they had arrived on US soil by the trip organisers, were prematurely put ashore on remote islands in the Turks and Caicos and the Bahamas. Unknown numbers died as overcrowded and leaky boats sank, while others were simply thrown overboard by the crew.

Despite the campaigns of refugee advocates who highlighted the catalogue of human rights violations attributed to the Duvaliers, in the eyes of the US immigration authorities the boat people were economic rather than political refugees, and therefore did not qualify for asylum. Among the Haitian population resident in North America, the boat peoples' desperate attempts to escape from economic misery and political violence made the issue a *cause célèbre*. Protests against the way the boat people were treated featured in the disapora press and in the songs of emigré Haitian musicians. (10)

With the overwhelming election victory of President Aristide in 1990, and the expectation that, with the demise of military rule and the advent of democratic government, the lot of the poor majority would improve, the number of boat people leaving Haiti dwindled. This correlation between the political situation and the boat people exodus was starkly underlined when during the year following the coup some 37,000 Haitians were interdicted. Although the US administration of President Bush tightened the procedure so that all those intercepted would be returned without even a cursory screening to establish their eligibility for political asylum, the boat people kept leaving. The contrast between US policies, which rejected fleeing Haitians but admitted Cubans attempting to escape from Castro's Communist regime, was pronounced. (11)

During the three-year long period of military rule in Haiti, thousands of Haitians took to the seas. Most hoped to reach the United States, but few made it past the flotilla of US craft deployed to block their passage. Many ended up in the nearby islands of the Turks and Caicos and the Bahamas, while smaller numbers drifted off course to land in Cuba and Jamaica. By mid-1994, as a United Nations economic embargo eroded living standards in Haiti still further, as political repression intensified and as hopes of return to democracy evaporated, a new wave of departures by boat threatened to overwhelm the US Coast Guard. (12) As a stop-gap measure the US opened a holding camp at their military base at Guantánamo, Cuba, which was soon filled with 20,000 Haitians.

In the view of many analysts, the seemingly insoluble problem of the Haitian boat people was one of the main reasons for the US-led military intervention in Haiti in September 1994. With the re-establishment of democratic government in Haiti, a new chapter in the long story of the Haitian refugees began. The US repatriated the Haitians interned at Guantánamo, and other countries in the Caribbean region followed suit by starting to send back longer-term immigrants as well as recent arrivals. (13)

The repatriation programmes underline the uncertain status of thousands of Haitians who have left their country over the past decades. The typical pattern is one of host countries at first welcoming Haitians prepared to work hard for low pay when unskilled and menial jobs are plentiful, but then, in times of economic hardship, the migrants are quickly made 'scapegoats', and accused of taking jobs, depressing wages and putting an intolerable strain on social services.

By far the largest component of the Haitian diaspora, over one million people, live in North America, with the three main communities located in the metropolitan area of New York, in south and east Florida, and in Montreal, Canada. Composed of Haitians from every sector and class, these communities are far from homogenous, and divisions between older and newer immigrants have been commonplace. For example, in New York, upper-class Haitians who began arriving in the 1950s, live in the boroughs of Queens, Manhattan and Long Island, and are quick to distinguish and distance themselves from the newer, and poorer immigrants who have tended to settle in Brooklyn. Yet Haitian immigrants from all social backgrounds have had to deal with an established anti-Haitian prejudice in the US as well as the more recent stigmas associated with the arrival of the boat people, and the erroneous association between Haitians and the spread of the HIV/AIDS virus. (14)

The boat people coming ashore in the Florida faced an array of difficulties. Often arriving without money, or language skills, frequently illiterate and unskilled, they have had to forge an existence in the twilight world of the illegal immigrant – a problematic status that has been inherited by their children. (15)

In the face of an often hostile reception in their adopted homeland, and sharing a common opposition to the Duvaliers and the military regimes that succeeded them, Haitian exiles in the US have maintained strong links with the mother country. An enduring commitment to Haitian politics and culture among exiles living in New York was illustrated by the numerous large demonstrations in support of democracy in Haiti during the 1991-4 military coup regime, and the existence of Vodou houses. (16) In a more general sense, the diaspora has exerted an important influence in Haiti through the practice of sending remittances to relatives at home. During the 1990s it was estimated that as much as US$300 million were sent back to Haiti from the North American diaspora each year, a considerable sum that does much to sustain the stricken Haitian economy.

Many in the Haitian-American community have regarded their residence in the US as temporary, imagining that once the political problems in Haiti were resolved they would return. However, there are signs that this belief may be undergoing a significant change in the face of a growing realisation that the return of democratic government in 1994 has not brought the anticipated improvements. (17) At the same time, a second-generation, born of Haitian migrants or arriving in North America as children, has reached adulthood, and these young Haitian-Americans are noticeably more self-confident and publicly proud of their Haitian roots than their parents. This new mood is both expressed and reinforced by the commercial success enjoyed by the artist, Jean-Michel Basquiat, the writer Edwidge Danticat, and the rap music group, the Fugees. (18)

(1) A HISTORY OF MIGRATION

Félix Morisseau-Leroy, *Boat People,* 1991

A Haitian poet recalls that his countrymen have been sea-borne migrants since they were transported from Africa as slaves. In the context of the derogatory labelling of Haitians in the US as 'boat people', he reclaims the term, and attempts to set the record straight about the Haitian migratory experience.

> We are all in a drowning boat
> Happened before at St Domingue
> We are the ones called boat people.
>
> We all died long ago
> What else can frighten us?
> Let them call us boat people
>
> We fight a long time with poverty
> On our islands, the sea, everywhere
> We never say we are not boat people
>
> In Africa they chase us with dogs
> Chained our feet, embark us
> Who then called us boat people?
>
> Half the cargo perished
> The rest sold at Bossal Market[1]
> It's them that call us boat people
>
> We stamp our feet down, the earth shakes
> Up to Louisiana, down to Venezuela[2]
> Who would come and call us boat people?
>
> A bad season in our country
> The hungry dog eats thorns
> They didn't call us boat people yet
>
> We looked for jobs and freedom
> And they piled us on again: Cargo — direct to Miami
> They start to call us boat people
>
> We run from the rain at Fort Dimanche[3]
> But land in the river at Krome[4]
> It's them that call us boat people

Miami heat eats away our hearts
Chicago cold explodes our stomach
Boat people boat people boat people

Except for the Indians -
All Americans are immigrants
But it's us they call boat people

We don't bring drugs in our bags
But courage and strength to work
Boat people – Yes, that's alright, boat people

We don't come to make trouble
We come with all respect
It's them who call us boat people

We have no need to yell or scream
But all boat people are equal, the same
All boat people are boat people

One day we'll stand up, put down our feet
As we did at St Domingue
They'll know who are boat people

That day, be it Christopher Columbus
Or Henry Kissinger – They will know
Whom we ourselves call boat people

[1] The market where newly arrived slaves from Africa were put on sale in colonial Saint-Domingue.

[2] The ramifications of the Haitian revolution were felt in Louisiana, sold to the United States by Napoleon in 1803 after the failure to reconquer Haiti, and in Venezuela, freed from Spanish colonial rule by Simón Bolívar with Haitian assistance.

[3] The 'rain at Fort Dimanche' is a reference to the machine gun fire directed at protestors by Duvalierist forces at the infamous Fort Dimanche prison in April 1986.

[4] Krome is the immigrant detention centre in Miami, Florida, where many Haitian boat people were incarcerated before being deported.

2) THE LURE OF CUBA

Brenda Gayle Plummer, *Haitian Migrants and Backyard Imperialism*, 1985

From 1902, Haitians began leaving for Cuba's expanding sugar economy. Driven by a declining agricultural sector at home and the prospect of higher wages abroad, by 1916, 20,000 Haitians were travelling to find work in Cuba each year.

Haitian labourers in Cuba worked hard for little money. The dollar a day they could make in some Cuban fields surpassed the fifteen cents a day at home. Haitian justices of the peace, consuls and other functionaries laid away far greater sums, made by selling passports and collecting fees from workers. Even some veteran canecutters went into the business of labour recruitment.

Yet emigration did not please everyone. Some officials and upper class elements saw in the exodus the possibility of losing control over the rural masses. Travel and self-improvement had been prerogatives of the rich, and the newly rising expectations could prove subversive...The First World War temporarily overshadowed these concerns. Renewed demand boosted sugar production in Cuba and the Dominican Republic, which opened their doors to aliens on a massive scale to get the labour the plantations required. Consuls, customs officials and recruiters shared in the resultant profits...

The war's end, a steady supply of workers and the utter powerlessness of Haiti under US rule meant no particular care had to be taken of migrant welfare. The US claimed it had no jurisdiction over labour traffic, despite its complete authority over most aspects of Haitian civil life. Haitian officials remained generally indifferent to the worker's plight and, in any case, unable to help them. Some of them only cared about their share of the profits on each labourer shipped out.

Labourers were carefully documented so that recruiters and consuls could collect their fees. Migrants paid the cost of their own tickets, permits and visas. Labour organisers advanced the cash, and later subtracted it from workers' wages, or held mortgages on the migrants' farms in Haiti. The exploitative middlemen, the transport to the plantations on foul, densely packed ships and the backbreaking labour earned the labour recruitment business the nickname of 'the slave trade'.

Once at work, Haitians found themselves the victims of diverse abuse, which included physical assault by Cuban militia. Fraud accompanied violence, as informers, pimps and thieves preyed on the newcomers. Behind the criminal element stood the circle of compliant officials and the sugar companies which profited from cheap, demoralised labour. The vicious atmosphere in the Cuban fields retarded the development of protest and organisation among workers.

Conditions changed in the Caribbean economy by the late 1920s. Signs of weakness in the Cuban sugar industry were apparent, and as the world economic crisis intensified, Cuba expelled Haitians from every port. Each harvest witnesses the employment of fewer workers.

(3) THE MASSACRE

Rénald Clérismé, *Relations of Production in the Dominican Coffee Economy,* 1996

The interviewee, Titi Nana, is the son of Haitian parents living in El Fondo in the border region in the south of the Dominican Republic. He was seventeen years old in 1937 when security forces carried out the massacre of as many as 25,000 Haitian-Dominicans and Haitians living on Dominican territory.

Titi was very reluctant to give me an interview about the massacre. I went to his place three times over a period of four months without success. Finally one day when he was in a good mood, after returning from his nearby garden, he agreed to talk.

It was around three in the afternoon. Titi was sitting on a piece of wood among the debris of pots and pans scattered in a room six feet wide by seven feet long that serves as both bedroom and kitchen. Titi told me what he remembered of the massacre. He told his story in a half-joking half-dramatic way to disguise his pain. His account alone may underscore the gravity of the event in the Barahona region. He remembered that a few days before the massacre, the assistant mayor of El Fondo warned one of his Haitian neighbours to leave the mountains because life might become difficult for Haitians of the region. The Haitian did not care. He was murdered a few weeks later in the massacre. Dominicans took over his land.

The massacre started in October, Titi recalled, in the middle of coffee harvest period. Many Haitians engaged in harvesting coffee died. Only those who took refuge in the American-owned Barahona Sugar Company were spared.

Titi recounts how a wealthy Haitian by the name of Zaboka escaped to the Sugar Company leaving behind him pigs, cows, chickens and lots of vegetables. He was advised not to come back. A few days after he left, thinking that the massacre was over, he returned to his property in search of a pig to eat with his family. He was killed on his own estate.

Titi went on to recount that the Dominican *guardia* was killing all across *la loma* during a month-long period of killing Haitians. A Haitian father of two lovely daughters was offered life in exchange for his daughters, while two of his neighbours were to die. He refused the deal saying, "Either you spare my neighbours or you kill me along with them." *La guardia* killed all of them. [...]

(He) went on to explain how the massacre affected the lives of Haitians and shaped their identity in the border region. They lost all their wealth. They became suspicious and felt hatred towards the Dominicans who had taken away their estates. They felt outraged to come back as *jornaleros* on their former estates.

(4) NON-CITIZENS IN THE DOMINICAN REPUBLIC

National Coalition for Haitian Rights, *Beyond the Bateyes,* 1996

Haitians living and working in the Dominican Republic are periodically rounded-up and deported by the authorities.

Haitians (and Dominicans of Haitian descent) have always been subject to deportation at the whim of the army and the national police. In addition, they face repatriation for economic reasons, as the victims of powerful landowners, CEA [1] managers and construction companies who utilise the army and the police to deport Haitian workers in lieu of paying them the compensation they are owed. [...]

The odyssey of Pierre, a 48-year old cane cutter, is typical. He lived in the Dominican Republic for many years with his wife and seven children, cutting cane at Batey Gotuel near Santo Domingo. He was picked up by soldiers while walking in Santo Domingo with one of his children. The two were held in an outdoor detention pen for six days before being transported to the border crossing at Jimaní. They were again placed in a detention area, this time for two days, to await the arrival of additional Haitians. They were then deported with a large group and went to their hometown of Bon Repos, near

Port-au-Prince. The rest of the family sold all of its belongings in Santo Domingo and joined them eight days later. After two months without work in Haiti, they returned to the Dominican Republic, crossing on foot at Pedernales, an isolated border village. He found work and lodging on a private Dominican farm, but was subsequently picked up by the Dominican army and forcibly taken with his family to cut cane at a CEA mill. [...]

The Dominican army and national police traditionally have carried out arbitrary round-ups of "Haitian-looking" individuals to provide coerced labour for the sugar industry at the beginning of the harvest (normally in December) and to deport Haitians in the weeks immediately following the end of the harvest season (usually April or May) when the demand for labour declines. The pattern of abuse characteristic of the army round-up has been institutionalised: indiscriminate arrests, verbal and physical mistreatment, arbitrary confiscation and destruction of identification documents; theft of personal belongings; and the refusal to allow those rounded-up to notify family or friends before being transported to a sugar mill or deported...In April 1994, for example, the Dominican press reported on a series of round-ups conducted by the army and the national police in Santiago, the major city in the north-east of the country. Dominican security forces would arrive in a section of the city in large trucks and jeeps, detain anyone with black skin and, if the soldiers believed them to be Haitian, force them into trucks for immediate deportation at the border town of Dajabón.

[1] Consejo Estatal de Azúcar (CEA) is the nationalised Dominican State Sugar Council

(5) LIFE IN THE BATEYES

Maurice Lemoine, *Bitter Sugar,* 1981

Every year thousands of Haitians travel to the Dominican Republic to work as cane cutters during the sugar harvest. The labourers, known as *kongos* if they have recently arrived, or as *viejos* if they have worked on the harvest before, live in camps on the plantations – the notorious *bateyes*.

The sky was undulating in gloomy whorls, swept along by a nasty wind. It had rained. The batey, disgraceful human cesspool, foul blister of despair, was decomposing, lost in the dripping immensity of the cane. The miserable huts were huddled against one another along alleys transformed into sewers. You could hear fits of coughing. It would be cold that night. Kongos with vacant eyes were trying to light fires for the evening meal on the bare, mirey ground turned into a swamp by the rain. Others were working barefoot in the mud. They were coming out of the plantation, their faces ravaged, their clothes soaked, going along silently, expressions stamped with a painful dignity. Those with a pay slip in hand went to the bodega. Those without went to bed with nothing, or else gathered their last bit of strength to go and pound a few pieces of cane. They drank the cane juice down to the last drop. Others were passing silently like zombies. Near an open door a woman rubbed the skinny body of her child with a mechanical gesture.

An insistent odour was lurking around two cells curtained by a few rags. A broth of excrement was gently overflowing the camp latrine. An exhausted viejo swore with lassitude, went to shit far into the cane, holding his belly. Another, overcome with dysentery, brutally emptied himself into his barracon. No doctor, no clinic, no clergyman, no union. No money, no food. Their only relations were with the cane, the horses, the oxen, the bosses, living completely isolated – with no radio, no newspapers, no nothing. They felt very dirty, they who had been so clean in Haiti. Poverty and filth don't necessarily go hand in hand. They could go a week without bathing. The river was far, they didn't have the time, they didn't have the strength. At night, they scraped the mud and their skin off with the machete blade... In the evening, after their sorry homecoming, they talked about their conditions of existence and went to sleep... They didn't have leisure time. They got up too early, were much too exhausted... Sometimes they were so hungry they couldn't even speak. When you have gone two or three days without eating, drinking only water or cane juice, you can no longer even speak. You can stew, but you can't speak...

They dragged themselves around, destroyed by fatigue, crippled by humiliation, without joy, without laughter, without identity, completely alienated.

(6) MODERN SLAVERY

Paul Latortue, *Neo-slavery in the Cane Fields: Haitians in the Dominican Republic,* 1985

In January 1983, the International Labour Organisation sent a commission of enquiry to investigate the working conditions of Haitian migrant workers in the Dominican Republic's sugar industry.

D ominican Republic law fixes the agricultural minimum wage at 3.50 pesos a day. The migrants do not make this bare minimum, the wages of cane cutters not exceeding 2 pesos a day for at least 12 hours' work. The government of the Dominican Republic claims that cane cutters are paid according to output and thus are not subject to the minimum wage laws. One of the most widely mentioned abuses is the weighing system. Most workers complain that the weight of cane cut and loaded is understated by officials at the mills. The trade unions state that their representatives are not permitted to oversee the weighing process. They believe that the weighers make deductions, at times to benefit the plantation and at times for their own benefit.

The sugar mill cashes the workers' tickets every two weeks. Since most cane cutters can't wait that long, wage tickets become negotiable instruments that can be cashed at discount at the food store. If we assume that the store owner receives tickets every day and has to wait for one week, on the average to cash them, we must conclude that he is lending money to migrants at a rate of interest equal to 520 per cent a year.

The cane cutters do not receive daily a wage ticket for the full rate of 1.83 peso per metric ton of cane cut and loaded. This amount is divided in two parts: a wage ticket for $1.35 p. and a voucher of 0.50 p. payable upon departure to Haiti at the end of harvest time. Curiously this 50c voucher is called an "incentive". Unlike the wage tickets, the voucher is not negotiable. Migrants complained that the vouchers were valueless and they could not be cashed upon departure to Haiti. The commission concluded that the allegation of non-receipt was well-founded. The government of the Dominican Republic showed proof of payments made to the Haitian Embassy in Santo Domingo to cover the "incentive" costs. However these payments were made well after the end of the harvest and the departure of the migrants. There appeared to be corruption on both sides.

The migrants work at least 12 hours a day without stopping for meal. They had rest days but not according to any regular schedule, but only when the management stopped them from working because of operational needs. These long hours are related to the very low wage received: an increase in wages could induce workers to put in fewer hours. The mills probably know this and do their utmost to avoid measures that are both costly and diminish their labour supply. Obviously this is a no-win situation for the migrants unless the entire system is put down. One could hardly imagine longer hours of work under slavery.

(7) THE BAHAMAS CONNECTION

P. Anthony White, *One Haitian in the Hand and Two in the Bush,* 1994

For several decades the Bahamas underwent an economic boom, and as this Bahamian newspaper columnist remembers, Haitian immigrants were welcomed as cheap labour. But by the 1990s, with the boom over and thousands more refugees arriving from Haiti, attitudes towards them changed.

As late as the 1970s on the cocktail circuit, quite a number of Bahamian pseudo-socialites used to boast about their "French maid", or about how loyal "my Haitian" is. The acquisition and maintenance of one or more Haitian helpers was considered a step above, especially by the black bourgeoisie. Some even dressed up the Haitian drivers in caps and bow ties and insisted they accompany the master to the saloon where the Haitian would sit quietly observing from a stool near the door, lest someone should look upon their master with anything except friendliness.

On many a Saturday morning friends would "lend" their Haitians to others to do yard work, to paint fences, or to perform any other necessary chores, with the understanding that whilst the borrower may tip the fellow, the day's wages were already paid by the lender. In some households there was more than one Haitian connection, with a maid inside, a gardener/handyman outside, and an itinerant craftsman who would come once a month or so to touch up the paint on the outside mouldings of the house. Invariably those were the homes of upper-grade civil servants. It is perhaps safe to say that at all times 50 percent of the Haitian workers were on the job illegally.

They used to tell the story of a senior police officer who lived out east, and would hire a few Haitians to weed the yard, paint the outside of the house, wash the cars and even wash the dogs. At the end of the day when it came to dole out the wages, the officer would go inside the house, don his uniform, complete with cap and swagger-stick, and step briskly onto the front lawn. The poor illegal Haitians, caught in the vice of fright at the sight of Bahamian authority, would dash across the street into the woods and be never seen again... [...]

Twenty years later, the problem that had been considered no problem at all has escalated into a calamitous conspiracy of human rights, sovereignty, national security, foreign relations, public relations and a potential souring of the milk of human kindness. The Prime Minister noted this week that the number of illegal immigrants presently in the country is too high and uncontrollable, and that a great effort is being made to ensure that there is no increase in that number. The lion's share of that number are the Haitians in the community.

Not the Haitians of the 1970s who took to the bushes at the sight of a uniform, but the hundreds and thousands who have slipped ashore in the dark of many a night, and who are still filtering into the system even while new arrangements are afoot to repatriate others to their homeland... [...]

If you've been close to a Haitian individual and have become accustomed to their fierce loyalty, implicit fidelity, and unquestioning performance of assigned tasks, you will have a problem with a question of massive repatriation...It will also stir some silent rage in the hearts of the many Bahamians of Haitian heritage, or others who have entered into marital bonds or sweet-love relationships with Haitian nationals in this country. But at some point somebody has got to bite the bullet and try somehow to unravel the problem.

(8) INVISIBLE WORKERS

Laënnec Hurbon, *Le Migration haïtienne en Guadeloupe,* 1982

In the French Caribbean overseas department of Guadeloupe, large numbers of Haitian workers were allowed in to work in the sugar and banana industries from 1974 onwards. By 1980, the total number was estimated to be in the region of 10,000.

Preoccupied with surviving in the country for as long as possible, Haitian workers seemed not to question their contribution to Guadeloupe's economy. The inevitable comparison with his own country tends to blur the immigrant's vision when it comes to the reality of living and working conditions in the host country. Labour costs in Guadeloupe were ten times higher than in Haiti. On this basis, the Haitian worker automatically turned his back on any involvement with the unions, seeing them as their foremost enemy. The overriding need to find work was such that his ignorance of social mores and political structures seemed almost intentional. An examination of the consequences of this attitude would have amounted to useless and unnecessary speculation, as far as he was concerned. Finding a job and (any) salary was already a luxury, a dream come true. But it was precisely this situation which was to prove such a godsend to owners of both small and large businesses who were already experiencing difficulties as a result of the wages demanded by the various unions.

Haitian migration gave Guadeloupe's economy a breathing space. It slowed down the rise in labour costs, largely replacing a Guadeloupian work-force reluctant to return to working in the service industries, and disinclined to accept poorly paid jobs like cane-cutting or work on the banana plantations: always prepared, too, to emigrate to France when the going got tough.

In fact, the big cane and sugar planters were the first to find sound allies amongst the Haitian workers who did not know about calculating their working hours or demanding wage increases, let alone social security. Certain planters therefore made use of agents whose job was to "collect" groups of Haitians from the roadsides at dawn and take them to work on the banana plantations. Sometimes the owner would even lodge the Haitians in an on-site hut, so that the colonial/feudal relationship, somewhat eroded today, was unexpectedly resurrected.

On the other hand, there were few small-time plantation owners and building contractors, faced with the stiff competition, who could ultimately do without cheap Haitian labour, despite their own obligatory protests against the employment of Haitians by the big company owners. If all the Haitian workers had left Guadeloupe at the same time it would have spelt disaster for the small planters and contractors.

Translated from French by Emily Dunbar

(9) POVERTY AND PERSECUTION

Josh DeWind and David Kinley, *Aiding Migration,* 1988

Interviewed by US immigration officials, most migrants leaving Haiti by boat cited poverty and persecution as the explanations for their decision to leave.

François was 31 year old cultivator in a small village in the South when he ventured in a small and precarious sail boat to Miami with 195 other men and women. He, his common-law wife, and his daughter had made their living from a number of animals, including a cow, several goats, and a flock of hens, and from the coffee, potatoes, bananas, manioc, corn, and sugar cane which they raised on a *caro* (3.2 acres) of land. Although he owned more land than 80 percent of other landholders in Haiti, François saw that everyone was leaving the area and decided to leave as he could see no future for himself or his family in Haiti and felt as though he was accomplishing nothing. As he put it, "I don't have any money to work my land. I can't offer my child any future. Why should I want to stay?"

• Merlien's father, who had supported Déjoie for president against Duvalier, was abducted by Macoutes in 1964 and was never seen again. Her mother died in a hospital reportedly after being denied medicines on orders from Port-au-Prince. After Merlien told classmates she would like to shoot Duvalier for what he had done to her parents, the Macoutes came for her at her home. Merlien managed to flee by boat to the Bahamas. She returned to care for a sick aunt in 1977 after being assured by the Haitian consul that she would have no problems in Haiti. On arrival at Port-au-Prince airport, Merlien was arrested and imprisoned. Told that her father had supported Déjoie and that God had sent her "so that justice could be done," she was beaten until she lost consciousness every morning and evening for six days. Her cell was too small to lie down and she was given neither food nor water. Finally she was put on a plane to the Bahamas.

• Julie, age 56, had been a prosperous wholesaler in Port-au-Prince before she was forced to flee. Earning $300 per month, she was able to pay for children's education, build a house in the fashionable Soudalle neighbourhood, and save $100 monthly. When she tried to collect debts totalling $535 owed her by two Tontons Macoutes, they planned with two others to kill her. One member of the plot warned Julie' brother, who was then an army officer. Julie fled to Port de Paix and hid for three months until she managed to go by boat to Miami. Subsequently, her brother was murdered by Macoutes, one son was imprisoned for two years, and as of 1980, two other sons continue to hide in a small town in Haiti.

(10) THE VIEW FROM MIAMI

Magnum Band, *Liberty,* 1982

The plight of the boat people was taken up by Haitian artists in the disapora. In the lyrics of this song by a compas band based in Miami, the songwriter, Dadou Pasquet, contrasts his privileged situation in the United States with that of the boat people.

> *Chans pou mwen m pati depi lè m te toupi*
> I was lucky to leave when I was very young
>
> *M pa janm gen nesesite pou m te pwan kante*
> I never had to take a small boat
>
> *Kwak se lè m gade sa frè m yo ap pase*
> When I see what's happening to my brothers
>
> *Se zantray mwen fè mwen mal jistan m kriye...*
> My insides ache until I cry
>
> *Libète nou mande pou frè n yo*
> We're asking for liberty for our brothers
>
> *Yo vann tout sa yo genyen lakay*
> They sold everything they had at home
>
> *Pou yo vin chèche yo meyè vi*
> To look for a better life
>
> *Lè yo rive se nan pwizon yo mete yo*
> When they arrive they're put in prison[1]
>
> *Genyen nan yo ki pa menm rive*
> Some never arrived

Rekin manje yo depi wout
Sharks ate them en route

Move tan bare yo sou dlo
They sank in terrible weather

[1] This refers to the incarceration, in the Krome detention centre, of several thousand Haitians who made it to Florida but were apprehended by US immigration officers.

(11) HAITIANS AND CUBANS

Edwidge Danticat, *Children of the Sea,* 1993

This extract, from a short story by a Haitian-American writer, highlights the anxieties of boat people on the long journey north towards the United States, and their awareness that the treatment they receive will be different from that given to Cuban refugees.

Today was our first real day at sea. Everyone was vomiting with each small rocking of the boat. The faces around me were showing their first charcoal layer of sunburn. "Now we will never be mistaken for Cubans," one man said. Even though some of the Cubans are black too. The man said he was once on a boat with a group of Cubans. His boat had stopped to pick up the Cubans on an island off the Bahamas. When the Coast Guard came for them, they took the Cubans to Miami and sent him back to Haiti. Now he was back on the boat with some papers and documents to show that the police in Haiti were after him. He had a broken leg too, in case there was any doubt.

One old lady fainted from sunstroke. I helped revive her by rubbing some of the salt water on her lips. During the day it can be so hot. At night, it is so cold. Since there are no mirrors, we look at each other's faces to see how frail and sick we are starting to look.

Some of the women sing and tell stories to each other to appease the vomiting. Still, I watch the sea. At night, the sky and the sea are one. The stars look so huge and close. They make for very bright reflections in the sea. At times I feel like I can just reach out and pull a star down from the sky as though it is a breadfruit or a calabash or something that could be of use to us on this journey.

When we sing, Beloved Haiti, there is no place like you. I had to leave you before I could understand you, some of the women started crying. At times I just wanted to stop in the middle of the song and cry myself. To hide my tears, I pretend like I am getting another attack of nausea, from the sea smell. I no longer join the singing.[...]

There is a crack in the bottom of the boat that looks as though, if it gets any bigger, it will split the boat in two. The captain cleared us aside and used some tar to clog up the hole. Everyone started asking him if it was okay, if they were going to be okay. He said he hoped the Coast Guard would find us soon.

(12) MASS EXODUS

Haiti Progrès, *The Great Escape,* 1994

During 1994, the numbers of Haitians attempting to make the journey to the United States by boat dramatically increased, overwhelming the efforts of the US Coast Guard to intercept them.

Seizing one of the few opportunities for escaping from the unceasing repression in today's Haiti, thousands took to the seas this week, forcing the Clinton administration to re-open the US navy base in Guantánamo Bay, Cuba, as refugee screening camp. "It feels as if they have got all these boats and we don't have enough ships," Cmdr. Bob Reininger of the US Coast Guard ship Hamilton told *The Washington Post* June 27. "Some of the stuff happening here is just amazing."

From this past Friday to Monday, the US Coast Guard picked up some 2,500 refugees from dozens of vessels. On June 27 alone, the US ships intercepted 1,486 people, the second-highest one-day total since the September 1991 coup that ousted President Aristide. The exodus reportedly stunned the Clinton administration, who apparently hadn't realized the full implications of their policy of "keeping the lid" on Haiti by encircling the Caribbean country with ships and preventing people leaving this past year and a half.

The pressure cooker has now exploded with a vengeance, and on June 28, the Clinton administration decided to reopen the US navy base at Guantánamo...

The latest surge of escapees from Haiti, which President Aristide has likened to people fleeing a house on fire, has kept the Coast Guard working overtime. "This is far and away the largest Coast Guard operation since World War II," Coast Guard Lt. Cmdr. Jim

Howe told reporters, noting that 15 Coast Guard and 10 US Navy ships are involved. The Coast Guard has intercepted close to 50,000 refugees since the September 1991 coup and 60,000 more have applied for refugee status at "in-country processing centers." US officials allowed only 13,000 of those into the US, most under the administration of President George Bush, insisting the majority of refugees are "economic migrants." The question of political vs. economic continues to be a major source of struggle, with refugees and refugee advocates saying it is a false dichotomy. "Don't they understand that without a political system there is no economy? Don't they understand that if we go back we die?" one young woman aboard a Coast Guard ship asked a reporter from *The Washington Post*.

(13) UNHAPPY RETURNS

Dan Coughlin, *Life Still Hard After Aristide's Second Coming,* 1995

Some 30,000 Haitians refugees and migrant workers, expelled from more than half a dozen countries around the Caribbean region since Aristide's return in October 1994, had been returned home by August 1995.

Hope has turned into despair for those Haitian refugees persuaded to return after US military muscle restored President Jean-Bertrand Aristide to office last September. They are taking to the high seas again, threatening a replay of the refugee crisis that featured in world headlines up to a year ago – and stimulated the outcry that forced the US-led military intervention of the Caribbean nation.

Reports reaching here from Miami said on Monday the US Coast Guard intercepted an 80-foot freighter packed with more than 400 Haitians. Three refugees died in the crowded conditions. The Coast Guard said two others drowned when they jumped overboard.

In an interview with IPS before news of that interception broke, one former refugee who returned to Haiti hopeful, based on the promise of post-Aristide improvement, reflected the depth of frustration over the delay in attending to the needs of the returnees. "If we don't get a response, we're going to raise an American flag, get in some boats and head for the United States again," said Augustin Richmond.

Human rights groups say the problem of satisfying the demands of returning refugees is "overwhelming", and frustration levels are running high. [...]

"The refugees came back, they got almost no welcome, and they feel that their contribution to the return of Aristide has not been recognised and they feel entitled to something," noted Anne Fuller of the National Coalition for Haitian Refugees.

Earlier this month, the anger of the former refugees boiled over at a chaotic weekend meeting at a school in Port-au-Prince. Police had to be called as several dozen people demonstrated in front of the National Palace for two days, demanding government action to relieve their plight.

Santilla Olivier is symbolic of the plight of the returnees. In July of last year, Olivier, 38, reached the end of her tether. Her husband was dead, murdered by Haiti's military regime. A biting international embargo was causing her family to suffer. Olivier sold all of her possessions and packed her two children off to relatives. Paying about 100 US dollars, she boarded a boat in her home town in the southwest of the country and headed towards the United States. Her journey ended in confinement. For seven months she was held at the US navy base in Guantánamo Bay, Cuba. US authorities eventually persuaded Olivier to return to Haiti after the return of President Jean-Bertrand Aristide from exile.

"They told me to come back. They said the president returned and everything was going to be all right," she said. Returning to Haiti this past January with a sick infant born at Guantánamo Bay and little else, she found that things were far from being all right. Homeless and jobless, the former market woman now lives in this capital, scraping by to make ends meet.

"We're on the street, with our arms open, and we are demanding that the rulers of the country help us because we are suffering and because we struggled for the return of President Aristide," said 32-year-old Sidieu Paul. He was referring to the influence which the plight of Haitian refugees had in pressuring the international community to restore Haiti's first democratically-elected president.

(14) FACING PREJUDICE

Garry Pierre-Pierre, *Edwidge Danticat: Chronicling the Haitian-American Experience*, 1995

The Haitian-American writer, Edwidge Danticat, who moved to New York as a child, received critical acclaim for her first novel, "Breath, Eyes, Memory", published in 1994. The narrator of the story is Sophie Caco, a teenager who, after spending years with her aunt in rural Haiti, is reunited with her mother in Brooklyn.

Critics have praised Ms Danticat's vivid sense of place and her images of fear and pain, which have been compared with Alice Walker's. The New York Times Book Review said the book "achieves an emotional complexity that lifts it out of the realm of the pot-boiler and into that of poetry." [...]

Ms Danticat insists the story is not about herself, although she too was raised for several years by an aunt in Port-au-Prince after her parents – her father, André, is a cabdriver, and her mother, Rose, is a factory worker – left for Brooklyn in search of a new and better life. She says the most autobiographical aspect of the book is the heroine's emotional reaction to coming to America. Like Sophie, Ms Danticat says it left her feeling severed from her roots.

"The first time was when my mother left, when I was four," Ms Danticat said. "I remember being yanked from her as she was getting on the plane. The second time was coming here. My uncle had a laryngectomy. At that time I was the only person who could read his lips and understand what he was saying. Without me he would have had no voice."

Ms Danticat began working on what became her first novel soon after she arrived in Brooklyn, in 1981. Taunted at school for her Creole lilt and her not-so-hip wardrobe and coiffure, she found solace in writing. Even her dimpled and expansive smile faded as she recalled the painful memories of those early years in New York.

"It was very hard," she said, shifting in her chair as if to dispel an intense feeling that was still with her. "'Haitian' was like a curse. People were calling you "Frenchy, go back to the banana boat,' and a lot of kids would lie about where they came from. They would say anything but Haitian."

It was a time when the bodies of Haitian boat-people routinely washed up on the beaches of South Florida. The early 80s was also the time when Haitians were officially classified as a high-risk group for AIDS by the Center for Disease Control in Atlanta. [...]

During her high school years, Ms Danticat said she barely spoke above a whisper because she was embarrassed by her accent, which has now faded to almost nothing.

Having published her novel, she has to wear the mantle of being "the voice" of Haitian-Americans. It is a responsibility that she has accepted hesitantly. "I think I have been assigned that role, but I don't really see myself as the voice for the Haitian-American experience," she says. "There are many. I'm just one."

(15) HAITIANS IN MIAMI

Libète, *Interview with Monsignor Thomas Wensky*, 1997

Thomas Wensky, a Polish-American priest who has worked with Haitians in the diaspora for 18 years, was consecrated bishop in Miami in September 1997.

Libète: Today, how is the community doing, what are its problems, its needs?

It is an adult community, one that is strong. Its problem has to do with the legal status of its members, for not all came legally: they must put their papers in order. The first problem is to find a way to stay here, to obtain the residency. After that, it is work. The third priority is education: to learn English, to learn a profession. Thus, I can say that Haitian immigrants do not ask for more than that. They do not ask for state support, for welfare.

What is being done to solve these problems?

We try to satisfy these needs in the Pierre Toussaint Center. In that church, we have 5 masses every Sunday in Creole for the Haitian community. Next to the church, we have a school where close to 500 adults come daily to learn English. We also have a literacy center where the illiterate learn to read and write in Creole, because many in the diaspora face that situation. The diaspora is a snapshot of Haiti: it includes all social categories. Miami was the destination of boat people and that is why we find more of them there than in other cities. We have a center that deals with legal issues. Thanks to its work, we help people obtain residency or political asylum. We help about 60 people daily. We also have a large placement office to help those seeking work. Furthermore, we have a kindergarten for the small kids. It enables their mothers to work while we take care of their children. So, we can help out with these three problems. I recall many people I received straight from the boat, with wet pants on; today, 12, 15 years later they own a house, etc.

What opportunities do teenagers have upon completing high school?

Haitians are doing well because every year, among kids graduating from high school, Haitian kids have the top grades. This shows there is hope. Most graduates want to go on to college to learn a profession. With the proper papers, there is no problem. We always face the fact that many kids in the parish do not have legal status in spite of the fact that they grew up in Miami. This becomes a problem when they try and find scholarships to go to school or college.

Why aren't they legal, is it because their parents are not legal?

Some parents do not have legal status. Some do not have parents in the country; they were raised by an aunt. They do not meet the criteria to enable them to achieve legal status in the States. Early in the 80s, three quarters of Haitians were illegal. Today, maybe one quarter is illegal and this hinders their progress. Once they obtain legal papers, they are more at ease, they can go to school more easily, find work, and this enables them to get ahead. But, those without papers face a tough time. Their hands are tied. They do odd jobs, work under cover, or work for themselves, but there are limits to what they can do.

The way you explain it, those with papers are OK?

Life is not easy even for those with papers. They must work hard and they must study in order to find better work. But there is more hope for them. Today, the US economy is doing well though Miami has the highest rate of unemployment in the whole country. Possibly, because so many people come to Miami. Or possibly because the economy of the area depends on tourism. In any event, once one is willing to work, one can always find something.

Another problem has to do with the high cost of living, because the Haitian working in Miami is not working to support himself or herself alone. He must take care of the rent, telephone, and find a way to send money to his family back in Haiti. Without the remittances from New York or Miami, Haiti would have disappeared. These are the good people who sustain the country, in spite of the fact that they left home and some cannot go back because they do not have papers. Yet, they do not forget their family easily. Often, families in Haiti feel that those abroad ought to send more money, but if at times they do not, it is because they do not have the money. This is because the cost of living is high and those in the diaspora must make a big sacrifice to be able to send money home.

Translated from Creole by Max J. Blanchet

(16) SPIRITUAL LINKS

Elizabeth McAlister, *Serving the Spirits Across Two Seas,* 1992

One source of support for Haitians in New York is the social net-work of the Vodou house.

It is impossible to know how many people in New York serve the spirits, but there are Vodou houses in all the boroughs. Holding ceremonies in New York poses problems for a *mambo* or *oungan.* [1] Everything is expensive – foodstuffs, alcohol, and flowers. Paying the drummers can be so costly that most people go without drums and use handclapping and singing alone. Cramped apartments and prejudiced neighbours dampen the joy of dances, which are often held in basements to offer a modicum of sound proofing. Once seven police burst into a ceremony I was attending in Brooklyn. Their guns were already drawn; they thought the sounds of the sisal whip dur-ing the *Petro* rituals was gunfire.

Space and time becomes economised in New York *Vodou.* New York initiations must be done in three days to minimise lost work time. Any ritual that should be done outdoors – under trees, next to water, or in a cemetery with the ancestors – must be changed. Be-cause everyone works so hard, there are no free hands to help make the ceremony; the burden falls on a small few. For people who can afford to wait, it has become easier to do the truly important work back in Haiti. Since the uproooting of Duvalier in 1986, many peo-ple who could not go back for political reasons are now able to return.

Try booking a flight to Haiti during the November *Guede* season or around Easter and Rara. So many people go back and forth that Port-au-Prince and New York have become a continuous social sphere, with businesses and family relationships that span the two cities. It has become hard to find the person in Port-au-Prince who doesn't have someone in New York....

New York and Haiti are spiritually linked...Just because some-one lives "up north" does not mean they can forget their responsibilities to the spirits. Sometimes the spirits insist that a per-son return for a dance, or for one of the pilgrimages. It is thought that to ignore the call is to court misfortune. Maybe the spirits, like teachers, are trying to pass on their history. They are saying that ignorance, like disease, will make you sick.

Language reflects the preoccupations of a people. Haitians say that the spirits and the ancestors are *lòt boa,* "on the other side." They are across the water dividing the dead and the living. Now, speaking to "the other side" in Haiti can also mean somebody has gone to New York. Like the dead and the spirits, they are not here, but they may, sometimes, be back.

[1] Priestess or priest.

(17) ANGER IN BROOKLYN

James Ridgeway and Jean Jean-Pierre, *An Alienated and Angered Hai-tian American Community Fights Back,* 1997

The New York weekly, *The Village Voice,* reports on the new mood of the Haitian-American community in the aftermath of the alleged torture of a Haitian by New York policemen.

Nearly two weeks after the first revelations of police brutality against Haitian American Abner Louima, another protest in a stream of rallies was staged outside the 70th Precinct in Brooklyn last Saturday. A week ago, large crowds of Haitians waving toilet plungers maintained such a constant presence in front of the station house that the price of plungers in Flatbush was driven up three-fold.[1] [...]

On Nostrand Avenue, about a mile from the 70th Precinct, the lobby of the Creole-language station Radio Soleil was crowded with people over the weekend, talking, arguing, and waiting for the lat-est word on this Friday's march against police brutality from Grand Army Plaza to City Hall. To many Haitian Americans, the white police of Brooklyn's 70th Precinct are just another version of Duvalier's paramilitary thugs, the TonTon Macoutes: appearing out of nowhere, setting up night-time checkpoints, swooping down in unmarked cars to harass teenagers, and yelling insults at Haitian women on the street.

One reason the Louima case has become such a lightning rod among Haitian Americans is that this is an immigrant community in profound transition. In their hearts, many members of Brooklyn's huge (400,000-plus) Haitian community were for years just biding their time here, waiting for the moment when they could return home. But even after Aristide's presidency, economic conditions in Haiti have steadily deteriorated, and many Haitian Americans are now acknowledging that the long wait is over – they can never go home again. The future is here, and their battle must be waged amid political overseers they distrust and fear. [...]

At a citizenship class at St. Francis Church off Nostrand Avenue last Saturday, the mobilizing effect the Louima case has had on this community was apparent: "Although I am old and sick, I'm going to march as long as it takes for justice," said Emmanuella Augustin. "It could have happened to one of my sons or grandsons. Too bad I cannot vote this year." Added fellow student Rubin Unelus, "Since I am here, I must let the authorities know with my vote that we Haitians are not the poor and backward people they think we are."

More than any political leader, the Haitian American media has been the catalyst for the rising political consciousness among Brooklyn's Haitian community. The political presence of the "tenth department," as the Haitian diaspora is called, has been built, first, around newspapers like Raymond Joseph's conservative *Haiti Observateur* and the left-wing *Haiti Progrès*. But American radio, as in Haiti where there are more than 50 stations, is the real vehicle for information and politics. In New York, Creole radio provides the equivalent of a 24-hour non-stop talk show, from liberal Radio Soleil (which claims half a million listeners), to Columbia University's Sunday morning *L'Heure Haitienne*, Jocelyne Mayas's Tuesday evening WNYE commentary, and Long Island's Radio Tropicale.

"Most of those people have been here 15, 20, 25 years," said Jocelyne Mayas. "They have been living as transients all those years. Now things have changed because of new immigration laws. Some of them have worked here all their lives...They have been waiting here for 30 years to return...With Aristide, they thought that would be it. But Aristide returned in 1994 and things have not changed. This is home and they have no choice [but to fight]."

---

[1] Haitian-American, Abner Louima, alleged that following his arrest outside a nightclub, two police officers assaulted him by ramming the handle of a toilet plunger into his anus.

(18) FUGEE STAR

Karin Joseph, *A Night with Wyclef Jean and the Refugee All-Stars*, 1997

The rap group, The Fugees, two Haitian-Americans and one Afri-can-American, enjoyed massive commercial success and critical acclaim with their 1996 recording, *The Score*, which sold over 12 mil-lion copies in little over a year. The success of the group, which takes its name from the slang for 'refugees', was a great morale-booster for young Haitians in the diaspora. One of the singers, Wyclef Jean, who as a child had left his native Haiti for a life in New York, re-leased a solo album, *Carnival*, featuring four songs in Creole in 1997.

On the darkened stage of the Hammerstein Ballroom at the Man-hattan Center, Friday, October 24, 1997, a tall tuxedo-clad fig-ure wearing a white Carnival mask glides across the platform to the piano. The excited audience swells towards the stage as they cry out for their hero – Wyclef has arrived.

Wyclef Jean starts the concert with a piano rendition of John Lennon's "Imagine" and continues with a showcase of various art-ists which include: Blondine Jean, Wyclef's younger sister; Cannabis, a rap artist; Savion Glover, choreographer of Broadway's *Bring in 'Da Noise, Bring in 'Da Funk*; Run of Run DMC; Beenie Man, a Jamai-can Reggae artist, and a visit from his Fugees partner, Lauryn Hill.

The event was being taped for MTV's the 10 Spot and Wyclef wanted an energetic audience!... He scolded anyone who was sit-ting down, "this is not the opera," and the crowd cheered their agreement. For the duration of the performance, his fans were stand-ing, jumping and writhing with excitement. Haitian flags were waved in the air as those holding them moved to the music. One suave fan had even wrapped the red and blue flag around his shoulders as if it were an evening cape. Wyclef has made being Haitian popular and people are proud to claim their alliance with this performer. His opening act hailed him, "the Bob Marley of our [generation]," and the parallels are evident. Jean has enlightened American pop cul-ture to Haitian culture and in doing so has renewed the pride Haitians of all generations take in their country. After having endured more than four decades of negative press, Haitians, through Wyclef Jean, the Fugees and the Refugee All-Stars, are enjoying a more positive perspective in the media.

Back to the evening of the 24th, as the hour of the show was al-most over, Wyclef performed his new hit, *Guantanamera*, a Cuban folk song made popular in the '60s by Pete Seeger. Wyclef has re-

208 Libète: A Haiti Anthology

introduced this song to his generation giving it new meaning after 30 years. Even as the cameras were turned off the performance still continued. Wyclef invited an audience member to come onstage and rhyme for the crowd, tapping his foot and nodding his dreadlocked head in approval. Finally the stage-hands came forward and told him to wrap things up. It was time to go home. He got off the stage and came down to the main floor to sign autographs, shake hands, and exchange a few words, throwing in some Kreyòl for his Haitian fans.

CHAPTER SEVEN
FOREIGN INTERVENTIONS

From the moment of its birth, the independent nation of Haiti was immediately faced with hostility on the part of the European powers whose colonies surrounded it. They viewed the Haitian revolution as a dangerous example that threatened the colonial system and the institution of slavery upon which that system was built. For the colonial powers, and the United States too, the very existence of an independent black republic represented a subversive challenge to the ideology of white racial superiority. The great fear for Haiti's early leaders was that this antipathy would be translated into another foreign military invasion, and they took significant measures to counter this threat. Dessalines ordered most of the remaining French settlers killed, and included in the country's first constitution the famous provision prohibiting foreigners from owning any land in Haiti. His successor, Christophe, allocated substantial sums to strengthen defensive fortifications and to maintain a state of military preparedness. In the event, no such invasion materialised, yet Haiti soon succumbed to another form of foreign intervention.

Even while the world's great powers treated Haiti as a pariah, leaving it politically ostracised and diplomatically shunned, trade links were re-established. First British, and then French and American merchants came to monopolise the export of agricultural commodities and the import of luxury goods. When, in 1825, President Boyer agreed to pay a massive indemnity in return for French recognition of its former colony's independence, the extent of Haiti's economic dependence deepened. While the settlement reduced the threat of invasion, foreign loans were contracted in order to pay the French, and, to keep up with the interest payments, successive Haitian governments were compelled to borrow from French, German, British and American bankers. Haiti became immersed in debt, the repayment of which consumed an estimated 80 per cent of national revenue by the end of the nineteenth century. (1)

The extent of direct foreign economic penetration was limited by the break up of the plantations and the ban on foreign land ownership. However, during the latter half of the nineteenth century, Haitian leaders periodically granted commercial privileges to foreign business interests in exchange for diplomatic and material assistance in their struggles with rival elite factions. To protect these interests, and to ensure prompt repayment of loans and interest, foreign powers frequently sent their gunboats into Haitian territorial waters.

During this period of neo-colonialism, the ascendancy of the traditional powers, France and Britain, was increasingly challenged by the US, which finally recognised Haitian independence in 1863, and by Germany, whose merchants gained a majority control over the lucrative coffee export trade. Foreign domination of the Haitian economy was extended still further when during the latter years of the century Syrian and Lebanese immigrants established a significant presence as retail traders in the interior of the country. (2)

In the early years of the twentieth century, the US enforced its hegemony throughout the Caribbean/Central American region with military interventions, and in 1915 US Marines were sent to occupy Haiti. The invasion was prompted in part by the threat posed to US economic interests by the country's mounting political instability, but of more relevance was the concern to counter the growth of German interests and influence, particularly since Haiti had new strategic importance following the 1914 opening of the Panama Canal.

Opposition to the occupation in Haiti was muted at first, but resistance soon developed when the US authorities introduced the *corvée*, a system of forcibly recruited labour gangs, to carry out public works programmes such as road-building. (3) Resentment among Haitian peasants, for whom the corvée was painfully reminiscent of slavery, turned into an anti-occupation uprising in 1918. Several thousand peasants led by an ex-soldier, Charlemagne Péralte, launched a military campaign that overwhelmed the US-trained Gendarmerie, and obliged the US to commit more Marine forces. Employing guerrilla tactics of attacking with small commando groups that would then disengage and withdraw into the countryside before enemy reinforcements could be deployed, Péralte vowed to liberate Haiti from the occupying force. (4) After nearly two years of bloody warfare, Péralte was captured and executed by US troops and, although resistance continued under the leadership of Benoît Batraville, by 1920 the rebellion had been crushed.

During the occupation, the US came to dominate Haitian economic and financial interests. A new constitution, written by Franklin Roosevelt who was then an assistant secretary of the navy, ended the prohibition of land ownership by foreigners, and US companies acquired land for agricultural projects. (5) The economic influence of France was gradually eclipsed and, after Haiti declared war on Germany in 1918, German assets were seized and German businessmen were expelled. Direct US investment in Haiti tripled between 1915 and 1930.

While under US control, there was a period of relative political stability, and new technical and vocational schools were set up in line with US policy to encourage the growth of the black middle class. Yet the overall effect of the occupation was to reinforce the existing structures of power and the resulting inequalities. Apologists pointed to the development of the country's infrastructure, notably the construction of roads, hospitals, bridges and port facilities, but in reality these works were guided more by the need to make the country attractive to foreign investment than to benefit Haitians. Opposition to the occupation came not just from peasants forced to participate in the corvée, or moved from lands expropriated by US companies. The occupying forces treated Haitians of all classes with a thinly veiled racist contempt, and these offensive attitudes succeeded in uniting previously hostile mulatto and black elite factions in a nationalist opposition movement. (6)

The withdrawal of the Marines in 1934 ended 19 years of occupation, but the US maintained its influence over Haitian affairs through a series of compliant presidents – President Lescot (1941-6) in particular was a loyal servant of US interests – as well as by its continued control over the nation's finances and through its close links with the Haitian Army, a force that had been revamped and remodelled by the US military during the occupation.

US relations with Haiti were severely strained during the early years of the François Duvalier dictatorship. However, following the 1959 Cuban revolution, Duvalier successfully exploited US fears of the spread of communism to bring pressure to bear on Washington. Duvalier suggested that, without US support, Haiti would be obliged to look elsewhere for allies, and the US responded by granting generous aid allocations. For the US, Papa Doc's blatant disregard for democratic values and human rights, while unseemly, was nevertheless tolerable as long as he stood as a valuable bulwark against communism. Furthermore, Haiti under Duvalier continued to offer attractive possibilities to US capital. The American company, Reynold's, for example, enjoyed exclusive rights to the extraction of bauxite deposits in southern Haiti (7), and, at the end of the 1960s, US companies began to take advantage of non-unionised and low-paid labour by setting up offshore assembly plants in Port-au-Prince.

For all Washington's public pronouncements in favour of democracy, when Jean-Claude Duvalier inherited power on the death of his father in 1971, US warships patrolled Haitian waters to ensure an unchallenged transition. A short time later, US military advisers were dispatched to Haiti to help establish a new counter-insurgency unit, the Leopards. Under Jean-Claude, US economic interests in Haiti were extended through the expansion of the assembly plant sector in the free trade zones in the capital. By the beginning of the 1980s, approximately 200 mostly US-owned or subsidiary companies were employing over 60,000 Haitian workers assembling basic electronic components, clothing, and baseballs for the US market. At one time all the baseballs used in the North American professional leagues were manufactured by Haitian labour.

When, during the administration of US President Carter (1976-80), Washington pressed for improvements in the dire human rights situation and threatened to suspend US aid allocations, Jean-Claude responded by releasing some political prisoners, and briefly relaxing strict controls over the media. US aid money continued to flow into Haiti, and, following the election victory of the right-wing Republican Ronald Reagan, the Duvalierist system came to depend even more heavily on US aid. (8) At the same time, the US Agency for International Development and the US-dominated multilateral donors, the World Bank and International Monetary Fund, took on an increasingly dominant role in the planning of economic development in Haiti. As agricultural production declined, the foreign planners stressed that Haiti's future lay with the extension of the light industry sector and agri-business for export. (9)

The US-backed eradication of the entire native pig population (see chapter 3), and the provision of massive quantities of mostly US-produced food aid, appeared to make the planners' prophesies self-fulfilling by contributing to the deterioration of the traditional peasant agricultural economy. At the local level, foreign influence over the economy was also exerted through the interventions of evangelical church missions, mostly from the US, and the relief and development programmes carried out, or funded, by international non-governmental organisations (NGOs). The Protestant missionaries, whose presence had grown since the time of the US occupation, often utilised 'food for work' programmes in their efforts to seduce Haitians away from the practice of Vodou. (10) Many of the international NGOs also distributed food aid as emergency relief, although a significant minority attempted more progressive development programmes that bolstered, rather than undermined, the traditional local economy. (11)

As opposition to the regime of Jean-Claude mounted in Haiti, official US support in the form of aid was finally withdrawn in January 1986. The Duvalierist system could not maintain order, nor could it administer the economic reforms needed for the modernisation of the economy, and, as such, a continuation of the dictatorship was no longer compatible with US plans. Duvalier made way for a military regime headed by General Namphy, and US aid was restored and then doubled. The 'American Plan', as efforts to re-orient the economy became known in Haiti, took another step forward as the Namphy regime reduced the level of state protection for domestically-produced foodstuffs by opening the country's ports, and by declaring that it would drastically cut import tariffs. Although the resultant inward flow of both contraband and legally imported food met a need among a hungry population, it also damaged the agricultural production of peasant farmers by driving down the prices of domestic foodstuffs in local markets.

With the departure of Duvalier, US policy focused on supporting the interim military government that was expected to oversee the transition to democracy and political stability, thus creating the conditions favourable to economic reform and renewed foreign investment. This strategy ran aground when the military colluded with Duvalierists in the violent attacks on voters that succeeded in aborting the November 1987 elections. Although the US suspended aid to the Namphy regime, it was resumed when another military regime headed by General Prosper Avril took over in 1988. Meanwhile, other forms of US funding were distributed to conservative groups in Haiti with the intention of making sure that when democratic elections were held they would produce a government sympathetic to US interests. (12)

Elections, funded by the US and supervised by the United Nations, finally took place in December 1990. Contrary to expectations, the presidential election was won, not by the clear US favourite, the former World Bank official, Marc Bazin, but by the radical Catholic priest, Jean-Bertrand Aristide, who polled 67 per cent of the vote compared to Bazin's 14 per cent. The new president made friendly overtures to the Haitian elite, and convinced international lenders to pledge US$450 million in development aid, but after just eight months he was overthrown by a military coup d'état. Although the Bush administration publicly condemned the coup, and backed the Organisation of American States (OAS) economic embargo against the coup regime, in practice US government policy was less than forthright in supporting the restoration of the democratically-elected Haitian leader.

The embargo was never actively enforced by the US, and shipments of oil and other products needed to sustain the military regime continued to arrive in Haiti. Within three months, the US lifted the embargo on shipping by assembly plant operators. Even while the

Haitian military carried out a violent campaign of murder and beatings against Aristide supporters, the US State Department focused on alleged human rights violations attributed to Aristide while in power. The US position appeared increasingly to be based on the belief that the cause of the political turmoil in Haiti was Aristide and his proposed reforms in favour of the country's poor rather than the overthrow of Haiti's first democratically-elected government. Washington pressed Aristide to negotiate a settlement with the leaders of the military regime, most of whom had been trained by the US. Meanwhile, the US Central Intelligence Agency launched a public character assassination campaign targeting the exiled president. (13)

In 1993, with the involvement of a new US president, the Democrat Bill Clinton, and the United Nations Security Council, it appeared as though the international community would mount a serious attempt to resolve the crisis. A joint UN/OAS human rights monitoring mission was deployed in Haiti, and, in June 1993, a new, stricter, world-wide embargo on arms and fuel was voted by the UN. Three weeks later, the Haitian military leader, General Raoul Cédras, signed a UN-brokered accord containing a series of steps to be taken by the military regime that would culminate in Aristide's return to Haiti. With the embargo lifted, the Haitian military then cynically reneged on the accord, launching a renewed wave of repression of the democratic and popular movement in Haiti. A US ship carrying a UN force despatched to oversee the separation of the police from the army turned tail when a hostile crowd demonstrated at the port, and plans for Aristide's return were abandoned. Both the port demonstration and many of the killings of Aristide supporters were the work of a new paramilitary death squad force, known by its acronym, FRAPH. This military-backed front of hired killers had been created and was led by a Haitian who, it was subsequently revealed, enjoyed a close working relationship with the CIA mission in Port-au-Prince. (14)

Although the UN renewed the embargo, this measure merely increased the poverty of the general population, while providing the top military officers with the opportunity to grow rich through the control of smuggling, much of it across the border with the Dominican Republic. International diplomacy in search of a solution was spearheaded by the US, with Washington's efforts continuing to centre on pressurising Aristide to compromise with the military. The exiled president's 'intransigence' was increasingly portrayed by US policy-makers as the main stumbling block to a resolution of the crisis. To many in the Haitian democratic and popular sector it appeared as though the effect of the diplomatic initiatives pursued by the international community with the US at its head was to prolong, rather than end, the life of the coup regime. (15)

However, by mid-1994, an increasingly vocal pro-democracy lobby in the US and the potentially destabilising effect on the Caribbean region posed by the exodus of tens of thousands of Haitian refugees, prompted a new US policy. A UN resolution authorising a multinational force to use 'all means necessary' to remove the coup leaders from power was passed, but the Haitian military failed to show any signs of a climb-down. After nearly three years in power the military regime had been unable to establish any semblance of stability in Haiti, where support for Aristide remained strong. When Aristide's representatives agreed to proposals by international lenders for an economic reconstruction plan based on the neo-liberal reforms, the countdown to the invasion began. (16)

With the first airborne troops reportedly en route to Haiti, a high-level US delegation led by former President Carter sealed an eleventh hour deal with the Haitian coup regime to permit the unopposed entry of a 20,000-strong US intervention force on 19 September 1994. Although some on the Haitian left were convinced that the US military presence would permit the full application of the 'American Plan' and prevent a resumption of the popular organising seen prior to the coup, the majority of the populace welcomed the foreign troops as liberators from three years of violent political repression. (17)

Within four weeks of the intervention, the three main coup leaders went into exile and President Aristide returned. Initially, the role of the US troops and their relationship to the Haitian military was somewhat confused. For example, a Marine unit shot dead ten Haitian policemen in Cap-Haïtien yet, when members of the Haitian military and paramilitary forces attacked pro-Aristide demonstrations in Port-au-Prince, the US troops failed to intervene. Eventually a *modus vivendi* was established, and the two forces mounted joint patrols to the chagrin of many Haitians who had expected the Haitian military to be immediately disbanded and individual human rights abusers punished. Under pressure from the US, Aristide stressed the need for reconciliation between those who supported the coup and those who suffered from it, and when the pro-coup elite benefited from business arrangements with the US force, some commentators wondered what form of democracy had been restored. (18)

After six months, the UN took over responsibility for the intervention forces, although the commanding officer and the great majority of troops continued to be provided by the US. The US exercised a vast influence over important reforms such as the revamping of the judiciary, and the creation of a new police force separate from the military. Although Aristide carried out the highly popular disbanding of the army in early 1995, concerns continued to be voiced about the repercussions of the intervention forces' failure to disarm the former military and paramilitary squads. (19)

Neo-liberal economic reforms demanded by the international financial institutions in return for over US$2 billion in economic aid became a hotly contested issue, and again raised questions about Haitian sovereignty. (see Chapter 5) The sale of state-owned enterprises to foreign investors, and the elimination of import tariffs, opened up the Haitian economy to outside interests as never before. Further integration into the global economy and culture poses a growing challenge to Haiti's hard won independence. (20)

(1) CONDEMNED TO DEBT

Jean Métellus, *Haïti: Perspectives*, 1996

When President Boyer agreed to pay a massive sum in return for French recognition of Haiti's independence, the country became involved in an endless cycle of debt and loans. The creditor nations intervened repeatedly to enforce repayments and to impose other financial penalties.

The independence of 1804, despite being won with great courage, was not consolidated, and the very people expelled from Haiti by the first black government in history did their best, with the help of the whole world, to destroy the Haitian State. In Article 2 of the decree of 17th April 1825, signed by Charles X, it is written that: "The current inhabitants of the French part of Saint-Domingue will pay to the federal deposit bank of France the sum of one hundred and fifty million francs, in five equal yearly instalments, the first being due on the 31st December 1825. This will be used to compensate former settlers claiming an indemnity. Subject to the conditions of this decree, we will grant full and absolute independence to the government of the current inhabitants of the French part of Saint-Domingue." It was not enough to have taken up arms in the struggle for independence, it had to be paid for too, and its cost was high. As Jean-Marie Drot wrote: "One hundred and fifty million francs represented exactly ten times the entire annual revenue of Haiti, the equivalent of 3.4 billion francs today, according to the experts."

And what did Haiti do to satisfy such demands? She took out three loans in fifty years from French capitalists: 30 million francs from the first loan (the lenders retained a premium of 6 million) passed directly from the coffers of the banks of Laffitte Rothschild, Blanc Colin and the Syndicat des Receveurs Généraux to the Caisse des Dépôts et Consignation in Paris .

We will not dwell on France's vow to occupy a portion of Haitian territory, Môle Saint-Nicolas, as a guarantee, because Haiti was unable to honour her debts with sufficient haste.

It is enough to recall that the double debt owed to France (the indemnity and loan of 1825) were not settled until the end of the 19th century. Penalties for late payments amounted to an interest charge of five percent. This indemnity, which had further profited the bankers and colonists, had placed an overwhelming burden on the young independent state. President Boyer (1818-1843) paid 2 million francs per year from 1838 to 1842 from an average annual revenue of approximately 12.5 million francs [...]

One by one, Germany, Great Britain, France and the United States demanded compensation for their nationals, backed by the threat of armed force. In 1872, 15 thousand dollars was paid out for the German, Batsch; 251,275 francs went to France; 217,755 francs was paid out for English residents; 89,260 for Americans...In 1879, the United States demanded 2,466,480 dollars for a bandit of American nationality who was selling Haitians to Cuba, because he had been convicted under Haitian law. In 1883, Haiti had to pay compensation amounting to 3 million francs in three years, on a budget of seven million. Jules Ferry arrogantly threatened military intervention. For the arrest of an American smuggler, Haiti had to pay 6,000 piastres. She then had to pay 160,000 dollars for Luders, a German convicted of the assault of a policeman.

During the nineteenth century, within the country itself, Haiti was faced with professional compensation claimants, foreign businessmen who shrewdly burnt or looted their property in order to demand twenty times its value from the Haitian government at a later date, threatening action by their consul and its guns. What is more, these merchants lent and sold on credit to critics of the government in order that they might take up arms and start their own 'revolution', while simultaneously doing the same for the government in order that they might combat the general discontent. In other words, they were making sure that they made big profits no matter who won.

The consequence of this second phase was that Haiti inaugurated Third World debt.

Translated from French by Emily Dunbar

(2) THE 'ARAB INVASION'

David Nicholls, *Economic Dependence and Political Autonomy. The Haitian Experience*, 1974

Haiti was one of a number of Caribbean and Latin American countries to receive Syrian and Lebanese immigrants in the latter part of the nineteenth century. Their decendants continue to play a significant role in the Haitian economy today.

These Arab traders were concerned more with small retail trade than with foreign commerce, and they penetrated the interior of the country in a way which the European merchants rarely did. Although there were laws going back to the earliest days of independence prohibiting foreign merchants from operating in the interior, and from engaging in retail trade, they were not strictly enforced. Also, many Syrians had become naturalised Haitians, and were thus free from discriminatory legislation of this kind. The constitutional provision prohibiting whites from owning land had been modified in 1867 to become an exclusion of foreign ownership; also the naturalisation laws had been liberalised in 1889. Many of the Arab traders, however, remained British, French or United States subjects, thus claiming protection from foreign consulates. It has been estimated that by 1905, there were between 10,000 and 15,000 Syrians in the country. Although at first the commercial challenge was felt by the small Haitian traders, the foreign commercial houses soon began to feel threatened by Syrian activity. A journal called *L'Anti-Syrien* demanded the expulsion of these foreigners, and an end to the "Syrian invasion". Other journals joined the campaign: "With our valiant market-women *Le Devoir* cries: Down with the Syrians!" In 1903, a law was enacted in Haiti to prevent further Syrian and Lebanese immigration, and to restrict foreign retail traders...The Syrian colony as a whole decided to seek the protection of the United States, feeling that the French consulate, to which the colony had looked for protection in the past, was increasingly hostile to Syrian interests because these merchants constituted a growing challenge to French merchants in the Republic.

Vitriolic attacks on the Syrians continued throughout the period of Nord Alexis's rule (1902-08). They were called "Levantine monsters" and "descendants of Judas", "a people essentially defective and immoral."...

The issue remained an important one into the second decade of the twentieth century. In 1912, the Haitian foreign minister, J.N. Léger stated that: "It is necessary to protect nationals against the disloyal competition of the Easterner whose nationality is uncertain; it is also necessary to protect public health."...

In the same year, the British ambassador to Washington informed the United States government that unless the Americans were able to bring influence to bear on the Haitian government to change its hostile policy towards the Syrians, the British would take unilateral action to protect the interests of those Arabs who were British nationals, by sending a gun boat... The Syrian colony, however, continued to believe that the USA was its most effective guardian, and cabled President Taft in May 1912 calling for American intervention to protect their interests.

(3) THE CORVÉE

Roger Gaillard, *Les Blancs débarquent*, 1982

In this 1980 interview, Nestor Dorisca remembers how he was forcibly recruited into a labour gang (a *corvée*) and set to work building a road in the Central Plateau. The '*blanc*' – the Haitian word for a foreigner – was one of the American soldiers who during the early years of the US occupation used the corvées to carry out public works programmes.

❞ It was in 1918, when I was 20 years old...Early one morning some *gendarmes* suddenly entered our house. I didn't have time to move. They grabbed hold of me, and, without offering any explanation, told me I was under arrest. I protested and even resisted – they beat me... On the other side of the hedge which separated our house from the path I saw some other young guys in a line. The gendarmes made me take my place among them and they drove us, roped together, to Hinche, where they put us in prison. Still nothing had been said to us about the reason for the arrests [...]

The next morning, before the sun was up, a sergeant came to announce that we had been placed under his orders to work on the construction of the road for which he was responsible. He distributed some pickaxes, shovels and wheelbarrows. It was the first time that many of us had seen the latter. At first, I found it hard to push it correctly, and it turned over when I filled it full of rocks. Eventually, I worked out how to use it.

We were taken to Passe-Bonbon, a river ford between Maissade and Hinche, where there was an old track. The work wasn't difficult, but all the time we were urged to work faster. We cleared the trees from each side, cut down the plants and grasses...and dug out ditches. The excavated earth was shovelled onto the track, then packed down and covered with sand [...]

You couldn't rest. From the moment you were 'arrested', the truncheon knocked you down, and the same truncheon made you get up again. There was no question of even opening your mouth... Nevertheless, there were some brave ones. I remember the torture inflicted one day on the late Estimon. It was at pay time, and an argument started between him and the blanc.

"You've already been paid."

"No."

"Your name's in the book."

"But I tell you, I haven't been paid."

"You've been paid."

"No."

Then the furious blanc, grabbed hold of him, hung him by his wrists from a tree, and beat him – beat him without stopping. The blood ran down Estimon's body. He clenched his teeth, and didn't cry out. Then the blanc had had enough. He ordered him to be taken down, to have his blood-stained shorts taken off, and for him to be sent naked back to work. I can recall that day the silent anger, deep down in the heart of the late Estimon. When they gave out the food, he refused to take his portion. It was his way of continuing to defy the blanc. Soon after, he ran away..."

Translated from French by Charles Arthur

(4) AGAINST THE YANKEES

Charlemagne Péralte, *Lettre*, 1919

Charlemagne Péralte was the commander of several thousand peasant irregulars who fought the US Marines in the regions around the town of Hinche. In this letter to the French consul in Port-au-Prince, written in July 1919, Péralte claims that military resistance to the US occupation was consistent with the principle of national self-determination proclaimed by US President Woodrow Wilson at the end of the First World War.

Honourable Minister,

Contrary to the principles generally agreed to by civilised nations and to the rules of international law, the American government, taking advantage of the great European war, has intervened in the affairs of the small Republic of Haiti by imposing a convention whose ratification in the National Assembly was assured by a military occupation. In spite of the threats to our autonomy and our dignity as a free and independent people, we were disposed to accept this convention and execute our obligations as we were directed to. However the false promises made by the Yankees on disembarking on our territory are being realised, after only four years have passed, by perpetual antagonisms, outrageous crimes, murders, thefts and acts of barbarism of which only the American, in the whole world, is capable. Today our patience is at an end and we demand our rights, unrecognised and flouted by the unscrupulous Americans who, by destroying our institutions, deprive the Haitian people of all their resources and thrive on our name and our blood. With cruelty and injustice, the Yankees, have for four years cast ruin and desolation on our territory. In this day when, at the conference for peace among civilised nations, they have sworn, before the entire world, to re-spect the rights and sovereignty of small nations, we demand the liberation of our territory and the right of free independent states, as recognised by international law. We ask you, consequently, to observe that we have been struggling for ten months with only this end in view, and that our weapons until now victorious, permit us to ask you to recognise our right to violence. We are prepared to make any sacrifice to liberate Haitian territory and create respect for the principles adopted by President Wilson himself, concerning the rights and sovereignty of small nations. Please note, Sir, that the American troops, by virtue of their own laws have no right to wage war against us.

Sincerely,

Charlemagne M. Péralte, Commander-in-chief of the Revolution, and 100 other signatories

Translated from French by David Nicholls

(5) OPEN FOR BUSINESS

Suzy Castor, *L'Occupation américaine d'Haïti*, 1988

American companies took advantage of the US occupation and the subsequent changes in legislation permitting foreign land owner-ship to establish plantations on the northern and Artibonite plains.

The peasantry became the victim of compulsory purchase orders, the principal form of capitalist exploitation in an occupied colony or country. Starting in July 1915, several businessmen became inter-ested in establishing agricultural plantations. To this end, several commissions travelled to Haiti to examine its potential, and the re-sults of the studies sent back to the State Department seemed favourable...The success enjoyed by investors in Cuba, Puerto Rico, the Dominican Republic and Central America was to spread to Haiti.

In the first wave of euphoria, concessions were obtained on the pretext of providing the population with work and ensuring economic development.

In order to ease the penetration of American capital, several legal measures were taken during the occupation, according to the various complaints, suggestions and demands of potential investors in the country. In 15 years, from 1915 to 1930, 33 legislative measures were adopted...The first measure was the deletion of Article 5 of the Constitution, which prohibited the ownership of property by foreigners [...]

... Capitalists arrived in large numbers to solicit concessions. In this way, thousands of carreaux[1] of land were sacrificed to businessmen who wanted to maximise profits in as short a time as possible by means of large-scale agricultural development...

Thanks to figures gathered from a variety of different sources, the compilation of the following list of some of the concessionary companies and their respective concessions has been possible:

W.A.Rodenburg	125,000 acres
Haytian American Sugar Co.	24,000
Haytian Corporation Pineapple Co.	1,000
Haytian Corporation of America	15,000
Haytian American Development Co.	24,000
Haytian Agricultural Corporation	14,000
Haytian Development Corporation	2,200
Société Commerciale Haïtienne	9,000
United West Indies Corporation	16,000
Haytian Products Co.	16,000
Haytian American Co.	20,000
North Hayti Sugar Co.	400
	266,600

Without giving precise details as to the extent of their territory, the following concessionaires are also worth mentioning: The Haytian Fruit Co.; Société des Plantations de Saint-Marc; The Haytian Filer corporation; The Plantation Company of Hayti; The Verrettes Plantations Corporation; La Société de Terre-Neuve; the concession of the island of la Gonâve; The Haytian American Development Co.; The American Dywood Co.; The Company of l'Attalaye. Most of the allocated land was in the fertile northern plains of the Artibonite valley. "In the north", wrote Georges Séjourné, "50,000 Haitians were expropriated, a large number of whom, having emigrated to the Dominican Republic, became victims of Trujillo in October 1937."[2]

[1] A carreau is a unit of measurement equivalent to 1.29 hectares or 3.19 acres.
[2] This refers to the 1937 massacre of tens of thousands of Haitians living in the Dominican Republic.

Translated from French by Emily Dunbar

(6) A COUNTRY BEING KILLED

Normil Sylvain, *A Haitian View of the Occupation,* 1927

This letter, written to a member of the Women's International League for Peace and Freedom who visited Haiti along with five other Americans in 1926, reveals the hostility to the US occupation among Haitian intellectuals.

...A civilisation was in process of development. That is what the men of your country do not understand. They came and interrupted it. They act like barbarians, for they have established nothing but a coarse materialism, the religion of money, the worship of force and success. I do not hate them, because it is not my turn of mind nor the way my feelings have been trained. I cannot any longer hate, but I despise them. That does not trouble them I know; but I despise them for their sterile lack of understanding, for their vanity, men who are parvenus in matters of intellect and feeling.

Although foreign domination is never a good thing, medicine teaches us that painful operations sometimes effect a cure. The American invasion might have been a good thing if, although unjust and even infringing for a time upon our independence, it had been temporary and had led ultimately to the reign of justice and liberty. But such is not the case. The Americans have not even this excuse. They have made themselves the allies of the evil past of oppression and tyranny; they have abolished liberty, justice, independence; they are bad administrators of the public funds; they offer a peace of degradation and subjection, shame and dishonour. They push forward like the rising tide; they attack our traditions, our soul. Is it not claimed that they want to change our culture, our religion?

Even the good that they do turns to hurt, for instead of teaching us, they do it to prove that we are incapable. They are exploiters.

How can they teach us when they have so much to learn themselves? I am not bitter as I may appear. If when you were here I seemed less emphatic than I do now, it is because I was not well informed then. Every day I learn more, and the things that I had felt and suspected prove to be true. It is not that I have been disillusioned unless you understand that to mean that I formerly hoped for a change peacefully brought about by mutual consent; in that sense – yes. I do not aspire to propose any plan. I do not desire to be given any government place. My social position and relations put fortune and honour within my reach, but I should feel myself an accomplice. I have long accepted poverty and obscurity. Poverty is painful only when you see those that you love suffering.

The present regime, an American occupation with a false facade of Haitian government, is a pretence and a lie.

It is a pathetic sight, a country that is being slowly killed.

(7) UNDERMINING THE ECONOMY

Ernest Bernadin, *L'espace rural haïtien*, 1993

The American company, Reynold's, had an exclusive concession to exploit bauxite deposits in southern Haiti. Over a period of 25 years the company made good profits but the local people enjoyed little benefit and the environment was seriously damaged.

Reynold's is an American company which has been mining bauxite in the Miragoâne region of Haiti since 1957. It benefits from a concession of 844.40 hectares of land. Everything pointed to the belief that the company's arrival would raise the standard of living of the peasant masses, or at the very least contribute to the development of the area and, in particular, to basic infrastructure. The company proposed it would be participating especially in the social development of the region. However, obsessed by the pursuit of maximum profit, it gradually reduced its personnel, despite its promise to create more jobs. From 800 in 1957, the workforce was reduced to 222 in 1971, and 180 in 1980. Reynold's could be regarded as a breeding ground for all sorts of problems: dispossession of peasant farmers, rural exodus, prostitution, etc. The deterioration of rural life in Miragoâne began when the arrival of Reynold's provoked a profound disequilibrium. The few who survived were forced to sell their land for derisory sums. To offer more and more land to

Reynold's, the Haitian state had started evicting the majority of farmers – contributing to the rural exodus to Port-au-Prince where an urban sub-proletariat was fed by the northern and southern departments, and the Artibonite valley.

Notable too is the growth of prostitution in Miragoâne since the arrival of Reynold's: young peasant women no longer take an interest in selling agricultural produce, preferring to prostitute themselves. There are a great number of prostitutes in and around Miragoâne...

Agriculture was formerly flourishing (until the sixties) – Miragoâne produced a lot of coffee and root crops, but this time is no more! These days the region is supplied by the coastal towns...The situation will continue to deteriorate as the years go by unless significant action is taken by the authorities.

From the economic point of view, during the period 1957 to 1973, bauxite exports totalled 7,598,039 tons with a revenue of 44,444,655 gourdes, whereas in the period 1976-80, following a revision of the contract with the Haitian state, the taxes levied were valued at 252,178,060 gourdes from an output of 2,486,846 tons. On the social level, Reynold's did provide electricity, drinking water, medical care, and medicines to the populations of Miragoâne and Paillant.

But all things considered, apart from a few all-weather roads, the dilapidated condition of most houses in Miragoâne and the proliferation of shacks at the entrance to the town clearly demonstrate that the standard of living of the population has barely changed. (Also) the mining of bauxite disturbed the ecological balance. The result was an increase in dust over a large area which led to many cases of lung disease.

Translated from French by Anne McConnell

(8) AIDING DICTATORSHIP

Alex Stepick, *The New Haitian Exodus*, 1982

During the latter half of the twentieth century, Haiti received huge amounts of foreign aid assistance, but rather than helping the poverty-stricken population much of it was wasted or stolen by corrupt governments.

Haiti received $137 million in international aid in 1980 and is scheduled to receive 20% more than that for 1981. This gives it the highest per capita assistance in the Western Hemisphere. Two-thirds of Haiti's development budget, $81 million in 1979, was provided by external sources: 50% through multilateral sources (primarily the UN, World Bank, and the Inter-American Development Bank), and the remainder bilaterally with the US in the lead followed by France, West Germany and Canada. In addition, more than 130 non-governmental organisations provided an estimated $15 million.

Indeed virtually all development agents who have been in Haiti over a year are completely cynical, with most concluding that corruption is so extensive that the Haitian people would be better off if all the international agencies abandoned Haiti. One US official in Haiti complained, "no one knows why we are here, what our interest is or what we are trying to achieve. By maintaining a large mission here we are just condoning the practices of the Duvalier government."

Many development experts argue that "more compulsive giving" is not what Haiti needs. The country cannot absorb it and most is wasted. Indeed most international development agents who have worked in Haiti recount endless stories of money and goods simply disappearing. Massive amounts of "Food for Peace" sent to Haiti in bags marked "Not for Sale" are found on sale in Haitian markets throughout the country. Much of the food which is not appropriated for sale is used in "Food for Work" programmes which many claim are used by wealthy landowners for projects to benefit them, increase the dependency of the peasants, and works to undercut prices and incentives to produce for small agriculturists.

At the end of 1980, after drifting into a foreign exchange crisis, Haiti approached the IMF for a budget supplement. On December 5, 1980, IMF granted $22 million to Haiti. Shortly thereafter $20 million was withdrawn from the government of Haiti's account. A cable to the US Secretary of State, Alexander Haig, states that "about $4 million may have been diverted to the VSN," the Volontaires de la Sécurité Nationale, the official name for the Tonton Macoutes. Many believe the other $16 million went into Duvalier's personal accounts. The IMF bluntly states, "The fund's staff (IMF) attributed excessive unbudgeted spending as the most important cause of Haiti's financial crises." Still, Baby Doc's wife, Michelle Bennett Duvalier, reportedly draws a $100,000 monthly salary for her duties as "Mrs President." Last year (1980) between 5 and 7 million dollars was spent on their wedding. Yet, the US and other international aid establishments feel compelled to continue helping.

(9) THE AMERICAN PLAN

Haiti Info, *Haiti's Agricultural Production,* 1996

This alternative newsletter, produced in Port-au-Prince, attributes the decline of the rural economy and the country's increasing dependence on foreign food imports to the liberalisation measures that began in the early 1980s. Successive Haitian governments agreed to economic plans proposed by the US through its Agency for International Development (AID) and the multilateral agencies it dominates, the World Bank and the International Monetary Fund.

The liberalisation, or application of 'neo-liberalism', quickly became known here as "The American Plan." At that time, Ernst Verdieu put out a 21-page document ("The American Plan for Haiti") that circulated widely and explained the US objectives by citing US and World Bank documents..."The American Plan" was and remains: – to re-orientate the rural economy, already in crisis, by replacing (1) hill side and mountain slope food production with fruit, coffee and cacao trees for export, and (2) replacing sugar, rice and other cereal and food crop peasant plots in the plains with agro-industries of non-traditional products for export, and – to promote what they call Haiti's "comparative advantage": a poor population ready to work at rock-bottom wages.

AID experts acknowledged that liberalisation of the economy would cause "massive" rural-to-urban displacement, increasing urban populations by 75% by the year 2001. All of those landless workers would find a job in the "Taiwan of the Caribbean", as one AID man called it, and during the 1980s US and Haitian incentives pushed US companies to locate here. "We get it done for less," the Association des Industries d'Haiti promised in one of its brochures. In the 1980s, 30,000 to 50,000 minimum or less-than-minimum wage jobs, which do little for the workers or the national economy, were produced for a few years, but they soon disappeared as investors moved to more stable, or cheaper countries...

In the meantime, the planners' own documents recognised that the population would suffer. A 1985 World Bank paper called for cuts in "misdirected social objectives", defined as health, education, support for small farmers, and for assistance, not to peasants but to large growers with a greater "growth potential." AID acknowledged in 1982 that the reforms would produce "a decline in income and nutritional status, especially for small farmers and peasants," and that the new, open economy would have "a sharply growing need to import grain and other consumer products." AID called the result of this new situation paradoxically, "an historic change toward deeper market interdependence with the US."

AID did have something to say about the need for 'food security' in Haiti, but for AID, food security is actually "food and agriculture self-reliance", meaning the country would miraculously have enough agricultural and manufacturing jobs so, while it would not have "food self-sufficiency in the narrow sense", it could satisfy needs through local production combined with "importation of food at commercial terms paid for from export earnings." Naturally, the subsidised US agri-businesses stood ready to fill those needs...

(10) SAVING SOULS

Ian Thomson, *Bonjour Blanc,* 1992

This extract from a travel book, written by a British author, highlights the influence of foreign Christian missionaries whose humanitarian relief work is often carried out with the ulterior motive of 'saving' Haitians from Vodou.

One day I struck up conversation with two Mormons – the Elders Walsh and Cumming – while having my hair cut by Monsieur Célestin Excellent, chief barber to Jérémie since 1962. One after the other we sat on a high, old-fashioned black leather swivel chair, talking as blond hair fell to the floor amid woolly curls shorn from the heads of Haitians.

"Well whaddeya know! So you're gonna write a book about Hay-di, huh? Boy, that's a tough one, real tough. For a start, you got the Voodoo. Man, that can really put the whammy on a guy."

"The what?"

"Elder Walsh's talking about the evil spirits abroad at night," explained Elder Cumming from Las Vegas. "Gotta watch out for them, with the dark-skinned thousands all around you. Yes sir, you gotta watch out for the spirits."

"It was a real shocker, when they told me I was gonna be posted to Hay-di. Didn't even know where the place was, let alone that it was a ... Black Republic. I figured there might be Red Indians here, or like a variety of Hispanic folk. But blacks? No-o sir."

As missionaries in the Church of Jesus Christ of Latter-Day Saints, the Mormons are here to prepare the people for the Grand Millennium. ("You never know when it's gonna happen,' said Elder Walsh. "The Second Coming, I mean. But we're waiting, we're ready.") Servants of the Lord, they feel it's their duty to dress with becoming moderation – "We are not here to swim or ride motorbikes or drink alcohol" – and are proud to announce that no single convert to Mormonism will ever revert to Voodoo...

American missions are to found everywhere in Haiti: Larry Jones's Hands of God Ministries, Mission to Haiti Inc., Mission Possible...There are Baptists, Methodists, Jehovah's Witnesses, Seventh Day Adventists. All are devoted to the extirpation of Voodoo and scorn this religion in much the same way that Dr. Johnson scorned the ideal of Rousseau's Noble Savage: "The savages have no bodily advantages beyond those of civilised men. They have not better health; and as to care or mental uneasiness, they are not above it, but below it, like bears."

The Eglise Baptiste Conservatrice of Pastor Wallace Turnbull, built half a century ago in the green hills above Port-au-Prince, is particularly virulent in its missionary preachments. "The Haitian people are caught in Satan's grip," says Pastor Wally in his Middle American twang. "Voodoo divides with mistrust, requires unnatural acts."

Two hundred and fifty baptised Haitians work for Pastor Wally and his mission, tilling the fields in return for food, rarely for dollars. This Food-for-Work programme is typical of US missionary endeavour in Haiti. It conserves money for the evangelists and has enabled Pastor Wally to run the Mountain Maid Gift Shop (where one may purchase embroidered garments as well as hamburgers, French fries and peanut-butter cookies.) Thus Haitians become dependent on food supplied by Christian aid agencies, usually imported from the United States, and neglect to produce their own.

(11) VERSIONS OF DEVELOPMENT

Robert Maguire et al, *Haiti Held Hostage: Quest for Nationhood 1986 to 1996,* 1996

Hundreds of international and local non-governmental organisations have been active in Haiti over several decades. While some merely dealt with humanitarian relief, others attempted programmes intended to help poor Haitians to resolve their problems themselves.

These organisations carried out a dizzying array of humanitarian assistance and socioeconomic development programmes throughout the country, most of them bringing little durable improvement to the lot of ordinary Haitians. Little coordination existed either among or between funders and implementing agencies. The absence of accountable government structures spurred the evolution of what was widely described as a "Republic of NGOs."

Partners could be found to accommodate the objectives of donors to reverse, contain, or expand change. Indeed, the panoply of funders and implementers exhibited the full spectrum of objectives and activities. Persons interviewed for this report agreed with the categorisation of bilateral and multilateral donors, international NGOs and their local partners, and Haitian NGOs and grassroots groups into two broad groups.

The first group was composed of organisations directing their efforts toward emergency relief and the provision of goods and services. These organisations met certain pressing needs in times of disaster but stopped short of addressing the root causes of suffering. Also in this category were agencies that actively supported recidivistic forces thwarting legitimate popular aspirations for change.

The organisations in this first category tended to be affiliated with Haiti's economic, political, and religious elites, often employing Haitians from the country's leading families. USAID and various intergovernmental organisations provided them with significant amounts of funding. CARE and an array of major religious organisations and missionary groups carried out their own such programmes and funded indigenous partners as well. Broadly speaking, these activities supported the status quo or sought to introduce modest changes in it, although their stated objectives may have been more reform-orientated.

The second category was comprised of organisations whose interventions sought to bring about fundamental social, economic, and political change. Their programmes, often mixing human resource development with economic empowerment, embraced more active decision-making roles for participants. The local groups receiving aid tended to be either community-based or linked through professional or technical associations with grassroots membership organisations and entrepreneur groups, the disenfranchised, and the religious rank and file. Funders included progressive religious groups, NGOs such as Oxfam, or autonomous government-supported entities such as the Dutch Catholic Organisation for Development (CEBEMO) and the Inter-American Foundation (IAF).

An example of the second category is provided by Oxfam UK, an international NGO that began work in Haiti in the 1970s. During the Duvalier era, it had worked largely with church groups in training and literacy. In 1986, it took advantage of the political opening to begin work with a newly formed federation of "base groups" in income-generating projects. These activities contrasted with those of NGOs in the first category, which emphasised food-for-work and other assistance programmes.

(12) FUNDING THE TRANSITION

William Robinson, *Low Intensity Democracy in Haiti,* 1994

US policy towards post-Duvalier Haiti centred on support for the military in order to ensure that the transition from dictatorship to constitutional rule would produce a friendly civilian government. A vital part of this approach was an aid programme to fund a conservative elite faction and so create an alternative to Duvalierism.

The Clinton administration's hypocritical diplomacy around Jean-Bertrand Aristide is a high-profile manifestation of a ten-year campaign of "low intensity democracy." Conducted through the State Department, the Agency for International Development (AID), the Pentagon, the CIA, the National Endowment for Democracy (NED), and other US agencies, this programme is part of a post-Cold War shift in methods of social control over Third World populations.

Touted as "democracy promotion," it aims to blunt the most scandalous abuses and create a democratic facade. In fact, the policy defuses mass movements for democratisation while preserving the exploitative economic and social order. It relies less on outright coercion than on sophisticated mechanisms of ideological hegemony, political co-optation, and new forms of domination in the global economy.

Imposition of "low intensity democracy" in Haiti has not gone smoothly. Since 1986, when a civic uprising sent Jean-Claude ("Baby Doc") Duvalier into exile, Washington began a new programme to facilitate a "transition to democracy" which involved economic, political, and military aid. The programme was intended to replace the Duvalier dynasty with less discredited elements of the tiny elite that has dominated the country since its independence in 1804. The downtrodden majority would again be bypassed.

Between 1986 and 1990, AID funnelled $300 million to Haiti for "development" while the Pentagon provided smaller amounts for "security assistance that helped sustain the military as an institution until the 1991 coup."[1] "You've got a problem with that army," said a State Department official in justifying the aid, "but it's the only institution in Haiti at the present time." [...]

The linchpin of the programme...was some \$3 million, spent in strategic doses between 1986 and 1990 by NED. These funds went to a variety of strategically placed organisations in civil society, including the Haitian Institute for Research and Development (IHRED), the Human Rights Development Resource Centre (CHADEL), the Association of Journalists, and the Federation of Unionised Workers (FOS), among others.

NED completely ignored the hundreds of grassroots organisations that eventually coalesced into Lavalas. Instead, it judiciously funded and cultivated an elite alternative to Duvalier-style authoritarianism, which provided the base for the September 1991 coup. For instance, IHRED head Leopold Berlanger and CHADEL leader Jean-Jacques Honorat both applauded the coup. Within a week of the take-over, Honorat became provisional prime minister. Similarly, NED provided \$2 million for "party building" and "civic education" in 1989 and 1990. This campaign spawned among others, Marc Bazin's Movement to Install Democracy in Haiti (MIDH). Bazin also would serve as one of the military regime's provisional prime ministers.

The US plan for a Haitian "transition to democracy" aimed at bringing Bazin and the conservative elite to power in the 1990 elections. The US had successfully pulled off "transitions to democracy' in the Philippines, Chile, Nicaragua, and elsewhere, but in Haiti, Lavalas and Aristide unexpectedly triumphed.

[1] Thomas Carothers, 'The Reagan Years: the 1980s' in Abraham Rosenthal, ed., *Exporting Democracy: the United States and Latin America, Themes and Issues* (Baltimore: John Hopkins University Press, 1991), p.113.

(13) THE CIA PAYROLL

Haïti en Marche, *Tous les 'nationalistes' agents de la CIA,* 1993

An article in *The New York Times* published on 1st November 1993 with the headline, "Key Haiti Leaders Said to Have Been in the CIA's Pay", added to the suspicions, long held by Aristide supporters in Haiti and among the Haitian diaspora, that an influential sector of the US government backed the coup regime.

According to the article, these men, "generals and politicians", have been in the service of the CIA during the last decade, from the mid-1980s until the coup d'état that overthrew Haiti's first democratically elected government in September 1991. They have supplied information about everything: drug trafficking, contraband, the political situation.

The New York Times' source was an American government official who, without naming names, said that "several of the principal players in the present situation were compensated by the US government". The official had not found out how much money had been involved nor when (or if) the payments ended.

President Aristide's lawyer, the former Maryland congressman, Michael Barnes, said that as "the CIA was working with the very enemies of the head of state," this explains the blatant injustice and partiality of the CIA reports on Aristide and his administration."

The New York Times, recalling that the CIA's recent briefing to the US Congress portrayed President Aristide as "a psychopath", noted that Brian Latell, the (CIA's) chief analyst for Latin American affairs, had declared in a 1992 report on the situation in Haiti under the coup regime that General Raoul Cédras, "the current dictator", is "one of the most promising leaders to have emerged in Haiti since the 1986 fall of the Duvalier dictatorship".

The lone champion of these "generals and politicians" – agents of the CIA – is the Congressman Robert Torricelli from New Jersey, who during the Bush administration had been one of the architects of the "return without a return" project for President Aristide.

Another member of the Congress mischievously commented that if there is one area about which these "informants" should have been able to supply precise information to the US government that would be on the trafficking of drugs.

Meanwhile, the CIA, which seems full of revelations these days, has made available the secret report that had formed the basis for the scandalous "psychological profile" of President Aristide. The author of this report – control yourselves – goes by the name of Michel-Ange Montplaisir, a neuro-surgeon.1 It is he who claims that a certain Dr Hervé Martin had prescribed tranquilisers (of lithium) to Father Aristide in a Montreal psychiatric hospital in 1980. However, Aristide was not in Canada in 1980, but in Israel. Dr Hervé Martin, a Haitian, does exist, but he maintains that he has never practised in Montreal. A CNN researcher found that no doctor of this name had ever been registered in that city.

[1] Dr Michel-Ange Montplaisir was a Haitian doctor living in Port-au-Prince.

Translated from French by Charles Arthur

(14) PARAMILITARY ALLIES

Allan Nairn, *Our Man in FRAPH: Behind Haiti's Paramilitaries,* 1994

Emmanuel Constant, was the leader of the Front for the Advancement and Progress of Haiti (FRAPH), a paramilitary group that acted as a front for the military coup regime in 1993-4. The FRAPH membership, composed of former Tontons Macoutes and attachés – gunmen working in tandem with the police and army – was responsible for thousands of acts of violence against individuals, organisations, and residential areas thought to be sympathetic to the exiled Aristide. Constant fled from Haiti to the US in late 1994 when murder charges were brought against him following the return of constitutional rule. With the US Central Intelligence Agency (CIA) subsequently confirming Constant had been a paid informant, the US declined the Haitian Government's request for his extradition.

Interviews with Constant and with US officials who have worked directly with him confirm that Constant recently worked for the CIA and that US intelligence helped him launch the organisation that became the FRAPH. Documentary evidence obtained from other sources and confirmed in part by Constant also indicates that a group of attachés – some of them implicated in some of Haiti's most notorious crimes – have been paid for several years by a US government-funded project that maintains sensitive files on the movements of the Haitian poor.

In my October 3 *Nation* article ("The Eagle is Landing") I quoted a US intelligence official praising Constant as a "young pro-Western intellectual...no further right than a Young Republican" and saying that US intelligence had "encouraged" Constant to form the group that emerged as the FRAPH. Reached at his home on the night of September 26, Constant confirmed the US official's account. He said his first US handler was Col. Patrick Collins, the US Defence Intelligence Agency attaché in Haiti, who he described as "a very good friend of mine" (Constant spoke of dealing later with another official he called "(the United States') best liaison", but he refused to give a name.) Constant said that Colonel Collins first approached him while Constant was teaching a training course at the headquarters of the CIA-run National Intelligence Service (SIN) and building a computer database for Haiti's notorious rural section chiefs at the Bureau of Information and Coordination in the General Headquarters of the Haitian coup regime.

Giving an account that dovetailed closely with that of the US official, Constant said that Collins began pushing him to organise a front "that could balance the Aristide movement" and do "intelligence" work against it. He said their discussions had begun soon after Aristide fell in September 1991. [...]

...a well-informed intelligence official confirmed that Collins had worked with Constant and had, as Constant says, guided him and urged him on. Collins has, in recent weeks, spoken quite highly of Constant and has said that Constant's mission from the United States was to counter the "extreme" of Aristide. ....

When the relationship started, Constant was working for the CIA, teaching a course at the agency-run SIN on "The Theology of Liberation" and "Animation and Mobilisation". The SIN, at that time, was engaged in terrorist attacks on Aristide supporters, as were Constant's pupils, army S-2 field intelligence officers. The targets included, among others, popular church catechists. Constant says that the message of the SIN course was that though communism is dead, "the extreme left", through the *ti legliz*, the grass-roots Haitian "little church" was attempting "to convince people that in the name of God everything is possible" and that, therefore, it was right for the people to kill soldiers and the rich. Constant says he taught that "Aristide is not the only one: there are tens of Aristides".

(15) THE REAL COUP-MONGERS

Fourteen Popular Organisations, *Position of the Popular Organisations on the Country's Crisis,* 1994

In this extract from a press release from July 1994, a group of grass-roots organisations express their belief that the coup regime was receiving the backing of certain US institutions, and that a US military intervention in Haiti would only serve American interests.

Faced with this tragic situation [we are compelled to ask the following questions:] Are the Tontons Macoute solely responsible? Did the Tontons Macoute stage the coup d'état alone? Where did the Macoutes obtain the strength to maintain such resistance and hold on to the rotten power they got through the September 30th coup d'état? Where did the coup leaders get the strength to withstand a supposed embargo by the entire international community over the past 33 months?

Notwithstanding the doubts expressed by many with respect to possible US participation in the coup d'état, the present arrogance displayed by the Macoutes along with the US role in the lame UN/OAS negotiations have confirmed that the coup leaders would not have been able to remain in power for so long without assistance – even with their access to money via contraband, drug trafficking and the pillaging of state coffers.

While the Haitian Army executed the plan of the coup d'état; the anti-democratic bourgeoisie financed it; and unscrupulous parliamentarians and politicians helped to entrench it, it is crystal clear that the US Embassy in Port-au-Prince – headed by Alvin Adams – planned and directed the September 30th coup d'état. In essence, the Macoutes – acting as lackeys of the US within the country – executed the order given to them by their boss...The major author of the coup is the US Embassy, the CIA, the Pentagon and the Bush Administration. Having conceived, planned, and directed the coup, these same US institutions are today seeking to consolidate the coup d'état under the Clinton Administration.

This is not the first time the US Embassy participated in organizing a failed or successful coup in Haiti. To be sure, since after the US occupation from 1915 to the present, the US Embassy has always installed, removed, and supported dictators in Haiti... The US Ambassador is the supreme director of political life in Haiti. S/he is a veritable colonial governor with the full power to do as s/he pleases in the country. S/he has even more power than did the French governor during the period of colonization.

Thus, we understand the reaction of US Ambassador Alvin Adams against the changes that the December 16, 1990 elections would have brought to the political life of Haiti, and his motivations for planning a bloody coup d'état against President Aristide in which more than 5,000 people have been killed.

Any observer of the political situation in Haiti could see that immediately after the September 30th coup, the US government adopted a hedgy policy with regard to the crisis. Officially, the US government, the OAS and the UN all condemned the military coup d'état of Cédras/François. In addition, they all took positions calling for the restoration of President Jean-Bertrand Aristide to power.

On the other hand, the US continues to covertly support and guide the coup; they continue to serve as advisors to the Macoutes in their repressive campaign against the forces struggling for change – particularly against the popular sector. The US Embassy continues to advise the coup leaders on initiatives to conserve their power. The emergence of FRAPH and the killing and disappearing of popular leaders is not an accident. It is the same policy adopted by the US in El Salvador with the extreme right ARENA political party. [...]

The US is using the Macoutes in the framework of its neo-liberal plan for Haiti. The US is responsible for the duration of the crisis by trying to find its own solution to resolve the crisis to benefit its own interests. The US is ultimately responsible for the trials and tribulations of the Haitian people.

List of signatories:

Solidarite Peyizan Ayisyen (SOPA), Tèt kole ti peyizan Ayisyen, Kominikasyon, oganizasyon pou edikasyon ak devlopman (KOPED), Komite Popilè Jan Jak Desalin (KPJJD), Solidarite Ant Jèn (SAJ), Veye Yo, Asanble Popilè Nasyonal (APN), Konbit Komilfo (Grand Goâve), Federasyon Mouvman Demokratik katye Moren (FEMODEK), Asanble fòs popilè (AFPO), Komite Defans Enterè Nasyonal (KODENA), Komite Leve Kanpe, Federasyon Jèn Limonad (FEJEL), Kowodinasyon oganizasyon kiltirel ak atis popilè.

(16) STRUCTURAL ADJUSTMENT

Allan Nairn, *Aristide Agrees to Austerity*, 1994

At a meeting with the main multilateral and bilateral donors in August 1994 President Aristide's representatives agreed to a structural adjustment programme to be bankrolled by a massive injection of aid.

The Aristide government of Haiti has agreed to a structural readjustment plan which adapts the economic approach favoured by the World Bank and IMF and appears to veer away from the more populist line he took before being ousted in a 1991 army coup. The plan was presented in August by Aristide advisers Leslie Voltaire and Leslie Delatour to a Paris donor meeting held in World Bank offices.

Under the plan...Haiti commits to eliminate the jobs of half of its civil servants, massively privatise public services, "drastic(ally)" slash tariffs and import restrictions, eschew price and foreign exchange controls, grant "emergency" aid to the export sector, enforce an "open foreign investment policy," create special corporate business courts, "where the judges are more aware of the implications of their decisions for economic efficiency," rewrite its corporate laws, 'limit the scope of state activity and regulation," and diminish the power of Aristide's executive branch in favour of the more conservative Parliament. In return, Haiti is to receive $770 million in financing, $80 million of which goes immediately to clear up debt owed to international financial institutions. [...]

Axel Peuker, a World Bank Haiti desk officer, said that the plan was written in consultation with "relevant donors" and that the final product was "well received." He added that "there is this tension between the public image of Aristide" and the "rather conservative approach, financial and otherwise" adapted by his Ministers when his government was still in Haiti. Peuker noted that the new plan "goes a step farther in this direction."

Asked about the fact that the plan seems to have abandoned Aristide's past efforts to substantially increase the Haitian minimum wage, Peuker dismissed it as a "non-issue." He said the same applies to Aristide's old attempts to create and enforce a Haitian Social Security pension system: "it's not on the agenda."

Peuker contends that the Haiti structural adjustment "is not going to hurt the poor to the extent that it has in other countries." He said the plan would benefit the "more open, enlightened business class" and would help "make Haiti interesting for foreign investors."

When asked for a comment, Chavannes Jean-Baptiste, a Haitian peasant leader who is also a member of Aristide's cabinet said that he had not been consulted about the plan. He said that though his portfolio in the cabinet included rural development and agrarian reform, "I don't know anything about this document."

(17) WELCOME INVASION

Paul Farmer, *The Significance of Haiti*, 1995

An American doctor, resident in a village in rural Haiti, found that local people, although suspicious of the motives for it, did endorse the US military intervention of September 1994.

If the US occupation was launched, then, to prevent further immigration of Haitian refugees to the United States and restore business as usual, what do we make of the obviously widespread satisfaction among Haitians of all classes? Many prominent Haitian intellectuals – all of whom are regarded as "pro-democracy" and thus suspect by the elite from which they sprang – have come out in support of the US action. "It is an intervention desired and demanded by the mass of Haitian people," asserted Jean-Claude Bajeux, director of the Ecumenical Centre for Human Rights...

On the ground in Haiti in the autumn of 1994, popular enthusiasm for recent developments was widespread. For the poor who were victims of most of the repression during the dictatorship, support for the US landing might be likened to an endorsement of less painful methods of torture. Any change in the balance of power – at times, one thought even a cataclysm of nature would do – represented an improvement for the perennial victims of state power.

Shortly after Aristide's return, I interviewed a number of friends, patients and co-villagers, most of whom I'd known for many years, about their attitudes toward the US occupation. In one small village in the Central Plateau, some people were downright effusive about the troops' presence, regaling me with stories about the humiliation of certain Haitian officers by US soldiers. Several people said to me, "This is what we call 'ipokrit yo sezi', meaning "the hypocrites are shocked," or less literally, "what goes around, comes around."

"We've been hit hard, but we're still here, as ready as ever," reported a young man who was a member of one of the local popular organisations. His analysis of current events was in many ways typical of the comments I elicited in October and November:

"The Americans would have been happy to have the coup succeed, we know that. The Bush Administration was probably involved in (the coup). But they didn't understand Titid's (Aristide's) power. He's very small, compared to them, but much smarter. He said to resist, and we did. The military killed a lot of people, and a lot of people took to the sea. Americans didn't like that, so they saw it would be good for them to give Titid back to us. They made him sign a bunch of bad papers, but the point is, he's back and the guys who were killing us are gone. So it's not perfect, but it's a lot better."

(18) BUSINESS AS USUAL

Noam Chomsky, *Democracy Restored?* 1994

From the early days of the US intervention in 1994 it was apparent that the rich Haitian elite families that had supported the coup, and had grown richer still by exploiting the commercial possibilities created by the UN embargoes, would also prosper from the US-engineered return to democratic rule.

**// **Senior US officials have initiated large-scale business negotiations with some of the most powerful and wealthy Haitian supporters of the military overthrow of President Jean-Bertrand Aristide," Kenneth Freed reported in the *Los Angeles Times* as US forces were "supposedly engineering a new political environment to undermine the power of the same anti-democratic elite." One case is General Shelton's arrangements with Haiti's influential Mevs family "about leasing a large waterfront plot for construction of storage tanks and a pipeline." It only makes sense, given that these leading coup backers had already built "a huge oil depot here to help the army defy the embargo," as the *New York Times* had reported earlier.

Parallel arrangements are proceeding with the other wealthy families that had financed fuel shipments, among other techniques to benefit from the "sanctions." The "powerful Haitian clan" of the Mevs "has positioned itself well to keep doing what it does best – make money," Jose de Cordoba reports in the *Wall Street Journal*. The Mevs had met with Aristide in Washington to induce him to "moderate his position and reach out to the tiny, mostly anti-Aristide, Haitian middle class" – an intriguing notion of "middle", when we consider the proportion of those who own almost all of the nation's wealth. Inexplicably, the Mevs have been able "to build a huge tank farm to store fuel" during the embargo, backed by "loans guaranteed by Haiti's Central Bank"; a fairly typical example of "free market" capitalism. They had "profited from their cosy ties to the Duvalier dictatorships," and therefore found it easy to deal with the US, and to adapt to the form of "broadly-based democracy" that they see the Clintonites fashioning.

While still "nervous about Aristide", the enlightened business sector is "counting on the Americans," the London *Financial Times* reports. Reasonably enough. Unlike educated Americans, it is not sufficient for them to chant ritual phrases; to pursue their interests, they must attend to historical and institutional facts. This "baronial class" of "several dozen families," generally light-skinned, recognises that the military forces coming to "restore democracy" will prefer to deal with them – our kind of folks, after all, unlike the people rotting in the slums. It is "not surprising that the US should do deals with powerful interests," as in the days of the Duvalier family dictatorship when these interests gained their power, benefiting from similar "deals' with the US government and foreign enterprise while the population sank deeper into misery. Why should anything change, now that the traditional benefactors have returned? [...]

Clinton's policies have generally been praised as successful, and rightly so. They achieved what the US has sought ever since the disaster of the free election of December 1990. The previous status quo has pretty much been restored, with one vital difference: civil society has been devastated, and its leading figure has (it is hoped) been trained to become more "pragmatic" and "realistic". The way is clear towards restoring the power of the core sector of Civil Society: foreign investors and "enlightened" elements of the Haitian business community, those who are offended by the sight of mutilated corpses as they are driven by in their limousines, preferring that the poor waste away quietly, out of sight, while the remnants perhaps find a place in the assembly plants where they may even survive the regimen of democracy and capitalism for a few years, if lucky.

(19) THE DISARMAMENT ISSUE

Laurie Richardson, *Haiti: Disarmament Derailed,* 1996

Haitian human rights advocates and grassroots activists contend that the failure of the US/UN forces to carry out an effective programme of disarmament means that former members of military and paramilitary forces will continue to exert a destabilising influence.

II An absolute success story," said US General John Sheehan in February as the last US soldiers, which topped 20,000 at the height of the occupation, pulled out. Indeed, with casualties practically non-existent, and ugly Somalia-type clashes with the population kept to a minimum, the US-led operation has helped the UN counter an image of impotence and given Bill Clinton a foreign-policy victory.

But this "success" is holographic. Although it may look three-dimensional from the perspective of international diplomats, Haiti's democratic popular movement sees it as little more than manufactured illusion. The passive and active resistance of Haiti's grassroots activists finally succeeded in forcing the United States to return ousted President Aristide on October 15, 1994. But the ensuing "soft invasion" scenario – coupled with the policy of political and economic reconciliation which Aristide agreed to espouse – prevented both invading US soldiers and the Haitian people from truly reversing the balance of forces established at the time of the coup.

Disarmament stopped before it actually started. The occupation troops confiscated only 30,000 weapons, many of which were heavy artillery not used against the general population and arms of questionable operability garnered through a controversial "buy-back" program. Haiti's military and paramilitary forces remain heavily armed, and ongoing impunity allows them to continue to repress and extort an unarmed population. As the mandate of the international troops winds down, Haitians are wary of what will occur when the "coco-rats" – the latest derogatory slang here for foreigners – finally clear out, leaving behind a US-trained police force to maintain "law and order."

UN spokesperson Eric Falt ended his rosy evaluation of MINUHA by beaming that its motto is "to be useful every chance we get." Asked about its chances of being useful by disarming Haiti's thugs, Falt replied that there was "a lot of confusion" around this issue. "Haitians think we have wrist watches that can literally see through walls," he said. "We don't have this sort of gadgetry here. We depend on the population to find out where large arms caches might be. Despite our repeated calls, we have had no serious information that could help us seize these large quantities of weapons."

According to human rights advocates such as Daniel Roussière, the Belgian priest who heads the Justice and Peace Commission of the Catholic Diocese of Gonaïves, the problem is not lack of information, but rather the absence of political will. "There would have been nothing easier than to disarm the macoute-military system," said Roussière, "because the UN Civilian Observers Mission was here [during the coup]. They had all the names of the FRAPH, the attachés, the soldiers – and the US soldiers themselves had all the information. Nothing would have been easier than to cull, quietly, those macoutes and soldiers who, for their part, were not particularly courageous individuals."

UN spokesperson Falt dismisses the fears of Haitians that the military and the paramilitary squads have not been vanquished. He contends that with the umbilical cord that connected these elements to the military now severed, they no longer pose a threat. "Instead of being scared, Haitians ought to realize that nobody will take anything away from them any more," he counsels. "It's still what you hear among the weak, those who have the least money, the least say in what is going on. It's normal, we understand, we sympathize, but there needs to be more education on the part of the government and the media."

In reality, the repression and extortion are growing, with violent acts in the capital increasing from an average of 75 a day to over 200, but this is now called "common crime." Far from counting on the international community to disarm Haiti's repressive forces, many in the popular movement blame them for exacerbating the problem. "We understand that everywhere the UN goes, they leave behind a trail of complete destabilisation," says Frantz, a young peasant organizer from Limonade in northern Haiti. "For example, we can see that they came to Haiti to protect the Haitian military. They came here to protect the privileged sectors of Haitian society."

(20) THE POWER OF CULTURE

Jean-Claude Martineau, *Haitian Culture: Basis for Haiti's Development,* 1996

Linking culture to the struggles for political and economic independence, the writer remembers past attempts to destroy Haitians' African legacy and culture, in particular, the anti-Vodou campaigns. In this extract, culture is a battleground in the modern-day struggles over economic development.

Out of the ten radio stations in Port-au-Prince, seven play foreign music all day long – the same music that can be heard in the background in every hotel and restaurant. Aside from the local news, 90% of the TV programming is from and about the outside world. Without translation, without adaptation, the TV stations relay exactly what the average North American viewer is watching in his/her living room: the talk shows, the basketball games, the violent movies. Haitians in Port-au-Prince are as informed as North Americans about the latest affair of such and such actress, or the current salary of certain sports figures.

A few months ago, the state-owned Tele Nasyonal had a choice to broadcast either an international football match played in Cap-Haïtien between Cuba and Haiti, or the final of the European football championship taking place in England. Need I say which game was televised?

Meanwhile, there is no programme about our cuisine, our medicinal herbs and plants, our fruits, our music, out theatre, our folk-tales.. It is as if a concerted effort was being made to give our youth foreign heroes who know nothing about their life, their aspirations and their plight. It is no wonder that a sizeable portion of the Haitian youth aspire to leave the country instead of working to make a better life where they are. There is a clear connection between this "foreign is better" campaign and the economic future of the country. If instead of consuming locally-produced goods we are bombarded with images of foreign goods, we are doomed.

Not too long ago, across the street from the general hospital in Port-au-Price, one could observe dozens of shops making footwear, from children's sandals to dress shoes for men. A wave of second-hand imported shoes has completely destroyed this industry. The shoe-making trade has disappeared, affecting the livelihood of thousands of Haitians. Imported second-hand clothes have killed Haitian tailoring, not only in the capital, but also in the most remote villages. When Haitian peasants no longer wear their traditional garb, the first question should be "what are the tailors doing to survive?" And the list could go on, from the imported rice, destroying the Artibonite Valley's production, to the imported popcorn, pushing the roasted peanut vendor out.

Is it poverty that has allowed this foreign penetration, or the penetration that has created the poverty? The truth lies somewhere in between. It is a vicious cycle in which one element reinforces the other. In a world in which everybody is talking about the global economy, exchanges are inevitable. But if we let others determine our country's place in that new world order, Haiti will end up working exclusively for exportation while importing everything needed for its survival. Fundamental adjustments will have to be made in every aspect of Haitian life. The culture that has allowed us to survive as a nation for almost two hundred years will be put aside. It has been tried before. It has failed before. Vodou is still practised despite years of vilification and repression. Creole is still spoken in spite of the imposition of French as the country's official language. Everything has been tried against Haiti's independence, from isolation to occupation. It is still there as a nation!

The Haitian people cannot be satisfied outside of their culture, meaning the pride in their history; the respect of their traditions; the taste of their food. Even away from their homeland, they speak, live, act and react as Haitians. The solution, therefore, is not the eradication of Haiti culture. Rather, it should be the basis for future development.

HAITIAN PORTRAITS

These photographs are from a set of over one hundred portraits that were taken in Haiti over a period of nine years. The market for photographs from Haiti is predominantly provided by aid agencies, newspapers and magazines. All of these organisations set, to a greater or lesser extent, their own visual agenda, and this collection of portraits was an attempt to represent Haiti from a less commercial angle. All the portraits were taken on a medium format camera which is laborious to operate, needing more time and greater participation from the subject than most modern cameras. This is the antithesis of much photojournalistic practice, and produces photographs quite different in appearance and atmosphere. Many of the pictures were taken outside Port-au-Prince in smaller towns where this method of working is easier.

Some of the subjects are strangers encountered on the streets, and some are old friends. When the picture of 'Big Foot and his Family' was taken, most of the small community in Fond de Bouden queued up to have their portraits taken in different family groups. The unique and strange costumes worn by the participants at the annual Carnival in Jacmel have been a constant source of inspiration for many of the shots in the set. Other photographs, such as 'On the road to Oboy' are chance sightings, just two young boys mysteriously carrying a cross on an otherwise deserted road.

Most people are pleased to have their portraits made in this way, and the only pity is that more of them cannot receive copies of the final prints.

Leah Gordon

Boys dressed as Taino Indians at Carnival - Jacmel

Cayes Jacmel

On the road to Oboy

Pierrot Barra - artist - Iron Market, Port-au-Prince

Gwo Zago (Big Foot) and family, Fond de Bouden

Sunday in Cap Haïtien

Jacmel

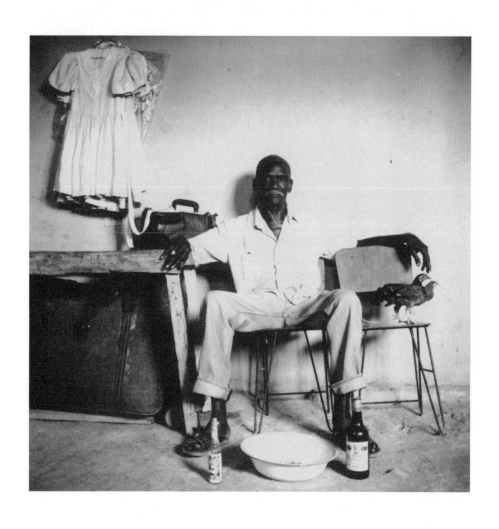

Edgard Jean Louis - Vodou priest - Bel Air

CHAPTER EIGHT
POPULAR RELIGION AND CULTURE

The economic and political division between Haiti's tiny elite and the mass of the population has its corollary in the realms of religion and culture. The roots of this division are located in the colonial era when, at the same time as the freed mulattoes emerged as a significant class, disparate influences began to coalesce into a distinct, and, in many ways, unique culture and sense of identity among the black slave population.

The mulattoes, the offspring of white planter fathers and black slave mothers, aspired to match not just the wealth and status of the white aristocracy, but also to emulate its society and culture. An intrinsic part of this process was the attempt to disassociate and distance themselves from the black slaves, to reject and deny connections to Africa, and to accentuate those with Europe.

On the other hand, the slaves, snatched from different regions of Africa and dispersed to far-flung plantations, were obliged to meld a great variety of languages, religions and customs together in order to forge a common social and cultural system. Two defining features of this embryonic new identity were an effective means of communication, and a shared set of beliefs. Elements of French, Spanish, English and African languages, with the majority of words having French origins, evolved into a common language – Creole. Although the slaves were forcibly converted to Catholicism, the influence of concepts and beliefs from West African religions remained strong. Drawing heavily on these influences, but also incorporating elements of both Catholicism and Freemasonry, a new religion emerged. Known in Haiti as 'serving the *lwa* (spirits)', it is popularly described as Vodou or Voodoo.

In the post-revolution society that developed in Haiti, these two currents persisted. A mainly urban and mainly mulatto elite wrote and spoke, at least in public, French, saw itself as European with its cultural roots in Paris, and was faithful to the Catholic Church. The vast majority, peasants in the countryside, and later, urban slum dwellers, communicated in Creole, kept their attachment to certain African traits and modes of social behaviour, and developed the ritual and ceremony to serve the spirits.

The importance of the role played by Vodou in the revolution against slavery is the subject of some dispute. There are those who highlight the leadership provided to the rebellious slaves by Vodou priests, and the inspirational qualities of Vodou in the war against the white, Christian slave-owners. They stress the importance of the Bois Caiman Vodou ceremony that ignited the revolution, and the influence of the experienced fighters from the Maroon communities where the essence of Haitian Vodou is believed to have evolved. (1) Others, however, point out that neither of the two great revolutionary leaders, Toussaint Louverture and Jean-Jacques Dessalines, had any evident sympathy with Vodou, and regarded the Vodou chiefs as a troublesome threat to military discipline and their centralised command structure.

When Dessalines became emperor, he prohibited Vodou services and shot its adherents. President Boyer too made the practice of Vodou illegal, but the new independent state had little authority over the populace outside of the coastal towns. Furthermore, Napoleon had withdrawn the French Catholic missionaries from Haiti in 1804, and although Boyer negotiated with the Vatican, it was not until after the signing of the 1860 Concordat that the Catholic Church began to reassert a significant influence. While Catholicism became the official religion, Vodou had already put down deep roots among the mass of the people.

A definition of Vodou is problematic. The tenets of the faith do not exist in a written form, and instead are passed on by word of mouth from one generation to another. Not only can variants of the belief system be found in different parts of the country, but rituals and services differ from one temple to another depending on the interpretation of the individual priest, the male *oungan* or the female *mambo*. (2)

There are, however, basic concepts that are widely accepted. The faithful believe in the existence of a God, but the supreme being, *Bondye*, is too great to be involved with the affairs of humans, and instead delegates this task to spirits, the lwa. (3) The Vodou pantheon contains hundreds of lwa, representing spirits from Africa, and the spirits of ancestors. They are conceptualised according to their sphere of influence, behaviour, associated symbols and colour, and the food that they prefer to be offered. (4)

The lwa are neither good nor bad, but display virtues and vices, just like the humans whose lives they administer. Many of them have counterparts in the roster of Catholic saints, a syncretism that harks back to the days when slaves disguised their worship of the lwa in the face of the Catholic missionaries' disapproval by incorporating Catholic iconography into their belief system. In the same way that Vodou is a flexible and changing faith, so too the significance of the lwa is open to interpretation. For example, Erzili Dantò can be seen as a revolutionary warrior and at the same time as a symbol of Haitian womanhood to be contrasted with the male fantasy represented by her sister Erzili Freda. Likewise, the family of Gede spirits can be interpreted as spirits of the dead and/or as representations of rebellion against social conventions. (5 & 6)

The lwa communicate to the faithful in their dreams, but are also invoked by priests through the means of ceremonies held in a temple, or *oufò*. These ceremonies are held either so that the congregation can honour or 'serve' a particular lwa or group of lwa, or to facilitate the interaction between a lwa and a believer, if the latter seeks to curry favour or hopes to remedy a transgression. The service, which lasts many hours is directed by the oungan or mambo, and involves elaborate rituals, singing, drumming and dancing, as well as the offering of cooked food and animal sacrifices. During most services lwa that have been summoned or are being honoured will 'arrive' and 'mount', or possess for a time, the body of one or more participants. (7)

Aside from the services for the lwa, the oungans and mambos also carry out an important role healing the sick. This is achieved either by administering natural, usually herbal, remedies – most priests are also 'leaf-doctors', or by invoking the lwa in a form of faith healing. (8)

A minority of priests, often known as *bokors*, use magic, or, as it is known in Haiti, 'practice with the Left Hand'. In the minds of the believer, the priest can deploy supernatural forces, enclosed in bottles or packets called *wanga*, as defensive or offensive magic. Among many Haitians, the explanation for most misfortunes and illnesses is that an enemy or rival has 'sent' an evil force, and belief in the power of magic plays an important role in disputes between neighbours.

The most extreme version of this magic is the practice of zombification – the belief that sorcery can be used to inflict a state of living death on a victim. It remains unclear whether some oungans know the exact dosage of a poisonous concoction that can make a person appear dead, administer it, and then retrieve the 'dead' person from their grave; whether the belief in zombies is a way of explaining away little understood forms of mental illness; or is even a method of dealing with unresolved grief for the death of a relative. Whatever the explanation for the belief in the phenomenon, the foreigners' interest far outweighs the importance accredited to it by Haitians.

The use of magic and the casting of curses are the best-known aspects of Vodou outside of Haiti. In the view of many commentators, this emphasis is a manifestation of the negative propaganda about Haiti generated by hostile colonial powers after the Revolution, and in particular, a reflection of the continuing battle for religious affiliation waged in Haiti by the Catholic, and later, Protestant, Churches. The Haitian government, and, from 1860, the Catholic Church, periodically mounted attacks on Vodou, notably with the anti-superstition campaigns of 1925-30 and 1941-2, when temples and religious objects were destroyed, and priests were persecuted. This hostility merely drove Vodou underground, and prompted Vodou priests to deepen the secrecy and mystery surrounding the religion as a means of defence. The dreaded secret societies, believed to hold sway at night in the countryside, are seen by some as a facet of Vodou self-defence. (9)

Throughout much of Haitian history, Vodou has been vilified by members of the elite who regarded it as an expression of a primitive and backward culture and society to be contrasted with their own embrace of European concepts of civilisation and modernity. However, an intellectual current, sympathetic and supportive of the religion and culture of the peasant masses, developed in the 1920s and 1930s. The proponents of this cultural nationalism advocated recognition of the value of Vodou and the Creole language as essential components of an authentic and unique African-based Haitian identity. Writers such as Jean Price Mars castigated the elite for denying their heritage. (10)

Several decades later, François Duvalier drew on some of these ideas to develop the ideological justification for his dictatorship. He also deployed his understanding of Vodou to appeal to, and, at the same time, control the peasantry. Many Vodou priests, for instance, were recruited into the Tonton Macoute network, and it was surely not coincidental that the Macoute uniform of blue denim and red neck-tie is the outfit associated with the lwa of agriculture and harvests, or that the black top hat and tails worn by Duvalier himself, are the trademarks of Baron Samdi, the powerful head of the Gede family of lwa.

The association with the Duvalier dictatorships contributed to a negative appraisal of Vodou, particularly among outsiders. In a more general sense, some Haitians commentators, while recognising its cultural and nationalistic values, have perceived Vodou as an inherently conservative religion, in which the overwhelming fatalism of believers represents a significant obstacle in the struggle to improve the lot of the Haitian poor. (11)

The Catholic Church, having failed miserably with its attempts to suppress Vodou, adopted a new, more tolerant approach from the 1950s onwards. Some of the participatory aspects of the Vodou ceremony, such as songs in Creole and the use of drumming, were incorporated into the services of many churches. The Protestant churches, increasingly prominent with the influx of evangelical missionaries during the mid- and late twentieth century, however, took up the anti-Vodou crusade. (12) Even so, Vodou has displayed a remarkable capacity to withstand these challenges and co-exist with the Christian competition, and it remains the dominant religion in Haiti. The fact that many Haitians have no problem considering themselves to be Christians, as well as servants of the lwa, is reflected in the oft-repeated cliché – Haiti: 80 per cent Catholic, 20 per cent Protestant, 100 per cent Vodou.

The influence of Vodou extends far beyond the realm of religious faith and worship, and informs many aspects of Haitian culture. Nowhere is this more apparent than in the richly creative and prolific field of artistic expression, for which Haiti has become world famous. The origins of Haitian art can be traced back to the decoration of the temple walls, and the creation of artifacts and accoutrements for the Vodou ceremony. The murals and models representing interpretations of the lwa, and the flags identifying a temple society, have, with the arrival of foreign art buyers and the emergence of a previously non-existent market, developed into the paintings, wooden and metal sculptures, and sequin flags, that are now successfully exhibited and sold in galleries both within and beyond Haiti. (13)

The country's musical tradition, too, owes much to the drumming and rhythms that form a central part of the Vodou ceremony. Rhythm-driven music has long formed the soundtrack for the celebrations surrounding pilgrimages to certain sacred sites, and for the street parties of the annual pre-Lenten carnival and the subsequent 'rara' season. (14)

There are, of course, many aspects of Haitian culture that are not directly intertwined with Vodou. The different musical styles, *troubadour* and *compas*, form part of a vibrant music and dance scene in both rural and urban contexts. (15) Sports, requiring facilities and equipment, have necessarily remained the preserve of the elite, with the exception of soccer, which is immensely popular with all classes. Despite the dearth of properly prepared pitches and the cost of footballs, there are hundreds of small teams, with the top clubs competing in leagues for both men's and women's football. The game received a considerable boost when, in 1974, Haiti became the first Caribbean nation to qualify for the World Cup finals. (16) Other favoured past-times are cockfighting, and betting on the lottery. (17 & 18)

In both rural and urban areas, schools have been a rarity, and the lack of formal education has had a significant bearing on the life and culture. With few people outside the elite minority able to read or write, an oral culture has developed, reflected in the popularity of jokes, riddles and storytelling. (19 & 20)

A high illiteracy rate of approximately 60 per cent means that books and newspapers are scarcely found outside the cities. Those that do exist are almost exclusively written in French. The Creole language, although spoken by all Haitians, was not recognised as an official language until the adoption of the new Constitution in 1987. Attempts to develop a standardised and universally recognised form of the written word have made some advances in recent years, and a weekly newspaper entirely in Creole has appeared since 1990. With the high level of illiteracy leaving much of the population with a relatively small vocabulary, idioms and proverbs are frequently used to convey more complex ideas and concepts. (21) Since the 1970s, radio has partly filled the void in the dissemination of news and ideas, but the use of FM transmissions that are impeded by high mountain ranges continues to limit access to this medium. International and local news, as well as rumour and gossip, are relayed by word of mouth, a phenomenon known as the *teledjòl*.

(1) BLACK MAGIC

Thomas Madiou, *Histoire d'Haiti*, 1848

In Madiou's highly subjective account of the 1791 slave uprising, superstition and sorcery were significant tactics used to inspire and unify the slave forces, and to terrorise their enemy.

At their head, the slaves placed Jean-François whose lieutenants were Boukman and Flaville. They led them to victory to the sound of African music which everywhere spread terror. All of the Plaine du Nord was put to fire and blood...Jean-François took the title of Grand Admiral of France and General-in-Chief and his lieutenant, Biassou, that of Vice-Roy of the conquered country. They dominated those bands composed of Congos, Mandigans, Ibos, Senegalese by both superior intelligence and superstition...Biassou surrounded himself with sorcerers and magicians, who composed his staff. His tent was filled...with objects symbolic of certain African superstitions... At night great fires were kept burning in his camp; naked women performed horrible dances of frightening contortions around these fires, singing words known only in the African deserts. When exaltation had reached its zenith, Biassou, followed by his sorcerers, stood before the crowd and cried forth that he was inspired by the spirit of God; he told the Africans they would be transformed to life in their old tribes in Africa if they fell in combat. Then in prolonged echoes their frightful cries carried through the distant woods; chanting and the sombre drums began again, and, exploiting these moments of exaltation, Biassou would urge his bands against the enemy, surprising them in the dead of night. Jean proclaimed himself the avenger of Ogé and Chavannes. He commanded under Jean-François. Like Biassou, he was influenced by sorcerers...

The cul-de-sac [1] insurgents (an army of two thousand maroons) had at their head an African of great height and Herculean strength. He ruled by superstition, always carrying under his arm a large white cock, which, he pretended, transmitted to him orders from heaven. He marched preceded by the music of drums, lambis, trumpets, and sorcerers, or papas, who chanted that he was invulnerable, that the enemy's cannon were only bamboo, powder, and dust. His guard carried long cow-tails, which they claimed deflected bullets...

The Léogâne quarter was laid waste by Romaine Rivière, who had assumed the title of prophet, calling himself the godson of the Virgin Mary. He signed himself Romaine the Prophesier. By superstition he dominated the slave bands he had raised in the mountains. He said Mass, subjected whites to all sorts of tortures, and pretended that this was ordered by the Virgin.

[1] The region east of Port-au-Prince

(2) WHAT IS VODOU?

Sidney Mintz and Michel-Rolph Trouillot, *The Social History of Haitian Vodou*, 1995

Vodou has fascinated anthropologists and sensation-seekers alike. Few, other than believers, know exactly what it is.

...In the words of one of the more thoughtful students of the religion, "Qui dit Haiti, pense 'Vaudoux', c'est un fait devant lequel on doit se contenter d'émettre une vaine protestation." [Whoever says Haiti thinks 'voodoo', a state of affairs over which one can only protest in vain.]

Most Americans and Europeans think they know what "voodoo" means. The meaning of the phrase "voodoo economics," for example, associated with ex-president George Bush, appears to be understood and is clearly recognised as pejorative, even though it has never been defined. The apparent collective assurance that the meaning of such words and phrases is already known makes it unusually difficult to write informatively about the history of Vodou and about problems connected with the label. There are many experts on Vodou and they do not all agree. In fact, it is easier to provide a sober ethnographic account of a contemporary ceremony than it is to make good sense of the religion's history.

Vodou was created by individuals drawn from many different cultures. It took on its characteristic shape over the course of several centuries. It has never been codified in writing, never possessed a national institutional structure – a priesthood, a national church, an orthodoxy, a seminary, a hymnal, a hierarchy, or a charter. It runs no day camps, athletic contests, or soup kitchens. And until the creation of the organisation called ZANTRAY, explicitly for the defence of the Haitian cultural tradition, Vodou has never had "public relations" either. It is widely dispersed nationally, in the form of what appear to be local cult groups. It has no geographical centre or mother church. Its practice seems to be highly variable locally. Though lacking a national apparatus of any kind, so widely is Vodou practised and so powerful are the premises of its underlying cosmology that it is usually considered by the Haitians themselves to be the national religion.

Subtle political elements are also involved in the image that Vodou projects. A strong ideological current among Haitians centres on the idea of Vodou's importance in the revolutionary creation of the Republic of Haiti, nearly two centuries ago. The religion continues to be lauded (and sometimes damned) in contemporary accounts of all sorts.

Since its beginnings in the New World, Vodou has always stood in some counter-posed dialectical relationship to other (European) religions, particularly Catholicism. It appears never to have excluded these other faiths from its own means for organising belief, and for squaring life with the demands of the daily world. But there are differences of opinion concerning the contribution of Catholicism to Vodou, and at least some authorities discount that contribution.

To document the history of Vodou is to define as much as to explain it. Yet because that history is murky – shrouded not only in myth but also in a million printed pages written by non-practitioners, both infatuated and violently hostile – a comprehensive picture is elusive.

(3) WORLD OF SPIRITS

Laënnec Hurbon, *Voodoo: Truth and Fantasy*, 1995

The spirits, or *lwa*, are an intrinsic part of the Vodou belief system.

The *lwa* are supernatural beings that can enter the human body, and they are thought to be present in all realms of nature: in the trees, the streams and the mountains; in the air, the water and fire. This belief is foreign to a modern sensibility, which does not ascribe God's hand to all events and elements of nature.

The *lwa* of voodoo establish a web of linkages between human activities – agriculture, war, courtship – and various aspects of the natural world. They create the structure of time and space, and they take control of an individual's life, from birth to death. It would seem that listening very carefully for their messages would enable the faithful to learn and realise their facets. The spirits provide a way of classifying the different provinces of the universe, as well as of life in society. Order and disorder, life and death, good and evil, favourable and unfavourable happenings – all take on meaning through the *lwa*, leaving nothing to strike the faithful as absurd.

The superior and invisible spirits are born into the world. They may have been important people who made a mark on the history of their clan or tribe, ancestors whose memory endures among their descendants, animals or natural elements such as thunder or storms. They act as links between the visible and invisible. They explain the origins of the world, representing its hidden side, shadowed and deep: the very essence of life [...]

The faithful believe that the *lwa* come from Africa, more specifically, a section of Africa confined to Guinea, irretrievably lost and considered purely mythical. According to the deported slaves, the lwa in their turn made the voyage out of Africa to the Caribbean [...] Whether they originated as the protective spirits of clans or deified ancestors, the categories of *lwa* in Haiti reflect the various African ethnic groups. They are regrouped into families called nations, or *nanchon*, which are divided by different rituals. Each ritual has distinctive ceremonies, with its own greetings, cheers, dances, musical instruments and type of animal marked out for sacrifice.

There are three important rituals. The ritual known as Rada honours spirits from Dahomey, in principle considered the 'good *lwd*', called *lwa* from Guinea, or *lwa-Ginen*... The Kongo ritual relates to the *lwa* of Bantu origin. They are less popular than the Rada spirits... The *lwa* celebrated by the Petro ritual mostly come from the colony of Saint-Domingue itself. These are called the Creole *lwa*. Highly vengeful, they are considered 'bitter' as opposed to the Rada *lwa*, which are 'gentle'.

(4) SYMBOLS AND SIGNS

A basic introduction to some of the most well-known *lwa*

Lwa	Role	Symbols	Representations/Associations	Catholic counterparts	Colours	Offerings
Legba	Lwa of rituals, keepers of the gates, crossroads, & paths	cross, keys, walking stick	a crippled old man	St Peter St Anthony St Lazarus	red orange yellow	rice plantains
Dambala	Lwa of wisdom, wealth & luck	snake, rainbow	a wise, successful man	St Patrick	white	white eggs, milk, rice, hens
Ogou	Lwa of war & authority	sword driven into the ground	a warrior, an authoritarian politician	St James the Greater	red	red cocks, rum
Azaka	Lwa of agriculture & harvest	knap-sack, straw hat, machete, pipe	a simple hungry peasant, hard-working & good-natured	St Isidore	blue red green	bread sugar brandy
Erzili Freda	Lwa of love & luxury	heart	a sensual mulatress, jewellery, fine clothes	The Virgin Mary	pink	gifts, sweet food & drinks, perfume, make-up

Erzili Dantò	Lwa of motherhood	heart, knife	a passionate, fierce mother	The Black Madonna	red blue	black pigs, rum Florida water
Simbi	Lwa of fresh water	snakes in a field of crosses	shy, clairvoyant	The Magi	grey green black	speckled hens, grey animals
Agwe	Lwa of the sea & sailors	boat	a sea captain or admiral	St Ulrick	blue white	rams, liqueurs, cakes, rum
Gede	Lwa of the dead, resurrection, & procreation	tomb, skull & crossbones, top hat	a mischievous, lascivious & obscene family	St Gabriel St Gérard St Expedit	black purple	black goats, black cocks
Gran Bwa	Lwa of the forest	tree	healing, initiation	St Sebastian	green	wood, leaves

(5) ERZILI DANTÒ

Karen McCarthy Brown, *Tracing the Spirit,* 1995

The *lwa* Erzili Dantò, a mother figure and fighter, represents many of the experiences of the poorer women of Haiti.

The stories that are told about Dantò capture much of the reality of the lives of poor women in urban Haiti. Dantò is a single mother who raises children on her own. The men in her life are unreliable and sometimes violent. Hard-working, resourceful, and fierce in her defence of her children, she nevertheless makes a habit of hiding her personal suffering. Yet Dantò, while modelling self-sacrificing maternal love, can become an abusive parent herself. There are times when her righteous anger against anyone who threatens her children suddenly and inexplicably turns on the children themselves. They call her Erzili of the red eyes, and she must be handled with care.

During the Haitian slave revolution (1791-1804) Erzili Dantò fought on the front lines, right beside her "children", and, she is said to have been wounded. Dantò lost her tongue. The tragic turn in this story is that it was her own people who cut off her tongue. They did it because they feared she would betray their military secrets. Dantò is thus a voiceless mother, a woman warrior, wounded not by the enemy but by those closest to her. Yet Erzili Dantò, unlike her beautiful and sensual sister, Erzili Freda, is fertile. She has born many children, while it is questionable whether Freda has any progeny. Freda's womanhood centres in sexuality, but Dantò's is rooted in productivity.

Erzili Dantò is almost always represented by the image of the Polish Virgin, Our Lady of Czestochowa. The chromolithograph of this black Virgin can be found from one end of Haiti to the other. Our Lady of Czestochowa is a particularly apt choice to stand for Erzili Dantò, not only because she is black, but also because she appears to have parallel scars on her right cheek, scars that function both as reminders of West African scarification and as external signs of the emotional wounds sustained by this archetypal mother.

(6) ZOZO

Donald Cosentino, *Envoi:The Gedes and Bawon Samdi,* 1995

The Gede *lwa* are celebrated each year on 1 and 2 November, a national celebration both of the dead and departed, and of procreation and renewal. They are also interpreted as manifestations of a barely concealed, anti-establishment and rebellious streak among young people.

Gede has become the most ubiquitous lwa, at once the closest and most revealing personification of the *pèp ayisyan* (Haitian people) at the century's end... Gede's role has increasingly become associated with the antics of social rebellion: *vagrancy, pilfering, lewd and lascivious behaviour, public drunkenness, impersonating officers of the state and priests of official religions, practising medicine without a licence...* The list goes on, but the point is clear, the Gedes are bums, louts, *mal élevé,* everything *honneur et respect* is not. And they are all the more popular for their bad manners... [...]

When he manifests as Gede Brave, the people sing:

> Call him brave-o – he's a bold fellow
> His banana butt is bold
> His bit of chicken is bold
> His cup of kleren is bold
> His sweet potato bit is bold
> I call Brave-Gede:
> Come and Save the Children

When his hips mime intercourse in the dance called *banda,* Gede sings:

> My dick says to my cherie's clit
> Come and get it, my dick is hard
> I spend the whole week working:
> Monday, Tuesday, Wednesday, Thursday, Friday.
> On Saturday, I give you money to buy some food
> On Sunday, I must fuck you all day long.

[...] *Zozo...Zozo:* the word means cock, and it means fuck, and everyone – men and women, sweaty faced, laughing hard – was shouting it in Carnival. Just as every character – political, military, or celestial – stripped of his pretences is an avatar of Gede, so finally is every motive and action reducible to *zozo*. Not *l'amoooour*...or *la vie*...or even *l'honneur* – only zozo. Gede may be foul-mouthed, but he is the sworn enemy of euphemism. He lives beyond all ruses. He is master of the two absolutes; fucking and dying. Group after group danced down the rue Capois, singing the grossest of his anti-love songs:

> When you see a smart ass chick,
> Pick her up and throw her down,
> Pull down her pants,
> And give her *zozo*....wowowo!

One could wonder that women as well as men were shouting these misogynist lyrics. But Gede rides women as well as men. And among the Fon of Dahomey, whose descendants brought Vodou to Haiti, it is young women who strap the dildos on in masquerade. *Zozo* means cock no doubt, but what else does it signify? Is the *zozo* a flip-off of established order? Of *la misère*? The antidote of life in death? Since everything is reducible to Gede, and Gede cannot lie, he makes it possible to laugh even at the most terrible things.

(7) SPIRIT POSSESSION

Alfred Métraux, *Voodoo*, 1959

A central feature of most Vodou ceremonies is the phenomenon of possession in which a *lwa* or spirit takes temporary control of a believer.

The explanation of mystic trance given by disciples of Voodoo is simple: a *loa* moves into the head of an individual having at first driven out 'the good big angel' (*gwo bon ange*) – one of the two souls that everyone carries in himself. This eviction of the soul is responsible for the trembling and convulsions which characterise the opening stages of trance. Once the good angel has gone the person possessed experiences a feeling of total emptiness as though he were fainting. His head whirls, the calves of his legs tremble; he now becomes not only the vessel but also the instrument of the god. From now on it is the god's personality and not his own which is expressed in his bearing and his words. The play of his features, his gestures and even the tone of his voice all reflect the temperament and character of the god who has descended upon him. The relationship between the *loa* and the man seized is compared to that which joins a rider to his horse. That is why a loa is spoken of as 'mounting' or 'saddling' his *chwal* (horse). Possession being closely linked with dancing, it is also thought of in terms of a spirit 'dancing in the head of his horse'. It is also an invasion of the body by a supernatural spirit; hence the often-used expression; 'the *loa* is seizing his horse'.

The symptoms of the opening phase of trance are clearly psychopathological. They conform exactly, in their main features, to the stock clinical conception of hysteria. People possessed start by giving an impression of having lost control of their motor system. Shaken by spasmodic convulsions, they pitch forward, as though projected by a spring, turn frantically round and round, stiffen and stay still with body bent forward, sway, stagger, save themselves, again lose balance, only to fall finally in a state of semi-consciousness [...]

The possessed are protected from the possible effects of their own frenzy by the crowd which surrounds them. They are prevented from struggling too furiously and if they fall, arms are ready to catch them. Even their modesty is shielded: a woman rolling on the ground, convulsed, is followed by other women, who see to the disorders of her dress. This sympathetic concern on the part of the crowd for the gambols of the possessed certainly provides an atmosphere of moral and physical security which is conducive to total abandon in the state of trance.

(8) HERBAL MEDICINE

Selden Rodman and Carole Cleaver, *Spirits of the Night,* 1992

Oungans and *mambos* serve communities without doctors or health centres. Their knowledge of herbal remedies is profound.

As "leaf-doctors", they must know how to cure colds with infusions, shock with salt, bleeding with spider-web applications, infections with garlic. And pectin, a remedy for diarrhoea, is found in the skins of many fruits. Lime juice is known to kill germs.

Michel, a Haitian boy working for our family in Jacmel one winter, had seen the pain and terror inflicted on our son when a licensed doctor lanced his boil. When Michel suffered a similar affliction and we offered to call in the same doctor, he threatened to run away.

That night he visited a houngan on the edge of town and came home with a leaf attached to the ugly sore. The following morning the boil had begun to drain and subsequently healed.

A Haitian friend of ours in La Boule sprained her ankle badly. We recommended hot and cold compresses, but a local houngan wrapped the swollen ankle in a bandage containing leaves, and the next day it was almost normal. There is even a case of a houngan on La Tortue island off Port-de-Paix, who is said to have cured yaws with poultices of mould – which of course is the basis of penicillin.

When illness is beyond their capacity, reputable houngans or mambos will send the patient to a licensed physician. But many of the houngan's or mambo's cures are in the realm of psychosomatic medicine. The psychosomatic therapy of vaudun is at least as remarkable as the medicine of these natural healers. No one who has attended a genuine ceremony can have failed to notice the exhilaration and sense of well-being with which most of the participants leave – especially, perhaps, those who have been possessed.

Milo Rigaud describes the great lengths to which a société once went to revitalise a young man struck down and near death from a disease none of the Port-au-Prince physicians could diagnose. When all else seemed to have failed, the ailing man, who had not eaten in weeks, was lowered into a hole in which a chicken had been buried alive. A young banana tree was placed beside him (if it survived, he would die). His body was next rubbed down with flaming alcohol. He was given a clove of garlic to hold on his tongue. The mambo spat, then gave this invocation:

> With the permission of God, the Saints, the Dead, by the power of Papa Brisé, Monsieur Agueroi-Linsou, Monsieur Guédé Nibo, Monsieur Guédé Nouvarou, and all the Guédés, I demand that you return the life of this man. I Mambo Yabofai, demand the life of this man. I buy for cash; I pay you; I owe you nothing!

And miraculously, after a dozen more esoteric ministrations, the young man did recover. In fact the following morning he was able to get up by himself and wash. He spoke and asked for something to eat. He was given tea and vegetable broth. For dinner he requested potato pancakes and red herring. Rigaud called his recovery "a veritable resurrection."

(9) SECRET SOCIETIES

Karen McCarthy Brown, *Serving the Spirits: the Ritual Economy of Haitian Vodou,* 1995

Vodou's secret societies have long exerted their influence over rural Haiti but their role is changing.

The ritual season for Haitian secret societies coincides with the New Year's holiday. A ceremony held in 1984 in the Artibonite Valley, an area known for secret society activity, brought together three local branches of one society. The night-long rituals, held in a flat and treeless rice-growing area, included powerful Petwo drumming and dancing so energetic the bodies of the dancers nearly disappeared in a cloud of dust. There was no electricity for miles. Complete darkness surrounded a dancing arena lighted only by a modest wood fire. Around midnight something startling happened: a ball of fire suddenly shot up in the distance, to the southeast of us. Immediately after it died out, another exploded toward the northeast. The dancing stopped and we all stood staring into the night. Back and forth the fireballs went, getting closer to one another with each volley, while also coming closer to us. At about the same time, we also heard distant drums, but it was hard to pinpoint the source of the drumming. The sound came and went as if tossed by a wind we knew was not blowing. Then suddenly the volume of the drumming increased dramatically. Two batteries of drums were in hot, loud conversation as two processions, moving on trajectories forty-five degrees apart, simultaneously pierced the skin of darkness and entered our circle of fire light. The leader of each of the neighbouring secret society bands had a soda bottle with a clear liquid in one hand and a burning candle in the other. A mouthful of gas sprayed into the air, the touch of a flame and...Whoosh!

Haitian secret societies – e.g. Sanpwèl, Bizango, Zenglendo – work hard at mystification. They have had to. For longer than one would think, the government of independent Haiti was effectively confined to the coastal cities; it lacked the means to impose its authority on the inaccessible mountainous interior of the island. During that period secret societies, which most likely already had a long history in Haiti, effectively governed the countryside. Secret societies have a related role in West Africa. Both African and New World secret societies tend to buttress their authority by promoting images of themselves as superhuman in power, and quite capable of enforcing swift and deadly justice. The arrival of roads, telephones and radios in rural Haiti, along with the development under Duvalier of a country-wide civilian militia, changed the role of Haitian secret societies. Today, Vodou secret societies run the gamut from political groups (several have recently been involved in organising peasant labourers) to benign local social clubs, to fronts for various kinds of organised crime.

(10) VODOU IS A RELIGION

Jean Price Mars, *So Spoke the Uncle,* 1928

Price Mars, a Haitian intellectual, broke with the traditional elite rejection of peasant culture, and in his seminal text, *So Spoke the Uncle,* defended Vodou as a legitimate religion.

Voodoo is a religion because all its adherents believe in the exist ence of spiritual beings who live anywhere in the universe in close intimacy with humans whose activity they dominate.

These invisible beings constitute an Olympian pantheon of gods in which the greatest among them bear the title of Papa or Grand Master and have the right to special homage.

Voodoo is a religion because the cult appertaining to its gods requires a hierarchical priestly body, a society of the faithful, temples, altars, ceremonies, and finally a whole oral tradition which has certainly not come down to us unaltered, but thanks to which the essential elements of this worship have been transmitted.

Voodoo is a religion because, amid the confusion of legends and the corruption of fables, we can discern a theology, a system of representation thanks to which our African ancestors have, primitively, accounted for natural phenomena and which lies dormantly at the base of the anarchical beliefs upon which the hybrid Catholicism of our popular masses rests.

We are aware that this statement will bring quick objection. You are, no doubt, wondering what is the moral value of such a religion and, as your religious education is dominated by the efficiency of the Christian moral philosophy, you use that as your standard of judgement. In the light of such rules you can only dutifully condemn Voodoo as a religion, not only because you reproach it for being immoral but, more logically, because you frankly declare it amoral. And since it is not known how an amoral religion can exist, you cannot accept Voodoo as a religion. Ah! Such an attitude would be worse than an intellectual injustice, it would be a negation of intelligence. For, in the end, we are aware that every religion has its moral code and that it is most often closely related to the mental evolution of the group in which this religion has been born and has taken root.

(11) THE CURSE OF VODOU

Rémy Bastien, *Vodoun and Politics in Haiti,* 1966

Some Haitian intellectuals see Vodou as a moribund religion, inhibiting moves towards the development of a modern state able to serve the population.

Houngans and *bocors* live by keeping their clientele on a constant alert and by sustaining belief in the supernatural interpretation of the environment. Should the peasantry, the urban proletariat, and a sector of the bourgeoisie lose their faith in the capacity of the Vodoun clergy to manipulate nature and its phenomena at will, *houngans* and *bocors* would face a serious loss of income and social power. But that loss of faith can only come when education, sanitation, and improved economic conditions alleviate the chronic insecurity. Such a programme is well beyond the national resources, both financial and human, of Haiti. As long as these improvements are not introduced, Vodoun will reign supreme over goods and lives. It will operate beyond class lines since it offers to some members of the educated minority a last hope against illnesses which the professional physician cannot cure. As long as insecurity prevails, urbanites and peasants will seek from the *houngan* the secret of wealth and the key to political and social advancement.

Thus, it is hard to see Vodoun in perspective. It unites and divides, cures and kills, protects and persecutes all at once. More than the state, it has succeeded in giving to the Haitian masses a sense of belonging. Perhaps more successfully than Creole as a unifying language, Vodoun has erased the tribal differences among the former slaves of the French colony by imposing coexistence on their divers gods... Yet when all has been said, good and bad, one condemning aspect of Vodoun remains. Historically the religion, like all religions, has evolved and then suffered a process of stagnation which is fatal to the interest of Haiti. It undoubtedly possesses a certain dynamism and undergoes superficial changes. But it has lost its original revolutionary impetus. It has turned into a conservative institution which condones and feeds upon the backwardness of the peasantry. Moreover, Vodoun lacks a hierarchy capable of formulating and imposing a new policy for the benefit of the rural population. It can only thwart or at least remain indifferent to the efforts to initiate changes which might menace the local control of the houngans over their flocks. To our knowledge, no *houngan* has ever sponsored the building of a school, promoted a programme of community development, sought to introduce new crops, or innovated an agricultural technique. His overspecialisation not only guarantees him relative power and wealth, but it also makes him unfit for the kind of *true* leadership which places the material and spiritual welfare of the community above personal advantages. The type of change needed today is beyond the comprehension of Vodoun and contrary to its interests.

Vodoun will remain the bane of Haiti and the arch-enemy of the progressive state until its clergy is curbed by a superior power and learns to cooperate with the rural teacher, the physician, and the agronomist. But should this metamorphosis occur, the *houngan* would cease to be a *houngan*; he would turn into a civil servant. The gods would die.

(12) POLITICAL MISSIONARIES

EPICA / Voices for Haiti, *Beyond the Mountains, More Mountains*, 1994

Since the US occupation (1915-1934) Protestant missionaries have grown increasingly influential, playing, some would say, a dubious cultural and political role.

As in the rest of Latin America, the Protestant church in Haiti has traditionally played a restraining role. Aside from preaching the message of the Bible, there has been little reason for Haitian pastors to challenge the status quo and strive for justice. Instead they have preached a theology of resignation which stressed the need for personal salvation and ignored the mandate for the people of god to work for justice. People were encouraged to accept their present circumstances, wait for their reward in heaven, and obey church and state authorities above all else. The soul and body were always viewed separately; in the final analysis, the only thing that mattered was eternity. It was easy to ignore any social or political situation with the rationalization that one is mainly concerned with saving souls.

The theology of resignation kept people from desiring justice from dictatorships. All they wanted was relief, and the Protestant church was in an excellent position to provide it. Millions of dollars in food and medical aid came into the country through mission organizations, and memberships soared. Since most of the relief work was being done by foreign organizations, Duvalier's government was freed of any social responsibility for the country. Instead, he could use foreign money to arm the Macoutes and consolidate his power.

Missionaries share a large part of the blame for this distorted theology. The spiritual and physical development of the Protestant churches has been seriously hampered by the paternalistic attitudes of many missionaries, mainly from right-wing churches of North America that have a colonialist approach to mission work. While mission organizations are responsible for an enormous amount of relief and development, these services are often seen as a means to an end and are provided with the intention of luring people into the churches so they can be saved. Not only is the work unsustainable, but it perpetuates the Haitian concept of the "patron" who provides everything for his charges...

The Protestant church sees itself as competing with the Catholic church, the official religion of Haiti. Success is determined by the number of converts a pastor wins. Since the Protestant membership increases only at the expense of Catholic membership, the Catholic church feels threatened in return, even though most of the Catholics who become Protestant are inactive members of any church. Instead of working together as Christians, Catholics and Protestants fight one another, making the church extremely easy to control and manipulate by outside forces.

Many Haitian pastors and missionaries claim that voodoo is the root of all Haiti's troubles and are very uncomfortable with what they see as the Catholic church's current tolerance of voodoo...Most Protestants also violently oppose liberation theology, considering it Marxist, too social, and unconcerned with personal salvation.

(13) HAITIAN PAINTING

Patrick Leigh Fermor, *The Traveller's Tree,* 1950

Haiti has enjoyed a reputation for producing so-called 'naive art' of the highest quality ever since foreign visitors began persuading Haitian artists to commit their creativity to canvas in the late 1940s.

They are astonishing pictures. The influences that lie behind them are manifold and diverse. The dwindling hangover of African traditions, the painted drums and banners of Voodoo, the obsessive, *kris*-like writhings of the serpent Damballah, the multi-coloured plumage of the globe-shaped Congo charms, the heraldic and geometrical precision of the maize-flour *vèvèrs*, and the horned head-dresses, the bats' wings and the great animal masks of carnival are some of the most apparent. To these must be added the sleek formalism of religious oleographs from Europe and Latin America, cinema posters, the covers of dime-magazines, and the omnipresent portraits of the Haitian heroes. These things are all registered and remembered in brains that abound with the miracles of Voodoo and Wanga[1] and Christianity and the deeds of the great Lwas, the *loups-garous* [2], Haitian battles, zombies and African fairy-tales, while all around them, as a permanent and unconscious background, lie the mountains, the forests, the intricate forms of the leaves, the sea and the luminous thin atmosphere of Haiti.

The pictures that emerge from this maelstrom of currents prove once more the overwhelming primacy in the Haitian mind of the imaginary world over the real. Less than a quarter of them are recordings or transpositions of what lies before the painter's eye, and portraits are scarcely attempted. There is a profound unconscious wisdom in this choice of themes, a true feeling for the limitations of their scope, and a reluctance to force it beyond itself into alien channels. One has the feeling, too, that many of the landscapes – the cross-roads or crowded markets or those wooded mountain-sides with their dazzling angular scaffolding of roads – are inventions or memories. The others are all, as it were, literary: the recording of a great event in Haitian history, as in the case of Philomée Obin – a procession of heroic rebels, the funeral of a patriot, an historic incarceration, a ball – or an imaginary scene drawn from religion, mythology, folklore or magic. Once the subject is chosen, nothing – absolutely nothing – daunts these artists, and the paint is applied with the strength , conscientiousness and diligence of a grown man, and all the intrepidity of a child; and with regard to any academic rule of thumb, with a flair for the combination of colours and a pristine and almost miraculous heterodoxy that makes the observer gasp.

These painters reflect the brilliant colours of their habitat, and their pictures are filled with an aura that appertains to the worlds of dream and nightmare...Many of the group pictures – market-places, wakes, Voodoo ceremonies, bamboches, the pursuit of runaway slaves – are packed with tiny figures placed among hills and trees and stilted palm roofs, as though they had been cut out and glued

on, so immobile are they; or so agitated that each animal and mani-
kin is whirling, leaping or gesticulating in an epileptic and
independent access of activity which has suddenly been frozen into
silence and immobility by the baleful stare of Medusa. Such are the
pictures of Rigaud Benoît, André Bouchard and Wilson Bigaud.

[1] The practice of magic and sorcery
[2] Werewolves

(14) RARA

Verna Gillis and Gage Averill, *Caribbean Revels*, 1991

Rara is a traditional folk music and celebration unique to Haiti. During the 1980s, it influenced the development of a new commercial
musical style, known as roots, or *racines* music, that has become an
increasingly popular alternative in a music scene hitherto dominated
by the *meringue*-influenced, *compas* music.

In the week before Easter, roads all over Haiti swell with bands of
revellers, dancers, singers, percussionists, and players of bamboo
and tin trumpets followed by the ubiquitous vendors of fresko
(shaved ice with sweet syrup flavouring) and kleren (cheap cane
liquor that provides some of the stamina needed for gruelling pa-
rades under the hot Haitian sun). These bands are led by presidents,
colonels, queens and other members of the complex rara band hier-
archies. After preparatory rituals in the Vodou temples, they move
from house to house and from one neighbourhood to another collecting money and occasionally engaging in low-level conflict with
other groups. This time of year, this type of group, and this type of
music is known in Haiti as rara. Despite its seasonal association,
rara can take place at any time of the year and animates political
rallies, demonstrations, and celebrations of all types...
   Rara songs can be obscene, satirical, political, or religious and it
is often many or all of these at once. Sacred / secular, Vodouist / Christian, African / European, political / religious / obscene, playful /
dangerous...rara incorporates all of these contrasts. It is always, however, exuberant and noisy. To fè rara (make rara) is synonymous in
Haiti with "to make a big racket..." [...]
   The peak of rara takes place in Haiti from Holy Wednesday
through Easter Sunday. Most rara activity occurs at night, usually

beginning at about 9pm and continues through early morning. The bands gather and set out on foot from the ounfo (Vodou temple) onto the streets where they attract their followers...

Single-note bamboo trumpets of varying lengths, called vaksins, are the most distinctive instrumental sound of rara. A node at the end of a bamboo tube is pierced to form a mouthpiece and the tube is blown through and struck on its side to produce a rhythmic timeline called a kata (the kata can also be played on small iron beaters called fè). The individual pitches on the different trumpets are interlocked in short melodic-rhythmic patterns, or "hockets."...The konet is an instrument similar in function to the vaksin but made of hammered zinc ending in a flared horn...

On the heels of the 1986 rebellion against Duvalier came a musical movement based primarily on rara and Vodou. A rara song critical of the political elite won popular acclaim as the best carnival song in the 1989 carnival, and the group that sang it, Boukman Eksperyans, along with the groups, Foula, Sanba-yo, Rara Machine and others helped to spark a roots-orientated, populist music. Rara has been at the centre of the process of cultural renewal in this period. It is seen as a uniquely Haitian symbol – a celebratory, socially-engaged expression of group power by sectors of the population that have traditionally wielded neither political nor economic power. The exuberant ambience of rara – summed up in words that denote unrestrained emotion and display: antyoutyout (worked up, excited), anraje (enraged), debòde (overflowing) – is a feature of Haitian social life that continues to resonate and carry meaning for Haitians from a wide spectrum of social classes.

(15) HAITIAN RHYTHMS

Katherine Dunham, *Dances of Haiti*, 1957

Although dancing forms a central part of the Vodou ceremony, it also exists as an important social activity away from the temple.

A *bamboche* is any get-together, or "blow-out," not connected with religious rites and not categorised as a seasonal dance. It may have as its primary feature a wedding celebration, or it may be organised to fete the departure of a notable in the community. It may be a part of a feast-day entertainment for a Christian saint (curiously enough, though the ceremonies for the cult gods[1] are sacred and according to ritual, the scene at a feast for a Christian saint is one of decidedly secular entertainment); or someone may simply decide to give a *bamboche,* making the necessary preparations and notifying people. Or it may simply be an instituted Saturday or Sunday night dance. In town, dances are in the houses of prostitution or along the lower waterfront in rum shops. On the outskirts of town and in the country, they are held in fairly permanent shelters, occasionally in the same tonelle that serves the community for *vodun* dances.

In the organisation of a social dance, a striking difference exists between groups in town and country. In the town at the rum shops and public houses, the common dance is the *meringue,* the national dance of Haiti. This might be described under the general term of ballroom dance but, as is true of the closely related national dances of the other islands, the *meringue* has undergone radical changes in character on being introduced to an urban setting. These dances in town call for no unusual knowledge or skill and no leader. Men pay to enter an establishment and dance with the women, or they buy rum for the privilege of dancing, and they leave at will. All are young or middle-aged people, still very sexually active, who seek stimulus and outlet for a definite localised urge. It is a matter of two people, who are not interested in the rest of the group and who have no contact or association with the others, often having themselves met only by chance. They have no particular feeling of interest in the dance, excepting as it serves the secondary purposes of sensory stimulus and an excuse for physical and social contact.

In the country, to the casual observer the *bamboche* bears some resemblance in outward appearance to the *vodun* or other sacred dance gatherings, probably because it takes place under a *tonelle.* This perhaps accounts for much of the confusion in descriptive accounts of *vodun* dances. Undoubtedly many of the sins of the *bamboche,* such as the excessive rum drinking and the sexual character of the dances, have been attributed to the priest of *Damballa.* But to one who frequents the two gatherings, they are as distinctly different in structure as they are in form and function. In place of the special clothes, the imposing *hounci,* and the officiating *houngan* or *mambo,* one finds a self-appointed *maît-la-danse,* usually one of the best dancers in the neighbourhood. He must have a female partner and she, too, must be outstanding as a dancer. In the country, the same people appear time after time at a *bamboche,* not only because it is a neighbourhood affair but also because of the limited opportunity to travel any distance in the short time between sundown Saturday and sunrise Monday, when every peasant is faced again with the practical problems of existence... At these dances young and old are equally active. Usually the older ones lead the dances and the young follow.

[1] Vodou lwa

(16) UP FOR THE CUP

Charles Arthur, *'The Man Who Beat Dino Zoff'*, 1998

Manno Sanon's goals put Haiti on the footballing map when, in 1974, it became the first Caribbean nation to qualify for the World Cup finals.

Manno Sanon, Haiti's first soccer superstar, is a modest man. Of the goal he scored against Italy in the 1974 World Cup finals he says, "It was nothing special. I scored a lot of goals." His goals, an astounding 47 of the 106 scored in the four years after he broke into the national team, helped Haiti top their qualifying group and become the first Caribbean nation to qualify for the World Cup.

He was already a hero in Haiti, but his powerful run and strike against Italy, a goal voted the best of the entire tournament by international football writers, turned him into a legend. Now twenty-four years since that goal, and back in Haiti after a long time living abroad, Manno is clearly chuffed by the reception he has received, "When I go to do something that should take five minutes, it takes an hour, because everyone wants to ask me about that goal."

Haiti's qualification was made possible by the patronage of the dictator, Jean-Claude Duvalier, who through the Haitian Football Federation, paid the squad of talented amateurs a monthly retainer during the long qualifying process. Nevertheless relations between team and benefactor were far from cordial.

Manno recalls the euphoria and tensions when Mexico's failure to beat Trinidad in the qualification tournament played in Port-au-Prince meant that Haiti was through to the finals in West Germany,

"It was the first time a small country like Haiti had qualified for the World Cup. At that time there were only 16 teams in the tournament, so it was quite something. The night we knew we had qualified, well, the country was upside down. It was crazy."

Then the successful players demanded a bonus of more than $5,000 and the furious dictator sent a message saying the strike threat deserved a death sentence. His representative let it be known that they would be pardoned but would be expected to do their patriotic duty by representing Haiti in the finals.

The team's first game was against Italy, finalists in 1970, and led by goalkeeper Dino Zoff who had just completed 12 consecutive internationals without conceding a goal.

"Everybody was asking who would beat Dino Zoff. The newspapers mentioned European and South American players, but nobody thought a Haitian could do it. That upset me because I knew I could do it."

The Haitian team surpassed all expectations by holding Italy to 0-0 in the first half. Two minutes into the second half, Manno shocked everyone but himself.

"With my pace, you can't leave me with just one defender, but that is what happened. I was one-on-one with Spinosi. I received a pass from Phillipe Vorbe. I beat the defender with my speed. One-on-one with Dino Zoff, and the goal was wide open. I dummied to go left, and then went right. I rounded him, and rolled the ball into the net."

One of the biggest upsets in World Cup history was on the cards, but it was not to be. Five minutes later Italy equalised. The Haitian team began to tire, and the relentless Italian attacks brought two more goals. Worse was to come. After the game a Haitian player tested positive for drugs – a cold-cure like Maradona in 1994? Later that night a fight broke out between some of the Haitian players and Duvalierists in the Haitian delegation who were furious that the country's honour had been besmirched.

The demoralised team lost its two other matches with Poland and Argentina, but Manno's goal against Zoff had made him a star. After the tournament he signed for the Antwerp club, Beerschoot, at that time a force to be reckoned with in Belgian football.

After seven years in Antwerp and 16 in the US, Manno has now returned to live in Haiti, and is trying to revitalise Haitian soccer.

"The country is in a state, and Haitian football is in poor shape too. Me and some of my teammates from before are talking about what we can do to make those good times come back again. We have pure talent in the street – it's like Brazil. You don't have to send them to school or coach them. They know it themselves. But the conditions are not right."

(17) COCK-FIGHTING

Blair Niles, *Black Haiti*, 1926

The cock-fight is a popular 'sporting' activity on Sundays.

The heat was heavy in the crowd about the cockpit. The sun forced its way through the great dried palm fronds which, laid one upon another, formed a flat roof over the circular arena. It came through in slender fingers of light, which lay upon the earth floor, separated one from the other by the pinnated shadow of the leaves. Only uprights of bamboo supported the leafy roof; the sides, but for a two-foot high enclosure, were open to the crowd which after the game begins must leave the arena to the cocks and to official personages in charge of the fight.

Now, before the game was called, the spectators swarmed in the pit itself, examining the birds and endlessly discussing how each would place his money, while to heap confusion upon confusion the owners were going about, cock under arm, comparing points, seeking suitable adversaries for their contestants, raising objections, suspiciously inspecting spurs to see that they were not poisoned, and feathers to make certain that they had not been larded to turn aside attacking beaks...

And still new combatants were arriving, not carried any old way, upside down, suspended by feet or wing, as on week days the vulgar among fowls travel to market; not thus, but held tenderly and close against the body of the owner or stage manager, held carefully with head pointing forward. Occasionally a cock arrived on horseback, and then its owner was a person of importance; frequently an elderly man with a head-handkerchief twisted like a Mohammedan turban, and with a Panama hat to top it off.

And each new arrival increased the tumult and added a new note to the deafening challenging crows.

In Haiti on Sundays the peasant woman sits under the pleasant shade of a bread-fruit tree while some relative or friend combs and dresses her hair. The only women who obey the cock's summons are those who gather to do a bit of trading, bringing their low rattan chairs and sitting with their usual wares spread out before them on wicker or wooden trays. They are there to sell tobacco and rum, kola and cookies and plantains, and to carry on a bantering talk among themselves. They are obviously unconcerned with sport. [...]

Within the ring, all but the two cocks and their human seconds, squatted close to the bamboo railing. Outside we, the spectators, were packed in a perspiring circle. The confusion died down to a buzz of excitement...The sign of the cross was then scratched on the floor of the pit, and a pinch of dust from the sign rubbed on the cocks' bills. The tethering cords had been released from their legs. All was ready.

The men placed the birds on the ground, advancing and withdrawing them back until they showed voluntary pugnacity, when the men withdrew. The battle was on...

(18) THE FINAL HOPE

Charles Arthur, *Banking on Shit*, 1997

The *borlette*, the Haitian version of the lottery, is a popular pastime for many Haitians.

Lucien regularly 'bets' a few gourdes at a borlette shop – the brightly-painted kiosks selling lottery tickets found on nearly every street in town and at junctions of many country roads and tracks. He explains that, like most Haitians who play the borlette, he chooses the number to bet on according to what he dreamt about the night before.

"I dreamt about shit last night, and I know the number for shit is zero seven. So I'll put five gourdes on zero seven. That was a good dream. If I don't have a good dream, I don't play the borlette."

Lucien doesn't trust the borlette operators and remembers the time he had dreamt about making love to a woman, and the next day asked for the number.

"They told me it is twenty-six or sixty-two, but I found out it's twenty-seven or seventy-two. They were tricking me."

Many gamblers consult a pocket-book, called the Tchala, which gives a number for a whole host of objects and symbols that can be matched to significant features from dreams.

The winning lottery numbers used to be taken from the draw made for Venezuela's national lottery and everyone used to know how to count from 0 to 99 in Spanish so that the borlette sellers wouldn't be able to fool them. Then it was discovered that borlette organisers were switching numbers so that they wouldn't have to pay out so much. Now, in the interests of fair draw, the numbers are taken from the daily New York State lottery and the weekly draw made on Sunday in the Dominican Republic, and the results are broadcast on Haitian television.

The borlette shops have names such as Lesly Bank, Chez Polo Bank, and Toto Bank, corresponding to the owner who runs the game. For the Haitian poor, who in the past would 'invest' by fattening up a pig or a goat and sell it to raise cash in an emergency, the borlette is the only form of 'banking' available. A winning bet can make all the difference.

Lucien hopes his number will come up in the draw and that with his winnings he'll be able to reclaim the gold chain he had to pawn a month ago. He plays the borlette when he is desperate, which nowadays is most of the time. With no steady income, he lurches from one crisis to another: in 1994 a hurricane blew the roof off his house; then he had to hire a lawyer when his son was arrested and accused of involvement in a fraud scam; and just recently he had an eye-infection and had to pay a doctor 60 Haitian dollars for treatment.

Now he has just a few gourdes saved up, and the borlette is his only hope of breaking out of a downward spiral of poverty.

(19) THE ORAL TRADITION

Various Sources, *Riddles and Jokes*

Haiti is an oral culture. There is a long tradition of proverbs, jokes, riddles and stories which people have been telling around the evening fire for centuries.

Perhaps the most popular form of humour and amusement are riddles. There is a definite form to the riddles: The person "throwing" the riddle says: *Tim Tim*. Those who want to hear it reply: *Bwa Seche*. Then the riddle is given. If they get it, they announce it. If they give up, they say *Bwa Seche*, which means they eat dry wood (the penalty for not getting the riddle.) The riddles themselves are very difficult. They require a transition from the literal problem to quite fanciful and figurative answers.

They serve it food, it stands on four feet, but it can't eat.
I enter white, I come out mulatto.
Three very large men are standing under a single little umbrella. But, not one of them gets wet. Why?
When I sit, I am taller than when I stand.

How many coconuts can you put into an empty sack?

Ou bwa seche? (You give up?) The answers are:
A table.
Bread.
It's not raining.
A dog.
Only one. After that the sack's not empty.

More Riddles:
Tim Tim (a challenge)
Bwa seche (bring it on)
What has four legs, eats straw, has a single heart, and can see just as well in the dark as it does in the day?
Why is it that when you lose something, it's always found in the very last place you look?

Ou bwa seche? (You give up?)
Answers:
A blind donkey.
Because after you find it you quit looking.

Stories are introduced by the invitation to hear a story. The person willing to tell the story shouts out: *Krik*. If people want to hear the tale, and they nearly always do, they answer in chorus: *Krak*. The most popular folk tales concern the smart, but mischievous Ti Malice and his very slow-witted friend Bouki.
Two examples:
Krik? Krak!
One day Ti Malice went over to Bouki's house. When he arrived at the lakou (farm yard), he was shocked at what he saw, and watched for some time. Bouki was playing dominoes with his dog! Ti Malice said, "Bouki, what a brilliant dog you have! He can play dominoes." "I don't know," said Bouki, "he's not so smart. I beat him 3 out of 5 games already!"
Krik? Krak!
Bouki: "Did I tell you that Madame Joseph had triplets two weeks ago, and now she has twins!"
Ti Malice: "But that's impossible! How can it be?"
Bouki: "One of the triplets is staying at her grandmother's house."

(20) TALL TALES

Diane Wolkstein, *Papa God and General Death,* 1978

This story, ostensibly about the harsh reality of survival in the countryside and, in particular, the perennial problem of water scarcity, also suggests something of the fatalistic yet pragmatic outlook common among the peasantry.

One evening, two men were walking on a hillside, Papa God and General Death. As they walked along, General Death pointed to a large yellow stone house overlooking the valley and said, "Last week I took one from there." Then he pointed to a smaller house down the path: "Tomorrow I shall take one from there."

"You are always taking from people," said Papa God, "and I am always giving to them. That is why the people prefer me."

Oh, I wouldn't be so certain of that," said General Death.

"Well let's see," said Papa God. "Let's ask the man you will be visiting tomorrow for some water and see whether he gives more water to you or to me."

"Good evening," Papa God called from outside the gate. "Have you some water for a thirsty man?"

"I haven't a drop," the man answered.

"I beg of you," said Papa God. "I am very thirsty. And I am sure Papa God would be pleased if you would give me some water."

"My good fellow, don't talk to me of Papa God. Do you know how far I have to go for water? Ten miles! Five miles to the spring and five miles back! And Papa God makes places where there is so much water people are swimming in it. No, don't talk to me of Papa God."

"My good man," Papa God said patiently, "if you knew with whom you are speaking, I am certain you would give me some water."

"Who are you?" asked the man.

"I -I am Papa God."

""Papa God," said the man, "I still do not have any water. But I will tell you this: if General Death should pass this way, then I would have water."

"How is that?" asked God.

"Because Death has no favourites. Rich, poor, young, old – they are all the same to him. Last week, he took my neighbour's wife, the week before a young baby, and the week before that an old man.

Death takes from all the houses. But you, you give all the water to some people and leave me here with ten miles to go on my donkey for just one drop."

Papa God saw Death motioning to him. It was Death's turn. Shaking his head sadly, Papa God walked away.

Several minutes later, General Death walked up the path.

"Good evening," he said. "Can you give me some water?"

"If you please," said the man, "what is your name?"

"I am General Death."

The man excused himself and went into his house. He returned with a calabash full of cool water.

"Drink!" he said to General Death. "Drink as much as you wish."

And Death drank. He drank long and he drank fully. And he must have been pleased, for the next day he did not stop at the small house but he continued on his route down the hill.

(21) PROVERBIAL WISDOM

Various Sources, *Proverbs*

A sample of the hundreds of proverbs and sayings used to comment on and explain aspects of Haitian society and life.

Si travay te bon bagay, moun rich la pran l lontan.
If work were a good thing, the rich would have grabbed it long ago.

Lajan al ka lajan.
Money goes where money is.

Se lè koulèv mouri, ou konn longè li.
Only when the serpent dies, do you know its length.

Jan chat mache se pa konsa li kenbe rat.
The way a cat walks is not the same as the way it hunts a mouse.

Bourik swe pou chwal dekore ap dentel.
The donkey sweats so the horse can be decorated with lace.

Lè yo vle touye yon chen, yo di l fou.
When they want to kill a dog, they say it's crazy.

Si towo bèf te konn valè l, li pa ta kite yon kòd senk kòb touye l.
If the bull knew its strength, it would not let a five cent rope kill it.

Prizon pa fè pou chen.
Prisons weren't built for dogs.

Bourik fè piti pou do l poze.
A donkey has a child so she can rest her back.

Bwa pi wo di li wè, grenn pwenmennen di li wè pase l.
The tall tree says it sees far, the walking (travelling) seed says it sees further.

Bèl antèman pa di paradi.
A beautiful burial does not guarantee heaven.

Bèl dan pa di zanmi.
Beautiful teeth doesn't mean he's a friend.

Kay koule tronpe solèy, men li pa tronpe lapli.
The house that leaks can fool the sun, but it can't fool the rain.

Lè ou pa gen manman, ou tete grann.
When you lose your mother, you drink your grandmother's milk.

Kreyon pèp la pa gen gonm.
The peoples' pen has no eraser.

De mòn pa kapab renkontre, de moun kapab.
Two mountains can't meet, two men can.

Yon sèl dwèt pa manje kalalou.
You can't eat okra with just one finger.

Men anpil, chay pa lou.
With many hands, the load is not heavy.

Piti, piti, zwazo fè nich li.
Little by little, the bird builds its nest.

CHAPTER NINE
LITERATURE AND LANGUAGE

The declaration of Haitian independence, drafted by Boisrond Tonnerre in 1804, can be seen as the beginning of Haitian literature and arguably Caribbean literature as a whole. Much of Haiti's writing in the nineteenth century takes its cue from this document. Pride in the historic defeat of Napoleon's army, the need to inspire the ideal of nationhood and a celebration of Haiti's redemptive mission in a world where slavery still persisted dominated the *littérature de circonstance* of the early post-independence years. The need to create a literature that was profoundly original was driven as much by nationalist ideals as it was by the view that the new republic had to demonstrate its intellectual and literary achievement in the face of charges of barbarity and primitivism levelled against the former French colony. It is not surprising that the form favoured by many early Haitian intellectuals is that of the polemical essay, in which writers like the Baron de Vastey, Anténor Firmin (1), Louis-Joseph Janvier and Hannibal Price discuss such issues as the evils of colonialism, the fallacies of racial theorising and the system of government which would be most appropriate to Haiti.

Not only was literature seen to have this ability to demonstrate mental capacity, but the influence of the Romantic movement further encouraged the need to establish a racial and cultural uniqueness through the production of literary texts. In this desire to write the new Haitian world into existence, nature played an important role in that it established a referential validity for the new republic. The idea of the Haitian landscape as the territory of the marvellous and the magical has its roots in early writing, where nature is endowed with a capacity to ground an authentic national identity. Much early nineteenth-century poetry reads like an inventory of tropical flora and fauna, and the land, invariably feminised, is prized for its coherence and its harmonies. The poet who best represents this tradition is Oswald Durand, who is famous for his experiment in writing in Creole in the poem *Choucoune*. (2) These literary conventions also gave birth to the peasant novel in Haiti by the turn of the century. The emergence of the prose narrative in the early realistic depictions of Haitian life by Frédéric Marcelin (3) and Antoine Innocent would lay the groundwork for a strong tradition of politically motivated prose fiction in the twentieth century.

However, the political reality of Haiti was far from being that of a unified and homogeneous society. The increasingly bleak political climate began to be evident in the poetic movement entitled *La Ronde*, whose members at the end of the nineteenth century called into question the celebratory, nationalistic verse of their literary forebears. Chronic instability, which brought seven presidents to office between 1910 and 1915, eventually lead to the US occupation, which lasted from 1915 to 1934 and inaugurated a new phase in Haitian literature. The neo-colonial nature of the American presence in Haiti provoked a new wave of nationalism, which manifested itself in different ways. There was, firstly, a short-lived peasant revolt led by Charlemagne Péralte, which fed increasingly intense anti-American sentiments among the traditional elite. Protests against the occupation came to a head in 1929 with a series of strikes initiated by students at the School of Agriculture. It was a sign that a younger and more radical generation of Haitians was about to dominate Haiti's intellectual and literary activities. It was this generation that launched the movement known as *indigenisme* in the 1920s. The iconoclasm of the movement's adherents was inspired by the anti-establishment movements fashionable in France at the time and soon became apparent in the pages of their magazines *La Trouée* (1927) and *La revue indigène* (1927-28). Beyond the fashionably bohemian spirit of the times and their populist posturing, the major writers of this generation – Jacques Roumain, Carl Brouard, Emile Roumer and Philippe-Thoby Marcelin (4) – sought to end Haiti's cultural isolation by introducing contemporary writing from the Harlem Renaissance and Latin America.

Their interest in defining Haiti's national soul was influenced by the ideas of the French nationalist thinker, Charles Maurras, which led them to embrace the idea of cultural authenticity put forward by one of Haiti's most influential intellectuals, Jean Price Mars. His ethnographic study *Ainsi parla l'oncle* (1928), which accused the francophile elite of 'collective *bovarysme*' and advocated, in the face of such self-denial, that Haitian folk culture was the key to understanding the national soul, pushed *indigenisme* in the direction of *noirisme*, with its belief in the essential Africanness of Haiti's national identity. (5) The ideology of *noirisme* was articulated at this time by Louis Diaquoi, Lorimer Denis and François Duvalier in their journal *Les Griots* (1938-40), whose pages are filled with articles on black nationalism and Vodou mysticism. Carl Brouard's attempt to develop a non-elite national aesthetic is typical of the journal's concerns. (6) This movement remained essentially literary and ideological and did nothing to upset the political status quo.

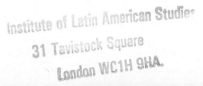

The reaction from intellectuals of the traditional elite, such as Dantès Bellegarde, was unmitigated scorn, but this preoccupation with race and ethnicity dominated the literary avant-garde in the 1930s and appealed to a sense of solidarity with a homogenous pan-African culture. Haitian *négritude* was expressed in the epic poems of Jean Brierre and Jacques Roumain. The 1930s also saw the beginning of the influence of Marxism, as the Communist Party was founded by Jacques Roumain in 1934. Roumain's ideas transcended the narrowly reductive nationalism and racialism of his contemporaries, and his work was inspired by a visionary Marxism that saw culture as dynamic and ever changing within a precise economic context. His most enduring work was the posthumously published 1945 novel, *Les gouverneurs de la rosée*, the best-known work by a Haitian writer. (7) Its reputation is justified as it tackles the issue of founding a new community on the ruins of an archaic culture and a divisive past. It revisits the idea of grounding a national identity in uncharted space, a theme that was a major preoccupation among Haiti's early writers. Roumain's unswerving adherence to Marxism and his sophisticated rewriting of the peasant novel would leave an indelible mark on the next generation of Haitian writers.

The 1940s in Haiti were a decade of intellectual effervescence. This atmosphere was heightened by the influence of World War II, the literary radicalism of the post-occupation period and intense exposure to surrealism through contact with such figures as Pierre Mabille, Wifredo Lam, Aimé Césaire and Alejo Carpentier. The remarkable visit of André Breton in December 1945, during which the founding father of surrealism gave a series of lectures to coincide with Lam's controversial art exhibition, was particularly influential. The lectures combined explosively with prevailing literary radicalism and contributed to the overthrow of the pro-American, conservative regime of Elie Lescot in January 1946 by the student activists of the newspaper *La Ruche*. Surrealism was of immense importance to the leaders of this movement, Jacques Stéphen Alexis (8) and René Depestre, as it both confirmed their interest in the culture of Haiti's dispossessed and encouraged their faith in Haiti's unique national identity despite an exploitative capitalist world order.

If the 1940s signified the success of Marxist and surrealist ideas in Haiti, it also meant the political ascendancy of *noirisme*. The revolution of 1946 put in power the black president Dumarsais Estimé, who would later be cited by François Duvalier as one of his political predecessors. Estimé soon rid himself of the firebrands of *La Ruche* by providing them with scholarships to study in Europe and banning the Communist Party. Alexis became one of the first black writers to challenge the doctrine of *négritude* in a paper entitled 'Concerning the Marvellous Realism of Haitians', read at the First Congress of Black Writers and Artists held at the Sorbonne in 1956. Depestre also ran foul of *négritude* in the form of an angry rebuke from the Martinican poet-politician Aimé Césaire for advocating a national poetics as opposed to a racially derived one in his *Introduction à un art poétique haïtien*. The political triumph of Haitian *négritude* with the electoral victory of François Duvalier in 1957 meant that Depestre would spend most of his life in exile and that Alexis would be killed by the Tontons Macoutes while taking part in an abortive invasion attempt in 1961.

The Duvalier dynasty lasted 29 years and had a devastating effect on literary and intellectual activity. François Duvalier died in 1971 and was succeeded by his son, Jean-Claude, who was overthrown in 1986. Duvalierism contained elements of xenophobia, racial mystification, militarism and authoritarianism, which were an extreme political manifestation of Haitian negritude. The doctrine of Duvalierism was articulated in François Duvalier's tellingly entitled *Oeuvres essentielles*, promoted as the only essential reading in Haiti during his regime. Meanwhile, Haitian writing shifted locale to the intellectual diaspora created by the Duvalier dictatorship. Haitian literature was now produced in Montreal, Dakar, Havana, Paris and New York and was predictably dominated by anti-Duvalier sentiment and nostalgia for the lost native land.

Within Haiti the only movement with any literary impact was the ill-defined doctrine of *spiralisme*, started by Franketienne (Franck Etienne). As much a reaction against the narrow nationalist feeling of the post-occupation period as a call to radical formal experimentation, *spiralisme* was never openly political and espoused a literature that could avoid censorship and offer an alternative to the closed discourse of Duvalierist politics. It was only under the more relaxed regime of Jean-Claude Duvalier that *spiralisme* began to confront the Haitian state and became associated with the use of Creole in literary texts. Etienne's novel *Dezafi* (1975) is the best-known work of fiction written entirely in Creole. (9) Outside of Haiti, however, writing was characterised by a strident anti-Duvalierism. Novels by Gerard Etienne, Anthony Phelps (10), René Depestre and Pierre Clitandre (11) were the most successful examples of this tendency but no single work attained the high quality of the Latin American dictator-novel. Both Depestre's *Festival of the Greasy Pole* (12) and Marie Chauvet's *Love, Anger, Madness* (13) are set within the surreal and disturbing context of an arbitrary dictatorship. To some extent, exile was beginning to make this writing less authentically Haitian, even as writing on the inside became more self-consciously Haitian in the use of a Haitian language and world view.

Perhaps the most interesting literature created in the Haitian diaspora was not the politically engaged prose, but those works which sought to treat the condition of exile itself and the emergence of a new supra-national sense of identity. This trend was heralded by two novels that both appeared in 1985: Dany Lafferière's *Comment faire l'amour avec un nègre sans se fatiguer* (*How to Make Love to a Black Man Without Getting Tired*) and Jean-Claude Charles's *Manhattan Blues*. Both texts deal with Haitians outside of Haiti and, particularly in the outrageous humour of the Laferrière novel, call into question the pieties of Haitian nationalism and the blind parochialism of cultural authenticity. This writing marked a major rupture with a tradition of literary nationalism with its roots in the revolutionary fervour of 1804. It also announced the emergence of a new generation of writers formed almost entirely outside of Haiti. The best known of this generation is Edwidge Danticat, whose acclaimed first novel, *Breath, Eyes, Memory* (1994), is likely to be the first of a new phase of writing by Haitians in English. (14) With the fall of the Duvalier dynasty in 1986 the anti-Duvalier theme understandably disappeared from writing in the diaspora and exile today is no longer a politically sensitive condition.

After 1986 a new theme enters Haitian writing – redefining the writer's relationship with a land he no longer fully understands and the real difficulty of returning to the native land. Very few of Haiti's writers returned home after Duvalier's departure. One of the most notable of these voluntary exiles is René Depestre, whose *Hadriana dans tous mes rêves* (1988) is a disavowal of Cuban Communism and a nostalgic evocation of the town of Jacmel where he spent his youth. Similarly, Dany Laferrière who lives in Miami has treated the theme of the writer's problematic relationship with Haiti in his 1996 *Pays sans chapeau* (15). The most prolific novelist in this area is the Canada-based Emile Ollivier, who, most recently in his prize-winning novel *Les urnes scellées* (1995), revisits the question of rupture within particular linguistic and cultural contexts and suggests that there is much to be gained from the wider horizons and the new roots established through exile. (16)

Haiti, more than a decade after the end of Duvalierism, remains a grim and desperate country. Even more so, perhaps, because of the absence of a literary and intellectual culture which has remained outside the country. Literary traditions remain alive in the diaspora, but within modern Haiti the burning issues are no longer literary.

(1) THE FALLACY OF RACIAL SUPERIORITY

Anténor Firmin, *De l'égalité des races humaines,* 1885

Anténor Firmin was one of the best known of the essayists in nine-teenth-century Haiti. He had a distinguished and often turbulent career in politics. While in Paris in 1885, he wrote a massive refuta-tion of Gobineau's *Essai sur l'inégalité des races humaines* (Essay on the Inequality of Human Races), defending the universal nature of all human values.

After having reviewed all the arguments that could be advanced to support the doctrine of the inequality of the human races, it appears that none can withstand the slightest scrutiny. No doubt, there are several that we have unwittingly omitted, in this dispirit-ing survey of errors and prejudices so long spread among a great number of minds that it is impossible for them to return to more logical and impartial concepts. Nevertheless, when one has been walking for some time, after climbing many a summit and crossed many a precipice, one feels the need to stop for breath. Having ar-rived at a certain height, one notices that quite a lot of space has been covered and, casting one's eye over the journey completed, one contemplates with a certain relief the stages along the way. One is convinced that hidden paths still remain to be explored, but the complete panorama is enough to provide for the mind all the clarity one would wish for in appreciating the terrain where investigations have been conducted. Such is the sentiment I feel in bringing to a close the series of discussions that had to be initiated on the various scientific notions that, by a false interpretation, seemed to favour the hypothesis of the inequality of the human races.

In my recapitulation of all the objections which refute, as it were, in their very foundation, all the systems of establishing a hierarchy which every effort has been made to try and institute among the diverse groups of mankind, we can now affirm that natural equality exists among all the races. This equality is only further verified when a superior level of evolution brings along to one of them a develop-ment and new aptitudes which have not yet been attained by the others. But as if to prevent us from forgetting completely the origi-nal inferiority of those who have now attained the highest summit of civilisation, one can encounter not only in the annals of the past, but in the present time at different points in the world, a multitude of their fellow men living in a state that visibly proclaims their an-cestral temperament.

Translated from French by Michael Dash

(2) FOLK ROMANTICISM

Oswald Durand, *Choucoune,* 1880

Oswald Durand is recognised as the most important of the nationalist school of poets of nineteenth-century Haiti. Closely attached to
the Romantic movement and to Victor Hugo in particular, Durand
brought to poetry a range of themes especially the beauty of the
Haitian countryside. His poem *Choucoune* is the first major poem
written in Haitian Creole. It was later put to music and became a
popular song.

Behind a thick clump of cactus
The other day I met Choucoune;
She smiled on seeing me.
I said: 'Lord! Oh! What a beauty!'
She said: 'You think so, dear man?'
The little birds in the air heard us...
When I think of it all I am so sad,
For since that day, in chains my two feet I've had!

Choucoune, she is a marabout,
Her eyes shine like candles.
She has firm breasts too.
Ah! If only Choucoune had been true!
We stood there talking for a long time,
Till the birds in the woods seemed content!...
I'd like to forget it all, the pain is too great
For from that day, my two feet in chains I've had!

Choucoune's little teeth like milk are white;
Her mouth the colour of our star apple:
She's not a fat girl, she is plump:
Such women for me are sweet.
Bygone days are not those today we meet!...
The birds had heard all she said!...
If they think of that day it must make them sad,
For since that day, my two feet in chains I've had!

To the house of her mother we went
An old woman honest and kind!
She gave me the once over and said:
'Ah! this one really pleases my heart!'

We drank chocolate with nuts, as we should...
Is that all over, little birds from the wood?...
I'd like to forget all that, it makes me so sad
For since that day, my two feet in chains I've had!

The furniture's ready; nice lit-bateau
Rattan chair, round table, rocker,
Two mattresses, one porte-manteau
Tablecloths, napkins, muslin curtains...
There were only two weeks to go...
Little birds who are in the woods, listen, listen! ...
You too will understand if I am sad.
If since that day, my two feet in chains I've had!

You see, some little white guy came our way:
Little red beard, nice, pink face,
Watch by his side, good hair too...
He was the one who caused my misfortune!
He finds Choucoune pretty,
He speaks French...Choucoune falls for him...
I'd like to forget all that, it makes me so sad,
Choucoune left me, since then my two feet in chains I've had!

But the saddest thing of all,
That which will surprise you all,
Despite what she did, it's Choucoune I love still!
She will have a little quatroon!
Little birds look close! Her little belly has grown quite round!
Be still! Shut your beaks! It makes me quite sad:
The two feet of little Pierre, his two feet in chains he will have.

Translated from Creole by Michael Dash

(3) VODOU OBSESSIONS

Frédéric Marcelin, *Au gré du souvenir,* 1893

Marcelin was one of Haiti's leading novelists in the nineteenth century. He had an active career in politics and is known for his realistic depictions of the Haitian landscape and mores. In this review of a book on Haiti, he laments the obsessiveness with which foreigners reduce all of Haitian culture to Vodou.

I have right here under my eyes a large work of 338 pages, written by Eugène Aubin, and entitled *En Haïti.* The author obviously wanted to be interesting at all cost. How could he be unless he describes scenes of vaudou, of fetishism because it is the framework within which the country was always displayed and because, moreover, this framework lends itself to various treatments? Therefore, in these 338 pages, hardly a line on our towns, on our economic and moral development, on what could constitute our social structure...Well! I am afraid that, despite the 32 photographs which it boasts, his book, without him suspecting, is a fake, because the peasant played him for a fool. He has long since learnt to trick the white man who, pencil in one hand and his objective in the other, travels through his mountains, with the sole purpose of seeking out the strange and the picturesque. He furnishes him with it, rest assured, for his money. Just like in the Libyan desert, where someone who has hidden it with you in mind, digs the sand and pulls out a statuette of Isis, the Haitian peasant knows how to improvise, with the jingle of coins in his ear, a vaudou temple to satisfy the traveller who demands one. In one way or another he will also simulate, if you are so inclined, a propitiation sacrifice with a rooster or a goat, on condition that the price is right.

I do wish to claim, however, that, in certain remote parts of the island, there do not perhaps exist a few vestiges of former superstitions...Where is this not the case? Without even mentioning Russia where the peasant is enslaved by barbarous ancestral rites, it is known that in Brittany, in the heart of intellectually refined France, you can sometimes come across surprising practices. But what I am protesting against, is the generalisation that is meant to be established. I know my country well, I have done much travelling through it. Well! I declare that, with a few exceptions, that fetishism is nothing but a way of exploiting the credulous foreigner. It is no longer a belief. It is a form of underhand speculation.

Translated from French by Michael Dash

(4) THE POETIC RENAISSANCE

Thoby-Marcelin, Brouard, Laleau and Roumer, *Five Poems,* 1920-1940

The 1920s and 1930s produced a surge of poetic creativity in Haiti. The themes of these poems ranged from celebrations of landscape to protests against western materialism, evocations of primitivist fantasies to the African past. Much of this writing is marked by the influence of radical movements in Europe as well as the Harlem Renaissance. Some of the best writers were Philippe Thoby-Marcelin, Léon Laleau, Carl Brouard and the highly innovative Emile Roumer.

Philippe Thoby-Marcelin, *Young Again*

This morning my heart is bursting with youth,
Seething with violence
My cheek resting against the freshness
Of the dawn,
Swearing an eternal scorn for European refinements,
I wish henceforth to celebrate you
Revolutions, shootings and massacres,
The sound of the coco-macaque stick on black shoulders
The roar of the lambi, the mystic sensuality of vaudou;
To celebrate you in a delirium three times
Lyrical and religious
To strip myself of all classical finery
And stand up naked, savage
And very much a descendant of slaves
To sing with a new voice the de profundis
Of rotting civilisations.

Carl Brouard, *Nostalgia*

Drum
When you resound
My heart howls for Africa
Sometimes
I am dreaming of a mighty jungle
Bathed in moonlight
Of naked, sweating, dishevelled bodies
Sometimes of a filthy hut
Where I savour blood from human skulls.

Léon Laleau, *Betrayed*

An obsessive heart which does not relate
To my language and my customs,
And on which bite, like a spike,
Borrowed sentiments and European customs
Do you feel this suffering
And this despair with no equal
In taming, with words from France,
This heart which has come to me from Senegal?

Emile Roumer, *Marabout of my Heart*

My beloved Marabout with breasts like tangerines
you are sweeter to taste than crab in eggplant
you are the piece of meat in my calalou
the dumpling in my pea soup, my aromatic herb tea,
You are the salt beef stored in the fat of my heart
syrup flavoured cane juice flowing down my throat.
You are a steaming dish of mushroom cooked with rice
Crisp fish fritters and sprat fried dry...
My hunger for love follows you wherever you go
Your bottom is a cauldron stuffed full of good things to eat

Emile Roumer, *A Black Girl Walks By*

Night-dark girl of the swaying hips...
Your walk sacred and slow, undulating
And weary – as you go by with an air so nonchalant,
Your grace will for a long time my memory haunt;
Feline smooth your fine hips sway
Bringing to mind the vision of a black panther in their way
Leaping, shuddering at the metal touch of javelin tips.
And my soul is cradled in moired silky crepe
To the carnal rhythm of this woman's hips.

(5) FOR A FOLK LITERATURE

Jean Price Mars, *So Spoke the Uncle,* 1938

Price Mars was the recognised theoretician of the indigéniste and noiriste movements that were created from the nationalist backlash against the US occupation. His *Ainsi parla l'oncle*, which was essentially the publication of a series of lectures given in the 1920s, chided the elite for their snobbishness and argued for a recognition of Haitian peasant culture.

Tales, legends, riddles, songs, proverbs, beliefs thrive here with an extraordinary exuberance, generosity and openness. Magnificent human raw material from which has been molded the warm heart, the teeming consciousness, the collective soul of the Haitian people! Better than the accounts of famous battles, better than the telling of the great events of official history always shaped by the constraint of expressing only a part of the elusive Truth, better than the theatrical posturing of men of state with their affectation of authority, better than the laws which are but borrowed finery ill suited to our society in which temporary holders of power secrete their hates, their prejudices, their dreams or their hopes, better than all these things which are more often than not the trappings of chance imposed by contingency and adopted by only a part of the nation – tales, songs, legends, proverbs, beliefs are works or products spontaneously generated, at a point in time, by inspired thought, adopted by all because they faithfully translate a common feeling, cherished by all and ultimately transformed into original creations through the mysterious process of the unconscious.

If a childish ditty which does no disgrace to the lips of the aristocratic female with her puffed-up pride in her nobility happens to sound identical in the emotionally tender voice of the peasant woman bending over her sleepy infant...if this belief in miracles which forms the basis for life in Haiti and confers on it its own identity – its mystical quality – if all of that is drawn from the common reservoir of ideas, feelings, events, gestures which constitute the moral patrimony of Haitian society, it is in vain that the arrogance of various people will react against the shared responsibility for faults and transgressions, for the bovarysme of dilettantes to dictate their acts of cowardice and lies, for stupid class antagonisms to unleash attitudes of hostility and measures of ostracism – nothing can prevent tales, legends, songs come down to us from the past or created and transformed by us, from being a part of who we are, made visible to us as an externalisation of our collective ego, nothing can prevent latent or formal beliefs come down to us from the past , recreated, transformed by us from having been the driving force in our behaviour and from having shaped the contagious heroism of the crowd which was slaughtered in the time of glory and sacrifice so as to implant black freedom and independence on our soil; nothing can ultimately prevent, in the period of transition and disquiet we are experiencing at present, these same intangible factors from being the most accurate reflection of the look of anxiety in our nation. They constitute in an unexpected and startling fashion the raw material of our spiritual unity. Where then could one find a more genuine image of our society?

What else has ever expressed the Haitian soul more completely?

(6) LITERATURE AND IDEOLOGY

Carl Brouard, *L'art au service du peuple,* 1938

Brouard was one of the main figures in the renaissance of Haitian literature produced by the nationalist self-scrutiny which followed the US occupation. His involvement with the *noiriste* movement led him to theorise in the pages of the Griots magazine about the new role for literature in its celebration of the Afro-Haitian soul.

To my way of thinking, Art in the service of the people has not yet been seriously contemplated, although the only viable Art possible comes from the people. But they cannot read, you say to me? No one is unaware of that, my friend. But they must be able to one day, and then what an everlasting honour it will be for us to have celebrated their joys and their suffering, for it is in the soul of a people that permanent values reside...Everything else is written on water, all is illusion and a wind howling in the desert. In any case, I have had the occasion sometimes to read poems to an auditorium of illiterate people. The result of doing this was overwhelming. Naturally they did not understand much, but they sensed the innate beauty. The reader can easily be convinced of this. Just choose for this purpose certain very simple and very musical poems by Verlaine. Everyone's soul has access to beauty, in the Platonic sense of the word. It is not a matter of intelligence but of intuition. The most ignorant peasant feels which vaudou temple is more artistic than another, that such and such a hounsi sings better than that other one, just as he will obey a dictatorship that works for order, truth and well-being because those are innate ideas. You might feel that I am too insistent on dictatorship. The fact is that I am of the firm opinion that a people only gradually attains, step by step, liberalism. Otherwise, it is simply marking time. Pétion's liberalism sank into despotism. You do not violate with impunity the laws of nature. In order to learn the alphabet, you must know the letter A! But this has nothing to do with where I started? Sorry. Education will be widespread only if this condition is fulfilled. And then I set my sights coming from the distant past, that is our link of continuity, (for only tradition makes a people strong) on the future. Let us create so that later we can perfect. Ultimately, and in spite of the pedants who, at every turn and out of turn, invoke dialectic materialism, the values of the spirit will live on. And it is through them that we rise to supreme beauty.

Translated from French by Michael Dash

(7) THE PEASANT NOVEL

Jacques Roumain, *Masters of the Dew*, 1944

The acknowledged masterpiece of literary nationalism is *Masters of the Dew* by the Marxist ethnologist Jacques Roumain. He used the form of the peasant novel, developed in the late nineteenth century, to examine the question of Haiti's rural culture, as his protagonist, Manuel, who has returned from years in Cuba, tries to communicate a new consciousness to the peasants of his native village.

// Here, we've got to struggle hard with life, and what does it get us? We don't even have enough to fill our bellies, and we've no rights at all against the crookedness of the authorities. The justice of the peace, the rural police, the surveyors, the food speculators live on us like fleas. I spent a month in prison with a bunch of thieves and assassins, just because I went in town without shoes. And where could I have gotten the money to buy them, I ask you, brother? What are we, us peasants? Barefooted Negroes, scorned and maltreated."

"What are we? Since that's your question I am going to answer you. We're this country, and it wouldn't be a thing without us, nothing at all. Who does the planting? Who does the watering? Who does the harvesting? Coffee, cotton, rice, sugar cane, corn, bananas, vegetables, and all the fruits, who's going to grow them if we don't? Yet with all that we're poor, that's true. We're out of luck that's true. We're miserable, that's true. But do you know why brother? Because of our ignorance. We don't know yet what a force we are, what a single force – all the peasants, all the Negroes of the plain and hill, all united. Some day, when we get wise to that, we'll rise up from one end of the country to the other. Then we'll call a General assembly of the Masters of the Dew, a great big *coumbite* of farmers, and we'll clear out poverty and plant a new life."

"You're talking sense, *oui*." Laurelien said.

He had almost lost his breath trying to follow Manuel. A wrinkle on his brow marked the effort of meditation. In the most inarticulate corner of his brain, accustomed to slowness and patience, a curtain of light began to rise. It illuminated a sudden hope, still obscure and distant, but as certain as brotherhood. He spat a jet of saliva through his teeth.

"What you're saying is as clear as water running in the sunlight." He was standing, and his hands were contracting as if to try to hold on to fugitive words.

(8) THE CONQUISTADORS RETURN

Jacques Stéphen Alexis, *Les arbres musiciens* , 1957

Alexis's novel *Les arbres musiciens* is the most celebrated work by this Marxist writer who was deeply influenced by the ideas of the Cuban 'magical realist' Alejo Carpentier and who died tragically at the hands of the Duvalier regime. In this novel the character Gonaibo who represents the spirit of the Haitian hinterland witnesses the invasion of the countryside by American heavy equipment, repeating an eternal cycle of exploitation.

What Gonaibo saw that morning in the heartland, he has never seen, nor heard about, and he would never forget it. A great cavalry of white men, in khaki, galloped on strange iron horses, at a crazy speed, like a cloud of avenging archangels, tearing through the countryside still wet with the dew. Everything fled before the squadron's frantic rush. How many were there? He could not say, but were there only eight or ten, he saw fifty, a hundred and more. These iron horses, low slung, carried long shiny horns on their foreheads which the riders grasped with their hands. The creatures had haunches decorated with brilliant, chrome plates, smoke, from harsh explosions, escaped from behind these strange mounts. They drove madly in circles across the trembling landscape and the horsemen with their leather helmets had pale faces on which he could make out only the dark line of a strap across the chin. They spoke to each other in a language which sounded hard and grated on the ear...They were exploring the entire countryside!

The heavens were filled with a panic-stricken uproar. There explosions, groans, grating noises, as if an army of mad ironmongers had begun to work in the countryside...Now, here it was his home had been violated! He looked at the sky filled with whirling birds and dirty smoke. A pervasive odour of burnt gasoline floated in the air. He then had the premonition that these apparitions meant the end of his uninterrupted dream, the end of his life of freedom, the end of his control over the uninhabited heartland. No man had ever dared to cross this secluded area with such arrogance. There apparitions behaved like conquerors, masters. He was torn by a feeling that shattered his entire being...Five centuries ago, the warriors of Anacaona the Great must have had the same impression when, in an apocalyptic rush, appeared before their very eyes the horsemen of Ojeda violating the frontiers of the realm of the cacique.

Translated from French by Michael Dash

(9) DEFIANCE AND DREAD

Franketienne, *Dezafi*, 1975

Franketienne's *Dezafi* is the best known fictional work in Creole. Experimental in form, it is structured around multiple voices that turn on a narrative dealing with the zombification of the people of 'Bois Neuf'. It is as much an example of the technical originality of the Spiralist movement as it is an indictment of political tyranny.

A tangle of branches of trees in an old yard. Tough earth, veins hardened by stone and sand. Serpent entrails/ coiled in hunger. Entrails knotted in pain. Each day stomach empty, Rita slaves away at her chores. Locked in his house Gedeon spits out his curses. In the middle of the night, shrill cries pierce our eardrums, penetrate our brains, fear in our guts, we tremble to our roots. Electrical shivers. Our hair stands on end. Suddenly we leap out of bed.

Saintil sits importantly in his official chair. At his feet a herd of zombis kneeling under the peristil. On his right, Sultana, seated on a straw-bottomed chair. On his left Zofer, motionless and rigid, a riding whip in his hand. Three candles light up the poto-mitan. Suddenly, Saintil begins to shake his calabash rattle and bell.

- Sultana, my girl! The dark waters are bubbling in the court of Gran Brigit and forbid any further delay!

- Yes, papa.

- Listen to me carefully. The nests will be undone in the middle of the night. The wind will blow away silent birds and fragile butterflies. The nest must be ready to catch the lost souls .

- Yes, papa.

- You are responsible for the preparation of food and the feeding ritual of the zombis. Never forget the use of salt is strictly forbidden. Never forget it my child, a zombi can only escape if he swallows salt.

Saintil shakes the calabash rattle reciting in a hoarse voice words from a secret language. Then he looks to the left.

Zofer!

Yes, master.

In the cracked egg in the sacred chamber, I hear the breathing of the chick torn between life and death.

Yes, master. Nothing escapes you. Since you possess the power to change human beings, you are infallible, undefeatable. Your august person is capable of enormous powers.

The season of the rice harvest approaches. It is time to honor the marasa. The night is writhing in all directions.

Yes, master.

Tomorrow at dawn, shave the skulls of the zombi properly. Before sending them to work in the mud of the rice fields, whip them until they bleed. General Linglessou is thirsty and impatient.

Yes, master.

At the slightest sign of insubordination on the part of any zombi, slash his skin, squeeze his flesh to pulp, break his bones, crush his head until it is reduced to powder. Then refresh yourself with his blood.

Yes, master. I will carry out your orders to the letter. Silence and peace will spread throughout your lands for another century. And nothing will stop your plans.

Translated from Creole by Michael Dash

(10) A DREAM OF REVENGE

Anthony Phelps, *Mémoire en colin-maillard,* 1976

The narrator of Anthony Phelps's novel has been tortured by the
Tontons Macoutes and dreams of avenging himself by killing the
President in the national Palace. Duvalier's name is never mentioned
but Claude remains obsessed by the fantasy of revenge and a long-
ing for heroism which were typical of much of the literature written
in exile in the Duvalier years.

One day. I. I will perform these acts. I will kill him with these
hands. My black man's hands full of fingers, hard, rough, solid
like iron sausages. I will strangle him.

I will slip in through the main entrance to the palace. The sentry
will not see me go by him. The most he will feel is a light breeze
brush against him. I will cross the stretch of lawn and climb the
main staircase. Inside, I will look for his office. He will certainly be
seated behind an imposing table, in the process of writing one of his
many stupid and incoherent speeches. I will go behind him and make
him a collar of flesh with my fingers. My black man's hands will
close around his neck, I will squeeze in a deliberately slow way until his forked tongue begins to stick out of his mouth. Then, I will
relax the pressure, just enough for him to hang on to life by a thread,
for him to begin feeling himself suffer. Once, twice, five times, I well
bash his head against the corner of the desk then with one blow
from a paperweight I will split his forehead and, grabbing hold of
the revolver which he always keeps within reach, I will empty the
barrel in his mouth. His sick black head will then be filled with terror, violence and death.

I, one day like today, will perform these acts. I will get up from
my armchair, leave the balcony where I survey my surroundings,
go into my room. I will put on my grey pants and my white shirt as
well as my tennis shoes. It has been a long time since I have worn
them, these pliable shoes. Silently I will make my way down the
corridor. No one will be in the rooms. Mesina will have finished
tidying up upstairs, she will be in the drawing room, in the process
of cleaning the furniture and polishing. No one in the corridor. At
the end is the staircase; the bay window will be wide open but in the
pool of sunlight, I will not see Mesina against the light, only the
particles of dust will begin to swirl as I enter the flood of light. I will
hold the railing and go down the steps one by one, with neither

hesitation nor haste for I must not be heard. I will step over the fifth stair, the one that creaks whatever you do. My rubber soles are discrete and bring me to the drawing room which I cross quickly. The yard is filled with sunlight. No one in sight. The maids are busy, the cook is looking after her pots, the yard boy is catching up on sleep behind the garage. It feels good to be in the sun.

Translated from French by Michael Dash

(11) DEATH AND RESURRECTION.

Pierre Clitandre, *Cathedral of the August Heat,* 1987

Clitandre's novel is a sad yet poetic tale of contemporary Haiti. Using all the devices of 'marvellous realism', the story uses a luxuriant, oral and carnivalesque style to evoke life in the slums of Port-au-Prince. Through the main character, a bus driver who ferries people from the country to the capital, whose son Raphael is eventually killed by a Tonton Macoute, Clitandre reflects on the sacrifice of innocence in the struggle for liberty.

John spent the whole night weeping beside the body. He couldn't bear it. His reason for living was there. When the first light of morning swept into the refuge in the old fort, his face was so ravaged with grief and reduced so suddenly to skin and bone that the new expression of harshness and power coming from him was almost unrecognisable. Passiona and old Dormelia came back with water, leaves, powder and perfume to lay Raphael out. They perfumed him with sweet basil water, sage bush and lotions, then laid him out on a bed of banana leaves. Surrounded by bouquets of white and pink rose laurel, Raphael had recovered as if by magic the purity of his features, the fullness of his lips and at moments John could believe that he was only resting

It was in one of those fleeting moments that John seemed to see his boy rise slowly from his bed of banana leaves, climb the little time worn stair and search frantically for something in the long grass of the courtyard of the old fort. Then he came back sadly, climbed down the little stair and stretched out again. John who, the first evening of this vision, believed he could hear some plaintive sobs which must be coming from his son, searched his memory for what it could be that was so important to Raphael. He thought of the pigeons. But at that time it was impossible to find any in the ghetto. Big migrations of doves always preceded the bad times: reprisals, drought, floods, famine, as if to warn the race who were no longer nomads. He thought of the old kitchen knife. Dormelia had given it to him. John had thrown it in the grass, still stained with the blood of the man Raphael had cut before he was hit by the bullet. The last time the boy must have seen it was on the afternoon of the third day he lay sick.

John remembered that the boy had bent down to pick up the knife and had gone forward toward the old cannon.

He had scraped it with the blade, as if he wanted to remove the rust of the Season of Neglect, as if to tell his father to keep his promise. That those brave ancestors who had forged this free nation, floating like a bird on the blue of the Caribbean Sea, should not be forgotten.

John would remember the sound of that old blade on the old cannon in the ruined fort.

(12) PAPADOCRACY

René Depestre, *The Festival of the Greasy Pole*, 1979

Duvalierism never produced an outstanding 'dictator novel', but did provoke a remarkable work of satire, which can be read as a *roman à clef* of the Duvalier dictatorship. Depestre's *Le mât de cocagne* (*The Festival of the Greasy Pole*), written in exile in Cuba, pits an ageing revolutionary against 'Papadocracy' and is centred around a competition to climb and conquer the greasy pole and thereby resist 'state zombification'.

Postel went down the steps and headed along the main street of Tête-Boeuf. He followed the galleries that served as sidewalks, protecting himself both from the sun and from the fierce agitation of the neighborhood. By now, the heat was rising from the asphalt in overwhelming waves. The air was pale with dust, boredom and fear. The passersby were a spectacle of a closed overdone world – teeming, jabbering, nervous in the depths of its degradation. From St Joseph's Gate to the Street of the Caesars, minicommerce was dominant, the secondhand trade at bay, odds and ends, jumbles of items, peddlar's wares, used clothes, little buying-and-selling operations. At every step it was a melee that deafened and stifled, and in which the passion for life seemed to get its strength from the very misery that saturated every square centimeter of the city. He cut through Fronts-Forts street, toward Monseigneur Guilloux street, up to the Square of Heroes, where the National Office for the Electrification of Souls was located.

In front of the brand-new, three storied building, there was a constant swarm of agents coming and going. Some were wearing blue uniforms, others the combat fatigues of a paratrooper. Some were to be seen in the style launched by the Great Electrifier himself: a black suit of light wool, an impeccable white-collared shirt, a pomegranate red tie with matching handkerchief, black glasses, a gray felt Stetson or Borsalino, butter-yellow gloves, and machine gun in hand. The two guards posted at the entrance to the building came up to Postel. They felt along his sides, in his armpits, along his legs, and in his trouser pockets.

"What's your business?" said one of the men

"The greasy pole," answered Postel.

"Follow the arrow," said both agents at the same time.

At the end of the corridor on the second floor, Postel came to a large, bare room where the portrait of the Great Electrifier loomed on the wall. A number of men in tattered clothes and shoes were standing in line in front of desk where two NOFESians were holding court.

"This for the mast?" asked Postel.

"Yeah, sure," replied the last man in the line.

Postel took his place at the end of the line...

(13) LOVE AND MURDER

Marie Chauvet, *Amour, colère, folie* , 1968

Marie Chauvet's trilogy *Amour, colère, folie* is set against a background of state terror. 'Amour' is written in a diary form by the main character, Claire, who is the dark-skinned daughter of a once important mulatto family. Claire, a frustrated spinster, longs to replace her sister in her brother-in-law's arms and is finally is driven, albeit ambiguously, to a political act.

I am lifting my arm with the weapon against my left breast when the screams of an angry mob shatter my state of delirium. With the dagger clasped in my outstretched arm, I strain my ears. Where are these screams coming from? There it is my attention has shifted from my objective. Life, death, don't they simply depend on coincidence? I hide the dagger in my blouse and I go downstairs. There are so many beggars that the stink of sweat and filth they exude makes breathing impossible. The street is lit with torches brandished by the peasants. They scream: "Down with Mr. Long" and head off to the American's house. The latter aims his machine gun: twenty bodies fall to the ground. Caledu and his policemen come running from the police post and appear to want to reestablish order by shooting in the air. I get the impression that a shot has just been fired from Jane's house. Pierrrilus pulls out his revolver from his rags and aims at Caledu; others follow suit: three policemen collapse. The bullets whistle close by me and, I am sure now, they are coming from Jane's balcony: I recognise Joel and Jean crouching behind the railing. Uniforms are scattered on the ground. The commander retreats shooting all the while. He is afraid, alone, in the dark, pursued by the beggars whom he himself has armed. Stepping backwards, he gets closer to my house. Does he realise this? Behind the drawing-room jalousies, I watch and wait.

I pull the dagger from my blouse and open the door slightly. He is on the porch. I see him hesitate and turn his head in all directions. There he is within reach. With extraordinary force, I plunge the dagger into his back once, twice, three times. Blood spurts. He turns around holding on to the door and looks at me. Will he die here under my very roof? I see him stagger off and fall full-length in the street, in the middle of a rut. The beggars, led by Pierrilus, hurl themselves on his corpse like mad men.

No one has seen me except, perhaps, Dora Soubiran whose house is so close to mine. I carefully close back the drawing-room door.

Translated from French by Michael Dash

(14) REAL NIGHTMARES

Edwidge Danticat, *Breath, Eyes, Memory*, 1994

Danticat's first novel traces the troubled lives of three generations of Haitian women. Written in English and set against a background of Macoute terror in Haiti and migration to New York, the novel chronicles the psychological trauma of the protagonist who must live within a new environment while coming to terms with memories of home.

W*ho invented the Macoutes? The devil didn't do it and God didn't do it.*

Ordinary criminals walked naked in the night. They slicked their bodies with oil so they could slip through most fingers. But the *Macoutes* did not hide. When they entered a house, they asked to be fed, demanded the woman of the house, and forced her into her own bedroom. Then all you heard was screams. Until it was her daughter's turn. If a mother refused, they would make her sleep with her son and brother or even her father.

My father might have been a *Macoute*. He was a stranger who, when my mother was sixteen years old, grabbed her on her way back from school. He dragged her into the cane fields, and pinned her down on the ground. He had a black bandanna over his face so she never saw anything but his hair which was the color of eggplants. He kept pounding her until she was too stunned to make a sound. When he was done, he made her keep her face in the dirt, threatening to shoot her if she looked up.

For months she was afraid he would creep out of the night and kill her in her sleep. She was terrified that he would come and tear out the child growing inside her. At night, she tore her sheets and bit off pieces of her own flesh when she had nightmares.

My grandmother sent her to a rich mulatto family in Croix-des-Rosets to do any work she could for free room and board, as a *rèstavèk*.[1] Even though my mother was pregnant and half insane, the family took her in anyway because my grandmother had cooked and cleaned in their house for years, before she married my grandfather.

My mother came back to Dame Marie after I was born. She tried to kill herself several times when I was a baby. The nightmares were just too real. Tante Atie took care of me.

The rich mulatto family helped my mother apply for papers to go out of Haiti. It took four years before she got her visa, but by the time she began to recover her sanity she left.

Tante Atie took me to Croix-des-Rosets, so I could go to school. And when I left, she moved back here, to Dame Marie, to take care of my grandmother.

[1] A Creole term for a child who is sent to live with a wealthier family as an unpaid servant.

(15) A PRIMITIVE WRITER

Dany Laferrière, *Pays sans chapeau,* 1996

Laferrière's semi-autobiographical novels are deliberately provocative attacks on literary tradition, national identity and conventional morality. They are marked by attempts to introduce new narrative styles to an old-fashioned and excessive literary rhetoric. In his most recent work he argues for an abandonment of traditional perspective and viewpoint for a more chaotic aesthetic.

Twenty years ago I wanted silence and privacy. Today, I cannot write if I do not feel people around me, ready to intervene at any moment in my work and give it a new direction. I write in the open air in the middle of the trees, people, cries and tears. In the heart of the Caribbean energy. With a basin of clean water, not far away, in order to refresh my body (face and chest) when the atmosphere becomes unbearable. The air unbreathable. The water splashes everywhere. A rare commodity. After this brief clean-up, I return hurriedly to my unsteady table in order to begin typing again like a mad man on this typewriter which has never left me since my first book. An old couple. We have known hard times, old dear. Days with. Days without. Feverish nights. Curiously, it is a machine which has allowed me to express my rage, my pain or my joy. I do not believe it is only a machine. Sometimes, I hear it groan when it feels that I am sad, or grind its teeth when it hears the growl of my anger. I write down all I see, all I hear, all I feel. A true seismograph. Suddenly, I lift the Remington with my extended hand towards the hard, clear midday sky. Write more quickly, always more quickly. Not that I am in a hurry. I am, in a mad rush while, around me, everything happens so slowly. I am barely finished with one story when another hurtles by. Overflow. I hear the neighbour explain to my mother that she knows of this kind of disease.

- Yes, dear, ever since he arrived, he spends his time typing on the cursed machine.

- It appears, says the neighbour, that this disease strikes only those who have lived for too long abroad.

- Has he gone mad? My mother anxiously asks.

- No. He must simply learn to breathe again, to feel, to see, to touch things differently.

The neighbour adds that she knows a remedy which could help me regain a normal rhythm. I want no brew to calm me down. I want to lose my head. Become a four year old again. Look, a bird crosses my field of vision. I write down: bird. A mango falls. I write down: mango. The children play ball in a street between the cars. I write down: children, ball, cars. You might say a primitive painter. Yes, that's it, I have it. I am a primitive writer.

Translated from French by Michael Dash

(16) THE IMPOSSIBLE RETURN

Emile Ollivier, *Les urnes scellées*, 1995

Ollivier's novel deals with the return of an archeologist and his wife to a Haiti now freed from dictatorship. In the tense and violent atmosphere of upcoming elections, a Haitian from a wealthy family is gunned down. Adrien using his professional instincts tries to unearth the reasons for this murder. Ultimately his homeland remains a mystery to him and he leaves with a sense of bewilderment.

A t sunset, when the silence was broken only by the chirping of insects and the trees stood petrified in the dark, an extraordinary anxiety gripped Adrien, an acute, piercing anxiety which made him want to go down on his knees and say a prayer. He had the unpleasant feeling of being nowhere, of being in a world made of tulle, gauze, wadding. This town had revealed to him its full incongruity. The mountainside bloomed with satellite dishes, billboards from dealers in Japanese, German and American cars, banners advertising Prestige, the locally made beer, signs publicizing charters for New York, Miami, Montreal. At the crossroads of Quatre Chemins, on Remparts-de-L'Eternité road, around the market, the flickering light of torches, lanterns around the fritters stalls. And the deep gash of the Gully that slices through it. Town-image of death where children in rags, tiny skeletons clinging to their mothers' dried up beasts, died from neglect, eyes eaten by flies. Town that knows only departures and never returns. Is this culture of leaving which has spread throughout the town a response to distress in the face of the fratricidal violence, repression, tyranny? It outstrips that of Somalia, of all the Rwandas and the Bosnia-Herzegovinas. Town-garbage bin of the ages, with its ruins, its colonial-style houses floating on blue waves. Town of queues: queue for rice, peas and oil coming from Food Care which is pillaged by the mafia and their bosses: they seize the emergency aid and sell the products; queue in front of the bank to cash the cheque coming from relatives living abroad; queues suddenly turned murderous when impatience breeds madness; queues for water; queues in front of the office where passports are delivered. Town of eternal queues! Marginalised town, town of misery filled with consumption, shooting stars and shadows. Town on its way to extinction, exploded town, mourning in the dawn. Yet it is swarming with life under this morning sky tinged with pink and streaked with light blue.There is the timid irony of flowers, and the rustle of wings, and birdsong which are made in the image of a rosy dawn, of creation, of the first dawning, of the divine appearance of the breath of life, of the first light, which first made the waters shimmer, the plants grow, the animals play about.

Translated from French by Michael Dash

CHAPTER TEN
THE VIEW FROM ABROAD

It is not an overstatement to say that Haiti began as an inadmissible phenomenon. The only successful slave revolt in recorded history was considered impossible at the end of the eighteenth century, when such an act both challenged the prevailing view that blacks were incapable of revolutionary insurrection and the system of plantation slavery in force at the time. Writing on Haiti ever since can be seen as a sustained attempt to come to terms with or, quite often, to distort and deny the reality of a black state, which emerged through the unimaginable feat of black slaves securing their freedom through armed resistance.

The world's difficulty with acknowledging the emergence of the first black state to emerge from plantation slavery is evident in the reluctance with which international recognition was bestowed in the nineteenth century. France imposed a crippling indemnity before recognition of Haitian sovereignty was granted in 1825. The United States, even more concerned over the effect of the example of black insurrection on the plantation south, recognised Haiti only in 1862. Consequently, it is not difficult to see how, from the outset, Haiti could have generated images of revulsion and hostility in the western imagination. It would, however, be a simplification to state that Haiti simply stood for some ill-defined and obsessive notion of black barbarity. Haiti has always had the lure of the extreme case, so that as much as a source of images of the unspeakable and the mysterious, the first black state in the western hemisphere also produced associations of heroic struggle and a salutary primitivism.

Fascination with Haiti actually predates the revolution, and perhaps one of the most famous visitors to Haiti was Moreau de Saint-Méry who visited Saint-Domingue on the eve of the outbreak of insurrection and wrote extensively about the colony's plantation society and about Vodou in particular. (1) After the revolution, much early writing on Haiti concerns itself with the leaders of the struggle for Haitian independence. There were the predictable accounts of black barbarity and monstrous acts perpetrated by frenzied blacks, in which Jean-Jacques Dessalines was invariably implicated. In stark contrast, the portraits of Toussaint Louverture presented him as statesman and martyr. He became the epitome of man's desire for freedom in the imagination of the Romantic poets, Victor Hugo and William Wordsworth. He was equally favoured by missionaries and abolitionists as epitomising the virtues of heroic self-sacrifice and the black's capacity for self-improvement. (2) To this extent, Haiti came to be seen as a place to which freed blacks from the United States could emigrate. Even though migration to Haiti was overtaken by the US Civil War which raised the prospect of an American future for emancipated black slaves, this early experience may well have formed the basis for a sense of solidarity between black Americans and Haitians.

The belief that unrestrained blacks would lapse into savagery, which blocked Haiti's recognition in the nineteenth century, acquired a new currency after the US occupation of 1915. By then a whole new school of sensationalist journalism had emerged, fed by stories of sorcery and cannibalism in Haiti. Much of this writing was provoked by a much read and lurid account of Haiti entitled *Hayti or the Black Republic* by Spencer St John, who had spent twelve years in Haiti as Britain's consul general. The prominence of St John's work is evident from the reference made to it by apologists for the American occupation. The two best known of these were the marine officers John Houston Craige and Faustin Wirkus, both of whom served in Haiti during the occupation. The very titles of some of their accounts of their experiences in Haiti, *Black Baghdad* and *Cannibal Cousins*, betray their racist intent. Filled with smug digressions on the subject of white supremacy and hypersensitive to the mystery and menace of Haiti, this writing served to justify the occupation in the minds of the outside world.

Along with these decidedly racist marine memoirs, there emerged another tendency in writing about Haiti, which was single-mindedly negrophile in its celebration of the marvellous strangeness of Haitian culture. Easily the most widely read of these travel books that painted Haiti as a primitive Eden was William Seabrook's *The Magic Island* which was published in 1929. Seabrook depicted Haiti as elemental and earthy and launched a vision of the country complete with throbbing drums and gyrating bodies that would become the stock in trade of travelogues and adventure stories. (3) Typical of this sensationalist travel writing, for instance, was Alec Waugh's *Hot Countries* (1930), but the most notorious of the travel books which followed Seabrook's was Richard Loederer's *Voodoo Fire in Haiti* which was translated from the German original in 1935. Seabrook's German successor was even more extreme in his depiction of black eroticism as Haiti became the scene of one long orgiastic spectacle. These stereotypes never entirely disappeared and would influence writers as diverse as the Cuban novelist, Alejo Carpentier and the Harvard-trained ethnobotanist, Wade Davis.

The prurient picture of black sensuality was only challenged in the 1940s with the publication of anthropological studies of Haitian popular culture by Melville Herskovits, Harold Courlander and Alfred Métraux. Then Haiti was rediscovered in terms of the power of the folk imagination, as DeWitt Peters promoted Haiti's self-taught artists and Katherine Dunham introduced Haiti's indigenous dances to Broadway.

The US occupation also attracted a number of black American writers and intellectuals to the Haitian cause. Prior to the 1920s, the most prominent black American commentator on Haiti was Frederick Douglass, but during that decade the interest of the National Association for the Advancement of Colored People and the visit of James Weldon Johnson meant that Haiti was increasingly seen in terms of black solidarity and not merely as an outlandish travel destination. Critical accounts of the US occupation could be found in the pages of *The Crisis*, edited by W.E.B. Dubois, and in the wake of Johnson's visit a number of leading black Americans including Dubois, Rayford Logan and Alain Locke, also published accounts of their visits to Haiti in the press. The most controversial impressions of Haiti by a black American artist took the form of Langston Hughes's report on his 1932 visit, which appeared in the pages of *The Crisis* under the title 'White Shadows in a Black Land'. (4) Hughes was not only critical of US imperialist designs on Haiti, but also of the francophile Haitian élite and their contempt for the masses, whom he described as 'people without shoes'. Hughes's sympathy for the Haitian working class was not, however, shared by another important black American visitor in the 1930s, Zora Neale Hurston. Hurston's effort to document Haitian folk culture in *Tell My Horse* is filled with approving comments on the American occupation and a Seabrook -inspired account of Vodou. This anthropologically questionable study seems at times to outdo even Craige and Wirkus in its depiction of the volatile and unpredictable nature of the Haitian personality. (5)

Haiti's image as a society whose values were profoundly different from those of the western world made the country attractive during the Second World War to various European surrealists because of that movement's interest in dream, the occult and the unconscious. It was the appointment of Pierre Mabille in 1940 to a post at the Port-au-Prince general hospital that cemented the contact between French surrealism and Haiti and facilitated the visits of a number of important figures from that movement. Mabille studied Vodou and helped to found the Bureau d'Ethnologie. (6) In the 1940s Aimé Césaire and his wife Suzanne (7) visited Haiti, as did the

Cubans Alejo Carpentier and Wifredo Lam. Haiti left its mark as much on Aimé Césaire as it did on Carpentier in that both writers were drawn to the drama of its revolutionary past and, in particular, to the figure of Henri Christophe and his monumental Citadelle. (8) Yet no encounter between surrealism and Haiti was as dramatic as that featuring André Breton, who was in invited to Haiti in 1945 by Mabille. It was Breton's public lectures in which he appealed to the importance of Haiti's cultural values in the face of American domination and oppressive local interests that contributed to the overthrow of the Lescot government in 1946. These visits also produced a more complex and creative depiction of Haitian culture than was available from American commentators during the occupation. This meant the arrival of the idea of the marvellous and the magical as notions of enormous literary and ideological value among contemporary Haitian writers.

The advent of Duvalierism in 1957 led to the undoing of the mainly positive images of the 1940s and the re-emergence of the stereotypes of Haiti as a land of danger and evil. The myth of Haitian barbarism was accentuated by the cruelty of the Duvalier regime and provoked a number of lurid works in the 1960s, of which the most notorious must be Graham Greene's 1966 novel *The Comedians*. (9) Greene's novel presents a gloomily oppressive picture of Haiti, complete with demonic head of state and malevolent Tontons Macoutes. The salutary disorientation that inspired the surrealists to celebrate Haiti now becomes the sinister prism through which the narrator views a society that has reverted to wretchedness and barbarity. Greene's evocation of Papa Doc's tyranny presents Haiti as a place of aberrant political culture and abnormal psychology. This view is also prevalent in the travel writing of Francis Huxley, whose interest in mental illness took him to Haiti in 1966, where he found his world of black magic and zombies. At the same time, a political commentator like Robert Rotberg could explain Haiti's 'politics of squalor' in terms of mental deviancy and a dependency complex that made Haitians particularly susceptible to dictatorship. Perhaps, the most widely read work on the Duvalier period was Bernard Diederich and Al Burt's *Papa Doc and the Tontons Macoutes*. (10) This supposedly objective account of Duvalier's reign of terror simply substantiated some of the more colourful episodes in Greene's novel, and its introduction was obligingly written by Greene himself. Unfortunately for Haiti, the Duvalier dynasty would last 29 years, during which time Greene's synthesis of the grotesque and the comical would fix Haiti in the minds of outsiders as the 'nightmare republic'.

Jean-Claude Duvalier fell from power in February 1986, thereby ushering in a new phase in the country's political life as well as a new chapter in foreign perceptions. The 1980s, however, did not begin very promisingly for Haiti's image abroad, as the dramatic increase in 'boat people' arriving in Florida and the mistaken, but widespread, belief that Haitians were carriers of the Aids virus increased its notoriety. In one sense, this was nothing new to Haiti, which has always been seen as 'high risk' in the western imagination, but the Aids crisis spelt disaster for a tourism industry that was just beginning to recover from the bad press of the 1960s. To further complicate matters, the time-honoured clichés of the supernatural were reworked in 1986 by the ethnobotanist Wade Davis, whose ostensibly scholarly and very popular book *The Serpent and the Rainbow* perpetuates the image of Haiti as the land of the zombie, where black magic reigns supreme. (11) Fittingly, *The Serpent and the Rainbow* was turned into a horror movie in 1988, directed by Wes Craven, the maker of *Nightmare on Elm Street*.

The political turbulence sweeping Haiti in the 1980s and 1990s as the last vestiges of Duvalierism were painfully swept away and the need for democratic reform violently manifested itself, had a profound effect on those writing about Haiti. Replacing Davis's 'possessed Haiti', contemporary politics with its violent conflicts, aborted elections and military coups, became the subject of a more informed and balanced journalistic treatment. The journalist Mark Danner 's description of the post-Duvalier period accurately conveyed the social and political forces in contention. (12) Amy Wilentz's *The Rainy Season* is among the best examples of this more objective perspective. (13) She is both acutely sensitive to the stigma attached to Haiti by writers such as Greene and Davis and asserts that Haiti is bigger and more complex than either of these demonising accounts would allow. Wilentz is particularly drawn to the display of 'people power' in Haiti and to the radical priest, Jean-Bertrand Aristide, who came to power in the elections of 1990. In *The Rainy Season* the ominous and ever-threatening thunderstorm of Greene's earlier novel becomes a metaphor for Aristide's *lavalas* movement which promises to cleanse Haiti of its corrupt past in a political flash flood. Equally attracted to the figure of Aristide is the Irish novelist Brian Moore, whose *No Other Life* is closely based on Aristide as a Messiah figure and his struggle again the forces of Duvalierism. (14) If there is a life beyond death in this novel, it is a political one and, as the title suggests, the only valid struggle is in the here and now.

Another work of fiction, less tied to contemporary events and published earlier, is Russell Banks's *Continental Drift*, which may point the way to a reconceptualisation of Haiti within the region and the hemisphere. (15) Banks presents a world of constant movement and unpredictable drift in his novel and draws startling parallels between the life of a native of New Hampshire and that of a Haitian refugee who sets out on a small boat for a better life in Florida. The author frames the story in terms of a personal journey of understanding, not the thrill-seeking expedition of the travel writer. As in Brian Moore's novel, Haiti provides a salutary lesson, this time in defining the position of the US in terms of the changes sweeping the hemisphere. Once more, as was the case in 1804, Haiti is presented as the key to remapping the identity of the Americas.

(1) SUBVERSIVE RITES

Moreau de Saint-Méry, *A Civilization that Perished: The Last Years of White Colonial Rule*, 1985

Both the strengths and weaknesses of colonial Saint-Domingue were apparent to Martinican-born Saint-Méry who practised law there for a number of years. He was one of the first foreign observers to pay detailed attention to Vodou, which he characterised as a diabolical spectacle with revolutionary potential.

Faintings and raptures take over some of them and a sort of fury some of the others, but for all there is a nervous trembling which they cannot master. They spin around ceaselessly. And there are some in this species of bacchanal who tear their clothing and even bite their flesh. Others who are only deprived of their senses and have fallen in their tracks are taken, even while, dancing into the darkness of a neighbouring room, where a disgusting prostitution exercises a most hideous empire. Finally weariness brings an end to these afflicting scenes. This is not before a decision has been announced as to the time of the next meeting.

It is very natural to think that Voodoo owes its origin to serpent cult, to which the people of Juida are particularly devoted. They also say that it originated in the kingdom of Ardra, which, like Juida, is on the Slave Coast. And how far the Africans push their superstitions in regard to this animal, the adder, is easy to recognise from what I have just told.

What is very true of Voodoo and at the same time very remarkable, is the spirit of hypnotism, which brings the members to dance right to the edge of consciousness. The prevention of spying is very rigorous. Whites caught ferreting out the secrets of the sect and tapped by a member who has spotted them have sometimes themselves started dancing and have consented to pay the Voodoo queen to put an end to this punishment. I cannot fail to add, however, that never has any man of the constabulary, who has sworn war upon Voodoo, not felt the power which compels him to dance and which without doubt has saved the dancers from any need for flight.

In order to quiet the alarms which this mysterious cult of Voodoo causes in the Colony, they affect to dance it in public, to the sound of the drums and of rhythmic handclapping. They even have this followed by a dinner where people eat nothing but poultry. But I assure you that this is only one more calculation, to evade the magistrates and the better to guarantee the success of this dark cabal. After all, Voodoo is not a matter of amusement or enjoyment. It is rather a school where those easily influenced give themselves up to a domination which a thousand circumstances can render tragic.

One would not credit to what extent the Voodoo chiefs keep other members in dependence on them. There is no one of them who would not prefer anything to the evils with which they are threatened if they don't go regularly to the assemblies or don't blindly do what they are ordered to do. One can see that fright has influenced them, to make them abandon their use of reason. In their transports of frenzy, they utter shouts, flee from other people's eyes and excite pity. In a word, nothing is more dangerous, according to all the accounts, than this cult of Voodoo. It can be made into a terrible weapon – this extravagant idea that the ministers of this alleged god know all and can do anything.

(2) HEROIC TOUSSAINT

John Greenleaf Whittier, *Toussaint Louverture*, 1969

Whittier's *Anti-Slavery Poems, Songs of Labor and Reform* are examples of the abolitionist view of Haiti's struggle for independence. Inspired by the Romantic evocation of Toussaint by William Wordsworth, Whittier celebrated in 1833 the nobility of the cause and the heroic nature of the 'black chieftain of Haiti', while denouncing the treachery of the French.

> Sleep calmly in thy dungeon-tomb,
> Beneath Besançon's alien sky,
> Dark Haytien! For the time shall come,
> Yes, even now is nigh,
> When everywhere, thy name shall be
> Redeemed from color's infamy;
> And men shall learn to speak of thee
> As one of earth's great spirits, born
> In servitude, and nursed in scorn,
> Casting aside the weary weight
> And fetters of its low estate,
> In that strong majesty of soul
> Which knows no color, tongue, or clime,

Which still has spurned the base control
Of tyrants through all time!
Far other hands than mine may wreathe
The laurel round thy brow of death,
And speak thy praise, as one whose word
A thousand fiery spirits stirred,
Who crushed his foeman as a worm,
Whose step on human hearts fell firm:
Be mine the better task to find
A tribute for thy lofty mind,
Amidst whose gloomy vengeance shone
Some milder virtue all thine own,
Some gleams of feeling pure and warm,
Like sunshine on a sky of storm,
Proofs that the negro's heart retains
Some nobleness amid its chains,-
That kindness to the wronged is never
Without its excellent reward,
Holy to human-kind and ever
Acceptable to God.

(3) AUTHENTIC ECSTASY

William Seabrook, *The Magic Island*, 1929

Apart from Graham Greene, William Seabrook must be the most influential travel writer on Haiti. His widely read *The Magic Island* presents an alluring picture of a mystical country, largely given over to Vodou and ritual sacrifice.

And now the literary-traditional white stranger who spied from hiding in the forest, had such a one lurked near by, would have seen all the wildest tales of Voodoo fiction justified: in the red light of torches which made the moon turn pale, leaping, screaming, writhing black bodies, blood-maddened, sex-maddened, god-maddened, drunken, whirled and danced their dark saturnalia, heads thrown weirdly back as if their necks were broken, white teeth and eyeballs gleaming, while couples seizing one another from time to time fled from the circle, as if pursued by furies, into the forest to share and slake their ecstasy.

Thus also my unspying eyes beheld this scene in actuality, but I did not experience the revulsion which literary tradition prescribes. It was savage and abandoned, but it seemed to me magnificent and

324   Libète: A Haiti Anthology

not devoid of a certain beauty. Something inside myself awoke and responded to it. These, of course, were individual emotional reactions, perhaps deplorable in a supposedly civilized person. But I believe that the thing itself – their thing, I mean – is rationally defensible. Of what use is any life without its emotional moments or hours of ecstasy? They were reaching collective ecstasy by paths which were not intrinsically peculiar to their jungle ancestors, but which have been followed by many peoples, some highly civilized, from the earliest ages, and will be followed to the end of time or until we all become soulless robots. It is not necessary to look backward to the Dionysian orgies, the bacchanalia, the rites of Adonis, or frenzied David dancing before the Ark of the covenant. What, after all, were they doing here in these final scenes, when formal ritual had ended, that was so different from things which occur in our own fashionable night clubs, except that they were doing it with the sanction of their gods and doing it more successfully? Savage rhythm, alcohol, and sex excitement – yet there was an essential difference, for here was a mysterious something super-added. Lasciviousness became lust, which is a cleaner thing, and neurotic excitement became authentic ecstasy, the divine frenzy of the ancients... Here certainly in these mountains, where sacrificial blood flowed free and all things were done in the name of the gods, the gods magnificently descended.

(4) A DARKER WORLD

Langston Hughes, *White Shadows in a Black Land,* 1932

Haiti had always had a special appeal for Hughes, who visited the country towards the end of the US occupation. Yet he confessed to being disappointed by Port-au-Prince and the general level of poverty, and was particularly repulsed by the arrogance of the Marines as well as the deep class prejudices of the Haitian elite.

Imagine a country where the entire national population is colored and you will have Haiti – the first of the black republics, and that much discussed little land to the South of us. To a Negro coming directly from New York by steamer and landing in Port au Prince, the capital, it is like stepping into a new world, a darker world, a world where the white shadows are apparently missing, a world of his own people. The customs officials who examine his baggage will be Negroes, the taxi drivers will be black or brown, his hotel keeper will probably be mulatto. In the shops, clerks of color will wait on him. At the banks, Negroes will cash his travelers' checks and explain the currency of the country to him. Should he visit the Chamber of Deputies, he will find the governing body filled with dark races and even the President of the Republic will have a touch of color in his blood. In the country districts, the peasants who make up the bulk of the population, will smile at him from kind black faces, and the dark visitor from America will feel at home and unafraid.

It is doubly disappointing then, to discover, if you have not already known, how the white shadows have fallen on this land of color. Before you can go ashore, a white American Marine has been on board ship to examine your passport, and maybe you will see a U.S. gunboat at anchor in the harbor. Ashore you are likely to run into groups of Marines in the little cafes, talking in "Cracker" accents, and drinking in the usual boisterous American manner. You will discover that the Banque d'Haiti, with its negro cashiers and tellers, in really under control of the National City Bank of New York. You will become informed that all the money collected by the Haitian customs passes through the hands of an American comptroller. And, regretfully you will gradually learn that most of the larger stores with their colored clerks are really owned by Frenchmen, Germans and Assyrian Jews. And if you read the Haitian newspapers, you will soon realize from the heated complaints there, that even in the Chamber of Deputies the strings of government are pulled by white politicians in far-off Washington – and that the American marines are kept in the country through an illegal treaty thrust upon Haiti by force and never yet ratified by the United States senate. The dark-skinned little Republic, then, has its hair caught in the white fingers of unsympathetic foreigners, and the Haitian people live today under a sort of military dictatorship backed by American guns. They are not free.

(5) UNRELIABLE HAITIANS

Zora Neale Hurston, *Tell My Horse*, 1939

Hurston visited Haiti in 1937 to carry out what was supposed to be the first serious study of Vodou by a black American. There is little solidarity with the Haitian people in her book *Tell My Horse*, but a strong sense of her vulnerability as a woman alone in a country she does not fully understand.

Then again under the very sound of the drums, the upper class Haitian will tell you that there is no such thing as voodoo in Haiti, and that all that has been written about it is nothing but the malicious lies of foreigners. He knows that it is not so and should know that you know that it is not true. Down in his heart he does not hate voodoo worship. Even if he is not an adept himself he sees it about him every day and takes it for a matter of course, but he lies to save his own and national pride. He has read the fantastic things that have been written about Haitian voodoo by people who know nothing at all about it. Consequently, there are the stereotyped tales of virgin worship, human sacrifice and other elements borrowed from European origins. All this paints the Haitian as a savage and he does not like to be spoken of like that. So he takes refuge in flight. He denies the knowledge and the existence of the whole thing. But a peasant who has been kindly treated will answer frankly if he is not intimidated by the presence of a Gros Negre or a policeman. That is if the policeman is strange to him or is known to be self-conscious about voodoo. But that same peasant who answered you so freely and so frankly about voodoo, if you paid him in advance for the simplest service would not return with your change. The employer class in Haiti continually warn their foreign friends not to pay for any service in advance nor to send anyone off with change. The peasant does not consider this as stealing. He prides himself on having put over a smart business deal. What he might lose by it in future business never occurs to him. And while this applies particularly to the servant class, it is just as well not to pay any money in advance to anyone in Haiti unless you know them very well indeed.

This self deception on the upper levels takes another turn. It sounds a good deal like wishful thinking out loud. They would like to say that Haiti is a happy and well-ordered country and so they just say it, obvious facts to the contrary. There is a marked tendency to refuse responsibility for anything that is unfavorable. Some outside influence, they say, usually the United States or Santo Domingo, is responsible for all the ills of Haiti.

(6) RURAL HAITI

Pierre Mabille, *The Haitian Panorama*, 1945

Mabille may have been the most important European visitor to Haiti in the twentieth century because of his impact on Haiti's intellectual life. His interest in Vodou went beyond mere sensationalism as is evident in his involvement in the Bureau d'Ethnologie. He was, moreover, a perceptive observer of rural Haiti and published his panorama of rural Haiti in 1945.

Twenty miles or so from the towns and especially from the capital, in the escarpment of Kenscoff or the morne at Cabrits, you start to meet long lines of barefoot peasant women, balancing their heavy baskets on their heads. They go their way singing, chatting, laughing and even dancing, never setting down their enormous loads which do nothing to diminish the suppleness of their gait. They walk like this for hours, days, nights, years, for their whole lives. If I had to leave Haiti for good, the image I would retain of it would certainly be that of these women walking the length of eternity, descending the footpaths, effortlessly scaling the highest peaks, winding across the plain, taking with them mountains of herbs, carrots, sweet potatoes, cabbages, pineapples, baskets of poultry, piles of hats, stacks of chairs, cans of milk. Here the procession is accompanied by a few asses, there by some thin Caribbean horses, bent under their excessive burdens.

Wherever you go there are people walking. They run in modern cities; they step with heavy tread in our own countryside; in North Africa they advance slowly in caravans which criss-cross the desert fleeing famine; but nothing compares with this possessed tramping of the Haitian peasant, a legacy of the African forest, possessed like the struggle of impoverished existence against the renewed assaults of poverty. This muttering old woman, a clay pipe between her teeth and her tinware on her head, climbs more than ten miles down the mountains each morning to carry milk to her customers. That one over there has travelled more than twelve miles to get to market so she can sell her basket of mangoes for no more than a gourde. Don't be surprised if in a few moments you see her crouched asleep in a shady corner, and don't speak too hastily of nonchalance. And if, retracing her path with rapid steps, the rain takes her by surprise, she will bundle up her sackcloth dress, leaving a shirt which the falling water will plaster against her black body. Then, tomorrow, perhaps you will hear coming from a hut the howls that accompany a death and which, according to tradition, succeed each other throughout the night over the corpse. Don't speak too hastily of a negro's sensitivity to pulmonary ailments.

(7) PRESENCE OF THE CARIBBEAN

Suzanne Césaire, *The Great Camouflage*, 1945

Suzanne Césaire visited Haiti with her husband Aimé Césaire in 1944. This was the first of a series of intense encounters between Haiti and surrealism. Césaire's lectures had an enormous impact on Haitian intellectuals, while Haiti's mark would be left on Césaire's writing as well. Suzanne Césaire published this impressionistic prose poem on a cyclone in Haiti in 1945. It was among the last things she would write before lapsing into silence.

In the eye of the cyclone everything is snapping, everything is collapsing with the rending sound of tumultuous events. The radios fall silent. The great palm-tree tail of fresh wind is unfolding somewhere in the stratosphere where no one will follow its wild iridescence and waves of purple light.

After the rain, sunshine.

The Haitian cicadas consider chirping out their love. When not a drop of water remains on the scorched grass, they sing furiously about the beauty of life and explode into a cry too vibrant for an insect's body. Their thin shell of dried silk stretched to the limit, they die as they let out the world's least moistened cry of pleasure.

Haiti remains, shrouded in the ashes of a gentle sun with eyes of cicadas, shells of mabouyas, and the metallic face of sea that is no longer of water but of mercury.

Now is the moment to lean out of the window of the aluminium clipper on its wide curves.

Once again the sea of clouds appears, which is no longer intact since the planes of Pan American Airways pass through. If there is a harvest in process of ripening, now is the time to glimpse it, but in forbidden military zones the windows remain closed.

Disinfectant or ozone is brought out, but it hardly matters, you will see nothing. Nothing but the sea and the confused lay of the land. You can only guess at the uncomplicated loves of the fishes. They stir the waters, which give a friendly wink at the clipper's windows. Seen from high above, our islands assume their true dimensions as seashells. The hummingbird-women, the tropical flower-women, the women of four races and dozens of blood ties, have gone. So too have the canna, the plumiera, and the flame tree, the moonlit palm trees, and the sunsets seen nowhere else on earth...

Nevertheless they're there.

Yet it was fifteen years ago that the Caribbean was disclosed to me from the eastern slope of Mount Pelée. From there I realized, as a very young girl, that, as it lay in the Caribbean Sea, Martinique as sensual, coiled, spread out and relaxed, and I thought of the other islands, equally beautiful.

I experienced the presence of the Caribbean once more in Haiti, on summer mornings in 1944, which was so much more perceptible in the places from which, at Kenscoff, the view over the mountains is of an unbearable beauty.

And now complete lucidity. My gaze, going beyond these perfect forms and colours, catches by surprise the torment within the Caribbean's most beautiful face.

(8) CHRISTOPHE'S SUICIDE

Alejo Carpentier, *The Kingdom of This World*, 1957

Carpentier's visit to Haiti in the 1940s took him to Cap Haïtien where he was overwhelmed by the ruins of King Henri Christophe's palace and the Citadelle. In his description of the tragic suicide of the king he catches the grandiose, egotistical and surreal world of Haiti's first king.

Calling to one another, answering from mountain to mountain, rising from the beaches, issuing from the caves, running beneath the trees, descending ravines and riverbeds, the drums boomed, the radas, the congos, the drums of Boukman, the drums of the Grand Alliances, all the drums of Voodoo. A vast encompassing percussion was advancing on Sans Souci, tightening the circle. A horizon of thunder closing in. A storm whose eye at the moment was the throne without heralds or mace-bearers. The king returned to his chamber and his window. The burning of his plantations had begun, of his diaries, of his canefields. Now the fire outran the drums, leaping from house to house, from field to field. A flame shot up from the granary, scattering red-black embers into the hay barn. The north wind lifted the burning husks of the cornfields, bringing them nearer and nearer. Fiery ash was falling on the palace terraces...

The drums were so close now that they seemed to be throbbing there, behind the balustrades of the main entrance, at the foot of the great stone stairway. At that moment the fire lighted up the mirrors of the Palace, the crystal goblets, the crystal of the lamps, glasses, windows, the mother-of-pearl inlay of the console tables – the flames were everywhere, and it was impossible to tell which were flames and which reflections. All the mirrors of Sans Souci were simultaneously ablaze. The whole building disappeared under this chill fire, which reached out into the night, making each wall a cistern of twisted flames.

The shot was almost inaudible because of the proximity of the drums. Henri Christophe's hand released his pistol, to touch his gaping temple. His body stood erect for a moment, as though about to take a step, before it fell face forward amid all its decorations. The pages appeared on the threshold of the room. The king was dying sprawled in his own blood.

(9) HAITIAN HOMECOMING

Graham Greene, *The Comedians*, 1966

Graham Greene visited Haiti in 1963 during the darker years of the presidency of François Duvalier and made Haiti the setting for one of his better-known tales of betrayal and despair. Haiti emerges as a modern-day *Heart of Darkness*, in which shadows darken everything that Greene's narrator observes.

I was returning without much hope to a country of fear and frustration, and yet every familiar feature as the *Medea* drew in gave me a kind of happiness. The huge mass of Kenscoff leaning over the town was as usual half in deep shadow; there was a glassy sparkle of late sun off the new buildings near the port which had been built for an international exhibition in so called modern style. A stone Columbus watched us coming in – it was there Martha and I used to rendezvous at night until the curfew closed us in separate prisons, I in my hotel, she in her embassy, without a telephone which worked to communicate by. She would sit in her husband's car in the dark and flash her headlights on at the sound of my Humber. I wondered whether in the last month, now that the curfew was over, she had chosen a different rendezvous, and I wondered with whom. That she had found a substitute I had no doubt. No one banks on fidelity nowadays.

I was lost in too many difficult thoughts to remember my fellow-passengers. There was no message waiting for me from the British Embassy, so I assumed that at the moment all was well. At immigration and customs there was the habitual confusion. We were the only boat, and yet the shed was full: porters, taxi-drivers who hadn't had a fare in weeks, police and the occasional Tonton Macoute in his black glasses and his soft hat, and beggars, beggars everywhere. They seeped through every chink like water in the rainy season. A man without legs sat under the customs-counter like a rabbit in a hutch, miming in silence.

A familiar figure forced his way towards me. As a rule he haunted the airfield, and I had not expected to see him here. He was a journalist known to everyone as Petit Pierre – a metis in a country where the half castes were the aristocrats waiting for the tumbrils to roll. He was believed by some to have connections with the Tontons, for how otherwise had he escaped a beating or worse? And yet there were occasionally passages in his gossip column that showed an odd satirical courage – perhaps he depended on the police not to read between the lines.

He seized me by the hands as if we were the oldest of friends and addressed in English, 'Why, Mr Brown, Mr Brown.'

'How are you Petit Pierre?'

He giggled at me, standing on his pointed toe-caps, for he a tiny figure of a man. He was just as I remembered him, hilarious. Even the time of day was humorous to him. He had the quick movements of a monkey, and he seemed to swing from wall to wall on ropes of laughter. I had always thought that when the time came, and surely it must one day come in his precarious defiant livelihood, he would laugh at his executioner, as a Chinaman is supposed to do.

(10) VODOU PRESIDENT

Bernard Diederich and Al Burt, *Papa Doc and the Tontons Macoutes*, 1969

Diederich and Burt's book, colourfully subtitled 'Atrocities in the Realm of a Madman', was perhaps the most widely read account of Duvalier's presidency in the 1970s. It freely combines actual events with outrageous speculation and mere hearsay. Typical of the book's reportage is its sensationalist account of Vodou, while noting accurately that the religion was cunningly manipulated by Papa Doc.

Every *houmfort* or temple is autonomous. The *houngan* and the *bocor* each runs his own show and sometimes adds the personal touches and frills to his ceremonies and services. The priest takes orders from the *loas*.

From the very beginning Duvalier set out to bring to his side the thousands of priests from the most isolated villages – from Bombardopolis to Anse Hainault – in the desire to have them regard him as their supreme master.

He hired a knowledgeable Haitian for the sole purpose of arranging visits to the National Palace of notables and *bocors* from the most isolated areas of Haiti. No other President until Duvalier had taken such pains to dominate this influential group.

One such visit in 1962, designed to impress a *bocor* and his community that the 'supreme being' was Papa Doc, ended disastrously. The ancient *bocor* from Aquin in Southwest Haiti became so terrified at the sight of all the armed soldiers and militiamen in the halls of the palace that was seized by a sudden attack of diarrhea. He never did get his audience. Instead, he was given medical treatment and a new pair of pants and permitted to return home.

These visits have their effect not only on the *bocors*, but on their communities. Rural Haitians have always taken the state for granted and expect nothing from it but a hard time. They accept the white Catholic priest, *monpere*, but they reserve their reverence for his voudou counterpart. Duvalier has managed to supercharge that reverence. *Houngans* and *bocors* fear him; their flocks see him as a kind of super-*bocor*.

It is not unlikely that Duvalier himself began circulating the stories of strange practices going on at a calvary in the Bel Air section which he ordered rebuilt shortly after taking power. Port au Prince, Fignolé's traditional stronghold, needed to be impressed. Stories of Papa Doc burying people alive at the base of the giant cross took care of that. And when his adversaries disinterred his father's corpse and took to smearing excrement on the calvary, Papa Doc was made.

After the 1963 rebel attack on the village of Ouanaminthe was beaten back, Duvalier ordered that former Army Capt. Blucher Philogenes' head be cut off, packed in ice, and brought to the palace on an Air Force plane. News spread around Port au Prince that Papa Doc was having long sessions with the head; and that he had induced it to disclose the exiles' plans.

(11) SINGULAR HORROR

Wade Davis, *The Serpent and the Rainbow*, 1986

Davis' book appeared in the very year in which a popular uprising
ended the Duvalier dynasty, but you will find no evidence in it of
Haiti's new political consciousness. Davis' Haiti is a neo-African
society in which *Bizango* secret societies control the lives of ordinary
Haitians. As much fiction as field work, the book is made up of a
series of adventures, during which the wide eyed narrator wanders
through the wilds of Haiti in search of zombies, led by a local Ariadne,
Rachel Beauvoir.

In the summer in Haiti the spirits walk, and the people go with
them. For weeks in July the roads come alive with pilgrims, and
we followed them.

Leaving Gonaïves, Rachel and I drove north across the mountains to the lush coastal plain, calling first at the sacred spring and
mudbaths of St Jacques, and then moving on to the village of
Limonade and the festival of St Anne. Here they had gathered, literally thousands of them dressed in the bright colors and clothes of
the spirits, fused in hallucinatory waves that flowed across the plaza.

The seething edge of the throng enveloped us even as we stepped
from the jeep. We were carried, flesh to flesh, by the collective whim
of the crowd. It was like being pushed through the stuffed belly of a
beast, and soon we were ploughing through the throng to the nearest refuge, the stone steps of the church standing firm like a jetty
above the madness.

Our senses numbed, we entered the church and were well inside
the nave before we realized what was going on. It was the mass of
the Invalids, and at our feet lay the most diseased and wretched
human display imaginable. Lepers without faces, victims of elephan-
tiasis with limbs the size of tree trunks, dozens and dozens of dying
people, collected from the length and breadth of the country to seek
alms and redemption at the altar of this church. It was a scene of
such singular horror, we could think only of escape.

Rachel stepped ahead of me toward an open door, and then
gasped. There in the shadow of a cross, her head covered by a black
shawl was a single woman, and draped across her legs was her
daughter, a teenage girl whose shattered legs crossed like sticks. Her
skin was jet black and her head a grotesque melon, so swollen with
disease that you could see the individual follicles of hair. It was a

sight so terrible that we could not pass. We turned back to wade through the brown-frocked beggars carpeting the front of the church, and as we passed they tugged at our clothes. There was nothing for them, and the real horror of the moment was less their condition than our fear.

Then, on the steps of the church the scene turned into an epiphany. A healthy peasant woman, dressed in the bright-blue-and-red solid block colors of Ogoun, swirled through the beggars possessed by her spirit. Over her shoulder was slung a brilliant red bag filled with dry kernels of golden corn. She twirled and pranced in divine grace with one arm stretching out like the neck of a swan, she placed a small pile of corn in each of the begging bowls. When she was finished, her bag empty, she spun around to the delight of all and with a great cry flung herself from the steps of the church. Rachel and watched her flow into the crowd. Wherever she went the people backed away, that Ogoun might have space to spin. Our eyes followed her until she was gone, and then without speaking we dropped back into the crowd.

(12) VIGILANTE JUSTICE

Mark Danner, *Beyond the Mountains*, 1989

Danner's three-part series covered the first three years after the fall of Jean-Claude Duvalier for *The New Yorker*. He does not focus on Haitians as an atavistic, tribal people but as participants in an often bloody struggle to construct a modern, democratic state. In its own desperate way, vigilante justice became the only means of dealing with the Macoutes left in Duvalier's wake.

Pushing through the crowd, we discovered a tall, lean young man, several hours dead, laid out carefully on Haiti's Route Nationale 1. His body had been prepared for its role: a rope had been twisted about his neck, and above the frayed noose a metal necklace had been pulled tight around his chin, but most of it had disappeared into the gaping maroon slashes around his mouth and throat. Distinct, deep machete cuts in a V-shaped pattern above and below the mouth, they seemed almost an attempt to construct for the victim, after death, a parody second mouth. A partly smoked cigarette had been placed between his lips, a charred wooden match balanced jauntily on his chin. Within easy reach next to his stomach, which, left exposed, was already dense with flies in the rising heat, were a handful of rice, a can of tomato sauce, and a slab of cheese, all displayed on a scrap of brown cardboard. "That's so he can eat," an old man said laughing, bringing on the laughter of the crowd. "And the cigarette, that's to keep him happy." There was no blood on his shirt, the old man said, because when they spotted him near the La Saline marketplace early that morning, as gunshots echoed in the distance, this tall young man had been wearing a dress – the all-purpose Haitian disguise – and carrying a can of gasoline. He was a Tonton Macoute, they said, a member of Jean Claude Duvalier's militia – one of the thousands who had gone into hiding after the fall of the dictator, nearly two years earlier, and who now, during the months of growing violence, had begun to reappear in the neighborhood. He had come to spread terror by bringing to the people of La Saline what they dreaded most: a fire that in seconds would roar through the dense labyrinth of scrap-wood hovels, leaving scores of people dead and thousands homeless.

But the *brigades de vigilance* – neighborhood committees that had formed themselves in these last days of terror – had been watching. And when the Macoute appeared in that dark and now deserted marketplace, wearing his dress and carrying his can of gasoline, the *brigade* slum boys let out a shout and gave chase, pursuing him down the tiny alleyways, over the ditches filled with pale-green waste, until at last they caught him, dragging him to the ground beneath the black mountains of the vast charcoal yard. There, in front of the angry shouting crowd, the slum boys stunned him with their machetes, then lynched him. They prepared the body and left it on the road for Guede, the voodoo lord of the Crossroads to the Underworld, to attend to in his own good time – for Guede, despite his great power, often appears as a poor wandering beggar, a famished traveller, who would be sure to look kindly on the sumptuous meal of rice and sauce and cheese that had been left beside the young man's lifeless hand.

(13) THE VIEW BEYOND THE PALACE

Amy Wilentz, *The Rainy Season,* 1989

Wilentz covered post-Duvalier Haiti for *Time,* and in *The Rainy Season* she charts the rise of the grassroots Catholic Church and Aristide. Wilentz's coverage of Haiti is remarkably sensitive and well informed. She is acutely aware of the way in which images of Haiti have been manipulated in the past and always insists on looking at the broader human picture.

There was something about it, that palace. Our cameraman couldn't get away from it. Each time he pulled back to show us the long view, the whole range of the city – the black waters of the bay, the tin shanties and cardboard shacks of La Saline, the bright foliage that covered most of the capital, the hills of Bel-Air – he zoomed back to the palace. Look at this over here, he would say, pointing his lens at the graveyard. But only for a moment, and then back to the monolith. Look at this new hotel, he said, panning up to a point above the cemetery; that cross up on the hill, the mountains in the distance, that little road you can see winding over there – but then, back to the palace.

This obsession with the seat of power was an outsider's obsession, the obsession of the U.S. government, the obsession of foreign correspondents; that was the lesson I learned from the cameraman's failure to keep his eye on the long view. The place exerted a singular attraction for him, the way Dr Duvalier had for Graham Greene, the way elections have for the State Department and the New York Times, the way the zombi has for foreign anthropologists. Most Haitians try to look away from the palace, try to avoid it. They know that Haiti is bigger than that. The evil power is not the only thing. Of course the chef de section still rides through the Haitian hills with his revolver at his hip, and the President still travels in a twenty-car motorcade, armed to the teeth. But the long view sees more than a trail of Mercedes limousines twisting through mountains of misery, more than Dr Duvalier riding through town and tossing bright coins to the children of La Saline.

The long view sees those children, not the dictator. It takes into account the villages and the slums and the pretty houses of Pacot, as well as the palace and the Casernes Dessalines. If you cast your eyes wider than the palace grounds, you can see dozens of small churches, with their paper flowers hanging behind the altar, and their broken fans, their makeshift seating arrangements and slatted windows. You'll see rifles too, and revolvers, grenades and tear gas, there are also tailors' sewing machines and beauticians' hairdryers, doctors' stethoscopes and accountants' computers. Besides the Macoutes and the Police and the Army, there are the car salesmen, the dry cleaners, the jewelry-store owners, and the poor relations who work for free in the homes of their wealthier aunts or uncles or cousins. Duvalier is present, certainly, or Namphy, or Avril now, or the colonel or general who is next in line. There are the people who profit from power, but also the people who take a loss.

(14) HAITI'S MESSIAH

Brian Moore, *No Other Life*, 1993

In Moore's novel, closely patterned on Aristide's rise to the presidency and his conflicts with the Catholic Church, a radical priest called Jean-Paul Cantave, known to his followers as Jeannot, is elected president. Moore manages to capture very convincingly Jeannot's mystical appeal.

The dead man was seated at a table dressed, as was the custom, in his best clothes, a clean white shirt, denim trousers, sandals. His old felt fedora was perched jauntily on his head. On the table was a funerary wreath fashioned from white frangipani and red immortelles. A dish of plantains, beans and rice had been set before him and an unlit cigarette drooped from his lips. He was a peasant in his thirties, scarecrow thin, as were most of the others in the room. And then I saw the bullet hole in his temple. The blood had been cleaned away.

People nodded humbly to me, the priest. They looked with curiosity at Jeannot, not recognising him.

Jeannot smiled at them and said, 'God is with us.'

It is as though he had spoken his name. There was at once an amazing stillness in the room. In a chorus, voices answered.

'C'e Mesiah. C'e Mesiah.'

People came forward touching him as they might touch a sacred object. 'Mesiah! Mesiah!' They wept, they smiled, they bowed to him in reverence.

Jeannot moving through the crowd, went to the table and gently touched the dead man's hand.

'Who killed our brother?'

Stumbling, interrupting each other in their eagerness to tell, the villagers explained that they had gone down to Papanos two days ago to join other peasants in a protest against parliament's refusal to accept Jeannot's choice of premier. The dead man was carrying a poster with Jeannot's picture and had been shot by soldiers when he tried to hoist it up over the entrance to the town hall.

And now, as in a biblical miracle, Jeannot had appeared at the dead man's wake. The villagers did not ask why he had come or how he knew of the death. The Messiah is not a man. He co-exists in the world of the flesh and the world of the spirit. To them, Jeannot had appeared in their village as the Virgin might appear. He was

God's messenger. Because of this the room was filled with a strange exaltation. These lives of poverty, of endless toil, of children's early deaths, of storms that washed away the meagre crops, of soldiers and *bleus* who beat and pillaged, were, in that room, on that day, transformed into the promise of a future life. Now, with the Messiah come among them, they believed anew. Paradise would be theirs.

(15) THE HAITIAN OTHER

Russell Banks, *Continental Drift,* 1985

Banks' novel is a highly original treatment of the mysterious bonds that hold together Haitians and North Americans. The drifting, no-madic, migratory impulses of inhabitants of the western hemisphere are revealed in an encounter between Haitian boat people and the white American smuggling them into Miami.

From the moment he first saw them ride out from the beach at New Providence in the dinghy, saw how astonishingly black they were, African, he thought, and saw how silent and obedient, how passive they were, he was struck by the Haitians. There's a mixture of passivity and will that he does not understand. They risk every-thing to get away from their island, give up everything, their homes, their families, forsake all they know, and then strike out across the open sea for a place they've only heard about.

Why do they do that? he wonders. Why do they throw away everything they know and trust, no matter how bad it is, for some-thing they know nothing about. And can never trust? He's in awe of the will it takes, the stubborn, conscious determination to get to America that each of them, from the eldest to the youngest, must own. But he can't put that wilfulness together with what he sees before him. – a quiescent, silent, shy people who seem fatalistic al-most, who seem ready and even willing to accept whatever is given them.

He almost envies it. The way he sees himself – a man equally wilful, but only with regard to the small things, to his appetites and monetary desires, and equally passive and accepting too, but only with regard to the big things, to where he lives and how he makes his living – he is their opposite. It's too easy to explain away the Haitians' fatalism by pointing to their desperation, by saying that life in Haiti is so awful that anything they get, even death, is an improvement. Bob has more imagination than that. And it's too easy to explain away their wilfulness the same way. Besides, it's not logical to ascribe two different kinds of behavior to the same cause. There's a wisdom they possess that he doesn't, a knowledge. The Haitians know something, about themselves, about history, about human life, that he doesn't know. What to call it Bob can't say. It's so outside his knowledge that he can't even name it yet.

EPILOGUE

Jean-Claude Martineau, *Ayiti Demen*, 1991

Lè l a libere, Ayiti va bèl o!
W a tande, w a tande koze
Lè l a libere, Ayiti va bèl o!
W a tande, ala yon ti peyi mache o!
W a tande.

Nou kapab pèdi moun, nou kab pèdi batay
Men pèdi Ayiti, se yon lòt bagay
Nenpòt lè san yon patriyòt koule
Va genyen yon douzèn lòt ki pou leve.

Lit la di anpil, e l ka dire lontan,
Men, de jou an jou, l ape vanse.
Moman difisil ape tann nou devan
Men nou pape janm dekouraje.
Nou konn Ayiti a vini yon bon peyi
Kote avni pèp la asire
Kote sa k plante, se li ki rekòlte
Kote sa ki swe, se li k poze.

Lè sa a, fanm yo va gen choublak nan cheve
Kou gason yo va gen mouchwa wouj mare
Nan lari, tout timoun ape chante
Granmoun yo menm va di: men jou a rive.

Menm jan pye joumou pa janm donnen kalbas
Laparès pa donnen laviktwa
Yon sèl gout lapli pa ka fè lavalas
Zong kretyen vivan pa koupe bwa
Men nou pa kapab rete 2 bra kwaze
Si nou vle jou sa a rive vrèman
Yo pa janm fè moun kado lalibète
Libète se pou pèp ki vanyan.

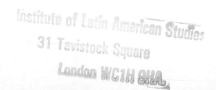

Haiti Tomorrow

Once free, how beautiful Haiti will be!
Wait to hear what people will say
Once free, how beautiful Haiti will be!
This little country has come a long way
That is what you will hear people say.

We may lose people, we may lose battles
But losing Haiti, that's a different matter
Whenever a patriot's blood is spilt
A dozen others will stand up to take his place.

The struggle is hard, and may last long,
But, day after day, we are moving forward.
Hard times lie ahead
But we will never be discouraged.
We know Haiti will be a great country
Where the future of its people will be safe
Where the one who sows is the one who reaps
Where the one who sweats is the one who rests.

When this time comes, women will wear hibiscus in their hair
Men will wear red scarves around their necks
In the street every child will sing
And the adults will say: the day has come.

Just as a pumpkin bush will never yield a calabash
Idleness will not lead to victory
A single drop of rain does not make a flood
A fingernail can't cut wood
We can't stay arms folded
If we really want this day to come
They never make a gift of freedom
Freedom comes to people who struggle for it.

Translated from Creole by Webber Emile

INDEX

ACKNOWLEDGEMENTS AND PERMISSIONS

N.B. Year dates in extract titles: the year refers to the first-known publication date or the publication date of the edition from which the extract is drawn.

Chapter One - Colonialism and Revolution
John Cummins, *The Voyage of Christopher Columbus*, Weidenfeld and Nicholson, London, 1992, pp 147-148. By permission of Weidenfeld and Nicholson, and St Martin's Press.
King Ferdinand, Letter to the Tainos, in Bartolomé De Las Casas, *History of the Indies*, Harper Torchbooks, New York, 1971, pp 192-193.
Benoît Joachim, *Les Racines du sous-developpement en Haiti*, Deschamps, Port-au-Prince, 1979, pp 9-10.
Dantès Bellegarde, *La Nation haitienne*, J. de Gigord, Paris, 1938, pp 54-55.
Harold Courlander, *The Drum and the Hoe*, University of California Press, Berkeley, California, 1960, pp 4-5.
C.L.R James, *The Black Jacobins*, Allison & Busby, London, 1994, pp 45-46, 55-56.
Baron De Vastey, *Notes à M. le Baron VP Malouet*, Cap Henry, 1814.
Gabriel Debien, Marronage in the French Caribbean, in Richard Price, ed, *Maroon Societies: Rebel Slave Communities in the Americas*, John Hopkins University Press, Baltimore, Maryland, 1979, pp 107-108, 110-111. Originally published as Le marronage aux antilles françaises au XVIIIe siecle, Caribbean Studies, Institute of Caribbean Studies, University of Puerto Rico, 1966.
Alejo Carpentier, *The Kingdom of This World*, Penguin, London, 1957, pp 17, 20-22.
Carolyn Fick, *The Making of Haiti: the Saint-Domingue Revolution from Below*, University of Tennessee Press, Knoxville, Tennessee, 1990, pp 31-32. By permission of the University of Tennessee Press.
Moreau de Saint-Méry in Ivor Spencer, *A Civilization That Perished: The Last Years of White Colonial Rule*, University Press of America, Lanham, Maryland, 1985, pp 22, 152-153.
Moreau de Saint-Méry, *Description de la partie francaise de l'île de Saint-Domingue*, Société de l'histoire des colonies francaises, Paris, 1958, pp 86-91.
H. Pauléus Sannon, *Histoire de Toussaint L'Ouverture*, Port-au-Prince, 1920, in Jean Fouchard, The Haitian Maroons: liberty or death, Edward W. Blyden Press, New York, 1981, pp 340-341.
Stéphen Alexis, *Black Liberator. The Life of Tousssaint Louverture*, Ernest Benn Ltd, London, 1949, pp 27-28.
David Geggus, The British Army and the Slave Revolt, in *History Today*, Vol. 32, London, July 1982. By permission of History Today Ltd.

René Depestre, Toussaint Louverture: Haiti's Tragic Hero, in *The UNESCO Courier*, 1981.
Toussaint Louverture, Letter to Lavaux, in CLR James, *The Black Jacobins*, Allison & Busby, London, 1994, pp 158-159.
Félix Morisseau-Leroy, Thank You Dessalines, trans, Marie-Marcelle B. Racine, *Haïtiad & Oddities*, Pantaléon Guilbaud, Miami, Florida, 1991, pp 34-36.
Boisrond Tonnerre, Declaration of Independence, in Thomas Madiou, *Histoire d'Haiti*, Cheraquit, Port-au-Prince, 1922, pp 103-106.

Chapter Two -The Status Quo: Elite, Soldiers and Dictators
David Nicholls, *From Dessalines to Duvalier*, MacMillan Education Ltd, Oxford 1996, pp 37-38. By permission of MacMillan Education Ltd.
John Candler, *Brief Notices of Hayti*, Ward, London, 1842, pp 30-32.
Michel-Rolph Trouillot, Haiti's Nightmare and the Lessons of History, in *NACLA Report on the Americas*, Vol. XXVII, No. 4, 1994, pp 47-48. By permission of the North American Congress on Latin America.
Heads of State, various sources.
Spencer St John, *Hayti or the Black Republic*, Frank Cass, London, 1971, pp 140-141.
Michel-Rolph Trouillot, *Haiti: State against Nation*, Monthly Review Press, New York, 1990, pp 105-106.
Jean Métellus, *The Vortex Family*, Peter Owen Publishers, London, 1995, pp 57-59. By permission of Peter Owen Ltd, London.
Graham Greene, The Nightmare Republic, in *The New Republic*, Vol 149, No 20, 1963. By permission of The New Republic.
The Jean-Claudiste National Action Committee, *Il était une fois...François Duvalier*, The Jean-Claudiste National Action Committee, Port-au-Prince, 1980, pp 38-39.
Marc Romulus, *Les Cachots des Duvalier*, Imprimerie Kopirapid, Port-au-Prince, 1991, pp 13-17.
Elizabeth Abbott, *Haiti: the Duvaliers and Their Legacy*, McGraw-Hill, New York, 1988, pp 171-172.
James Ferguson, *Papa Doc, Baby Doc*, Blackwell, Oxford, 1988, pp 174-175. By permission of the author.
National Coalition for Haitian Refugees, *No Greater Priority: Judicial Reform in Haiti*, New York, 1995. By permission of National Coalition for Haitian Rights.
Michel Laguerre, *The Military and Society in Haïti*, MacMillan Press UK, London, 1993, pp 151-152. By permission of the author and University of Tennessee Press.

Amy Wilentz, *The Rainy Season*, Vintage, London, 1994, pp 107-110. By permission of the author.

Catherine Orenstein, An Interview with Ben Dupuy, Aristide's Ambassador-at-large, in *NACLA Report on the Americas*, Vol. XXVII, No. 1, 1993, pp 12-14. By permission of the North American Congress on Latin America.

Alex Dupuy, *Haiti in the New World Order*, Westview Press, pp 120, 122-123. By permission of the author.

Jean-Bertrand Aristide, *Aristide: an autobiography*, Orbis Books, New York, 1992, pp 156-157, 160. By permission of Orbis Books.

Platform of Haitian Human Rights Organisations, *Resistance and Democracy*, Platform of Haitian Human Rights Organisations, Port-au-Prince, 1994.

James Ridgeway, Haiti's Family Affairs, in James Ridgeway, ed, *The Haiti Files: Decoding the Crisis*, Essential Books, Washington, and Azul Editions, Washington, 1994, pp 29-31. By permission of the author.

Chapter Three - Rural Haiti: Land and the Environment

William Seabrook, *The Magic Island*, Paragon House, New York, 1989, pp 28-30.

Harold Courlander, *The Drum and the Hoe*, University of California Press, Berkeley, California, 1960, pp 116-117.

Alfred Métraux, *Making a Living in the Marbial Valley*, UNESCO Occasional Papers in Education, Paris 1951, pp 33-34.

Madeleine Sylvain Bouchereau, *Haïti et ses Femmes*, Imprimerie les Presses Libres, Port-au-Prince, 1957, pp 162-164.

P. Baltenweck, Bulletin Météorologique du Collège Saint-Martial, Port-au-Prince, 1922, in Dantès Bellegarde, *La Nation haïtienne*, J. de Gigord, Paris, 1938, p 197.

Sidney Mintz, Markets in Haiti, in *New Society*, No.26, March 1963, pp 18-19. By permission of the author.

Commune of Borgne, *Haiti Info*, 28 November 1993. By permission of the Haitian Information Bureau.

Dany Laferrière, *An Aroma of Coffee*, Coach House Press, Toronto, 1993, pp 14-15, 17, 24-25.

George Eaton Simpson, Haitian Peasant Economy, in *Journal of Negro History*, Vol. 25, No. 4, Washington, 1940, pp 503-506.

San kontinye koule nan Latibonit, in *Libète*, No. 118, 27 December 1994.

Georges Anglade, Coup d'oeil sur le passé, in ed, Edwidge Balutansky, *Haïti, Terre Délabrée*, CRESDIP/NCHR/HSI, Port-au-Prince, 1990, p 69. By permission of the author.

Collectif Haitien pour la Protection de l'Environnement et un Developpement Alternatif (COHPEDA), *Causes de la Dégradation de l'Environnement en Haïti*, COHPEDA, Port-au-Prince, 1993.

Fédération des Amis de la Nature (FAN), *Quleques Données sur la Réalité Dramatique de l'Environnement en Haïti*, FAN, Petionville, 1986.

Leah Gordon and Anne Parisio, Interview with a charcoal maker, Research notes for the documentary film, A Pig's Tale, directors, Leah Gordon and Anne Parisio, London, 1997. By permission of the directors.

Bernard Diederich, Swine Fever Ironies, in *Caribbean Review*, Vol. XIV, No.1, 1985, pp 16-17, 41. By permission of the author.

Mats Lundahl, Underdevelopment in Haiti, in Mats Lundahl, *Politics or Markets?: essays on Haitian underdevelopment*, Routledge, London, 1992, pp 52-3. By permission of Routledge.

The Low Voice of Saint-Jules Clocy, A Haitian Farmer, in *Ideas and Action*, No. 173, Food and Agriculture Organisation, 1987, pp 6-8.

Gwo zago's gwoupman, Peyizan yo, Research notes for the documentary film, A Pig's Tale, directors, Leah Gordon and Anne Parisio, London, 1997. By permission of the directors.

Amy Wilentz, *The Rainy Season*, Vintage, London,1994, pp 144-145. By permission of the author.

Chapter Four - Poverty and Urban Life

Jean-Bertrand Aristide, *In the Parish of the Poor*, Orbis Books, New York, 1990, pp 6, 8-9. By permission of Orbis Books.

Famine and Food Aid, in *Haiti Briefing* No. 24, 1997. By permission of Haiti Briefing, the newletter of the Haiti Support Group.

J.P. Slavin, Restavèk: four-year-old child servants, in *Haiti Insight*, Vol. 17, No. 2, 1996, pp 4-5. By permission of Haiti Insight, the newsletter of the National Coalition for Haitian Rights (NCHR), and the US Committee for UNICEF.

P.J. O'Rourke, *All the Trouble in the World*, Picador, London, 1994, pp 270-272.

Catherine Maternowska, *Coup d'Etat and Contraceptives: A political economy analysis of family planning in Haiti*, PhD dissertation, Columbia University, 1996. By permission of the author.

Mike Kamber, Haiti: the Taiwan of the Caribbean breaks away, in *Z Magazine*, February 1991, pp 31-32. By permission of Z magazine.

Amy Wilentz, A Place called Haiti, in *Haiti: Feeding the Spirit*, Aperture, New York, 1992, p. 6. By permission of the author.

Michel Laguerre, *Urban Life in the Caribbean*, Schenkman Publishing Company, Cambridge, Massachussetts, 1982, pp 27-29. By permission of the author.

Charles Kernaghan, Living on the Edge of Misery, in *Open Letter to the Walt Disney Company*, National Labor Committee, 1996. By permission of the National Labor Committee.

The Bouretyes' Burden, *Haiti Info*, 7 May 1994. By permission of the Haitian Information Bureau.

Simon Fass, *Political Economy in Haiti: the Drama of Survival*, Rutgers, New Brunswick, New

Jersey, 1988, pp 331-332. Copyright © 1988 by Transaction Publishers; all rights reserved. By permission of Transaction Publishers.

Street Children, *Haiti Info*, 22 March 1997. By permission of the Haitian Information Bureau.

Ives-Marie Chanel: General Hospital: Ante-chamber of death, *Inter Press Service*, 10 March 1995.

Haiti Support Group, Interview with Rose-Anne Auguste, in Charles Arthur, ed, *Killing Us Softly*, Haiti Support Group, London, 1997.

George Leonard, AIDS in Haiti, in *Stretch*, No. 6, Summer 1991, pp 9-11. By permission of Robert Corbett.

Jamil Salmi, Equity and quality in private education, in *Haiti: the Challenge of Poverty Reduction*, Vol. II, Technical Papers No. 6, World Bank, 1998, p 2, p 5, p 10.

Zacharie Louis and Fred Montas, Comités de quartiers, *Haïti Progrès*, 28 May 1986. By permission of Haïti Progrès.

Chapter Five - Forces for Change

David Nicholls, *Haiti in Caribbean Context: Ethnicity, Economy and Revolt*, MacMillan, 1985, pp 175-176. Courtesy of Gillian Nicholls.

Lyonel Paquin: *The Haitians: Class and Colour Politics*, Multi-type, New York, 1983, pp 134-135.

Bernard Diederich and Al Burt, *Papa Doc and the Tontons Macoutes*, Editions Henri Deschamps, Port-au-Prince, 1986, pp 385-387. By permission of Bernard Diederich.

Arnold Antonin, *The Long Unknown Struggle of the Haitian People*, Ateneo, Caracas, 1978, pp 29-33.

Robert Maguire, The Peasantry and Political Change in Haiti, in *Caribbean Affairs*, Vol. 4 No. 2, 1991.

Interview with Father Hugo Triest, in *Unda News*, Vol. XX, No. 4, 1993.

Gonaïves: Symbole de la Résistance, *Haïti Progrès*, 19 May 1986. By permission of Haïti Progrès.

The Milot Land Struggle, *Haiti Info*, 27 April 1993. By permission of the Haitian Information Bureau.

Greg Chamberlain, Up by the Roots, in *NACLA Report on the Americas*, Vol. XXI, No. 3, 1987, pp 22-23. By permission of the North American Congress on Latin America.

Father Jean-Bertrand Aristide, Press Conference, in *International Viewpoint*, 12 October 1987, pp 8-9.

Marx-Vilaire Aristide and Laurie Richardson, Haiti's Popular Resistance, in *NACLA Report on the Americas*, Vol. XXVII, No. 4, 1994, pp 30-34. By permission of the North American Congress on Latin America.

Interview with a leader of the Tèt Kole Ti Peyizan peasant movement, in Charles Arthur, ed, *Killing Us Softly*, Haiti Support Group, London, 1997.

Press release, *Le Militant*, No. 18, March-May, 1989.

Leslie Griffiths, *The Aristide Factor*, Lion Publishing, Oxford, 1997, pp 138-140. By permission of Lion Publishing plc.

Laënnec Hurbon, L'insurrection du 7 janvier 1991, in *Lettre de Lucia*, Haïti Solidarité International, Port-au-Prince, 1993, pp 99-100.

EPICA/Voices for Haiti, *Beyond the Mountains, More Mountains - Haiti Faces the Future*, Washington, 1994, p 12. By permission of EPICA.

MPP programmes move forward, in *The Peasant*, Vol. 2, No. 2, 1995.

Interview with Camille Chalmers, in *New Internationalist*, November 1996. By permission of New Internationalist.

Lisa McGowan, *Democracy Undermined, Economic Justice Denied: Structural adjustment and the Aid Juggernaut in Haiti*, Development GAP, Washington, 1997. By permission of Development GAP.

Resurrection of the Popular Movement, *Haïti Progrès*, January 15 1997. By permission of Haïti Progrès.

Chapter Six - Refugees and the Diaspora

Félix Morisseau-Leroy, Boat People, trans, Jeffrey Knapp, in *Haïtiad & Oddities*, Pantaléon Guilbaud, Miami, Florida, 1991, pp 57-58.

Brenda Gayle Plummer, Haitian Migrants and Backyard Imperialism, in *Race and Class*, Vol. XXVI, No. 4, 1985. By permission of the Institute of Race Relations.

Rénald Clérismé, *Relations of Production in the Dominican Coffee Economy*, PhD dissertation, Yale University, 1996, pp 207-209. By permission of the author.

National Coalition for Haitian Rights, *Beyond the Bateyes*, NCHR, New York, 1996, pp 30-31. By permission of the National Coalition for Haitian Rights.

Maurice Lemoine, *Bitter Sugar*, Zed Books, London, 1985, pp 159-160. By permission of Zed Books Ltd.

Paul Latortue, Neo-slavery in the Cane Fields: Haitians in the Dominican Republic, in *Caribbean Review*, Vol. XIV, No.4, 1985, pp 19-20.

P.Anthony White, One Haitian in the Hand and Two in the Bush, *Punch* (Bahamas), 29 April 1994.

Laënnec Hurbon, La Migration haïtienne en Guadeloupe, in *Collectif Paroles*, No. 16, February 1982, pp 26-27.

Josh DeWind and David Kinley, *Aiding migration: the impact of international development assistance on Haiti*, Westview Press, Boulder, Colorado, 1988, pp 13-14.

Dadou Pasquet, "Libète", Magnum Band, from *Adoration*, Mini Records, 1983, trans, Gage Averill, A Day for the Hunter, A Day for the Prey, University of Chicago Press, Chicago, 1997, pp 152-153.

Edwidge Danticat, Children of the Sea, in *Krik? Krak!*, Soho Press (US), Little, Brown (UK), pp 8-10. By permission of Soho Press Inc, and Little, Brown and Company.

The Great Escape, *Haïti Progrès*, 29 June 1994. By permission of Haïti Progrès.

Dan Coughlin, Life Still Hard After Aristide's Second Coming, *Inter Press Service*, 22 August 1995.

Garry Pierre-Pierre, Edwidge Danticat: Chronicling the Haitian-American Experience, *The New York Times*, 25 January 1995. Copyright © 1995 by the New York Times Co. By permission of The New York Times Co.

Interview with Monsignor Thomas Wensky, *Libète*, No. 268, 26 November 1997.

Elizabeth McAlister, Serving the Spirits across Two Seas, in *Haiti: Feeding the Spirit*, Aperture, New York, 1992, p 47. By permission of the author.

James Ridgeway and Jean Jean-Pierre, An Alienated and Angered Haitian-American Community Fights Back, *The Village Voice*, 22 August 1997. By permission of James Ridgeway.

Karin Joseph, A Night with Wyclef Jean and the Refugee All-stars, *Haiti Observateur*, 5 November 1997.

Chapter Seven - Foreign Interventions

Jean Métellus, Haïti: Perspectives, in *Journal of Haitian Studies*, Vol. 2 No. 1, Spring 1996, pp 24-25. By permission of the Journal of Haitian Studies.

David Nicholls, *Economic Dependence and Political Autonomy: The Haitian Experience*, Centre for Developing Area Studies, McGill University, Montreal, 1974, pp 25-27. Courtesy of Gillian Nicholls.

Roger Gaillard, *Les blancs débarquent*, R. Gaillard, Port-au-Prince, 1982, pp 213-218.

Charlemagne Péralte, Lettre, in *Conjunction*, No. 115, 1971, p 102.

Suzy Castor, *L'Occupation Américaine d'Haïti*, Société Haïtienne D'Histoire, Port-au-Prince, 1988, pp 90-94. By permission of the author.

Normil Sylvain, A Haitian View of the Occupation, in Emily Balch, *Occupied Haiti*, ed, Emily Greene Balch, Writers Publishing Co, New York, 1927, pp 179-180.

Ernest Bernardin, *L'espace rural haïtien*, Editions L'Harmattan, Paris, 1993, pp 266-268. By permission of Editions L'Harmattan.

Alex Stepick, The New Haitian Exodus, in *Caribbean Review*, Vol. XI, No. 1, Winter 1992, p 55.

Haiti's Agricultural Production, *Haiti Info*, 28 February 1996. By permission of the Haitian Information Bureau.

Ian Thomson, *Bonjour Blanc: A Journey Through Haiti*, Penguin, Random House, London, 1992, pp 106-107. By permission of the author.

Robert Maguire et al., *Haiti Held Hostage: International Responses to the Quest for Nationhood 1986-1996*, Thomas J. Watson Institute for International Studies, Providence, Rhode.Island, 1996, pp 22-24. By permission of the Thomas J. Watson Institute for International Studies.

William Robinson, Low Intensity Democracy in Haiti, in *Covert Action Quarterly*, No. 48, Spring 1994, pp 6-7. By permission of Covert Action Quarterly.

Tous les 'nationalistes' agents de la CIA, *Haïti en Marche*, 3 November 1993.

Allan Nairn, Our Man In FRAPH: Behind Haiti's Paramilitaries, in *The Nation*, 24 October 1994. By permission of The Nation.

Position of the Popular Organisations on the Country's Crisis, Fourteen popular organisations, Port-au-Prince, July 1994.

Allan Nairn, Aristide Agrees to Austerity, in *Multinational Monitor*, July / August 1994. By permission of the author.

Paul Farmer, The Significance of Haiti, in ed, NACLA, *Haiti: Dangerous Crossroads*, Southend Press, Denver, Colorado, 1995, pp 223-224. By permission of the North American Congress on Latin America.

Noam Chomsky, Democracy Restored?, in *Z Magazine*, November 1994, pp 58-59. By permission of the author.

Laurie Richardson, Haiti: Disarmament Derailed, in *NACLA Report on the Americas*, Vol. XXIX, No. 6, 1996, pp. By permission of the North American Congress on Latin America.

Jean-Claude Martineau, Haitian Culture: Basis for Development, in *Roots*, Vol. 1, No. 4, Winter 1996/7. By permission of Roots magazine.

Chapter Eight - Popular Religion and Culture

Thomas Madiou, *Histoire d'Haïti*, in Jean Fouchard, The Haitian Maroons, Edward W. Blyden Press, New York, 1981, p 346.

Sidney Mintz and Michel-Rolph Trouillot, The Social History of Haitian Vodou, in ed, Donald J. Cosentino, *Sacred Arts of Haitian Vodou*, UCLA Fowler Museum of Cultural History, Los Angeles, 1995, pp 123-124.

Laënnec Hurbon, *Voodoo: Truth and Fantasy*, Thames and Hudson, London, 1995, pp 66-71.

Lwa chart, various sources.

Karen McCarthy Brown, *Tracing the Spirit: Ethnographic Essays on Haitian Art*, Davenport Museum of Art, Davenport, Iowa, 1995, p 32. By permission of the Davenport Museum of Art.

Donald J. Cosentino, Envoi: The Gedes and Bawon Samdi, in ed, Donald J. Cosentino, *Sacred Arts of Haitian Vodou*, UCLA Fowler Museum of Cultural History, Los Angeles, 1995, pp 401, 403, 413-414.

Alfred Métraux, *Voodoo*, Oxford University Press, and Schocken Books, 1959, pp 120-122.

Selden Rodman and Carole Cleaver, *Spirits of the Night*, Spring Publications, Woodstock, Iowa, pp 24-25. By permission of Spring Publications.

Serving the Spirits: the Ritual Economy of Haitian Vodou Karen McCarthy Brown, in ed, Donald J. Cosentino, *Sacred Arts of*

Haitian Vodou, UCLA Fowler Museum of Cultural History, Los Angeles, 1995, p 215.

Jean Price Mars, *So Spoke the Uncle*, translated and with an introduction by Magdaline W. Shannon, Three Continents Press, Washington, DC, 1983, pp 39-40. Copyright © 1983 by Magdaline W. Shannon. By permission of Lynne Rienner Publishers, Inc.

Rémy Bastien, Vodoun and Politics in Haiti, in Harold Courlander and Remy Bastien, *Religion and Politics in Haiti*, Institute for Cross-Cultural Research, Washington, 1966, pp 47-48.

EPICA / Voices for Haiti, *Beyond the Mountains, More Mountains - Haiti Faces the Future*, Washington, 1994, pp 35-36. By permission of EPICA.

Patrick Leigh Fermor, *The Traveller's Tree*, Penguin, London, 1984, pp 282-284.

Gage Averill and Verna Gillis, *Caribbean Revels: Haitian Rara and Dominican Gaga*, CD and cassette notes, Smithsonian Folkways Recordings, Washington, 1990. By permission of Smithsonian Folkways Recordings.

Katherine Dunham, *Dances of Haiti*, Center for Afro-American Studies, UCLA, Los Angeles, 1983, pp 35-37.

Charles Arthur, The Man Who Beat Dino Zoff, previously unpublished. Copyright © 1998 by Charles Arthur; all rights reserved.

Blair Niles, *Black Haiti*, Putnam's, New York, 1926, pp 35-36, 40-41.

Charles Arthur, Banking on Shit, previously unpublished. Copyright © 1998 by Charles Arthur; all rights reserved.

Jokes and Riddles, compiled from various sources by Robert Corbett and reprinted in Stretch magazine.

Diane Wolkstein, Papa God and General Death, in *The Magic Orange Tree and other Haitian Folktales*, Schocken Books, New York, 1980, pp 77-78.

Proverbs, various sources.

Chapter Nine - Literature and Language
Anténor Firmin, De l'égalité des races humaines, Paris, 1885.

Oswald Durand, Choucoune, Port-au-Prince, n.d.

Frédéric Marcelin, Au gré du souvenir, Paris, 1893.

Philippe Thoby-Marcelin, Carl Brouard, Léon Laleau, Emile Roumer, Five Poems, various sources. n.d.

Jean Price Mars, *So Spoke the Uncle*, translated and with an introduction by Magdaline W. Shannon, Three Continents Press, Washington, DC, 1983. Copyright © 1983 by Magdaline W. Shannon. By permission of Lynne Rienner Publishers, Inc.

Carl Brouard, L'art au service du peuple, Port-au-Prince, 1938.

Jacques Roumain, *Masters of the Dew*, Heinnemann, London, 1978.

Jacques Stéphen Alexis, *Les arbres musiciens*, Gallimard Jeunesse, Paris, 1957.

Franketienne, *Dezafi*, Fardin, Port-au-Prince, 1975.

Anthony Phelps, Mémoire en colin-maillard, Nouvelle Optique, 1976, pp128-30.

Pierre Clitandre, *Cathedral of the August Heat*, Readers International, London, 1987, pp.127-8.

René Depestre, *The Festival of the Greasy Pole*, University of Virginia Press, 1990, pp 30-31

Marie Chauvet, *Amour, colère, folie*, Gallimard, Paris, 1968, p126.

Edwidge Danticat, *Breath, Eyes, Memory*, Abacus, London, 1996, pp 138-140. By permission of Little, Brown and Company, and Soho Press Inc.

Dany Laferrière, *Pays sans chapeau*, Lanctot, Montreal, 1996, pp14-15.

Emile Ollivier, *Les urnes scellées*, Albin Michel. Paris, 1995, pp248-9.

Chapter Ten - The View From Abroad
Moreau de Saint-Méry in Ivor Spencer, *A Civilization That Perished: The Last Years of White Colonial Rule*, University Press of America, Lanham, Maryland, 1985.

John Greenleaf Whittier, Toussaint Louverture, in *Anti-Slavery Poems*, Ayer, 1969, pp18-19

William Seabrook, *The Magic Island*, Paragon House, New York, 1989, pp42-43.

Langston Hughes, White Shadows in a Black Land, *Crisis*, New York, No. 41, 1932, p157.

Zora Neale Hurston, *Tell My Horse*, Harper & Row, New York, 1938, pp104-5.

Pierre Mabille, The Haitian Panorama in *Messages de létranger*, Plasma, Paris, 1981, pp29-31.

Suzanne Césaire, The Great Camouflage in *Refusal of the Shadow*, Verso, London, 1996, p157.

Alejo Carpentier, *The Kingdom of This World*, Penguin, London, pp43-44.

Graham Greene, *The Comedians*, Penguin, London, 1967, pp 43-4. By permission of David Higham Associates.

Bernard Diederich and Al Burt, *Papa Doc and the Tontons Macoutes*, Editions Henri Deschamps, Port-au-Prince, 1986, p319. By permission of Bernard Diederich.

Wade Davis, *The Serpent and the Rainbow*, Collins, London, 1986, pp 159-161.

Mark Danner, Beyond the Mountains, *The New Yorker*, 27 November 1989, pp 55-56.

Amy Wilentz, *The Rainy Season*, Vintage, London,1994, pp 398-399. By permission of the author.

Brian Moore, *No Other Life*, Bloomsbury, London and Doubleday, New York, 1993, pp180-181.

Russell Banks, *Continental Drift*, Harper & Row, NewYork and Hamish Hamilton, London, 1985, p 305.

Epilogue
Jean-Claude Martineau (Koralen), Ayiti Demen, in *Pwezi, Kont, Chante*, Deschamps, Port-au-Prince, 1991, p 9.